"They Broke the Mold" *

The Mémoirs of Walter Birge

* The title comes from an expression that Walter Birge often used to describe people he found unique and interesting, yet most aptly can be applied to himself.
* These Mémoirs were written during 1990-1992 and edited by Virginia Birge (Birge's widow) in 2004-05.

THEY BROKE THE MOLD THE MEMOIRS OF WALTER BIRGE
Copyright © Virginia N. Birge 2007

First Published in the UK by
Paul Mould Publishing
p.mould@yahoo.com

In association with
Empire Publishing Service www.ppeps.com
P.O. Box 1344, Studio City, CA 91614-0344

All rights reserved. No part of this file may be reproduced or transmitted in any form or by any means without the prior written permission of the author, except by a reviewer who may quote brief passages in a review printed in a newspaper, magazine, journal or online.

A CIP Catalogue record for this book is available from the British Library or from the US Library of Congress.

Simultaneously published in
Australia, Canada, Germany, UK, USA

Printed in Great Britain
First Printing 2012

UK ISBN 9780956639-9-7
USA ISBN 978158690-121-9

Table of Contents

Introduction..5
1. The Early Years -Origins and Boyhood........................7
2. The Groton Years (1925-1931)......................................56
3. The Harvard Years (1931-1935)....................................75
4. Argentina, as Secretary to the Ambassador (1935)...........114
5. In Between Years (1936-1939)......................................125
6. Washington (1939-1940)...150
7. The Waiting Time (1941)..159
8. Tex-Mex (1941-1942)..169
9. Istanbul (1942-1944)...177
10. Baghdad (1944-1945)..226
11. Saudi Arabia (1945)..253
12. Iraq to Prague (1945)...266
13. Prague (1945-1949)..286
14. French West Africa (1950-51).....................................379
15. Munich – Radio Free Europe (1951-1953)...................387
16. Vignettes from the 1960's and 1970's........................391
Jim Gerard and Jean Shevlin..391
Belgium...396
Oliver..403
Addenda – Quotes about Walter Birge from three books.....409

Introduction

The question naturally arises as to why a relatively obscure person such as I should have the presumption to write about his past life. I have asked who would be even slightly interested in such a saga. I suppose that this literary effort stems from the after-dinner (or cocktail time) tales of bygone years I have sometimes told, for often one of my captive listeners would comment that I should write a book.

I suppose that the experiences, adventures, and occasional exploits of my life, such as they were, are still remembered by me and are of interest to some of those close to me; and I am conceited enough to reach for a sliver of immortality which might accompany the writing of such a book. The years to be covered stretch through World War I, the affluent 1920's, the depressed 1930's, World War II, and the parlous cold-war time of the late 1940's and early 1950's. Geographically, it is a potpourri, which includes New England, South America, Europe, and the Middle East.

In closing this brief introduction, I should like to add that of all the places lived in, the one which stands out as the most desirable for a permanent home is the Boston area – greater Boston, that is, plus New England in general. The basic reason for this feeling is that my so-called formative years were spent first as a resident of Connecticut and later at boarding school and college in Massachusetts. Moreover, some of the finest men I have known, all of whom had a definite and lasting influence on me, lived in Massachusetts.

Namely: Endicott Peabody, Fuller Albright, Ronald Beasley, and Crane Brinton.

Chapter One

The Early Years

I start with a little background about the Birge family. The first of that family to set foot in this hemisphere, Richard Birge, age eighteen, landed near what is now Dorchester, Massachusetts in 1630, having sailed over from Bristol, England, to the Massachusetts Bay Colony as the ward of a Puritan minister. Seven years after this landing, about one hundred and fifty of that group, including Richard and the minister, walked all the way to north-central Connecticut and settled in what was to become Windsor.

These energetic, hard-working farmers of yeoman stock were to prosper in their new home for they lived by the Puritan belief in "good work". Much later, they might have the time for "good works". Richard appears to have inherited enough money to enable him before long to buy land for a sizable farm. For almost two centuries, most of his descendants lived in or near Windsor and they thrived there. In 1837, about the time that the depression of that year struck the young republic, William Birge, my great-grandfather, accompanied by his brother, Leander, traveled to the Wisconsin Territory, then a wilderness.

At about the same time, Jeremiah Noble, a powerful ironworker of Canaan, Connecticut – "of remarkable strength and activity", also arrived in Wisconsin. He and his family had first traveled as far as Jamestown, New York (where he stayed a dozen years) in 1824 via the new Erie Canal on the first canal packet. He had a "winsome daughter, blue-eyed, blond, slender and vivacious", Mary Lavinia. The Nobles settled in Milwaukee.

Meanwhile, William and Leander had managed to establish a valid claim to a rather large tract of land in a small settlement, later named Whitewater. Occasionally, the Birge brothers traveled to Milwaukee to obtain provisions, and it was on one of those excursions that William met Mary Lavinia Noble. On the frontier, courtships did not often take long, for there were too many other pressing things to do. This seems to have been love at first sight and the couple was married in January 1839. Their first child, and the first Caucasian child to be born in this area, was Julius, my grandfather, who arrived on November 18 of that same year. By then, William had built a small log cabin, of which I still have a faded photo.

In those days, village fairs were sometimes held and there were feats of strength, horseshoe pitching, running, etc. William, who was about as powerful as his father-in-law, stood about 5'11" and weighed some 210 pounds. He was also a good wrestler. As fortune – or misfortune – would have it, there was another pioneer who lived near Whitewater, who was also a paladin of strength and known as the wrestling champion of that community. It was inevitable, therefore, that these two frontiersmen should meet at the village fair to determine who indeed was the wrestling champion. William had nothing personal against his opponent, whom he knew quite well. Sad to relate, however, he accidentally killed the other man when he threw him over his head, thus breaking his neck.

William had another interesting experience in that frontier village and had this one had a different outcome, I would not be writing these lines. There was an Indian chief whose camp was not far distant and thus was a frequent visitor in William's cabin, for in frontier days the latchstring was always out and it was customary for Indian neighbors simply to walk in and make themselves at home. On the occasion of one such visit, the chief, looking in the direction of Mary Lavinia, expressed admiration in the form of several grunts of approval. Not yet mindful that Indians did not share the white man's sense of humor, William suggested that he and the chief "swap squaws". The following day, while William was away helping a neighbor build his barn, Mary Lavinia, by chance looking out the door, spied the chief about a hundred yards away walking up the trail followed by his squaw, who was carrying a huge backpack, obviously laden with all her belongings. My great-grandmother barely had time to scoop up her infant son, Julius, scurry out the back window and flee to the nearest settlement, where she took refuge for weeks until the coast was clear and William could fetch her, for the chief presumably had been mollified in the interim. It need not be added that William did not joke with any Indian again.

William Birge died at the age of forty-seven in 1860. Julius, my grandfather, as the only surviving male in the family, undertook the management of his father's flourmill, an activity which provided for his mother and three surviving sisters and also prevented him from enlisting for service in the Civil War. In those days, that was not unusual, especially in the near-frontier areas. Apparently, the Birge flourmill prospered, not only owing to the rapidly increasing population in Wisconsin, but in view of the ever-urgent requirements of the army.

In 1866, at age twenty-seven, grandfather, ostensibly for reasons of health, having recently recovered from typhoid fever, joined a wagon train which was headed west and rode with them all the way to Salt Lake City where, according to his later accounts, he became quite friendly with Brigham Young, the head of the Mormon settlement in that city.

As I remember him a few months before he died, when I was ten, grandfather liked to tell jokes as he could always count on the apparently appreciative audience of his family; however, on reading both the diary he kept during the years of his youth, and *The Awakening of the Desert,* the book he wrote about his wagon-train journey, one would hardly know, from these writings at least. Everything is dead serious. In his book, however, one does learn how the pioneers crossed streams with covered wagons, how they fought off marauding mounted "Redskins". This long trip of some 3000 miles, mostly over trackless wastes, took place ten years before the massacres of Custer's detachment at Little Big Horn, and the Indians were always a potential menace in those days of the late 1860's.

Grandfather moved to St. Louis in about 1870. There, he met and married in 1873, Mary Jane Patrick, the diminutive (five feet tall and ninety pounds) and jolly daughter of a very prosperous owner of a Mississippi freight shipping line, lumber mills, and other successful enterprises. Julius and Mary Jane Birge had eight children. Jim, the eldest, died of tuberculosis at the age of twenty-seven, and a boy and a girl died very young. My father, born in 1877, was the third in age.

I well remember him regaling us with stories about his father's feats of strength and about his severity with his children. According to these tales, his father would occasionally demonstrate his strength by supporting three of his small children on his stomach while suspended with his head on one chair and his heels on another. He is also reputed to have walked under a clothesline and then high-jumped over the same line. Father would also make a point of explaining how discipline was maintained in the family. Serious misbehavior was almost invariably punished by the perpetrator being whipped with a strap behind the barn. It was perhaps because of this unpleasant memory that father never once meted out corporal punishment to any of us children.

Father, who could tell one amusing story after another far into an evening, was much more a Patrick than a Birge and he would tell any Catholic such as our Irish maids that he was half Irish, ignoring the difference between Catholic and Scotch-Irish. To him, County Antrim was just as Irish as County Cork.

Grandfather, with the financial help of his father-in-law, organized the St.Louis Shovel Company, which he eventually sold to Ames Shovel and Tool Company of Boston, remaining a director of Ames and vice-president and manager in the Midwest. He also bought into an Indiana tool firm (Seymour) and controlled this small enterprise all his life.

On Sundays in St. Louis, grandfather would spend the best part of the day in Pilgrim Congregational Church, teaching Sunday school, attending the morning service, and then going back for a long evening hymn-singing service. Considering that this was the atmosphere in which father grew up, I am amazed at how broad minded he was and this, I am sure, was mainly owing to the tactful influence of my beautiful mother, Mabelle Claire Brown, whom he had married in 1903.

My mother, who was from Kansas City, Missouri, was an only child whose mother had died when she was twelve. Father met this twenty-year old beauty at the "Veiled Prophets' Ball", to which she had been invited by St. Louis friends of her father. Father lost no time in having his self properly introduced to Mabelle Brown and he gave her a "big rush". Before long, a young man came up to father and in a stern and presumptuous tone stated that he and Mabelle Brown had an "understanding" and he wished to inform Mr. Birge of that situation. Father, according to his rendition of that episode many years later, replied, "Mabelle Brown is from Kansas City and you, sir, I presume are also from Kansas City. Notwithstanding that I am from St.Louis, I am going to take Mabelle away from you." And that is exactly what he did, and very soon.

Mother and father had four children: Claire, born April, 1906; Julius, March, 1909; Grace, September, 1911, and I, May 21, 1913. My first recollections are those of January first and second, 1916, when our family was traveling from St. Louis to New York, en route to Greenwich, Connecticut, where we were going to live. We were in a sleeping car compartment and there was a very black porter in a very white coat and I was ill with the croup.

Then I remember at first living in a rented house in Greenwich, which belonged to a family named Gaines. For some reason I also distinctly recall, while living in that house for a couple of months that I objected strongly to eating braised celery, a loathsome dish which was continually being foisted on me. We had an Irish maid called Delia and well I remember her and another maid carrying china and household items up the sidewalk and then across to number one, North Street, to a very large house, which father purchased soon after our arrival in Greenwich. What I remember about that house was that it seemed huge and in retrospect it had no charm or architectural elegance. But the ten acres of grounds surrounding it had beautiful trees and many well-kept flowerbeds. There was also a large garage, which housed our new twin-six Packard. Our chauffeur's name was Tommy Minogue, who had a red face, a seemingly perpetual smile and a way with children. Father also acquired two riding horses named Bob and Buttons. Bob soon came to grief when an automobile, moving too fast down Maple Avenue, ran into his front legs. His resulting death was my first heartbreak.

Mother went on a buying spree in New York shortly after we moved to North Street. She bought a Steinway grand piano and many oriental rugs, a few of which now grace my house here in the Bay State eighty years later. Mother had good taste and she did not compromise with quality, a luxury she was able to afford at that time.

Father had moved with his family east from St. Louis because two New York financiers, Percy Rockefeller and Sam Pryor, had been seeking an executive to organize and manage a new manufacturing company to be called Air Reduction Company. Father's name had come to their attention, probably owing to his record as general sales manager of the Plumb Company of Philadelphia, where my parents had lived from 1908 to 1910. These men probably interviewed father in St. Louis, for mother later remarked to me that it was there that she met Mrs. Pryor. While father, at age thirty-nine in 1916, was an attractive outgoing and articulate individual, mother, in her own way, was equally impressive. Even if mother had not met Ruby Pryor, father would probably have been chosen, but my gut feeling tells me that it was mother who clinched the deal, so to speak, by the special gift possessed of being able to get along well with anyone she wanted to impress, and applied especially to other women.

In a way, it was difficult for father to decide to leave St.Louis, which had been his home since his birth, except for the two years he and mother had spent in St. David's near Philadelphia. When he told his father of his decision to accept the position of president of Air Reduction, dad said that his father wept and commented, "Walter, in business I have drilled with a gimlet, but you drill with an auger." And so it was that our family came back to Connecticut from which state dad's grandfather had moved seventy-nine years before.

My parents chose to reside in Greenwich, as that was where the Pryors and Rockefellers lived, and it took little persuasion on Ruby Pryor's part to sell mother on the advantages of that attractive town. Many years later, mother told the story of how she visited several New York stores, such as the old DePinna, Brooks Brothers, and Saks, for the purpose of opening charge accounts. When she was asked what her husband's business was and what position he held, she was momentarily at a loss, as she never had more than a vague idea as to her husband's business ventures. "I think Mr. Birge's company has something to do with wind," said my beautiful mother. At that juncture, Mrs. Prior came to her rescue, explaining that the company involved was called "Air Reduction", and the account was opened.

Father's salary during the years 1916 to 1919 while he was CEO of Air Reduction was $25,000 a year. He had a fair income aside from this, but his total earned and unearned revenue probably did not exceed $35,000. That was affluence in those days. We had a cook, kitchen maid, and two parlor maids who doubled as waitresses. In addition to the gardener and chauffeur, mentioned above, there was also the governess. First, there was Mademoiselle Pitet, a young Swiss woman. This disciplinarian, who was pretty, athletic, and conceited, cared little for children and it subsequently came to light, as mother recounted much later, that her two absorbing interests were skating and getting out to meet men friends. As both of these pursuits necessitated her leaving whenever possible, it is understandable that she left much to be desired as a governess.

One day, she locked me in an unlighted closet, following some unremembered misdemeanor on my part – this probably involved my inability to pee directly into the toilet bowl. In any case, this was a bright, cold winter's day of 1916-17, and Pitet took herself off to skate at the Ice Company pond. My punishment enabled her to do this as she seldom paid much attention to Grace, then age five. I suppose that I must have let out plenty of howls, for eventually Claire, the oldest of us children, aged eleven, ascertained the source of that noise, unlocked the closet door and liberated me, thus ensuring her never-to-be relinquished prominent place in my affections up to the end of her life. Claire at once informed mother about where she had found me while the governess was off skating and that same afternoon mademoiselle Pitet was fired.

The really significant upshot of this event was the arrival of my new governess, Madame Espy, a lovable, sentimental French woman, who not only introduced me to the beautiful language of her country, but also poured out a never-ending stream of affection on the younger of her new charges, i.e., me. Grace was also under her guidance, but for some reason, there never developed more than a perfunctory rapport between Madame Espy and this stringy haired and rather plain – but later incredibly beautiful – little girl.

As for me, I became her *petit Napoléon*, after her hero, which doubtless influenced my life-long admiration of that great man. I well remember being driven with Gracie down to the railroad station by Tommy Minogue, our chauffeur. Dressed in the warmest winter clothing, (cars were unheated then) including a balaclava helmet, typical of that era, covering my bobbed locks, I was seated beside Gracie in the wide back seat of our Packard limousine. In those days, it was not unusual to have one chassis and to change auto bodies with the warm and cold seasons. This entailed a lot of work and I can see Tommy, assisted by a couple of men hired for that occasion, struggling with these car bodies. As one looks back on this custom, however, it seems logical to cope with winter and summer driving in this way, rather than owning two cars.

To get back to that trip to the station: Madame Espy was duly met by Tommy, whose normally red face was even redder on that bitter cold day, and escorted to the car where Gracie and I, conditioned to be frightened of a governess, were still huddled in the two corners of the back seat. Madame Espy dealt with that situation in short order by at once hugging each one or us to her very ample bosom and letting out a stream of French endearments. "Mon petit chou" or "le petit garçon de la mère il est" soon became household expressions. Love replaced fear and France became the epitome of everything wonderful, beautiful, and all-powerful.

One of the reasons this governess wielded such an influence on me – and somewhat less on Gracie – was that father was absent in New York all day and mother did not relate as many mothers do – to small children. She was unusually attractive and occasionally affectionate, but she was also somewhat unapproachable. The older I became, the closer became our loving relationship; but in those early years she had little direct influence on my comings and goings. Father, with his outgoing and jovial personality, was, despite his enforced absence at work, much closer to me, and I always awaited his return from New York each evening with joyful anticipation.

Madame Espy was fiercely loyal to France. She had one son who was in the French navy. So she saw to it that I was usually dressed like miniature French sailor, with a *gilet rayé* and with a *pompon rouge* on top of my blue and white sailor hat. One of the first things she did was to acquire a set of *La Bibliothèque Rose.* This was a series of short stories for children about little heroes who carried messages behind the German lines and then who cheerfully died for *la Patrie*, shouting with their dying breath, "*Vive la France*". If I was bad, which was not infrequent, the threat, which invariably brought me to heel, was that she would call the *gendarme* and I knew, from pictures of this terrifying officer, that he wore a Napoleonic style black hat.

In November 1918, almost two years after the arrival of Madame Espy, the Armistice was declared, putting an end to that needless war. Looking back on that time, there seemed to be a never-ending stream of parades, American, British and French flags flying everywhere, military bands and long speeches in the town square. One occasion was especially memorable. Madame Espy, Gracie and I were seated beside the Civil War monument overlooking the Post Road down which came a long parade of returning soldiers and sailors. This must have been early in 1919. My governess said, in a voice trembling with emotion, "*Si je vois des soldats français, je vais me casser les doigts en applaudissant.*" And then down that long road, along which had marched veterans of the Revolution, the Civil War and the Spanish-American War, there came a small detachment of French *poilus*, and the U.S. Navy band struck up the stirring French marching song, *Seine et Oise*. The crowd let out a roar of approval; then Madame Espy leapt to her feet and her dumpy body tore down that hill lickety-split. Forgotten for the moment were Gracie and me; for all she could see were those boys in sky blue, and she threw herself on each and every one, embracing them, weeping tears of joy at the sight of "*mes garçons français*", "*mes soldats glorieux*", etc. Those sons of France, now living in the land of the free, never knew what had suddenly hit them, but they took it in good spirit and they must have understood the love of a little middle-aged woman for her beloved France which they had helped liberate from *les boches.*

You can imagine what the relationship was between Hermann Grunert, the German gardener, and Madame Espy. Fortunately, Madame Espy spoke practically no English, so that communication between them was minimized. Herr Grunert, who had been in the United States since the turn of the century, considered himself a loyal American. Madame Espy at first referred to him as a *sale boche,* but before long, the two got along very well. He always called her *matmwassel.*

Not many who are still living will remember the war fever, which seized the United States during the First World War. The Second World War, while justified owing primarily to Hitler, never gave rise to the bitter anti-German feeling, which permeated America in 1917-18. No symphony would play Beethoven or other German composers during that time and anyone of recent German origin was sometimes suspect. In Greenwich, there lived a prosperous and esteemed family named Schwarz, the owners of F.A.O. Schwarz toy store in New York, a most impressive emporium, to which mother took me once a year to see the fabulous stuffed animals and a myriad of other toys. In May, 1918, the Schwarzes decided to build a tennis court, thus to enable Mrs. Schwarz to play more often with some of her women friends, including mother, who, incidentally, looked on the game as beneficial rather than especially enjoyable and as offering occasions for social contacts. The problem was that when the court was about half-completed, someone started a whispering campaign to the effect that what the Schwarzes were really building was a gun emplacement. "Of all the ridiculous stories I have ever heard," mother told father and some of her best friends, as soon as this piece of intelligence reached her. Mother then invited four or five of her newly made tennis-playing acquaintances to tea. At a suitable moment, she rose and in a few well-chosen words, as was reported much later, disposed of the rumor partly by casting ridicule on such a far-fetched idea and partly with the comment that a family which had contributed so large a sum to the American Red Cross and one of whose members was serving in the Home Guard with Mr. Birge could hardly be building a gun emplacement. And where would the gun point anyway?

When one looks back on those days of America's deep involvement in that Great War, it seems incredible that we ever allowed ourselves to be drawn in. Aside from a nostalgic feeling about France's having helped the thirteen colonies win their independence, few Americans had a high regard for that country except as a pleasant place to visit. Many Americans thought of Frenchmen as barbers, headwaiters or fortune hunters, and Paris was sometimes seen as a city of sex and bad drainage. Germany, on the other hand, had provided tens of thousands of young recruits for the Union armies, and German universities had provided a model for many American colleges, especially the singing groups, fraternal societies and musical clubs such as bands and orchestras. German and Austrian composers dominated symphonic music and the greatest ocean liners afloat had been built in Hamburg or Bremen. Indeed, until 1914, affluent families had usually hired German *fräuleins* to take care of their young children. England, of course, was favorably looked upon, but even this almost universal respect for the land of law and order, of the Magna Carta, of Empire and of the fundamental liberties in which we shared, was occasionally being sniped at by the millions of sons and daughters of Eire, even then concentrated in the eastern cities.

Then, as if by the waving of a magic wand, American thinking and prejudices were changed almost overnight. It was the masterful propaganda of England and France which ensured that Americans would be fully informed about the German atrocities and about the execution of Nurse Edith Cavell; it was the bombastic stupidity of the Kaiser and then a little later, President Wilson's desire to make the world "safe for democracy" that got American into the war. Had I been born in 1905 instead of 1913, my best foreign language would probably have been German instead of French, for my governess's name would have been Schultz, or Obermeyer instead of Espy. That having been said, I am glad that 1913 was the year of my birth.

Americans tend to be sentimental and romantic, as were the German immigrants who poured into this country following the revolution of 1848, soon to be almost immediately assimilated, and their proclivity to beer, group singing, joining societies and discipline became American characteristics. In 1917, few remembered that college songs, college societies, singing clubs and the American tendency to be joiners had a good part of their origin in the land of Karl Schurtz. But these things – important or not - depending on how one saw them, were at least temporarily forgotten. Now in 1917, Americans saw Germans as Huns, as the defilers of Belgian womanhood, as the murderers of Belgian and French *poilus.* One no longer heard *Ich hatt'einen Kameraden* or *Die Lindenbaum* or that majestic hymn by Haydn to which the words beginning with *Deutschland, Deutschland über Alles* had been affixed in the late nineteenth century. Now in 1917-18, Americans heard *It's a Long Way to Tipperary* and *Johnny Get Your Gun* and *Over There, Over There.*

The purpose of the above comments is not to praise or criticize any nation. American should probably not have become involved in World War 1. Sidney B., Fay, one of Harvard's great historians, led the reader of his *Origins of the World War* to the opinion that the blame for that war should be placed as follows: 1) Austria-Hungary (notably Count Berchtold), 2) Serbia, 3) Imperial Russia, 4) the German Empire and its blustering Kaiser, 5) France, and 6) England. Professor Fay, probably the greatest American authority on the origins of that war, thus ranked Germany fourth, closely followed by France. Yet President Wilson and the Hearst press painted one side all white and the other all black. The worst offender in that regard was Prime Minister Clémenceau of France. Thus, these two men together with Mr. Lloyd George and backed by Mr. Orlando of Italy, by forcing Germany to admit sole guilt for the war and by imposing impossible reparations, created the situation which led directly to Adolph Hitler's rise to power – that, plus indirectly to the Bolshevik revolution. If America had managed to remain neutral, no one can guess what would have taken place. It is perhaps safe to say that the end result could hardly have been worse.

Be that as it may, along with all the other boys and girls of my age, and perhaps more so in my case owing to the influence of Madame Espy, the early years of life had a backdrop of *la Marseillaise* and the *Tricolore,* along with the Union Jack and the Stars and Stripes. And the great men were General "Black-Jack" Pershing and Maréchale Foch. Not long after the war the latter visited the United States and was invited to attend a Yale football game in the Yale bowl. Unfortunately, the Yale band played the Yale anthem, which is sung to the same tune as *Die Wacht am Rhein;* Foch abruptly got up to leave and was only with some difficulty prevailed upon to remain.

Madame Espy stayed with us for three and a half years. I remember she accompanied us to Rye Beach, New Hampshire, the summer of 1919, when mother whisked us all away to that reputedly secluded resort in order to escape the fearful polio epidemic then raging in the greater New York area. At that time, it was called infantile paralysis. I well remember seeing children my age with shortened legs or withered arms, or even in wheel chairs. In retrospect, this move would probably have done little to protect us – as witness F.D.R.'s falling victim to this insidious disease on Campobello Island in far-off Canada.

What I remember best about that six-week stay in Rye Beach was fishing on the beach near the huge hotel in the company of Arzy Elder, the Negro waiter for our table. Mother probably arranged for Arzy to take me off the hands of my governess for an hour or so every afternoon. It was Arzy who did the fishing while I watched, though once in a while he would allow me to hold his pole after he had cast the weighted bait out into the generally quiet sea.

While I grew to love the sight of the ocean at Rye Beach, my real and lasting fascination with the water and boats started in the summer of 1920 when we spent the summer on Fisher's Island. By that time we had two cars: the big Packard twin-six and a recently acquired Model T Ford. Tommy Minogue drove the Packard with mother, Claire, Grace, and me, and most of our luggage, while Julius, (called Judy), at age eleven, drove the Ford, accompanied by Madame Espy, as father was unable to join us until a week later. In those days there was very little traffic on the Boston Post Road and auto license regulations, if any, were casually enforced. In any case, as Judy was a good and careful driver, all went well, even when Judy had to navigate the Ford onto the *SS Restless*, the ferry which was to take us from New London out to the island. The car had to be driven over two planks, one under each set of front and rear wheels. At one moment, Judy narrowly missed running into the Sound, but he succeeded in getting that Ford on to the *Restless* with characteristic aplomb.

The memories of our stay at Fisher's Island are still quite vivid after almost two-thirds of a century. "Uncle" Fayette Plumb, father's old friend from St. David's, Pennsylvania, came for a visit with his wife, "Aunt" Grace, for whom my sister was named. The Sunday morning following the annual Harvard-Yale crew race at New London was a celebrated occasion that year. Fayette, a Harvard graduate, had been coxswain of one of the Crimson crews back around 1900 and when the newspaper arrived that morning we all gathered around and Fayette read aloud the account of the Harvard Crimson victory. From that day on, and indeed from the time when my parents first met the Plumbs, we were a Harvard family.

The most dramatic – and almost tragic – event of that summer was when our cook, whom mother had employed locally, stabbed my beloved Madame Espy between the eyes with a carving fork. Fortunately, no serious injury was sustained. Sad to relate, my governess left us that fall. Upon our return to Greenwich, I was about to enter the second grade at the Brunswick School and there remained little for her to do, so we parted company that October, and painful was that parting. Children easily adapt their lives to new situations, however, and tend to forget easily. Even if those who have been very close to them suddenly move on, the ripples of disappointment and feeling of loss soon disappear. For me at that time, exciting events were to follow.

I shall now revert to an account of father's business activities, which led in unexpected ways to those exciting events.

Father started the Air Reduction Company with one salesman, a bookkeeper, and a secretary; yet within three years he had built it into a fifty million dollar enterprise. Those were the days when that figure in sales was the present day equivalent of approximately one billion dollars.

While no one could deny that father was an outstanding success as President of Air Reduction, many of his subordinates, as the firm rapidly grew, began to complain that he was pushing them too hard. I never learned the whole story, but what I do know is that when father had been at the helm of the company for almost four years, he and the directors parted company. It seems that the latter had decided to create a new position of General Manager without consulting father, who understandably felt that this placed him in an untenable position, especially as the lines of authority were not clear. So father resigned. As he had obtained an option on a large block of stock back in 1916, the price of which had risen considerably, he was not embarrassed financially. However, I cannot help but believe that had father kept his cool and worked things out with the new general manager, who, incidentally, became one of his best friends after he too left the company a year or so later, the stock he then owned in 1919 but sold when he left the company, would a few years later have been worth many millions.

Before father got back on an even keel emotionally following the business misadventure, he suffered what was akin to a nervous breakdown and he went with his younger brother, Stanley, to Arizona, apparently to recover. I sorely missed dad while he was away but rejoiced when he returned and brought me two Indian tomahawks, which I still cherish.

In the fall of 1920, two Italians from Turin, executives of the giant textile firm, SNIA Viscosa, came to New York with a view to finding a competent and experienced man of business to head up a United States company, which they planned to establish for the manufacture of artificial silk. Among the first men they called on were, perhaps fortuitously, perhaps owing to previous business contacts or bank recommendation, were Samuel Pryor and Percy Rockefeller. Apparently these two men held no hard feeling toward father and they strongly recommended him for the position these Italian executives had in mind, - "the ideal man for the job", they were later to report as Mr. Pryor's words.

I can imagine father's surprise when these two men from Turin telephoned him to suggest a meeting in New York. Father loved any challenge and especially one that involved getting in on the ground floor of a new business. He had self-confidence and ego, and the idea of being the president of the first artificial silk company in America intrigued him. When the position was offered to him at a luncheon a few days later, father, who prided himself on his readiness to make rapid decisions, accepted at once. The Italians, Mr. Treniaghi and Mr. Gurgo then suggested that father come to Italy to discuss final arrangements with the directors of SNIA Viscosa as soon as possible. The immediate result of the foregoing was that all four of us children, Claire, Julius, Grace, and I, ages fourteen, twelve, nine, and seven, were taken out of school and passage was booked for the six of us on the 20,000 ton Cunard steamer, *Caronia,* which was to sail from New York on January 1st, 1921, on its first cruise after the war. I shall never forget that wonderful adventure.

That voyage, which from our point of view was really not a cruise in the accepted sense, but rather a means of getting over to Italy in the most pleasant way possible, was quite uneventful. Father and mother seemed to have no worries in the world. Mr. Lavery, a jolly, middle-aged Englishman, befriended me, and presented me with a pocket compass to remember him by. Other highlights included a superficial bash on my head when I tripped and fell to the deck; a thrilling visit to the engine room where I gazed in fascination at the giant, roaring reciprocating steam engines; the stopover at Madeira, where we coasted down a hill in a sort of toboggan which slid over cobble stones. Then there was the visit to Algeciras, Spain, where seemingly countless peddlers entreated us to buy many marvelous items as we drove by in a carriage father had hired for a sightseeing excursion. One of these vendors managed to keep up with our moving vehicle and held up a beautiful dagger close to my eyes. I was at once captivated. "How much?" called out father. "Only three dollar!" replied the would-be seller, now out of breath. "One dollar!" was father's rejoinder, uttered with an unsmiling, straight face. The vendor kept running beside us, and father turned away. I saw my dagger being lost forever. The peddler cried out that at one dollar he would be ruined. But a few seconds later, the priceless weapon changed hands – first to father, and then to me, as a large, crisp one dollar bill was passed to the previous owner of my new treasure. I still have that dagger which now hangs on the wall in our downstairs hall, along with much more valuable and interesting weapons. But for that boy, in January 1921, and even for the man in his eightieth year that gim-crack dagger is still very special. By way of mention, the dollar bill of 1921 had some real purchasing power.

We left the *Caronia* at Monaco and at once boarded an express train for Turin. The six of us were able to find an empty compartment and I was at once intrigued at how we were warned in four languages about how it was dangerous to lean out the window. The conductor was one continual vast smile and in the dining car there were dishes I had never heard of and now could eat. When we finally alighted from this fabulous train at Turin, we were greeted by three executives from the big textile firm, including father's recent acquaintance, Mr. Treniaghi, elegantly attired in striped trousers and morning coat, whose name for the next few years would be a household word. The three Italians were carrying flowers for mother and when she – fabulously beautiful creature that she was – descended the steps of our car, the greeting of Mr. Treniaghi and his colleagues was effusive to say the least. "Che bella donna!" said the SNIA Viscosa delegation in unison. Then Mr. Treniaghi, taking mother's hand, now burdened with all the blossoms, added, "We had heard that American women were handsome, but we were not prepared for beauty such as yours!"

"Thank you, Mr. Treniaghi, thank you, gentlemen," mother replied, "Now I understand why my husband has expressed enthusiasm at the prospect of being associated with men such as you." We were then escorted to a palace of a hotel and presently to dinner at which our hosts insisted that we all be served wine, notwithstanding mother's politely expressed concern that Grace and I, at least, were much too young. Finally, she agreed to allow us watered wine; and so at the age of seven, I was introduced to the nectar of the Gods who had an Italian accent.

Our stay in Turin was short as Judy, Grace and I were to be put in Swiss schools: Sillig Institute for boys and Mlle Emerlin for girls. Moreover, Dad was scheduled to meet Dr. Fath, the chemist for SNIA Viscosa, in Vevey, the town where Sillig's (as it was generally called) was also. All went well until we spent the night in the Italian frontier town of Domodossola. Soon after leaving the train there I began to have difficulty in breathing – not because of any basic problem with my lungs, but apparently because I had all of a sudden developed swollen adenoids. The following morning, we continued on through the Simplon Tunnel and to Vevey.

Immediately upon arrival in that picturesque town it seemed essential to get me to a nose and throat doctor without delay. Apparently, the closest, well-recommended man in that field was in Lausanne, a Dr. Roche. I shall never forget that name. Mother, father and I traveled to Lausanne in a motorcycle sidecar, the first and last time I ever rode in such a conveyance. At that time taxis were not plentiful and the motorcycle-sidecar seemed logical.

The fearsome Dr. Roche, slender, grim, unsmiling, lost no time. After examining me, he announced that I had a "large clump of adenoids" which had to come out at once. I was given the choice of a local or general anesthetic. "Only", said the doctor, "if you choose general anesthesia you will have to take castor oil first." That made my choice easier as I had no intention of taking castor coil.

Suffice it to say about that operation, that it was terrifying and, as I look back on it, very painful; but a seemingly huge clump of adenoids did come out; and I never had any more trouble with adenoids again.

Soon after, father returned to the United States; Grace was put in Mlle Emerlin's in Bex; and mother and Claire left for Italy to visit the museums, churches and elegant hotels. I remained in Vevey with Judy in the Institut Sillig, the boys' school near the shore of Lake Geneva, that is, between Montreux and Lausanne. This school, which catered to foreign boys, notably the sons of diplomats stationed in Switzerland and nearby countries, took its name from Monsieur Max Sillig, the founder and headmaster. His wife, Madame Max, as she was called, was an elegant Frenchwoman who had style, good looks and a never-ceasing determination to ensure that all Sillig boys had good manners and gentlemanly ways. She sought to achieve this goal by having boys wait on her at every opportunity; at tea, when we sat by her at meals; when she invited a few of us to visit her in what was known as her boudoir. In that luxurious retreat, permeated with the smell of Turkish cigarettes and French perfume, we were taught to light her cigarettes, to pass chocolates, to pull out her chair when she was about to sit down, etc.

As I was the youngest boy in the school, I shared a room with my brother. The most vivid memory I have of this arrangement is the night when part of the school kitchen caught fire. It was not a very serious blaze, but it did entail all boys being required to get dressed at once and rapidly. I apparently had trouble finding my clothes, buttoning my trousers and, incredible as it may seem, tying my tie, for although part of the school might have burned down, the little gentlemen were expected to be properly dressed. Judy, that wonderful brother, ended up by performing most of these functions, and with such success that within three minutes I was dressed and standing with all students outside the school buildings.

I do not believe that I learned anything in academics at Silligs, except French, and that only by dint of having to speak it most of the time. Each Friday, every member of the school was obliged to report aloud how many sentences other then French he had spoken during that week. If he had spoken no English, or other non-French native language, he reported, "*sans exception*". If he thought he had spoken English, etc., a few times, he might report, "*excepté dix phrases*". I felt that I could report the "*sans exception*" only twice and I doubt that this optimistic summary was justified. Without doubt this exposure to the French language proved to be invaluable over the years to come.

Every morning before breakfast the whole school, that is, about thirty boys, was directed to the playing field, just across the road and by the lake, where all of us were put through strenuous sitting-up exercises. After this, we were paired off for wrestling matches. On one occasion, I had to wrestle against Bill Robinson, also an American, who was two years older than I. He put me on my back once, but finally I managed to pin him down. Perhaps because I was the youngest boy in the school, the older students liked me. Following my great victory in that match, I was carried into the dining room on their shoulders, a peak of popularity I was never to attain again. Those morning workouts taught me pretty well how to wrestle and defend myself and that, too, proved useful from time to time.

When spring came to Vevey, it was a beautiful place and I had no worries. We played cops and robbers in the nearby forest; we took walking excursions, with lunch breaks of Swiss cheese on large slices of delicious bread, and a sweet concoction called *bouchée Klaus*. The school had several four-oared crews and I was drafted to be a coxswain, which was enjoyable until I ran one of the shells into the dock. Fortunately, the damage was slight or I would never have lived it down. One activity, although sometimes exciting, was less enjoyable and involved "friendly" rock throwing contests between Sillig students and village boys. The beach near the school was strewn with rocks of all sizes. A group of village boys – the equivalent in the U.S.A. are sometimes called "townies" – would build a small fort of rocks, small enough to be lifted into place, and then, partially protected by their fort, they would start throwing small stones at Sillig boys who had built their own rock fort. Occasionally, one of the two groups would attack the other, throwing stones as they advanced.

Only once did I join our Sillig army, and when I saw one of our boys with a bloodied forehead, that was enough. The next day the Vevey gendarmerie put a stop to this mini-war.

In late May, mother and Claire, now fifteen, returned to Vevey from Italy where they had been visiting the museums and otherwise soaking up culture for three months. I remember that the school held a dance in June and Claire danced a tango, that daring and sensuous dance floor movement recently introduced from Argentina, with Roland de Graffenried, one of the young visiting graduates who was very good looking. Claire remembered this adventure for a long time for she always loved to dance, and this ability on the dance floor moved hand in glove with her beauty and sparkling personality.

As soon as school let out, the five of us - mother, Claire, Judy (Julius), Grace, and I – took the train from Montreux to Interlaken and thence to Grindelwald and the Bären Hotel. From this outstanding hostelry we could see the Wetterhorn, Eiger, Mönch, and, in the greater distance, the Jungfrau towering above. Of these, the terrifying Eiger was by far the most dangerous for mountain clumbers. Indeed, few mountains anywhere in the world present more problems that that *ogre*. I pressed mother to allow me to climb that mountain, but even at the adventurous age of eight, the lugubrious tone with which everyone questioned on the subject described the dangers of that soaring Alp was finally enough to divert my attention to the more friendly looking Wetterhorn. So, soon after our arrival at the Bären Hotel, Judy, Grace and I set out with Wolfgang, one of the hotel-recommended guides. We were to go only as high as the Gluckstein hut, the halfway stop to the summit. The only scary part was the glacier and this trepidation was caused mainly by Judy's graphic word-picture of an English bridegroom-climber who had fallen into one of the crevices of this same glacier almost a half century before while on his honeymoon, and just the year before our arrival had been harvested, so to speak, his body perfectly preserved, at the foot of the very slowly moving ice mass, as his widow, now an old woman, looked on.

We arrived at the halfway hut in time for lunch, which we were carrying with us. Our descent from that height was without incident and that evening, we prepared for our departure from Switzerland the following day. Exactly ten years later, I was to climb to the summit of the Wetterhorn, and narrowly escape serious injury or a gruesome death in doing so.

On our way back to the United States we visited Paris for a few days. There, I spent each afternoon under the supervision of a temporary governess while the other members of the family visited the Louvre, the book-stalls on the river bank, the Eiffel Tower, the Arc de Triomphe, the left bank, and other sights which mother presumed would have had no interest for her eight year old. And she was right.

On the day my governess reported for duty she took me to the Luxembourg Gardens where they had a carrousel. The children, as they went round, tried to put a small pencil-sized bar through a ring. Seated on the wooden horse just in front of me was a French boy of about my age. Almost at once we entered into animated conversation during which he asked how old I was. When I replied that I was eight, he at once informed me, "*Moi, j'ai neuf ans*", and he went on to say that he would be able to beat me in a wrestling match – "*Je pourrais te battre dans la lutte!*" I then assured this good-natured young braggart that I could have him his back in no time – all this in fluent French, of course. When the carrousel came to a stop, this French boy, with a polite wave of his hand and a "*Suis-moi, je t'en prie*", ushered me to a flat green space, which was close to the merry-go-round. We stopped and my young opponent bowed. Then I put to good stead all those pre-breakfast periods at Sillig's. Within ten seconds, I had this boy down and was in process of pinning his shoulders when first a young woman, soon identified as the French boy's mother, rushed over to us; then to me she cried, "*Ne lui fais pas mal!*" (Don't hurt him). My temporary governess then quickly materialized and started to pull me off. As I got up, the small crowd, which had quickly gathered around us, began to cry out, "*Vive l'Américain*", for in 1921, the French were still pro-American. My gentlemanly opponent then insisted that one of his shoulders had not been pinned down. Flushed with my victory gained before all those friendly people, I was walking on air and could afford to be magnanimous, so I put my arm around the shoulder of my new friend-antagonist and admitted that just maybe one of his shoulders had not been put completely down.

Then I noticed among the onlookers, some of them still cheering, a beguiling little girl who was looking at me with rapt admiration. I walked up to where she stood and asked her name and age, as children have a habit of doing: "*Quel âge as-tu? Comment t'appelles-tu?*" "*Je m'appelle Jeanne-Marie et j'ai six ans*", replied the adorable creature whose hair was like the gold of a Normandy wheat-field at harvest and whose admiring eyes matched the blue of that sunny sky above. Then I announced that I would like to see her again that day and asked if she could meet me at that same place at six that afternoon.

How I imagined that such a rendezvous would be possible, given the strict supervision under which I was operating, I have no idea. As for little Jeanne-Marie, she seemed entranced by my suggestion that we would meet so soon again. As I walked reluctantly away, I looked back at that lovable little golden-haired angel, her chubby hand waving goodbye and her clear, elfin voice calling, "*A bientôt l'Américain*". Alas, my first romance was nipped in the bud as my ubiquitous mademoiselle whisked me away, and I never saw Jeanne-Marie again.

We arrived back in Greenwich in mid-summer. In the interim, father had sold our large house at number one, North Street, having first rented it out during most of the time we had been overseas to Marjorie Merriweather Post, after her divorce from Edward Close, but probably before her marriage to Edward Hutton, (she later became Mrs. Davies, and Mrs. May). Father's new company, the U.S. subsidiary of SNIA Viscosa, the Industrial Fiber Company, was scheduled to begin operations in Cleveland that fall, so we took up temporary quarters in a rather small but comfortable inn called the Kent House. This hostelry, being close to Long Island Sound, reminded me of Fishers Island.

In September, father announced that the time had come for us all to move to Cleveland, where the new factory was almost ready to begin operations. There were seven of us to move west: the six members of our family and Jim, an attractive young colored chauffeur recently hired. All of us had to fit into that large Packard Twin-six, now permanently equipped with the summer "touring-car" body. I still do not figure out how we all fitted in that car, large as it was. Much of the luggage - most of which had been shipped ahead- was strapped to the running boards. I sat up front with Jim; mother, father, and Claire occupied the back seat; and Judy and Grace sat on the retractable jump seats. And so we were off, first to Binghamton, New York, where we spent the first night in a sorry looking hotel customarily patronized by traveling salesmen.

The second day, we drove to Buffalo, where we were to board the night boat for Cleveland. In those days, there were no through highways, and sadly inadequate road signs. One had to drive with the constant assistance of a *Blue Book*. We were guided by 7uch entries as: *Proceed on this road for one and a half miles until you come to a red barn on your left. Now turn right and proceed about five hundred yards until you reach a spreading oak tree; here you will see a fork in the road. Take the left bifurcation until you come to Elwood's General Store"*. Any speed of more than 35 miles an hour was like flying. I remember coming to a stop at a country cross road. A large Pierce Arrow drew up along side and a distinguished looking gentleman leaned forwards from the back seat and called to us that we were averaging better than 25 miles an hour, and he congratulated us on our excellent time which he had instructed his chauffeur to emulate by following us closely.

Upon our arrival in Buffalo, we proceeded directly to the port area and loaded the big Packard on the night boat destined to Cleveland. Father had reserved three cabins and after a large dinner of southern fried chicken with cream gravy, father's favorite meal, and one I would come to know all too well during later years in Greenwich, we all went right to bed. Jim slept in one of the cabins used by domestic help. The next morning, he reported that he had eaten and slept fine.

In Cleveland, father rented a medium size house on Monmouth Road in the Cleveland Heights district, and at once addressed himself to the consuming task of building the fortunes of the Industrial Fiber Company. Claire and Julius were placed in Hathaway Brown and University School, respectively – two excellent private schools which were to prepare them for entry into Farmington (Miss Porter's School) and Groton the following year. Grace and I entered the Fairfax School, my only exposure as a student to a public school, which I look back on as having been excellent.

I entered the third grade and established what I believe to have been a close rapport with Miss Hood, the unusually able and sympathetic teacher of that class. I remember that occasionally, she would have us listen to music played on an old Victrola; and without knowing the title to the piece, she would ask us to guess what the composer had been thinking of when he composed the music. I remember that one of those pieces was "A Whistler and His dog". I guessed correctly as to the whistler but not about the dog.

Of course, I acquired a bicycle and soon I had explored every section of that neighborhood. Every day, father drove the large Packard to and from the factory in West Cleveland. Shortly after our arrival, father bought a Lincoln sedan so that Jim, the chauffeur would be able to drive mother around, and Claire and Judy to and from school. In his spare time, Jim also carved toy boats for me, for he was also an adept carpenter.

Severe weather dominated that winter. There was a lot of snow and the temperature seemed always to hover well below the freezing point. We were beset by illnesses and came very close to suffering a tragedy in the family. One morning, Claire awoke with a bad stomachache. Our family physician, Dr. Taylor, strongly suspected appendicitis, but for most of that day was unable to establish contact with Dr. Russell Birge, a distant cousin who was a prominent surgeon and good friend since our arrival. He was finally found on the golf course and Claire was at once taken to Lakeside Hospital, where Dr. Birge operated on her without delay. It was almost too late, however. Her appendix had burst and peritonitis had set in. Within two days, her temperature soared to 106 degrees and she hovered near death for several days. Somehow, her system conquered the infection and she slowly mended. Had Claire died at that time, as well she might have, our lives, and certainly mine, would have been vastly different. The brightest of the family and in many ways its most cohesive force, she probably influenced my life in one way or another, more than any other person. She it was who married the great clinical scientist, Fuller Albright, and settled in Boston in May, 1932, my freshman year at Harvard. During my last three years in Cambridge, her small house at 9 Joy Street was always a second home and a ready refuge from the tumult and shouting that occasionally assaulted Harvard students. She it was who provided the anchor continually to link my life with Boston. How bleak would my early life have been without Claire.

In the spring of 1922, Judy took the competitive examinations for entry into Groton and passed easily; and that too was to have an impact – a happy one- on my life as will be pointed out later. Judy was struck down by scarlet fever that spring, a misfortune that happily did not adversely affect his Groton exam grades. Mother had planned to take a house in England for the coming summer, having begun these arrangements through the good offices of an English lady she had met in Switzerland the previous year. Owing to Judy's weakened condition resulting from his illness, however, these plans were given up, so in 1922, we returned to Greenwich, Connecticut.

In mid-June, Jim, the chauffeur, having been let go a short time before, and the big Packard having been bestowed on a member of the Industrial Fiber staff, dad drove us east in the new Lincoln ("By Leland") sedan. En route, we had an accident – fortunately not too serious – in eastern Pennsylvania necessitating our completing the last 150 miles by a hired car.

Immediately upon our arrival in Greenwich, we moved into the Augustus Blagden house, which father had arranged to rent for the summer months, well before our departure from Cleveland. This turned out to be a pleasant arrangement, as Bob Perry, the Blagdens' colored chauffeur, who lived over the garage, was available to drive for us that summer. Moreover, Bob's brother Dick worked for dad in the same capacity when we moved in early September into the Seton's place. That summer, my parents had searched assiduously for a suitable house to purchase, but without success, but as it turned out – for me at least – renting the Seton place for two and a half years worked out perfectly at the time when I was aged nine through eleven.

Dad joined three clubs that summer: the Field Club for tennis, the Greenwich Country Club, where dad occasionally played golf and which I hardly ever saw, and the Manursing Island Club in nearby Rye, New York, to which we used to drive in the hot days of July and August for swimming in Long Island Sound. For these excursions, we acquired a Ford station wagon with a wooden body – the first of that type produced. I used to sit on the floor at the back of this vehicle with my legs dangling half way down to the pavement. Of course, in those days, there were relatively few cars on any roads except in city streets, and even there, parking was never a problem. One just drove up to the curb – any curb – and parked. By way of mention: early in 1923, dad joined twenty or so friends and acquaintances as charter members of a new golf club on Round Hill Road, which was much more conveniently located for us; and I assume dad then resigned from the Greenwich Golf Club.

The Seton place, mentioned above, into which we moved in the late summer, was a most unusual house which had been built under the close supervision of Ernest Thompson Seton, the elderly – at least he looked pretty old to me – author of very well-known books on nature and animal lore, and children's books, such as "Wild Animals I Have Known". He was also an authority on the American Indian. His daughter, Anya Seton, also became a well-known writer.

Mr. Seton lived adjoining us in a smaller house. Father rented the main Seton property, which encompassed a rather large lake, circled by a rough road that measured a mile around. There was a small island in the middle of this lake where a floodlight made it possible to skate during the winter, even after sundown. As this body of water had been stocked with bass, I spent many happy hours trolling. I would just attach the line to the stern seat; throw the troll over board, and paddle or row, depending which boat I was in. I always caught something. I remember that Bill Arnold, a year or so older than me, who lived a half mile from us, used occasionally to walk over to try his luck. As he had no boat, he would cast a line off from one of the arched stone bridges over which ran our driveway. I do not remember that he ever caught anything but he would often ask me to give him one of the fish I had caught so that he would not have to return home empty handed.

In that fall of 1922, both Claire and Julius went away to boarding school – she to Miss Porter's School, in Farmington, Connecticut, which was always called "Farmington", and he to Groton, in Groton, Massachusetts, while I entered the fourth grade at the Brunswick School and Grace began her sixth grade at Greenwich Academy. During the time we lived in the Seton house, Claire and Judy were home only during the Christmas and Easter holidays during the school year. Grace did not enter Farmington until 1925, the year I went away to Groton at age twelve.

In those days, there was, of course, no television and practically no radio. Hence, there was little for me to do evenings except read; so I really ploughed through the "Book of Knowledge", geography texts, and the thrilling tales by G.A.Henty, most of which father had read in the late 1880's and early 1890's. Those were the days when I also read all about the battles of the American Revolution and the western frontier – events embellished by John Pringle, our butler.

Those were halcyon days. To a boy of my age, the great sprawling house next to the lake and otherwise surrounded by forest was heaven. Great foot-square beams supported the ceilings of the huge living room and the fireplace would easily hold four-foot logs for the roaring fires of winter. There was a large barn where we kept horses, and later, my beloved Welsh pony, Comanche. We had our own chickens, a cow and pigs, as well as an icehouse where we stocked blocks of ice cut from the lake. In winter, when the lake could often freeze to a foot thick, many neighbors would join us for skating.

I would roam happily through the woods with my Airedale, Spike, trying to emulate the young heroes of G.A.Henty's historical novels. I also loved to pretend I was a pioneer living among the Indians. How fortunate I was to have Mr. Seton living so close by.

Every winter evening, an open fire would roar and crackle in the living room. For a while, dad would stand in front of that fire and repeat several times, "How I love an open fire." Then he would often sit down on the large sofa beside mother and they might listen to Caruso's voice blaring out from the wind-up Victrola, as Grace and I played mah-jong.

Mr. Seton had founded an equivalent to the Boy Scouts, namely: the Woodcraft Indian League. He had built a circle of large stones in the woods; and two times a year he invited the members of his "Council" to an Indian powwow over which he presided. Of course, I was asked to join this select organization, if only because the Council rocks were situated on our rented property. We used to put on Indian wardress, have hand-wrestling contests, sing Indian songs, listen to Mr. Seton's stories and always had a good time. I became very adept at Indian wrestling and seldom lost a match. Once a year, father gave Mr. Seton permission to invite all members of his League – all parents included – to a big jamboree; and, of course, I enjoyed playing the role of the special guest.

In mid-May, some eight months after our arrival and just before my tenth birthday, Mr. Seton suggested that I be formally inducted into the Council by undergoing a special initiation which consisted of being led blind-folded at dusk to a sparsely-wooded area and left there until sunup the following morning. I was allowed to take with me only a penknife and a blanket. I was not allowed to have a compass, flashlight or food. Most important, I could not have my dog, Spike, to keep me company.

I did not get much sleep and I can vividly remember watching the stars as they moved across the sky and feeling totally alone far from home. While it was not very cold, the early morning dew began to dampen my only blanket and I feared that I might be forgotten. Then, to make matters worse, fearful wild-animal cries emanated from the surrounding woods. Though I guessed that Mr. Seton might be the source of these noises, they were nevertheless terrifying. Finally, after what seemed like an eon, Mr. Seton came to escort me home. As it turned out in the comforting light of the dawning day, I really had not been far from home the previous night. My ordeal was well worth the well nigh sleepless night, as Mr. Seton now pronounced me a full-fledged Indian scout.

During that time – 1922 to 1925 – we had colored servants. I use the term "colored" instead of "black" or "African-American" now in vogue, as that was the current word in use. The first group consisted of John Stull, the butler, Ada, the chambermaid, Ada's sister Sarah, the cook, Dick Perry, the big six foot-four chauffeur, (brother of Bob, who had driven us during the summer of 1922) and Bradley, the "outside man". Also living in the household was Henry Pringle, the nephew of Sara and Ada, who was one and a half years older than I. Henry's parents, John and Cora, had remained temporarily in Winston-Salem, North Carolina.

Just why Henry came to live with us I never asked. I think that his parents intended to follow the rest of the family up north. In any case, Henry became my great friend. We camped out together, played baseball with some of the ordinary "town" kids and, bearing in mind that we were not in school together, and that this was a different era, we had a fine and close friendship.

Hot-tempered John Stull stood about five foot eight and weighed a powerful 190 pounds, while Bradley, the "outside man" was wiry, mercurial and graceful. Sometimes he gave me boxing lessons in the basement. At that time muskrats abounded in and around the lake and very soon caught the attention of John and Bradley. One autumn day they decided to go out hunting with a view to acquiring skins from a few of those watery rodents. I doubt that father was consulted. Whatever the circumstances of the hunt, it seems that these two dark skinned nimrods somehow managed to bring home two muskrats. I spied them walking home along the lakeshore road, each gingerly holding one of the creatures by its rat-like tail. But then the trouble began, for there was apparently a considerable difference between two dead muskrats and two clean muskrat skins with the remains disposed of; and neither John nor Bradley, it seemed, wished to be the instrument in this transformation.

I never heard them arguing at length, but Henry reported, "They're mad at each other, yes, Walter, real mad!" Well, a few days after that hunt, with the muskrats still staying cool, covered with sawdust in the icehouse, Bradley walked into the kitchen on his way to the cellar door in order to shovel coal into the furnace. John was chopping up meat with the huge cleaver which father had recently acquired from the Plumb Hatchet Company. Henry and I were passing the time gabbing in the kitchen and Sarah and Ada were also there.

When Bradley had walked a few steps toward the cellar door, John said, "Say dere, Bradley, you done skinned dose muskrats yet?" Bradley, pausing an instant in his panther-like steps, turned his head on its skinny neck to look at John. "John, you know dat ah done most of de catchin', so, followin' owah agreement, you is meant to do duh skinnin'. 'Sides, you has de equipment and you gots de women folk to hep." "Listen heah, Bradley," replied John, "You are de outside man, so you's got to do de skinnin'".

The argument became increasingly heated with insults being shouted back and forth. Finally, John shouted, "Get out of mah kitchen!" as Bradley reached behind him for the cellar doorknob. John claimed later that he thought Bradley was reaching for a pistol. What then happened, I never forgot. John already had the big cleaver in his grasp, and with a sidewise fling of his arm, he struck that murderous implement at Bradley's head. Bradley's incredibly fast reflex saved his life, for he ducked with the speed of a mongoose and the cleaver sank into the cellar door a scant half inch above where the top of his head now was. At that instant, Henry and I, who had been watching this scene with speechless fascination, bolted out the back door and headed for the garage to report the goings on to "big Dick Perry", the chauffeur.

Sara later reported that John retrieved his cleaver from the cellar door and chased Bradley across the kitchen, chopping at this head as he ran. Ada rushed between the two men, thus doubtless saving Bradley's life.

Meanwhile, Henry and I were pouring out our frenzied account of the kitchen drama to Dick Perry. Then Bradley came running down the driveway from the house, his left cheek laid wide open by an ugly and bloody wound which had obviously been inflicted by that cleaver. "Lemme have yo gun, Dick," he entreated the chauffeur. "Ah'm gonna shoot John." Just then my father appeared, dressed in his old leather-hunting jacket, with his Smith & Wesson 38 revolver in its holster, strapped to his waist.

"If there is going to be any shooting, I'll do the shooting," stated dad. But when Bradley turned around to face him and dad saw his fearful wound, he turned abruptly and headed for the house to deal with John. As soon as dad re-entered the house by the kitchen door, (the nearest entrance), he informed John that he had twenty minutes to get off the place. But then the wily Ada, who we later found out was in love with John, persuaded mother and father that John had acted in what he thought was self defense when he saw Bradley reaching for a gun. Mother, who had not seen Bradley's wound and who was fond of Ada, persuaded father to change his mind about firing John, and the situation reverted to the status quo. Twenty-four hours later, I saw John and Bradley, now with twenty stitches in his cheek, exchanging pleasantries and seemingly the best of friends again. I never did find out who skinned those muskrats.

One of my dearest memories is my trip to New Haven to see my first Harvard-Yale football game in the fall of 1922. One evening in late November, father asked me whether I would like to see the big game on the coming Saturday. It seems he had a business acquaintance that would be staying with us that weekend – a Harvard graduate and former Crimson star of the gridiron. There would be four tickets and I could bring a friend along. I jumped at the chance of seeing that game about which I had already heard so much, even from my fourth grade school friends. At that time and until I left Brunswick School for Groton, my best friend was Dave Harrington, later to become a baseball pitching ace for Yale. So we set out on a frigid Saturday morning of that November, bound for New Haven. Of course, Dick Perry was driving. Father and his business friend sat in the comfortable back seat and Dave and I occupied the jump seats of the Lincoln town car.

Father's close friend and former Yale crew captain, Augustus Blagden, whose nearby house we had rented before moving to the Seton place, was also driving up to New Haven and dad had suggested that our two cars drive up in tandem. The Blagdens had a Marmon touring car and their chauffeur, it will be recalled, was Bob Perry, Dick's brother. Bob and I were old friends from the past summer.

The Perry brothers were looking forward to this excursion, notwithstanding the cold in the unheated automobiles of that era. We were fairly comfortable in the back, armed as we were with a huge raccoon skin robe and two monogrammed cashmere blankets, which had been especially made for the car. When the two cars reached Bridgeport, Dick Perry drew abreast of the Blagden's Marmon in the center of town where a red-faced cop motioned for us to stop to allow a few pedestrians to cross the Post Road. Bob Perry leaned out his driver's side door and called to Dick, "Hey, how about a little bet on the game? Mr. Blagden tells me the Big Blue is going to stomp Harvard." Dick replied,"Ah got two dollah that says de Crimson is going to ee-merge victorious. We got a fomah Hahvahd star who done tole me you all ain' got no chance." I remember that the Blagden family and dad and his friend thought this exchange hilariously funny.

We finally reached New Haven that blustery, frigid November afternoon. One of the rather silly memories of that day, having nothing to do with anything else, was going into the men's room in the Hotel Taft, then to discover that I did not have a dime to put into the lock-release mechanism on the door of one of the cubicles. So I crawled under the door, did my business and then started to crawl out, but as I was doing so, I found myself looking at the trousers of a very tall gentleman who was looking down at me with a wide grin. I had not yet reached the age when one saw an episode such as this in a humorous light; so I beat a hasty retreat. I was now ready for the game and we drove to the Bowl along with the streetcars and hundreds of automobiles, most of which displayed Harvard crimson or Yale blue banners.

No streetcar conductor attempted to collect a fare that day, for young people lined the running-board of those cars, and to do so the conductor would have had to edge his way along those jammed running boards on those swaying, bumping cars.

I do not remember too much about that game of so long ago, but one thing I do recall, and that was the great run up through the Yale line of George Owen, Harvard's ten-letter man. Fifty-five years later, when my sister Claire had the Owens and me to dinner, I asked George about that run and that game; and he remembered every step and every move he made on the play, which won the game for Harvard, 10-3.

We all drove back to Greenwich after the game, Dick Perry richer by four dollars and Dad's Harvard graduate friend overjoyed at the result. Dad was a light drinker in those days of prohibition, but whenever he had guests, as was the case that evening, there was always a cocktail for the men before dinner. No hard liquor "on the rocks" in those days. Those cocktails were carefully mixed and then shaken up with ice in a silver shaker. John Stull prided himself on his cocktail-shaking ability, as indeed did his successor, the great and good John Pringle, and on those special occasions when an extra butler was hired for dinners of perhaps ten or more, the visiting professional would invariably show off his cocktail-shaking ability by going into syncopated movements and catchy rhythms with the shaker. I was always fascinated by this traditional exercise, and that November evening was no exception. There was a roaring fire going and all was right with the world of the early twenties and of President Lowell's Harvard and of President Harding's America.

Not long after the events just related there was an important change in our household; that is, important as I saw it. The cleaver-wielding John Stull and Ada were replaced by Henry's parents, John and Cora Pringle who had recently arrived in Greenwich from Winston Salem. Now the Pringle family was united and for me, my life in that household became far more interesting and stimulating. John Pringle, now the butler, was a graduate of Lincoln University and far better educated than over ninety-nine per cent of the blacks of those far off days. He could discuss logic – though of course I did not understand anything he had to say on that subject – and he was a history buff with a lively mind full of battle dates and other important events. He could recite the Gettysburg Address and quote from both the Old and New Testaments of the Bible to anyone who would listen; and that was almost always I. He would fire questions at me such as, "Tell me about the Dred Scott Decision", or, "When was the battle of Tippecanoe?" Then he might intone, "What ye sow, so shall you reap." And he often commanded, "Reach for the stars, Walter!" And sometimes in the years ahead I would think back on John's words and remember with nostalgia and affection this very special friend of my boyhood. Indeed, I have never forgotten John Pringle over the ensuing seventy years for he was he was an influence for good and decency.

Henry, his son and my playmate during the three years between the ages of nine and twelve, was also a special friend. Many were the times when we played baseball with some of the public school village boys in an adjacent field; and then there were the occasions when Henry came to my assistance when I got into a fight with a boy too big for me, and he would say, "Walter, let me take care of this boy."

Cora Pringle, now the chambermaid, was tall, gentle and soft-spoken; indeed, it could be said that she was a *café au lait* edition of mother. Early in 1923, mother had her portrait painted by an obscure artist, Rachel Worrell, who had been recommended by an equally obscure acquaintance. Would that John Singer Sargent had been that artist. He would have done justice to mother's elegance, style, and patrician beauty. For her calm blue eyes, golden hair, perfect skin and her queenly carriage were indeed a sight to behold. I still have that portrait. It reveals that mother was beautiful, but it fails to bring forth the above-mentioned qualities of her beauty. The reason mention is made of that portrait is that mother sat for it in a handsome red velvet gown, and Cora often spoke to mother about how much she admired that gown. In the fall of 1924, word reached mother as well as all of us, that John and Cora were soon to attend a formal ball in town to be sponsored by their church. The same day mother heard about this upcoming event she presented the gown to Cora, a gesture which ensured Cora's total devotion; and this was perhaps logical for each was a beauty of her own race and time.

In July of 1923, my grandfather, Julius Birge, and grandmother, Mary Jane Patrick Birge, celebrated their fiftieth wedding anniversary in Charlevoix, Michigan, for many years their summer retreat from the withering heat of Saint Louis. In addition to the grandparents, there were four sons and a daughter of father's generation, and sixteen grandchildren. As two cottages had been rented for the occasion, every one of us was put up, many on sleeping porches. That celebration lasted a week. The first thing father did immediately upon our arrival was to rent a thirty foot sloop equipped with an inboard auxiliary engine which never functioned more than a few minutes at a time.

On Sunday, no one was allowed to engage in any activity other than going to church in the morning and then to a late afternoon hymn-singing service, which was conducted by grandfather who sat up on the raised stage of the high school auditorium. "Which hymn shall we sing?" grandfather intoned following the conclusion of the last musical rendition. The first time grandfather asked that question the hundred or more members of that congregation shouted, "Throw Out the Lifeline", and this loud cry was repeated at least three times. The great Calvin of the Reformation would have nodded in approval had he been present, for he was ably represented by that austere grandfather, the Senior Warden of Pilgrim Congregational Church of Saint Louis.

The anniversary celebration dinner was held in the evening before our departure. Uncle Stanley, the youngest child, and at age thirty-six still a bachelor, was the master of ceremonies and called on each and everyone present to get up and say something. As Judy was grandfather's namesake, his was meant to be the key oration and he spoke last. Before the dinner, the five other members of my immediate family asked me whether I had a speech prepared. Timidity was not one of my glaring faults and I remember feeling confident that at the last moment I would come up with a suitable few words. During the preceding days

I had entertained two or three of my cousins with a ditty I had learned from Sarah, our cook. One of these relatives, doubtless with tongue in cheek suggested that I sing that song at the celebration dinner.

At the dinner, most of the dishes had been cleared away and Uncle Stanley rose to call on the younger generation to make their renditions. As I was one of the youngest grandchildren, my turn came quite soon. The toastmaster rose and looked down on me seated half way down the table. "And now we will hear from Waltie." Mother and father looked in my direction with quiet smiles of expectant approval, benevolent expressions which soon evaporated.

I got up from my seat and launched into my contribution of the evening's entertainment thus: "Grandfather and Grandmother, a few weeks ago I learned a little song from Sarah, our colored cook. I think it is pretty funny and I hope you will think so too. Here it is."

> Hot Tomale, getting red hot
> She's a gal o' mine.
> Hot tamale getting red hot
> Steamin' down the line.
>
> My gal's sweet
> She tastes like turkey meat!
> She's got a great big head
> And little tiny feet.
> Good Lawd. Hot Tamale,
> *She's a gal o' mine.*

The tune to which the above words were sung was a jaunty one and quite fitting. As soon as I finished this contribution, I could see that mother was taken aback and mildly scandalized. Fortunately for me, most of my listeners laughed and loudly clapped their approval. At first grandfather looked a bit grim, but grandmother's Patrick heritage came to my rescue and she instantly blew me a kiss of amused approbation. I was fearful of what my parents were going to say later but their stern faces became smiling when Uncle Arthur, the super athlete and not-so-hot student, called out, "Walter and Mabelle, you have an actor in the family." Nevertheless, it took me awhile to live down that little histrionic episode. Thank God I had at least changed the original words, "great big teats" (to rhyme with "little tiny feets") to "a great big head"!

Grandfather died that winter of '23-'24 at the age of 84. Four years later, when I was fourteen, father, who had to travel on business to the Midwest, took me out to Charlevoix again to visit grandmother, and that occasion was much more enjoyable than the visit of four years before; for now I was fourteen and could go to a dance where I met a St. Louis beauty, Atwood McVoy. We exchanged a few letters during the ensuing year, but I never saw her again. I did not see my darling grandmother again either, as she passed away a few months later, aged seventy-seven.

Among my friends of that period was Alessandro Torlonia, the son of an Italian duke and an attractive and very well off American woman whose sister was the wife of Clair Chester, the chairman of General Foods Corporation, and a good friend of father.

I met Alessandro because one of his cousins, Mary Chester, was Claire's closest friend and his older sister, Olimpia, was a school chum of Grace.

For some reason, possibly connected with the advent of Mussolini to power, all the Torlonia family was living in Greenwich at that time. The Torlonias were tall and had prominent, aquiline noses, which gave them a certain air of distinction.

Alessandro was about a year or so older than I and was a year ahead of me at Brunswick School. Sometimes he and his sister would come to the house for supper after which we would be driven to the movies; but the occasion which prompted my mentioning this family was one which took place during the winter of 1924-25 when I was eleven. On the far side of the Brunswick football field there was a hill – not a very steep one - but a slope which was fine for coasting, as we then called sledding. On the afternoon I have in mind, Henry Pringle was also coasting with us, along with two of his "colored" friends, Allan Quartermaine and Joe Merritt. There were at least twenty other kids about our age coasting with us, for on that day the snow was perfect for those "Flexible Flyer" sleds. Alessandro, who doubtless had seldom if ever seen snow like this in Italy, was especially enthusiastic following his first coast down that

Brunswick hill. What now took place was that Alessandro was just about to take a running start before jumping on his sled, when Joe Merritt pushed ahead of him. The duke's son fumed with rage, stamped his large feet and shouted imprecations against Merritt and his race. When next Joe Merritt pulled his Flexible Flyer back up the hill, Alessandro strode up to him, demanded that he apologize and address him as a "Nigger". Even in those days that word was never used by any of us – certainly never by me. Joe Merritt did not hesitate for an instant, but socked Alessandro in the jaw, a blow that knocked him down, but did not do any serious damage.

This situation placed me in a difficult position as Joe Merritt was one of Henry Pringle's friends, and Alessandro had called Joe a "nigger", an insult not only to Henry's friend, but obliquely to Henry as well. Yet Alessandro was also a friend of sorts – a relationship that had been arranged by our respective mothers. What I did was get Alessandro away from that coasting hill as fast as I could, and Gustav, the Swedish chauffeur – who had succeeded Dick Perry – drove Alessandro and me to the former's house. Then, in today's parlance, all hell broke loose, when Alessandro's mother, the Duchess, heard her son's version of what had taken place. She grabbed the telephone and began calling everyone she could think of, including Dr. Carmichael, the headmaster of Brunswick; the Chief of Police; Mrs. Chester, her sister, and a few others. I took refuge behind my age of eleven and claimed that I really had not seen exactly what had happened.

The Duchess, as might have been expected, notwithstanding her ravings over the phone, got nowhere; so the crisis died down. When I got back home I immediately told Henry that my Italian friend had, of course, been gravely at fault, though I used eleven-year-old language to say this. "If anyone calls me a "nigger", I'm going to do just what Joe did," said Henry. "Sure thing", I replied. The sequel to this unimportant event is amusing. About two weeks after the Alessandro – Joe Merritt episode, Henry and I were about to enter the Greenwich Theater to see a movie; and Joe Merritt had also shown up. Most interesting of all, there, too, was Colby Chester, Alessandro's first cousin and son of the president of General Foods. Apparently, Colby suspected for some reason that it was Joe who had socked his cousin in the jaw; or maybe he had been tipped off. In any case, he walked up to Joe and said, "Was that you who socked my cousin Alessandro in the jaw a couple of weeks ago?" "Yeah, it was me," replied Joe in a truculent and somewhat menacing tone as though he expected to get into a fight with this stranger. "Congratulations", cried Colby, "I have been hoping that someone would take that insufferable cousin of mine down a peg."

During the immediately ensuing years, I ran into Colby a few times at debutante dances, but as he was two years older than me, went to a different boarding school, and then to Yale, our paths never crossed noticeably. But since that day in front of the movie theater I have thought of him as a "good guy" whom I would have liked to know better.

It is of possible interest to note that Alessandro returned to Italy with his father and I believe remained in that country during World War II. In 1935, he married Beatrice, the Infanta of Spain, and daughter of the former King, Alfonso.

It seems logical to comment here on Claire and Julius if only for the reason that each had a continuing influence on me.

Claire was always at the top of her class, wherever she was in school – i.e., at Rosemary Hall, at Hathaway-Brown during that one year in Cleveland, or at Farmington, where she graduated not only number one academically, but also was "Head of Little Meeting" – the equivalent of president of the student body – and head of the Players Club. I recall a friend of hers commenting that no student before that had ever been elected to those two top honors at that school.

Claire should have gone on to college. Several of her teachers urged her to do so. Perhaps the main reason she did not continue the academic life is that none of her best friends went on to college; moreover, mother often voiced the opinion that college dulled the sharp edges of a young woman's refinement – truly a very silly opinion and obviously based on her idea as to what was proper and fashionable for a socially prominent girl of the age for coming out in New York society.

In the retrospect of well over half a century, I think this decision to skip college was a big mistake. At Bryn Mawr or Vassar, or one of the other "seven sisters" colleges, Claire would almost certainly have tested her scholarly potential. Instead, she did prove that she was probably News York's most popular debutante, for she was not only very good looking, animated and outgoing, but a graceful dancer as well. However, from that coming-out year, 1925-26, until she got married in 1932, I think that she felt something lacking in her life. There was no intellectual challenge. She was elected chairman of the Provisional Members of the New York Junior League, but aside from this being a tangible indication of her popularity, it proved very little.

Claire always had a lot of beaux. The first and of course the most important, and understandably so, was Adlai Stevenson. In 1923, when we all journeyed to Charlevoix, Michigan to celebrate our grandparents' fiftieth wedding anniversary, Claire, aged seventeen, met Adlai, who was then a law student at Harvard. For five years Adlai pursued Claire, formally asked father for her hand in marriage and continued to try to persuade her to marry him, to no avail. "I was just not in love with him," said Claire, and I suppose this was reason enough. Claire had dozens of letters from Adlai, written during those years, 1923-28, and all of them were published in a chapter headed by "Letters to Claire Birge," in the book *The Papers of Adlai E. Stevenson, Vol. 1*, (Walter Johnson, Editor, Little, Brown, 1972).

I certainly do not imply that Claire should have married Adlai, for the man she did marry, the great Fuller Albright, of Harvard Medical School and Massachusetts General Hospital fame, was surely Adlai's peer, in his own field of clinical science. It is interesting to note that these two fine and highly successful men had much in common. They were thinkers, highly intellectual, and scholars, yet each had a wry sense of humor and perhaps as important, fully appreciated and understood what a superb person Claire was.

I do not believe that anyone ever disliked Claire. Women admired and looked up to her for her intelligence, good humor, and sterling character – those, among other qualities. Men respected, and were drawn to her because of her good looks and personality. I would not say that Claire had sex appeal, though a brother is hardly the best judge of that. Claire inherited her handsome facial bone structure and golden hair from mother, but her green eyes from father. She often had a serious and thoughtful expression, but in conversation at a dinner party, or just chatting with friends, her expression would light up and she was an entertaining hostess.

In short, Claire was, from childhood, an exceptional person. She did not have mother's calm Edwardian beauty; nor was she as devastatingly beautiful as Grace. As to character - she inherited mother's adroitness in seldom, if ever, antagonizing anyone. She certainly had father's executive ability.

As for Julius (Judy), he, too, was exceptional in most ways. He stood about 5'11" with a strong, but not powerful physique. He was quite handsome with a firm jaw, an undistinguished nose and kindly, compassionate eyes. I do not think he ever had an enemy. He was thoughtful, had good judgment and always weighed all sides before making a decision. In that regard, he was like mother and nothing like father. In fact, he was not like father at all, except that both were generous and kind-hearted, and had great courage. Above all, Judy was a scholar. At Groton he ranked number three behind his best friend, Douglas Dillon, who was always at the top of his form, and Lawrence Percival, who was editor-in-chief of the *Grotonia*, a prefect of the school, and rowed number four on the first crew.

The last time I saw Judy was at Thanksgiving time in 1957. We went for a walk near his home in Indianapolis. He told me that he was giving serious thought to leaving his position in the Bobs Merrill Company, where, as I recall, he was being paid the miserable salary of $6000 a year, in order to enter the ministry of the Episcopal Church; and he commented that he was studying Latin again, thirty years after his immersion in that language at Groton. He explained that an ability to translate Latin with ease was one of the required disciplines to an Episcopal clergyman.

Perhaps this impending or possible drastic change from a position in the publishing firm of which his father-in-law was president, to a ministry which might entail years of study and other problems was too much for him to cope with, handicapped as he was with the mental disorder he had never completely overcome since the summer of 1931.

Less than two months after our walk together, he purchased a box of shells, inserted one into his sixteen gauge shotgun, descended to the basement of his house and ended his life with one horrible blast. I could only be thankful that father had died five and a half years before that day, for he had been especially close to Judy during his last years and had known how near saint-like were Judy's qualities of goodness and how totally incapable he was of any act other than a kindly one.

Grace, who was a year and four months older than me, was at first unprepossessing, with straight, stringy brown hair and a gawky build; but, before long, that build was to blossom out into a tall, slender, elegant figure. Gracie was, I suppose, the rebel of the family. Neither father nor mother seemed ever to have understood her – or perhaps they understood her only too well. At an early age – of about twelve – she gave rapidly growing evidence of an acute awareness of the male sex; and this penchant continued to develop apace. As a young girl, Gracie had a few close friends, but this luxury, as far as I could see, did not continue to be enjoyed by her beyond her early teens. Other women, especially those with attractive husbands or cherished boyfriends, rarely trusted this unusually beautiful creature for long.

Grace was generous and often spoke of the *poor children* and once persuaded mother to allow her to bring a disadvantaged child home for a few days, but then her interest soon waned and the poor child was totally ignored. Grace was an excellent horsewoman and indeed looked devastating on her mount, which she named *Virginia Girl.*

Grace showed no interest whatsoever in school work. She was, however, the most artistically inclined member of the family, had the prettiest handwriting and a flare for interior decoration and tasteful adornment. She could put on a potato sack and it would look like a Balenciaga cocktail dress. In short, Grace always looked fascinating. She had mother's beauty, but added to that was a strong sex appeal, which mother, in her well-bred Edwardian way, never had. Grace liked to think of herself as interesting, and she was to most people, the first or second occasion they met, but then it would seem that her lack of education or scholarly interests or general knowledge began to wear thin. Beauty by itself is often not enough. Grace was popular on the dance floor as a debutante, but she was ruled by her heart and often, alas, her judgment of men was faulty, and this served to close a few doors to her. Had she been more appreciative of what a few of the more intelligent young men who courted her in those early days had to offer and less carried away by glamour, her later life might have brought greater rewards. She did, at age twenty, marry an unusually fine, well-educated and brilliant man of twenty-three, Manoel Bon de Sousa Pernes, because, as she later claimed, he was the first beau our parents approved of. Probably Grace was never in love with Manoel. Their first two years of marriage were spent in New York and the next year and a half in Montreal, to which city Aluminium Limited, the firm for which Manoel worked his entire life had transferred him. Finally, in 1935, the couple moved to Geneva and it was there in the following year that Grace fell in love with Mir Khan, a Moslem Indian from Hyderabad, who was an *observer* at the League of Nations. I shall tell more about this later in this story.

    Now, to return to the days at the Seton place; there was, as I mentioned, no television and almost no radio, and so I read voraciously, mainly about history, especially about the battles of the American Revolution and the expansion of the western frontier, events embellished by John Pringle. I was also drawn to the history and development of arms and armor from the early Middle Ages to the seventeenth century and became a young expert on that subject.

    Mother, while adorning the background with her calm presence, played little role in my life. During the day, I was either at school or riding my Welsh pony, Comanche. I never doubted her devotion, for she would come into my room when I was ready to go to sleep. She would kiss me goodnight and usually admonish me to be thoughtful of others. Father and I had a very close and affectionate relationship and he often spoke of the two of us as our *Chum Society*. However, as he was away in New York during the weekdays, I was rather undisciplined in that carefree time. This state of affairs came to an abrupt end when I went away to boarding school, as will be explained in due course.

    From the autumn of 1922, mother would periodically mention regret at having had to give up her plan to visit England that summer owing to the doctor's admonition to keep Judy quiet in order to ensure complete recovery from his bout with scarlet fever the previous spring. These references to a hoped for trip to Europe became ever more frequent until finally by early spring, 1924, father gave his permission and mother wrote to her English friends, Lady Boyle and her daughter, Mrs. Hallahan, an attractive woman of about mother's age, whom mother had met in 1921, to elicit their suggestions as to that part of our trip to be spent in England. The trip turned out to be a sort of "Grand Tour".

Mother and the four of us children aged eighteen, fifteen, thirteen, and eleven, sailed from New York on the *RMS Lapland* of the Red Star Line. The voyage to Southampton lasted seven and a half days. The second day out I got up before any other member of the family and decided to go out on deck to take a walk. Soon a middle-aged gentleman hove into view walking rapidly with the apparent purpose of taking his morning constitutional before breakfast. As he came up to the spot where I was standing, he called out in a peculiar accent the likes of which I had never heard before, "Say, laddie, why don't ye join me for a bit of a walk around the deck?" That idea seemed a good one, so I joined that genial new acquaintance. "My name is Harry Lauder and what's your, lad?" For the duration of the voyage, Harry Lauder and I became good friends. Indeed, the jovial Scot even launched me into a reasonable facility in talking like a Scot on special occasions. I have never forgotten the little song-ditty I learned from Harry. The reader may well know it also.

Just a wee doch an doris; just a wee yen that's aa.
Just a wee doch an doris before ye gang awaa.
There's a wee wifie waitin' in a wee wee but an benn.
If ye canna say, 'It's a braa bracht moonlicht nicht ta nicht –
Y'er aa-richt – ye ken.

I am sure that my phonetic spelling leaves much to be desired. That kindly Scot made the voyage interesting for the eleven year old; and since then I have greatly admired that intrepid race, highlanders and lowlanders alike. Of course, at that time, I was not aware of the international fame of Sir Harry Lauder, as a comic music hall singer.

There was another incident which took place during that voyage and in retrospect of the intervening two thirds of a century, comes across as pretty amusing. I became quite friendly with a young woman of about twenty who had a southern accent. The only previous contact I had had with that way of talking was with Sarah and Cora at home. So I remarked innocently, as Miss Ramsey smiled up to me from her deck chair that she reminded me of someone who spoke just like her. "And who is that, Walter?" the soft-spoken southern belle enquired. "Our colored cook", I replied ingeniously. It need hardly be added that this short interchange spelled finis to that shipboard acquaintance.

Gigli, the famous opera tenor, was also a passenger on that voyage of the *Lapland*. Mother, Claire, and Judy attended the two concerts he gave during the trip. (He was probably given first-class passage in exchange, as was customary then).

I do not remember about Grace, but I did not attend the second performance. Though everyone was insisting that Gigli was a worthy successor to Caruso, I was not ready for the classical repertoire at that age.

Our arrival in London coincided with the start of the Olympic Games. It did not enhance my popularity with the doorman, headwaiter, and desk clerk of our hotel by bragging to them about the prowess of certain American athletes who had just defeated their English opponents.

Claire enjoyed a memorable weekend; for "Duke" Sedgwick of Boston, one of her friends from back home, invited her to a dance being held in Cambridge on the occasion of *May Week*. This Duke Sedgwick was the younger brother of R.Mintern

Sedgwick, who played tackle for Harvard in the Rose Bowl game of January 1920, and taught at Groton in the mid 1920's.

Our stay in London lasted about two weeks, after which we set out on a tour of Great Britain in an Armstrong-Sidley sedan. Mrs. Hallahan suggested where we should stop in England and Scotland, and Claire and Judy had helpful ideas also. I sat in front with Robert, the chauffeur. Mother, Claire, Judy and Grace had ample room in back as it was a spacious vehicle. We visited Cambridge, Oxford, Stratford-on-Avon, Warwick, Chester, and Windermere in the Lake District, then, in Scotland: Edinburgh, Perth, Inverness, Oban, Lock Lomond, and Sterling.

Before we left England, I spied a small early eighteenth century blunderbuss in an antique shop to which mother had been drawn by the sight of a Wedgwood bowl in the window. She finally agreed to buy this ancient weapon that was a real bargain at twenty-five shillings. Not content with merely the acquisition of this addition to my already impressive weapon collection back home, I persuaded the chauffeur to assist me in a new game. While driving through a village, I would point the old gun out the window thus giving the signal to the chauffeur to make the engine backfire. Mother soon put a stop to this juvenile antic. Sad to relate, - that blunderbuss was stolen during our return voyage. Either a passenger or crewmember, having seen me at the fancy-dress party dressed as a pirate and bearing that old firearm, had taken the gun from my berth.

Our motor trip was enjoyed by all of us, especially the days in Scotland, notwithstanding the too-frequent rain. We stopped at the places where battles had been fought centuries before – notably at Killiecrankie Pass, and other battlefields, including those where "Scots wa hae wi Wallace bled." Especially beautiful was Loch Lomond where I overheard a lady's comment as she descended from a charabanc, "What a bonny wee village this is." What expressive words *bonny, wee* were.

We bid farewell to our Armstrong-Sidley and Robert, the chauffeur, when he drove us from Edinburgh to Leith, where we boarded the *Arcadia,* a five hundred foot long cruise ship which was to take us to Bergen, Trondheim and three of the fjords of Norway. I had a series of field-days on that excursion - mountains, cool, still waters in those fjords, short trips inland, interesting trinkets such as sheath knives to purchase, dances on board ship – one intriguing adventure after another.

Mr. Symington, an attractive fellow passenger from England who was about twenty-three years old took a fancy to Claire at the first of the ship's dances. Then he noticed Grace, and his attention began noticeably to be turned to her. When Claire then casually mentioned that Gracie was not quite thirteen, Mr. Symington shifted his attentive efforts back to Claire. Grace, however, was well on her way to the great beauty she soon became.

Also traveling on board the *Arcadia* was Prince Prajadhipok, heir apparent to the throne of Siam. Notwithstanding the prince's being about ten years older than I, we got on very well, perhaps because we were about the same height When the *Arcadia* stopped at Bergen en route back to Leith, our family left the ship and boarded the train about to leave on its one and a half day trip to Christiania, as Oslo was then called. Prince Prajadhipok also got on that train to travel in a private car.

When we were about an hour out of Bergen, I decided to pay a visit to my friend, the crown prince. Upon my arrival in his luxuriously appointed car, the diminutive heir apparent greeted me warmly and motioned me to a window seat so that we could look at the beautiful mountains together. Before long the train came to a stop in a small village and two young women entered the Prince's car. One of these females then came up to me and took us all aback by asking me, "Where were you born?" The prince and I looked at each other and then at the two strangers who for some reason in the middle of Norway wanted to know where an eleven year old had been born. All I could reply was, "St.Louis." The same woman then turned her attention to the prince. "Where were *you* born?" she repeated. "Why must you ask these questions?" was the prince's rejoinder. "Because we want to know," was the perhaps logical reply. It was finally ascertained that these were newspaper reporters who had been instructed to board our train and elicit from the prince how he was enjoying his visit in Norway. The only surprising aspect of this brief episode was that these young journalists questioned me first. Surely, they could not have mistaken me for a Siamese.

My friend, the prince, re-appeared twice in later years; the first time five years later when, now King Rama VII, he called on father in New York, where we were then living – having written first that he was soon arriving - to ask his advice as to which physician he would recommend to treat an ailment from which he was then suffering. On the second occasion, I met him by chance in 1937 in Berkeley Square, while I was studying at the London School of Economics. At that time this last absolute ruler was in exile, having abdicated in 1935, after a coup had established a constitutional monarchy in 1932. He died in England in 1941.

Our tour from the day we arrived in Christiania was of whirlwind rapidity. We traveled entirely by train and briefly visited Hamburg, Amsterdam, and Isle of Marken in Holland, (now no longer an island), Brussels, Paris, Venice, Florence, Rome, and Genoa. Venice left the most noteworthy impression because of its canals, swimming at the Lido, and the few beautiful pieces of antique furniture that mother purchased there, some of which are treasured in my house almost seventy years later.

We returned to America on the *Giulio Cesare* of the Italian Line, which we boarded in Genoa; and thence to New York, Greenwich and soon after into the sixth grade at Brunswick School.

In retrospect there were two episodes involving my special relationship with John Pringle, our butler, which seem amusing and worth the telling. In the fall of 1923, that is, during my tenth year, mother decided that I needed more discipline so she engaged an English governess. The name of this English woman was Miss Tootin. John at once showed this dislike for this rather stuffy female in several ways, mostly by telling me how he felt but also by being just polite enough, but no more. "What do you have to have Miss Tootin here for?" he would say to me in a conspiratorial and barely audible tone. As I knew that John was almost always right about everything and as Miss Tootin was singularly unimpressive, I, too, hoped that Miss Tootin would take her leave. At that time I was reading all about the American Revolution. One morning at breakfast, with Miss Tootin seated opposite me, I jammed my fork into the fried egg on my plate and said, "This is a British soldier in 1776!" The next day, Miss Tootin took her departure.

Mention has already been made of Bill Arnold who lived nearby. He had a sister, Rayella, who was about my age – perhaps a little older. Occasionally she would come over with her brother and on one of those days she suggested that we meet the next afternoon at the Indian Council Circle near the lake. I said I would be there. However, when I mentioned this plan to John, he said, "Walter, you are not to go there to meet Rayella. She has designs on you." I was then eleven and I had no idea what John meant. Of course, it may have been that Rayella was not as innocent – in her thoughts, that is – as I was. But I did not keep that engagement, and Rayella never showed up again. John was taking no chances that his young friend was going to stray from the straight and narrow.

Early in 1924, Dick Perry, the chauffeur was replaced by a huge Swede, Gustav, who was a heavy drinker. Somehow he managed to appear sober when he drove my parents, but once he was so drunk driving me home from school that I told father about how, on my way home, the car was weaving all over the road, so he fired Gustav at once. My parents heard about Jimmy Patterson, an American-born Scot, from the Scottish-American Moore family who used to hold Highland games once a year. Just at that time Jimmy, a chauffeur, was looking for a job so he came to us at once. I never forgot Jimmy, a six-foot four, kindly and efficient driver who became a special friend. When just the two of us were alone in the car he used to sing songs such as "I wonder what's become of Sally, that old gal of mine, ever since the day Sally went away..." I will tell about the tragic end of Jimmy later.

Father often mentioned the possibility of purchasing the Seton place, but Mr. Seton was asking $400,000 and that sum, even for father whose financial means were not exactly negligible in those days, was much too high. Therefore, he and mother kept looking for a permanent property. At length, one was found on Stanwich Road, some four miles distant. During the time following its purchase and before we left Lake Avenue, I often rode Comanche over to inspect the layout. In those days of country roads and little traffic, this was pleasant and, for a boy of just-past twelve, an adventure.

"Overbrook", the name of the newly acquired place, was quite impressive. Not rustic like the Seton house, it had been built in the early nineteenth century, that is, added on to a late eighteenth century farm dwelling. There was a rock garden in back of the house and a path leading down to an informal pool situated in a wooded glade, with two statues in the Greek style keeping watch over the scene. The property came with thirty acres to which father added thirty more, purchased soon after we moved in. Jimmy Patterson lived over the large garage and stable with his English wife.

We moved into Overbrook sometime during the spring of 1925. In addition to my pony, we had two thoroughbred hunters, one of which could jump six feet. The groom was a Scot named Smith who had been in the British army during the entire time of World War 1. Father hunted on a regular basis with the Round Hill Hunt, occasionally accompanied by Gracie, but, as I recall, her enthusiasm for equine activities began to wane, especially as soon as she left for boarding school. Hence Mr. Smith, the groom, did not have much to do.

Dad was quite pennywise, though often pound-foolish. He regularly turned off unneeded lights and he preached economy to the family. However, when it came to substantial expenditures, - that was another matter. He decided that many of the large rocks in the garden should be blasted out, and I can imagine what that must have cost. He also was not satisfied with the house as it was; so extensive alterations and additions were undertaken. In those days in the mid and late twenties, money came quite easily. For example, six months after dad bought the additional thirty acres (for $30,000), he turned around and sold this land to a Mrs. Weld for $60,000. "Overbrook" had been bought from a Mr. Tom Chadbourne who, however, kept quite a large adjoining acreage that included a barn. My father retained the caretaker of this acreage, Mr. Studley, to work part time caring for our gardens. It came to light that Mr. Studley liked to make elderberry wine, and as we had many elderberry bushes, he taught me how to make this wine; and this I proceeded to do with considerable success, and it was a very good substitute for bootlegged French wine, according to father and some of his dinner guests who sampled my vintage.

Mr. Studley was lazy and that is an understatement. One Saturday, dad asked him to perform a simple task; when Studley made silly excuses to avoid doing what dad wanted, dad fired him on the spot; but that was not the end of our experience with that character, for soon he managed to steal all the wine I had made, as he still had a key to our basement.

Tony, the Polish gardener, who had been with us during our last year at Seton's place, accompanied us to Overbrook for he was still needed to take care of the live-stock and to do the hard work. This was a man who was happy to undertake any chore, no matter how tedious. When we moved in, Tony was lodged in a small room over the stable. Not long after, Tony announced that he wanted to marry a young woman who had just arrived from the "old country", so dad told Tony that he would make necessary repairs to a small farm-house on the property for the use of the newly weds. Very soon, the intended bride came out to inspect this little dwelling as well as to look over our neighborhood. She was at least twenty years younger than Tony and it may well have been for that reason that he informed father after his intended bride's visit, that the marriage was cancelled. This did not appear to have upset Tony, who continued to work as hard as ever and with never a word of complaint about anything.

When we moved to "Overbrook", mother decided to make a complete change in our house servants. John Pringle, Cora, and Sarah were all let go and replaced by Irish-American help. Mother may have tired of fried chicken and cream gravy. I never learned the reason for the abrupt change, but I did know that I never forgot John and my friend, Henry, who had been so important to me at age ten and eleven. At the age of twelve, however, a boy quickly adapts to changed conditions. There is, however, an interesting and unexpected postscript.

Twenty-one years later, in the spring of 1946, I came back to the United States on my first home-leave in four years, following Foreign Service assignment in Turkey, Iraq, and Saudi

Arabia, and while I was stationed in Prague. I was driving from New York to Boston to visit Claire and when I drew up at the first toll station on the Merritt Parkway in Greenwich, a black toll taker stretched out his hand to take my quarter. There was something familiar looking about that parkway employee and when he bid me good morning, his voice was a grown-up version of my boyhood friend. "Is your name Henry, by chance," I asked. "You're Walter!" he replied as he grasped my hand. "Pull up over there. I'll get my noon replacement to fill in for me ahead of time." Twenty minutes later, Henry led me into his modest, but very neat row house in Greenwich and there I met his beautiful 'high yellow' wife, Clothilde, who was from New Orleans. The hour we spent during that luncheon sped past much too quickly. The pleasure of that reunion, however, was tempered by what he had to tell me about his parents. John Pringle had died of asphyxiation caused by a leaking gas jet; and Cora, he explained, just died of a broken heart. And I remembered how John had admonished over twenty years before: Walter, reach for the stars!" And then often, "What ye sow, so shall you reap", and "When was the battle of Tippecanoe?" On two subsequent occasions, I tried to re-establish contact with Henry, but to no avail. He had left with no forwarding address.

Chapter Two

The Groton Years

From the time I was about a year old, mother was determined that her sons were eventually going to graduate from Groton, and when mother made up her mind about something very important, nothing could dissuade her. It seems that Mr. Sherrard Billings, one of the founders of the school (1884), visited several cities in the Mid-West, including St. Louis, in order to encourage well-placed families to prepare their sons for admission to the by then well known Episcopal church school. Mother never forgot what Mr. Billings had said about *"mens sana in corpore sano"* and "building character" and "Christian virtues", etc.

    Without doubt, I would never have been admitted to Groton had my older brother Julius, who was a fine scholar, not gone there ahead of me. At Brunswick School in Greenwich and at the University School in Cleveland, he was at the top of this class and he had passed the Groton competitive exams with high marks. In the fall of 1922, he entered Groton in the second form (eighth grade) and he continued to do well.

    As for me, I was facile and in general a rapid learner, but not the scholar Julius was. At Brunswick, I was usually third in my class and athletic – but certainly no athlete. My parents did not realize until it was almost too late, however, that knowledge of Latin before entering Groton was advisable, if not essential. Hence mother arranged for Mr. Aiken, my sixth grade teacher, to tutor me in Latin every day after school. In spite of Aiken's efforts, however, I failed the entrance exam in Latin, and the other exams as well. My parents were devastated. "You flunked everything!" announced father. But all was not lost. Julius had become very *persona grata* with James D. Regan, the Senior Master and teacher of French, who was able to persuade the Headmaster (known as the Rector), Endicott Peabody, that Julius' brother might well be like him. Thus I was admitted at age twelve to the first form (seventh grade) on what was called a "chance vacancy", and on a mid-September day in 1925, mother took me by train from Stamford, Connecticut to Worcester,

Massachusetts, where we were to board a local to Groton. During the interval, while awaiting the train for Groton, I was led to a barbershop where mother saw to it that I was properly groomed tonsorially for my entry into "America's greatest school". In that hair-cutting establishment, I suffered the embarrassment of having mother continually intervene to prevent the barber from using the clippers on my neck.

Shortly after out arrival at that strange and, to me, forbidding school, Mother took her departure and I was on my own. My parents, as well as Judy and my sisters had told me repeatedly that Groton was the "Eton" of America, and there had never been any question of my going anywhere else. Indeed, I had not been consulted on the question. Now, over two-thirds of a century after the day when I became part of that school I look back – as I often have over the intervening time – to the years 1925-31 as having provided the discipline I sorely needed. While the time spent at Groton was not always enjoyable, fraught as it was with trying experiences, learning how to get along with boys whose sense of values often differed from mine and learning to conform when necessary, I left the school, I am sure, much better prepared for some of the trials which lay ahead, because of the formative years spent there.

What created a problem was that my *formation* - as the French would say – had been quite different from that of most of my form-mates. In Greenwich, I had grown up as an ear in a field of corn with a minimum of supervision, especially between the ages of nine to twelve. Most Groton boys had attended the well-known New York or Boston schools where discipline was strict and even after-school hours were supervised. Few boys in their pre-Groton years rode their ponies hither and yon or played baseball with the village kids or camped out with the son of their parents' colored (term then used for African-American) butler. Had I any thoughts of continuing my undisciplined and independent behavior, these ideas were soon snipped in the bud. When father came up for a first parents' weekend at Groton and asked how I was doing, Mr. Billings summarily informed him, "Either Groton will have to change or Walter will have to change, and I don't think it's going to be Groton."

It must be understood that the headmaster, Endicott Peabody, the main founder and absolute monarch of Groton, was indeed Groton. He was held in awe by and was even terrifying to every new boy and I am sure that few Grotonians ever outgrew their fear of those steely blue eyes, that stentorian voice and that imposing example of "muscular Christianity". The most frightening experience for any Grotonian – especially for any "new boy" – was to be summoned to the Rector's study. The story – probably apocryphal – has often been told about the young boy who, upon being informed that the Rector wanted to see him, remarked to form mates seated next to him, "I hope it's *only* a death in the family."

It is not my intention to leave the reader with the impression that Groton was a fearsome place. In some ways, at first, it seemed to be, but very soon, the first formers and the few members of the second form who were also "new boys" came to know the good, comforting and enjoyable facets of the school. For example, one evening a week, there was "parlor night" when Mrs. (Fanny) Peabody and one or both of her daughters, Marjorie and Betsey, would receive new boys in the parlor of the Peabody house which adjoined "Hundred House", the main school building. We would all play such games as "Who, sir? Me, sir? No, sir, not I, sir!" or charades, acting out the syllables of certain words (for example, cab-bage, or fright-ful, etc.). Mrs. Peabody and her daughters made us all feel at home and members of the Groton family. Then there was the half-hour of being read aloud to by the dormitory master (or prefect) before we went to bed.

Jimmie Roosevelt, the eldest son of Franklin D. Roosevelt, who at that time was governor of New York, was the only sixth former in charge of a dormitory, the one to which I had been assigned. Before we went to bed he would read to us such stories as "The Little Shepherd of Kingdom Come" and other tales of adventure. Another typical Groton diversion was the "sing-song" which took place about once a month in the library.

Mr. Peabody, many of the masters, and all boys took part in singing old ditties such as *Abdullah Bull-Bull Amir, Jolly Boating Weather, Solomon Levi,* or *Tit-Willow.* By far the most popular of these old songs was the one that told of the fights between Abdullah Bull-Bull, the son of the prophet, and Ivan Skavinsky Skiva, the cream of the Muscovite team. As the nickname of Mr. Nash, the very personable math teacher, was Bull-Bull, the boys would shout out that name and look at Phil Nash when that song was sung.

Twining Lynes, a superb organist, directed the choir, and as we all attended a chapel service every weekday morning and twice on Sundays, that group of about thirty-five, including three masters, played an important role in the school. I sang soprano my first form year, then alto the following year and finally, bass my last two years. I also carried the cross as a sixth former.

The pre-Christmas time of my first form year remains vivid in memory. For about an hour every evening during that mid-December the Rector read aloud from Dickens' *A Christmas Carol* to the whole school gathered together in his study. This had been a long tradition. For me, those readings by that great headmaster were a thrilling experience and I am sure that my emotion was shared by all of us. Mr. Peabody brought his characters to life in a way that will never be forgotten. The Rector was also adding in his special way fuel to the fires of our growing excitement at the prospect of the coming holidays. Then there was the learning of Christmas carols I had never heard before. During those rehearsals, I sang for the first time *The Holly and the Ivy, Bring a Torch, Jeannette Isabelle,* and that beautiful Bach hymn, *Jésu, Joy of Man's Desiring.*

These inspiring first-time boyhood experiences were a fitting and thrilling prelude to my first Christmas of the Groton years. At last on the morning when we were about to board buses that were to take us to the Boston & Maine station, we all formed a line to say goodbye and "merry Christmas" to Mr. and Mrs. Peabody. Then there was the joyous ride in our special Groton Railway car bound for New York and several towns in Connecticut on the way. When our train drew into the Stamford station, Jimmy Patterson, our chauffeur and my dear and very special friend, was waiting for me on the platform and during our twenty minute drive to "Overbrook", Jimmy sang three of his favorite songs, most notably, *I Wonder What's Become of Sally.* Two weeks following my return to school after the holidays, I received a letter from father informing me that Jimmy had died of pneumonia, presumably caught while waiting for my sister Claire in the unheated car to come from a debutante party. When I received this devastating news, I was in study hall and started to cry. A classmate, whose desk was next to mine, asked me what was wrong and when I explained to him that our chauffeur had died, he replied, "Oh, only a chauffeur. I thought it might have been a member of your family."

On the occasion of every Christmas since those first form Groton days in December, 1925, I have thought back with nostalgic joy to the pre-Christmas days, and also to the sad loss of my friend soon after.

The dormitories, washrooms, and compulsory cold showers at school were Spartan and were presumably intended to overcome any soft habits we might have acquired in our boyhood at home. Each boy slept in a cubicle that was about five feet wide and nine feet long. At one end was a window that was always open at night regardless of the temperature outside which in winter often descended close to zero. There was no door – just a curtain at the end opposite to the window. The sidewalls, which were about seven feet high, reached less than halfway to the dormitory ceiling. There was a bureau at the foot of the bed, a few hooks on the wall and a small chair. Nothing else.

Once a week each boy took a hot bath[*] in the lavatory, an ablution that was hardly necessary in view of the daily showers we all took, cold in the a.m., and warm, following afternoon exercise. Along one side of the large lavatory was a long soapstone trough where boys would brush their teeth and scrub their nails. The latter is especially mentioned as, during first form sacred studies class, the Rector always asked each student if he had scrubbed his nails every morning. If the reply was negative, the boy went to the bottom of the class. Just before lights in the dorm were turned off – at nine for younger boys and an hour or so later for older students, the dormitory master would walk up one side of the long dormitory and down on the other side, bidding goodnight to everyone, some of whom might well already be asleep.

When I arrived to enter the first form at Groton, the school was forty-one years old, having been founded by the Reverend Endicott Peabody and two close friends, the Rev. Sherrard Billings (the *Mr. Chips* of the school) and William Amory Gardner, a wealthy Bostonian and Greek scholar. It seems worthy of note that the first president of the school's board of trustees was the renowned Episcopal bishop, Phillips Brooks, and fellow trustees of that year of 1884 included William Lawrence, James Lawrence – household names at the school, and J. Pierpont Morgan.

---

[*] Bath night always reminded me of Gutzon Borglum, who at that time was sculpting the four presidents at Mt. Rushmore. We boys thought his name was hilarious, and one wit said that Borglum sounded like a fart in a bathtub, so from then on, that is what we always called it.

It is perhaps significant that 1884 marked the time when "Chinese Gordon" met his violent death in Khartoum at the hands of the Mahdi. The British empire was then at its height and the Rector must have had vividly in mind the English public school, Cheltenham, which he had attended in the early 1870's. The Rector remembered that the British empire owed much to the formation of its builders on the "playing fields of Eton." "Play up, play up, and play the game" were the watchwords which he never forgot. The school, figuratively, was built around the square-towered gothic chapel that was built in 1900 with money given by Mr. Gardner. There, services were held each weekday morning and twice on Sunday. While some of the hymns we used to sing are still in the modern-day Episcopal hymnal (1982), many have been removed. Some words of one of those great hymns (now deleted) come to mind; Kipling's "The Recessional"

The tumult and the shouting die,
The captains and the kings depart.
Lo, all our pomp of yesterday
Is one with Nineveh and Tyre!-
Lest we forget – lest we forget!

Although the boys became accustomed to the Rector's sermons, and when he preached, many of them could predict almost verbatim what he would say and how he would say it, it must be admitted that he was eloquent and obviously spoke from a complete sincerity and stalwart faith. His was the same steadfast character with no devious compromise with evil. I think he saw the Episcopal Church as marching forward in harmony with the Church of England. The "Battle Hymn of the Republic" and "Rule Britannia" both stood for what was good and courageous in the world. The Rector might compromise when relatively unimportant questions were involved, but never when an issue was basic and had to do with Christian teaching. It is doubted that any boy who went through Groton was not strongly affected by the Rector and who did not leave the school a better man, regardless of whether he liked the headmaster (many did not) or whether he had been happy at the school.

Sherrard Billings, as mentioned above, one of the three co-founders, was as different as could be from Peabody. To begin with, the Rector, at six feet-two and two hundred twenty pounds was a contrast to "Mr. B." as he was called, a small man physically, but an outstanding personality whose Latin class utterances were pronounced with meticulous clarity. He shared the Rector's devout faith and he often spoke of his absolute conviction that "the other side, bathed in steeps of light" awaited us. It was customary for the Rector and Mr. B. to take turns in preaching the chapel sermons. I think it was the consensus that Mr. B's sermons were, on the whole, better than those of Peabody – with exceptions, of course.

The third co-founder, as already mentioned, was William Amory Gardner. It is almost unbelievable that his $400,000 built the chapel, though, indeed, that sum was very large in 1900. Perhaps his most lasting contribution to the school was the stress he placed on the importance of the classics in the curriculum. Greek was his specialty and he taught that subject from 1884 until 1930, when he retired from the faculty. He died of a heart attack during my sixth form year, but until his passing he continued to be a very special personality, for two reasons among others. First, he lived next to the school and on his property there was a maze – perhaps not as large, or as famous as the maze of Hampton Court in England, but a continuing source of interest and enjoyment for the younger boys during the earlier days of the school. Second, every Sunday afternoon at four-thirty, all new boys were invited to Mr. Gardner's "Pleasure Dome", situated just behind the school and near his residence, where he served *google*, a sweet concoction of assorted fruit, sugar, and water. This was always a pleasant change to the normal routine.

Groton had, I think, the reputation of being a snobbish school, and with some justification. As was the case with most leading boarding schools of that time, Groton boys were mostly WASPs. While the Rector often inveighed against snobbishness, in a way he was a snob himself. The explanation for his seeming contradiction was that he apparently did not feel comfortable except in the company of those whose upbringing, education, and even forebears had been similar to his. Almost every Sunday morning the headmaster and his wife, the beautiful and always charming Fanny, would invite one or two boys to take breakfast with them in their house. A few of us who were from New York noted that the great majority of those invited were either from Boston or the sons of prominent New Yorkers known perhaps for their past and/or future potential generosity to the school.

Mr. Peabody would, I am sure, have been surprised had he realized how he was perceived by some boys and parents as possessing any element of snobbishness. As for me, I really never gave much thought to this, especially as the Rector was always completely fair and direct in this treatment of the boys of the "Groton Family"; and in spite of the Rector's prudishness, superior Waspish attitude, and view of the arts as somewhat unmanly, he had a superb sense of humor.

With regard to the Rector's less-than-enthusiastic feeling about the arts, a story has often been told about a mother who brought her son to Groton on the occasion of his entering the first form. Her boy had been a serious student of the violin and wanted to continue his lessons while at Groton. So, when she met Mr. Peabody, she said, "Mr. Peabody, I have a little problem. You see, my son is interested in the violin..." and before she could finish her enquiry as to continuing lessons, the Rector interrupted her peremptorily but politely, saying, "Do not worry, Madame, we'll soon get *THAT* out of him."

One rather amusing example of the snobbery of many of the boys at the school had to do with where one wore one's watch-chain. In those days – the twenties and early thirties – most Grotonians wore vests; at least, all the fathers of Grotonians wore vests. A watch was to be kept in the right hand, lower vest pocket; the chain was to be passed through a vest buttonhole and the (presumably gold) pencil or penknife placed in the left hand, lower vest pocket. Woe to him who used the upper vest pockets for the watch and pencil. That was just not done. Well do I remember when Thatcher Adams' mother and stepfather from Detroit came for a weekend visit with "Magoun", as we called him, for that was his middle name. The stepfather was not the Groton parent type. First of all, his accent was rather odd. Second, and even more important, his watch and chain were in the *WRONG* vest pockets. When some of us mentioned this to "Magoun", he assured us that his real father always used his lower vest pockets for his watch and chain. Nowadays, Grotonians dress casually. In the old days, they wore a coat and tie, and on Sundays a blue suit with a stiff white collar, and every evening, patent leather shoes. There was great emphasis placed on what was correct attire, with little choice for originality.

There were three forms of punishment in the school: demerits for tardiness or other minor infractions; black marks (a maximum of six at one time) for misdemeanors such as talking in study hall or in class, or for disobedience. If a boy was caught cheating or if he was a habitual problem, a total misfit, or a disturbing influence, he was likely to be suspended or even expelled; hence, the ultimate sanction served to discourage immoral behavior. Many years after graduating from Groton, I met a teacher who was a member of the faculty at the Columbus Academy (in Ohio) and who had attended a lecture given by Peabody at a National Teachers' convention. Someone asked whether he had any special words of advice for the gathering. Mr. Peabody replied, "Yes, - three rules! 1) Get rid of the bad boy. 2) Get rid of the bad boy. 3) Get rid of the bad boy." On the whole it must be admitted that this policy worked out pretty well at Groton, though I know that a few of these "bad boys" became quite successful in later life.

During my time at the school, the best example of this policy of the Rector took place during my second form year, which coincided with my brother Julius' sixth form year. Every other year when the Harvard-Yale game was played in Cambridge, members of the sixth form and upper-school boys with an 80- or-above scholastic average were allowed to attend "The Game". It might be added that in those far off days "The Game" was certainly one of the leading sports events in the country. Immediately after the 1926 game, ten to twelve members of the sixth form were invited up to the rooms of Harvard freshman, Guthrie Willard, who the previous year had been senior prefect, i.e., head of the school and the outstanding stroke oar of the crew. It seems that during that visit to Willard's rooms, several of the sixth form visitors broke a strict Groton rule by drinking an alcoholic beverage. These sixth formers then traveled back to the school by taxi and one or two of them compounded their previous infraction by smoking.

It was the Rector's invariable custom to shake hands with every boy who had been away from the school during this kind of special occasion. After all of the returning boys had supposedly checked in, the Rector noted that one boy, Ken Jenkins, was unaccounted for. He asked the sixth formers whether they knew of Ken's whereabouts and was told that as Ken had not been feeling very well, he might have gone to the infirmary. Mr. Peabody immediately called on Miss McLeod, the formidable and efficient head nurse from Prince Edward Island, who firmly stated that Jenkins was not in the infirmary.

The Rector at once marched his way to Ken's study, turned the doorknob to enter but found that the door was locked. Whereupon, with one blow of his massive fist, followed up by the effective kinetic use of the energy released by two hundred twenty pounds against that door, the latter gave way – lock, hinges, and all. And there revealed was Ken Jenkins half-passed out on the narrow six-foot long wall seat. When the Rector commanded, "Come to my study, boy," Ken, notwithstanding the depredations of alcohol and tobacco, managed to pull himself together and follow the Rector into that so-often terrifying place. The Rector then called John Adams, the Senior Prefect, and instructed him to see that every sixth former who had attended the Harvard-Yale game come at once to his (the Rector's) study. Once most of the sixth form boys were assembled there, the Rector ordered, "Any boy who took an alcoholic drink in Cambridge remain here. All others are to leave." No one dared lie, and the Rector summarily expelled the six boys who had remained in his office.

A tragic, though unrelated, aftermath of this event was that Guthrie Willard, a young man greatly admired by all who knew him, died of pneumonia shortly afterward, in December of his sophomore year at Harvard.

Four years later, two former Grotonians, then seniors at Harvard, drove out to the school at night and perpetrated several acts of vandalism, including dropping a huge rock onto the bottom of the motor launch, thus sinking it, and taking the large Bible from the chapel and dumping it into the bushes nearby. Ken Jenkins was later proved to have been the ringleader of this vandalism. What was especially unfortunate about this episode was that my brother Julius' Harvard roommate, Dan Merryman, son of Professor Roger B. Merryman, was the other involved in this revenge. Harvard at once expelled these students. Dan Merryman quickly rose above this temporary setback, finishing his college education at Yale and eventually becoming Master of Davenport College there. So much for getting rid of the "bad boy"!

The thought may naturally arise as to whether homosexuality was a problem at Groton in those far-off days. Let it be said at the outset that in the early and mid twentieth century no Gerry Studds (a former Grotonian, by the way) or Barney Frank could have lived down their coming out of the closet. Indeed, hardly anyone ever even mentioned homosexuality when I was growing up; that word was never uttered by my parents, brother, or sisters. Moreover, I do not remember having ever read in the nineteen twenties about what was then considered a perversion. When the subject was mentioned at all at Groton, it was voiced in whispers. There were, however, two exceptions to this, but even those were wrapped in silence.

The first occurred during my second form year. It was the school birthday, October 15, 1926, on which day we enjoyed a full holiday. After lunch, my best friend, Bill Kilborne and I, accompanied by Thatcher Adams and John Shallcross, set out for the Nashua River. There, we took two canoes and paddled upstream for a mile or so past an oxbow – Bill and I in one canoe and Adams and Shallcross in the other. There, we left our canoes on the bank and Bill and I proceeded on foot in one direction and the other two went a separate way. Bill and I knew that you could buy sweet apple cider at a roadside stand a half-mile down a nearby country road and so we set off. We stopped at that small store where we downed a whole gallon of cider.

Meanwhile Adams and Shallcross walked along the same road that Bill and I had started on, but in the opposite direction. Suddenly an unshaven, shabbily clothed man of about forty, who best could be described as a hobo, leaped from behind a tree by the side of the road, seized Adams and started to drag him into the woods. As Adams was almost two years older than me albeit in the same form, and thus about fifteen, he was strong enough to break loose from his derelict would-be captor and take off at full speed shouting to Shallcross to follow. The latter, however, just stood there, paralyzed by fear, and the hobo lost no time in grabbing hold of his second victim. Adams, looking back, saw Shallcross being dragged away. He raced the two miles back to school where he went directly to the Rector's study. It took him less than a minute to paint the picture, as only he could paint it, of what had happened – this with graphic exaggerations.

As soon as Peabody learned the salient fact that one of his boys had been seized by an obvious pervert, he cut Adams' recital short by raising his massive hand for silence and snatched the receiver off the stand of his old-fashioned telephone and in his adamant voice of command, instructed the operator to connect him at once with the Chief of Police. The latter was on the line within a few seconds. "Is that you, constable?" enquired the absolute monarch of Groton. The Rector then quickly and precisely, recounted what he had learned from Thatcher Adams and ended with the following:

"I want you to send some of your men to the school without delay and see that they are <u>well-armed</u>!" I am sure that none of us who were later regaled by Adams' recounting of his meeting with the Rector ever forgot that warning to the Chief of Police. The attacker was promptly arrested as he walked up the tracks of the Boston & Maine Railway. Shallcross made his way back to the school and we never found out the details of his experience, for undoubtedly the Rector had admonished him to remain silent.

Mr. Peabody, as already mentioned, had attended Cheltenham, an English public school (i.e., a private school) where he remained for five years, after which he studied at Trinity College in Cambridge. Having remained in close contact with several of his close English friends, it was inevitable that he learned about the "perversion" of Oscar Wilde. While, to my knowledge, the Rector never mentioned this scandal, it became clear to all that he had an abhorrence and horror of the "perversion" of homosexuality.

The second incident that comes to mind on this subject at Groton concerned a man whose last name was Cushing. Mr. Amory Gardner, as mentioned above, though retired, used to invite first and second form boys to his "Pleasure Dome" every Sunday afternoon for refreshments. Occasionally present also would be Cushing, a fellow bachelor and frequent houseguest of Gardner's who lived in Boston. One Sunday afternoon, this very tall, florid-complexioned Mr. Cushing began to make indecent advances to Thatcher Adams, who very soon afterward informed his fellow form mates as to what had happened. "First, Mr. Cushing placed his hand on my thigh which he began to massage; then, he took my hand and placed it next to his trouser pocket. At first, I thought Cushing had a flash-light in that pocket but as soon as I realized what it really was, I got out of there without delay and reported to Mr. Regan what had happened." Apparently, Jimmy Regan lost no time in bringing this information to the attention of Mr. Peabody. We never learned whether the Rector spoke to Cushing or to Gardner - probably he spoke to both. The upshot, however, was that Cushing was never seen again anywhere near the school.

At Groton there were three major sports: football, with a first and second team, baseball (a first team), and crew (a first crew). For those boys not involved with the school teams and crew there were intramural programs. All boys were divided into Wachusetts and Monadnocks, on the gridirons, baseball fields and on the Nashua River. In the fall of my first and second form years I played football with the Second Washusetts; my third and fourth form years, I was on the First Wachusetts team and my fifth and sixth form years, I played on the second and first football teams, respectively. As for baseball, my first two years I batted fourth in the batting order on the second Wachusetts and had I continued with that sport I might well have eventually made the first team in view of my good batting average. However, we were allowed to start rowing our third form year and Bill Kilborne and I decided to do so that spring. By way of mention, Bill's brother Stewart had been an outstanding oarsman at Yale until he left New Haven to get married (one could not remain in most colleges those days if married), and Bill eventually rowed on the Yale varsity for three years and was elected captain in his senior year.

When we started rowing, the Rector was the coach of the first crew, but before taking that boat out he spent some time each day teaching the fundamentals to the third form beginners. At Cambridge during the last three years of the 1880's he had been an outstanding oarsman and he was determined that every Groton crewman have perfect form. "Get those hands away, boy!" was his favorite comment on the river. The year before Bill and I began our rowing career on the Nashua, my brother Julius had rowed at number four on Peabody's first crew and I was determined to emulate him. Kilborne, relative to *his* brother, had the same idea.

The Rector's coaching of the beginner was carried out in a broad wherry that had the sliding seats and outriggers such as those in a racing shell, but had place for just two oarsmen, plus a cox's seat for the coach. Well do I remember the first day of rowing in the training wherry, the Rector in the stern, I in the stroke seat and Bill behind me in the bow. "Hands away fast, sit up straight, do not lean back, keep your back straight at the catch," intoned the Rector, and so on. Could those of us who started rowing in this way ever forget? Of course, Bill and I each tried to pull harder than the other and thus force the boat to starboard if rowing on the port side, or to port if rowing starboard. At that age, Bill and I were fairly evenly matched, but that was before Bill filled out and eventually – in college – became thirty pounds heavier. One late April day, I broke my oar when I took an especially hard pull, thus hoping to force the bow of the wherry to starboard. Perhaps that old oar had been weakened by dry rot over twenty years of hard use. In any event, the oar cracked with a most satisfying report. "Bother," said the Rector, and back to the dock we managed to go for another oar. In retrospect, and based on what I learned when rowing in England ten years after, some of the Rector's teaching of fundamentals was correct – namely; not to lean back more than just past the perpendicular, and to get a strong "catch". However, well do I remember the coach and captain of the Thames rowing Club in London – a year and a half before World War Two – keeping at me about *not* getting hands away so fast. Many Grotonians who rowed in England during graduate school days had the same experience. In short, the Rector's rowing style was dated even then. The outstanding Harvard crews coached by Tom Bolles and Harry Parker during the past forty years have seemed relaxed by contrast.

In the spring of my fourth form year (1928), the Rector – reluctantly, I am sure – gave up his head-coaching duties owing to the following circumstances; the senior prefect, John Bross, a rather small but determined bow oar on the first crew, was a close friend of Thomas Boylston Adams (called TB), the stroke and real leader of that crew. It is likely that Bross would have left things as they were, but then Adams apparently persuaded his friend that the Rector left much to be desired as a first – crew coach, albeit an excellent teacher of the fundamentals for beginners, and that the rowing program and future success of the first boat would be improved if he were replaced as first crew coach by Dick Richards, then coach of the First Wachusetts.

TB Adams' advice was probably good; moreover, most of the oarsmen agreed that "Mr. Dick" would be more effective at preparing a first crew for the big races. In any case, Bross allowed himself to be persuaded to undertake the very embarrassing task of suggesting to the Rector that he exchange places with "Mr. Dick". I can imagine how hurt the Rector must have been, but he hid his feelings and took over as coach of the First Wachusetts in which crew Bill Kilborne and I rowed that spring. That 1929 first crew might well have been one of Groton's greatest had the number six man, Elliott Roosevelt, (the second son of F.D.R.) not come down with appendicitis at the start of the season. This "smooth, powerful oar", to use Mr. Richards' words, would be sorely missed. But even without Elliott, it was a fine crew. Unfortunately, Roosevelt's replacement in the last and most important race of the season against Noble and Greenough caused Groton to lose the race. About a hundred yards from the finish, with Groton leading by a deck length, he heard the Nobles cox blow a whistle calling for their sprint, but for some reason he thought the race was over and he stopped rowing. Such things can occasionally happen in the heat of a close race.

The following spring, near the end of our fifth form year, Bill Kilborne, who now outweighed me by twenty-five pounds, was promoted to the first crew, while I continued to row with the First Wachusetts, - now as stroke.

As already mentioned, the Monadnocks were the intramural rivals of the Wachusetts and near the end of May our big race was held. We were fairly evenly matched although the Monadnocks, having more sixth formers in their crew were a slight favorite. I have never forgotten what happened that day. The Monadnocks were about a half-length or less ahead of us with two hundred yards to go, but we were gradually gaining on them when I started to raise the stroke, but in doing so I failed to get my oar cleanly enough out of the water as I moved forward before the next stroke. The result was that I "caught a crab", that is, the water caught my oar, thus forcing the other end of the oar with great force against my stomach and then chest, and preventing me from taking another stroke for several seconds. I should have recovered from that mishap more rapidly than I did, but the combination of surprise, chagrin and devastating disappointment delayed what should have been a much more rapid recovery. In any case, at the finish of that race we came in about a length behind the jubilant Monadnock crew.

The row back to the boathouse was the longest mile I ever spent on any body of water. The sequel was to be expected – that is, a summons that evening to the Rector's study, relayed to me by Mr. Regan, who was in charge of the Brooks House study hall that evening. What the Rector had to say was more devastating than I had anticipated. I walked rapidly along the circular path that led past "Hundred House" to Peabody's residence. "Sit down, boy," said the Rector as soon as I entered his study. The only seat available, and the one designated for such occasions, was a large, very low and deep armchair. As was his custom, Mr. Peabody remained standing directly in front of me. From where I was seated about a foot from the floor, he towered above me.

He lost no time in getting to the subject at hand. "Near the end of the race this afternoon you stopped rowing because you were pumped. Is that not so?" I had never heard that term *pumped* before, but the meaning – exhausted – was clear. I tried to explain that I had stopped rowing because the handle of my oar had knocked me flat on my back and I had been taken completely by surprise and also filled with chagrin and terrible disappointment. While my explanation did not appear to mollify Peabody very much, I think that he did understand that this experience for a boy still in his sixteenth year could have been pretty devastating.

Of course, I understood that my failure immediately to get the oar back into action was not to be excused. We all knew that when you are rowing a race, nothing interferes with reaching the finish line in the shortest time possible. I vowed to myself never again to allow such a thing to happen. I could only hope that the Rector would understand. Eventually, I think he did, but it took him more than a year to do so.

The following year, that of my sixth form, I rowed at number two in the first boat, alternating with Phil Cushing (owing to mutual problems of illness). Interesting to relate is that in that 1931 crew (if one counts Bill Kilborne who was unable to row in the last three races because of a painful boil on his seat), we had three future college crew captains: Ray Clark of Harvard, Francis Keppel of Princeton, and Bill Kilborne of Yale.

Aside from the Rector, whose towering qualities were apparent and whose influence, in one way or another, never ceased being felt throughout my life, the two masters I remember best and respected the most were "Jimmy" Regan and Ronald Beasley. Mr. Regan was a superb teacher of French - the only modern language taught in the school at that time. His accent was not perfect, but he knew how to teach grammar. I had been fairly fluent in French from early childhood and so tended to slide along with a minimum of effort. That was a mistake, for in my first two years in the study of that language, Mr. Mott was the teacher and, perhaps justifiably, he recommended that I be assigned to the *B* division in the fourth form. Presumably, the *B* division was for less able students. That demotion, I am convinced, was a blessing in disguise, for Mr. Mott taught the *A* division in the last three years. This was a logical arrangement in view of Mr. Mott's special interest in French literature and Mr. Regan's competence as a grammarian. I think Mr. Regan very soon recognized my weakness in grammar and concluded that the best way to prod me on was to mark strictly. It was a school custom to grade *A* division boys higher than those in *B* division. Hence, all through my last three years, my French grades remained quite mediocre. But then came the proof as to who were the best French scholars in the school. All twenty-seven in our form (out of thirty who had entered in 1925), of course, took the college entrance exams, of which French was one. About half of us were in one division and half in the other. I was the only boy in the *B* division to receive honors and only three boys in the *A* division received an honor grade. On one of the occasions when I returned for a visit to the school while I was at Harvard, I asked Regan why it was that practically all my grades in French had been below 80 (honors level) whereas I had received honors on the college entrance exam. "Well, Bishu," (his nickname for me) "if I had given you higher marks you would not have done as well on the entrance exam." I can still recite verbatim many of Jimmy's rules of grammar. He was an outstanding teacher as well as a disciplinarian and he made his stalwart contribution to Groton's reputation as one of our country's finest schools.

As for the second master mentioned above, he was, without a doubt and from the vantage point of over half a century, the ablest teacher in school or university with whom I came in contact. Ronald Beasley was an Englishman who came to the school to teach English history in the fall of 1928, at the beginning of my fourth form year. He never lost his English accent. On the first occasion when he made the customary announcements to a large study hall of which he was in charge, most of the boys laughed; but that was the <u>last</u> time anyone laughed at him. Mr. Beasley was not known as a disciplinarian in the generally accepted sense of that term, but he never had the slightest trouble keeping perfect order. How did he do it? I could not say. Some men and women have that knack; some do not. He was a born teacher, so that his students wanted to hear what he had to say. From the age of ten, I had loved history and long before entering Groton, I had read with glee about Lexington and Concord and the battle of New Orleans, and the British surrender at Yorktown. And there was "Old Ironsides" and "I regret that I have but one life to give for my country", but with Beasley, these men and events came to life and I can still hear this scholar tell of Pitt's campaigns.

Shortly before my fifth form year, Harvard, and perhaps Yale and a few other universities, changed the rule with regard to qualifications for entrance at the start of study for an A.B. degree. Up to then, one had to take entrance exams in English, math or physics, French or German, and Latin. Now, according to the new regulations, a student wishing to graduate from Harvard with an A.B. degree was allowed to take an easier Latin exam (CP3 instead of CP4) at the end of the fifth form (11th grade) year and history at the end of the sixth form year, along with the other required subjects. As far as I was concerned, this was a most welcome change as history and Latin had been my best and worst subjects, respectively, since the first form year. On the day prior to sitting for the Harvard history entrance exam, Mr. Beasley suggested that when the name of a king or queen of England was written in the blue book, I give that monarch's dates in parenthesis. As I had been taught all those dates, I followed Beasley's advice and this may have been a factor in my having received a "Highest Honors" grade in that test.

A few years after my graduation from Groton, Ronald Beasley accepted the post of headmaster of Mary Institute, a leading girls' private school in St. Louis. During my years at Harvard, I visited Groton several times and always met with Ronald on those occasions, but after 1935 I never saw him again, though we kept in touch. He died a year after retiring from Mary Institute. For me, he has been one of the three or four most influential men in my life.

My Groton years were those during which Germany was a defeated underdog of Europe; when the British Empire was still a power on which the sun never set; when a British Cape-to-Cairo railway was close to a reality; when the United States belonged to no League of Nations and looked upon any international entanglements as commitments to be avoided; when Japan had not yet become a menace to the West; when the star of F.D.R., while slowly rising, had not quite yet burst into the political sky with a bright light.

As for the Rector, I left the school that June of 1931 with a myriad of memories and impressions about him. He was decent, a man with deep sentiments, but with no sentimentality, a Victorian. For him, *the king* meant the king of England, and he looked upon Christmas in much the same way as did Charles Dickens. He was a moral rock and I admired him for that, though I was somewhat puzzled, at the age of fifteen, when he admonished a group of third and fourth form boys at one of his *Preparation for Communion* meetings: "Never use your wife as a means of enjoyment."

Mr. Peabody was an efficient executive rather than a scholar. He often expressed the hope that many Grotonians would eventually enter public life – and many did, notably F.D.R., Dean Acheson, Joseph Grew, Averill Harriman, Sumner Welles, Douglas Dillon and many others, including his own grandson and namesake, Endicott Peabody, who became governor of Massachusetts (as well as All-American guard at Harvard).

The Rector had been a superb athlete. Usually the fifth former he selected to be the school Senior Prefect the following year was an athlete- often a scholar-athlete as was Clive Duval, the Senior Prefect my sixth form year - and my close friend since that time- for Clive was at the top of our form academically and played well on our first teams in both football and baseball. The following year, he was a regular on the Yale freshman team and graduated from there *summa cum laude.* For many years, he was head of the Virginia Senate.

Notwithstanding the Rector's love of sports, not one of us doubted that scholarship always came first with him, for he was an outstanding headmaster and a great man. Perhaps he exemplified best the school motto, *cui servire est regnare.*

Chapter Three

The Harvard Years

My four Harvard years were prefaced by a bicycle trip I took in Germany with Charlie Butler, a fellow member of the form of 1931 at Groton. Charlie had not been one of my closest friends, possibly because we had not been on any team or crew together. However, he was very likeable with a good sense of humor and, for some reason, bought my idea of a bike excursion in Bavaria.

The period between the end of the First World War and the advent of Adolph Hitler saw Germany as the victim of the treaty of Versailles. This sad situation, coupled with the study of Wagner's music under Twining Lynes at school, fostered a pro-German bias in me. Everything German seemed very good during those years at Groton and during the first two years at Harvard.

So, in June 1931, very soon after leaving the sheltered life at school, Charlie and I boarded the *Olympic*, one of the great White Star liners. We traveled tourist class which cost father $200 for my round trip fare. We had already arranged for tickets to two performances of Wagner's operas in Bayreuth early in July. Traveling with us on the Olympic was Charlie's cousin, Dick Kernan, who was accompanied by his Harvard classmate, Charles Parker. These two had just graduated from Harvard and seemed to have a lot more money to spend than we did.

The experiences we had are still vivid. We landed at Cherbourg and traveled second class to Paris where we checked in at the *Hôtel de l'Université*. Charlie's cousin insisted that a visit to the city of light would be sadly unreplete without a visit to *cinq rue Daunou*, a house of ill-repute well known to many young American tourists in those peaceful days. A visit to such an establishment for a young and innocent boy did not mean necessarily that any sex was to be involved; in fact, I was rather frightened of the whole idea. However, we did witness a show put on by two women, one of whom impersonated a male (having strapped on the necessary equipment).

After a couple of days in Paris, Charley and I set out for Frankfurt on a night train. Unfortunately, all the second-class seats were occupied, so we entered a first class compartment. When the conductor came to collect our tickets, however, he informed us that we were not allowed to occupy a first class seat with a second-class ticket. "*Mais, il n'y a pas de place dans la seconde classe,*" I ventured. "*Très bien, vous n'avez que prendre une place dans un compartiment de troisième classe*" commanded the conductor. I suppose that logic, at least, Gallic logic, was on his side. In any event, we had no choice and had to spend all that night trying to catch some sleep on the third class wooden benches. Great, however, is the resilience of a boy of eighteen and we were none the worse for that wear.

Upon our arrival in Frankfurt the next morning, we lost no time in finding a bicycle shop and purchased two bikes which cost very little – perhaps ten or fifteen dollars apiece. And we set out on the road that led to Aschaffenburg. Shortly before reaching that town we came upon a small *gasthaus*, the owner of which had relatives in several Midwest American cities. He knew all about *ham-und-ekks*. Charlie, in preparation for this trip, had studied German with a tutor at Groton, so he knew how to say, *ein schlafzimmer mit zwei bett*. Apparently that was about all he had to know, for every innkeeper in Germany knew more English than Charlie knew German. In those days, I knew no German at all, a deficiency that has been rectified to a considerable extent since. The following day we reached Würzburg and the day after that, we sped on to Rothenburg, in most ways, the highlight of our trip. For here was a medieval town surrounded by thirteenth century walls. What a fabulous introduction to Germany. We stayed for the night at *Zum Grünen Baum,* the proprietor of which was Hans Schmidt. When I revisited that town twenty-three years later, I sought out Herr Schmidt whose inn had been destroyed during the war. I asked the owner of a small restaurant if he knew what had happened to Herr Schmidt and he pointed him out to me – sitting at a corner table with a few friends. I went up to him and said, "Do you by any chance remember me, Herr Schmidt? I stayed at your hotel in July, 1931, and you may remember that we talked about the Battle of Jutland." "Yes, of course, I remember the young American who wanted me to tell him all about that German naval victory." Of course, Herr Schmidt had aged quite a lot in those years and had survived the war, probably owing to his age which had kept him out of active military service.

After Rothenburg, we had an easy, level ride to Nürnberg. When we started to try to find a hotel in that then still-beautiful city (the larger part destroyed in 1945), Charlie, for some reason, asked for a *Krankenhaus* instead of an inn, and we soon found ourselves about to be ushered in the emergency entrance of one of the hospitals.

By this time we had no time to lose, even for that famous city, so we checked our bikes at the railroad station and proceeded to Bayreuth by train. The American Express Company had arranged for us to stay at a private house, owned by a distinguished middle-aged gentleman, who I believe was a teacher. He had reserved for us a double bedroom and an adjoining sitting room. The price for these two rooms was nine marks a day, at that time the equivalent of two dollars and a few cents. After one night we asked our host how much just the bedroom would cost. "Four marks," he replied, so we saved ourselves a bit over a dollar a day, which made sense, as we did not anticipate spending time in the sitting room.

The opera, *Tannhäuser,* was scheduled for the second day after our arrival, so I decided to go for a hike. Charlie had other plans. I left town by a country road where I encountered a young boy about fourteen years of age. He had only a rudimentary knowledge of English, but he knew Latin quite well, so we were able to converse quite adequately in pigeon English and Latin as we walked together for several miles. Beforehand, I had outfitted myself with what I considered the appropriate hiking garb: *lederhosen* with fancy suspenders and woolen knee socks, hoping that I cut quite a figure.

The opera started at five in the afternoon and as everyone was meant to wear evening clothes, Charlie and I (as well as Kernan and Parker who had come by rail) donned tuxedos and black tie. We drove to the *Festspielhaus* in a horse-drawn carriage and both sides of the road were lined with cheering and clapping villagers. I felt very important. Toscanini was the conductor and that was the last time he would conduct at that place. It was a memorable occasion for everyone, but perhaps especially for me, for everything was new and spectacular – the greatest composer of all time (as I was convinced then), the greatest conductor living, and the great German nation. Within a year and a half, those gifted people would be headed down the road to destruction and America would be on the path to becoming Germany's enemy, and I would lose good friends in that conflict: Hutch Robbins, my Groton form-mate; Jim Tew, my classmate at Harvard, and many others. But on that beautiful summer's day of 1931, though the economy of Germany was anything but robust and America was just about to enter its own economic tailspin, my own horizon was bright and I was enjoying a very special adventure experienced by very few Americans of my age.

The second opera we heard was *Lohengrin*, but as that was not the opening performance, we did not ride in state through a cheering crowd. While I remember this as having also been a great performance, in my opinion, fraught as it was by an all-consuming romanticism, it could not reach the heights of *Tannhäuser* and its powerful *Festmarsch*.

One perhaps very unimportant episode might be mentioned here. On the *Olympic,* I became intrigued by a fellow passenger, Lois Raggio, an attractive woman ten years older than me, but that did not prevent me from falling for her. This dark-haired beauty was very solicitous and seemed to understand how an eighteen-year-old boy could fall for an older woman. Lois had also come to Bayreuth and one bright afternoon, we went for a walk. We stopped for a rest and sat on a grassy knoll, but as I try to recapture that moment, I don't think I even had the courage to kiss her. About five years later, when I was in New York for a short time, I suddenly realized that a woman walking toward me was Lois. She also recognized me and we chatted for a minute or so. She had married a doctor and seemed very happy. I could only hope that her husband was worthy of this fine woman who had known just how to handle a youth of eighteen.

When our day of departure from Bayreuth came,* Charlie and I shipped two suitcases containing our tuxedos and other superfluous clothes to Paris in care of the American Express. We then boarded a train for Munich with our bikes in the baggage car. We could have bicycled to that city, but that would have taken the better part of two days over relatively dull country. At age eighteen, we knew very little about the contents of the Munich museums and I do not remember our visiting any special sights in that interesting city – except, of course, the renowned

---

* Curiously, two unused tickets for Bayreuth were found in 2005 tucked into a book that Walter Birge had won as a history prize at Groton at graduation that year; one for Parsifal on July 22, and one for Tristan und Isolde on July 23. They cost 30 marks each.

beer hall, the *Hofbräuhaus*. By that time we had acquired a taste for beer, but even so, the volume of our intake was miniscule compared to that of the patrons of that place who surrounded us. Twenty-two years later, I was to visit Munich again and remain there the better part of two years as Director of the "Voice of Free Czechoslovakia" of Radio Free Europe; but an eon of time, college and post-graduate years and the frightful war would come and go before that second visit was to take place.

We then decided to bicycle through the Bavarian Alps to Innsbruck. Well do I remember late in the afternoon of the first day, coasting down most of the winding road to a beautiful lake called Walchensee, where we came to a hotel on its banks and stopped to see whether we could find accommodations. In 1931, Germany was not a prosperous country; nor was any country in Europe. Probably for that reason we never had problems finding a place to stay. And such was the case in that simple but comfortable hostelry. During dinner the headwaiter came up to us and asked if we would like him to introduce us to two young German girls who were seated not far from our table. That was fine with us. They spoke a little English and Charlie and I each chose one of the girls to dance with as a small and rather poor orchestra played jazz of 1924 vintage.

What soon became apparent was that these girls were far more worldly than Charlie and me, for neither of us had more than a hazy idea as to what sex was. Moreover, Charlie, a devout Catholic, had been warned over and over again by his priest that illicit sex was a mortal sin. As for me, I did not exactly think of sex as a terrible sin, but a combination of Groton training, a conservative family, and complete innocence, as well as lack of experience in handling girls pretty much precluded forward behavior on my part. (I was also afraid of catching a venereal disease). The girls were careful to give us their respective room numbers. I recall getting into bed and thinking that as soon as Charlie fell asleep, I would steal out of the room and up to the room of the girl I had danced with. Things did not work out that way however, for the next thing I knew, it was a sunny morning. A whole day spent on a bicycle and the resultant fatigue had overcome the urge to experiment. At breakfast, the headwaiter asked what the matter was with us for apparently the girls had given him a negative report on our performance.

They were nowhere to be seen, having set out on a mountain hike. What became of them? Did they become enthusiastic Nazis? Were their future husbands killed on the Russian front? Did they meet an untimely end in an allied bombardment? Over the years, I often wondered about them, like many others I was to meet briefly and never meet again.

From Walchensee, we bicycled to Innsbruck. The problem with this mode of transport through the Alps is that you have to push your bicycle up the seep hills but when you go down the other side it is too tough on the brakes, so we ended up walking down as well as up some of the steep roads.

In Innsbruck, we checked into a small hotel, where we spent a pleasant evening at the so-called *nachtlokal* that was part of the hotel. With one notable exception, we were the only patrons of that spot. That exception was a middle-aged American of about fifty by the name of Porter, very much the "Ivy League" type, though that organization had yet to be formed. We ended up sitting at the same table and Porter, who seemed delighted at meeting young compatriots, ended up paying for everything, including drinks for a least a half dozen *artistes,* that is, young women who came to our table with instructions from the management to order as many drinks as possible.

After we had been there for an hour or so our new friend suggested that we now move on to a more rewarding kind of entertainment. Charlie, in fear of committing a mortal sin, declined and said he would go to bed. I, on the other hand, accompanied Porter and two of the less fearsome women to a bedroom. Porter, with no further ado selected one of the girls whom he led to one of the two beds, which were separated by about twenty feet – the width of the room. The other girl and I sat down on the opposite bed. I was curious but had no intention of doing anything more than sit there. In short, that female did not attract me in the least, but I remained there to keep Porter company of sorts. I guess the idea of intimate contact with a prostitute was revolting, and I must add that this has been the case ever since; that commercializing sex spoils the pleasure of its attainment. For me, even more important, without some sort of personal relationship, intimate contact is meaningless. It was to be a few years before I would be initiated into its mysteries.

We sold our bicycles the next morning and proceeded by train to Interlaken, Switzerland, and then on to Grindelwald. It was exactly ten years since my first visit to that beautiful place. Once more I marveled at the grandeur high above us: the Wetterhorn, the Eiger – perhaps the most dangerous mountain to climb in Switzerland - the Mönch, and in the distance, the Jungfrau. Charlie had never heard of these mountains or of Grindelwald and was awestruck.

As mentioned earlier, at the age of eight, I had climbed as far as the halfway hut – known as the Glückstein Hut – on the Wetterhorn and this time I suggested that we hire a guide and ascend all the way to the summit. The only clothes I had for this undertaking were my German *lederhosen* and a light wool jacket. I was to regret this inappropriate attire.

Our guide, Hans, was an attractive individual in his early twenties. We left the Bären Hotel at noon and when we reached the glacier which I had first crossed in July, 1921, Hans roped us together – Hans leading and Charlie between him and me. The gradually moving barrier of ice that we now began to cross seemed much less fearsome than I had remembered it; but still the crevasses were not to be taken lightly or carelessly.

We arrived at the Glückstein Hut in the late afternoon, where we planned to spend the night. Two couples were already there. I was surprised and somewhat shocked to be told that, while married, it was not to each other. We set out very early the next morning for the summit. It was then, as we were again being roped together, that Hans informed us that this was his first trip as a professional guide and that he hoped we did not mind. I felt a bit uneasy, but the die was cast; moreover, Hans seemed very competent.

I will never forget that climb, for in the first place, it was cold and with each additional hundred meters traversed – almost vertically it seemed – it was getting even colder. At first we scrambled over rocks, which was not very difficult; but then began the last steep ascent up hard-packed snow to the summit, and by then I was really congealed; and now I wished that I were dressed in woolen knickerbockers and heavy sweater as was Hans. But up we went and finally reached the top. There was not much space up there and no reason to remain more than a minute; so we took a photo and then started our descent. This time, I went first with Hans bringing up the rear, and it was fortunate that he did.

The descent was far more difficult than the climb up for we were told to face away from the mountain, dig our heels into the snow and look down onto that terrifying vast space outward and below. Slowly and with trepidation, we descended. All of a sudden, Charlie slipped. Fortunately the guide was prepared for such an eventuality, for at each step he had dug his ice ax into the snow so that in case one of us lost his footing he could quickly hitch the rope around the ax, thus preventing himself from being pulled down. For an instant I thought my last day had dawned. This might have been Hans' first official day as a guide, but thank heaven he knew what he was doing and almost surely saved our lives. At that moment, I vowed never to go serious mountain climbing again and I never have.

The following day, Charlie and I took a train to Basel and from there, as we were short of time, flew to Paris in a single engine plane which carried ten passengers. This, my first airplane trip, was a thrilling experience. The next occasion I would board an aircraft was eleven years later.

Charlie's mother, a member of the affluent Kernan family of Utica, had given a sum of money to him with the instruction that he was to use it in Paris to take us both to a fine restaurant. So we went to the *Tour d'Argent*, an establishment I could not afford to visit over a half century later. For about eight dollars, we had soup, *pâté en croûte, canard à l'orange*, a succulent dessert, and a not-too-expensive wine. That was a fitting wind-up for our voyage.

My summer ended at our summer "camp" in the Adirondack League Club Preserve at Little Moose Lake and Charlie's with his family at Alder Creek near Utica. We had bought our "camp" in 1929 because in 1927, we had sold "Overbrook", our country place in Groton, Connecticut and purchased a spacious apartment at 580 Park Avenue in New York City, where we lived during most of the year. At Little Moose that August, a New Zealander named Palmer, whom we had met on the ocean liner *Homeric* on our way home, paid us a visit. I learned a good bit about New Zealand and I think Palmer was happy with his American experience.

I reported to Harvard in mid-September with the class of 1935. That year of 1931 was the first when the new "house plan", made possible by the generous gift of Mr. Harkness (a Yale graduate) to Harvard, came into full effect. That fall, for the first time, the freshmen class was housed in the Yard and B-21 Wigglesworth was to be my home.

The change from Groton to Harvard was earthshaking. It was as though a move had been made from a pleasant, minimum-security prison to a great club where the intellectual stimulation was never-ending and where one made new friends every day. At that time, for an A.B. degree, you had to take a course in both French and German – of which one could be elementary and the other advanced. I enrolled in German-A as well as in Merriman's History-1 and in English-A, the compulsory writing course. I also signed up for Military Science. I took the required advanced French course the following year. In order to qualify for Second Lieutenant, one had to take Military Science all four years. Hence, I had second thoughts about that situation and dropped "Mil-Sci" after my freshman year. I was by then convinced that the United States would not again soon become involved in another conflict to "make the world safe for democracy." As I was not a good grammarian – albeit a good linguist – I did not do well in German, but I did obtain a passing grade. In subsequent years, my speaking proficiency in that language became quite strong. But this posed a problem. As my accent was excellent and as I could say what I wanted to express quite fluently, the person with whom I was speaking would usually assume that he or she could reply rapidly, often using colloquial expressions, with the logical result that I understood little of what had been said.

That first fall, I reported to football practice. What a change from school! The linemen all weighed over 190 pounds and many over 200; and most of the backs were tough and very fast. I had played against two of these halfbacks the year before, and as freshmen, they were even more formidable than they had been at Middlesex School. At 160 pounds and not very fast, I certainly did not expect to excel on the Harvard gridiron. As Henry Lamar, the Harvard freshman coach a few years later, was to comment about one his players, I was "light, but slow." I did, however, go back to Groton as an end on the second freshman team and we lost a close game, 7-0. I well remember one play when I tore into the Groton backfield and grabbed Edwin Pratt, their skilful quarterback; but before I could bring him down he flipped the ball back to their star runner, Charlie Potter, who took off around my end which was undefended and made a big gain. That over-zealous misplay on my part led me to the conclusion that perhaps I should drop football and go out for fall rowing.

Frank Picard, a former Harvard varsity player, was our end coach. His continuing admonition was, "No late nights and no drinking." It so happened, however, about two weeks before the above-mentioned Groton game, that Abby Beveridge, who had been Judy's best girl during his last two years in college and who lived in Beverly Farms, gave a small dinner-dance one Saturday evening to which I was invited as a generous gesture and presumably also to find out how Judy was doing, for she had learned about his undergoing psychiatric treatment and was obviously concerned.

Soon after my arrival, whom did I see but Frank Picard who just the afternoon before had warned us to avoid going to evening parties. I spent most of that evening avoiding him. If he entered a room of which there were many in that almost-palatial house, I left that room by another door. I suppose Picard would not have cared too much had he caught sight of me – especially as I was certainly not one of his leading candidates for a starting end position on the freshman team. But that evening in early October, it seemed very important that I not be kicked off the squad.

As all but one of my closest Groton friends had entered Yale or Princeton and as I knew that would be the case during my sixth form year at school – the year one was to choose roommates at college - at a New York dance I had approached two St. Marks acquaintances with a view to our rooming together at Harvard. Perhaps they felt that it would be embarrassing to refuse my suggestion; in any case, they agreed with my proposal, so in September, 1931, Jack Akin and Pete Haskins moved into B-21 Wigglesworth with me.

Jack and Pete were good-natured, attractive, rather irresponsible "good guys" in the generally accepted sense. From the outset, however, it was clear that we had little in common. The contretemps began when the three of us decided to rent a radio and a phonograph for which I signed. Then, as we needed a telephone, I made the necessary arrangements with the phone company. What ensued were seemingly countless long-distance calls for which I had to end up paying. Hence, I had the telephone disconnected. To make matters worse, neither Jack nor Pete would pay for their share of the rent for the radio and phonograph, so I got rid of those also. To top things off, these amusing characters threw three of a set of six fine old English hunting prints, which I had inherited from Julius' Harvard room, into the fireplace where a brisk fire soon consumed them.

At this juncture I came to the obvious conclusion that Jack and Pete were not intrigued with me and regretted having agreed to the rooming arrangement. So I made the best of that unfortunate situation – for which I was mostly to blame in view of my having made the first move – and I took down my remaining prints from the living room walls and hung them in my own small bedroom.

Shortly after this episode – in mid-November – I was operated on for appendicitis in Stillman Infirmary. When father came up from New York to see me and decided to take a look at B-21 and meet my room-mates, as mischance would have it, he entered B-21 in the late afternoon and found both Jack and Pete obviously drunk and sprawled stark naked on the floor. Father, despite his strict Midwestern, Congregational upbringing was broadminded. Nevertheless, from B-21 he made a beeline to Stillman Infirmary to see me and at once strongly urged that I do what I could to change rooms. That, of course, was out of the question, and when I saw Julius again at Christmas time he backed me up on my stand. It might be added that there was not much socializing with Jack and Pete the rest of that year.

All the above having been written, a few additional comments about these two men are in order. Jack was unusually attractive physically – a sort of Steerforth character. At St. Marks, he had sustained s serious football injury to one of his legs but had neglected to do anything about the doctor's prescribed treatment, with the result that when he entered Harvard the wound had not healed; he was thus unable to come out for freshman football. Nor the following year did he feel able to try out for the varsity. He had been an outstanding halfback at St. Marks and, had he followed his doctor's orders, he might well have played for Harvard. As he possessed social graces along with good looks and an easy-going manner, he got on very well in college, was taken into the Porcellian Club – the most exclusive of the "final clubs", and soon after graduation married a very attractive Boston girl, Dorothy Forbes. I have no idea as to what kind of business Jack entered following his graduation, but he did end up as manager of the New York Foreign Trade Council. As I attended every annual meeting of that Council during the ten years I was export sales manager of a manufacturing company in Columbus, Ohio in the late 1950's and early 1960's, I met with Jack again at those meetings. We also had a pleasant get together on the occasion of our twenty-fifth Harvard reunion in 1960. Finally, at the age of fifty, while vacationing with his wife in Jamaica, he was felled by a lethal pneumonia virus.

As for Pete Haskins, while he had little of Jack's easy charm, he was good natured and humorous. We occasionally met at reunions in the ensuing years but as old acquaintances, rather than friends.

Now in this narrative comes the brighter side of my freshman year. Within a week of my arrival in Cambridge, I came to know well the occupants of C-12 Wigglesworth, the entry adjoining mine: namely Burke Wilkinson of Llewelyn Park, New Jersey and Roger Hopkins, his taciturn Baltimorean room-mate, both graduates of St. George School. These two, as well as Joe Hoguet of New York who lived in a nearby entry became good friends. This was especially true with regard to Burke, a very special friend during the four Harvard years. We often played poker in C-12 and when we needed a bottle of liquor for drinks during the game, one of us would telephone Salvatore, our bootlegger. This swarthy individual, clothed in a tight-fitting Chesterfield overcoat, would soon make his appearance and utter in a low, seemingly menacing tone, "You men order a pint of rye? O.K., that'll be three bucks."

One afternoon in that fall of 1931, Burke received a telegram that his father had died suddenly. The four of us, joined by Bobby Jones, also a classmate and new friend, played poker until it was time for Burke to catch the midnight train for New York.

A few additional comments may be of interest about Burke, Roger and Joe. Burke won a Lionel de Jersey Scholarship for a year's post-graduate study in Cambridge, became a successful author of derring-do novels and biographies, most recently a life of Saint Gaudens. In addition, he served in London during World War II as an army liaison officer. Following the war, he was appointed to important posts in the State Department (Assistant Deputy Secretary of State) and later in Paris on General Norstad's staff. He was a speechwriter for several presidents. Roger settled in Baltimore where he became a successful banker and for many years up to end of his life was head of the annual "Cotillion", a post that must have given him great satisfaction, loyal Baltimorean that he had always been. Joe descended into alcoholism and finally committed suicide in his late forties.

One very enjoyable activity of that freshman year came from my joining the Glee Club. Not only did I get to know men I would otherwise not have met, but also singing with that group was a great experience – notably, our performing with the Boston Symphony Orchestra when we sang the Bach B-Minor Mass together with the Radcliffe Choral Society. Serge Koussevitsky was the conductor of that great orchestra and of our combined 250 voices. That experience I never forgot.

Near the end of our freshman year, we had to decide in which of the new "houses" we wished to live during our next three years. At the outset, Wilkinson, Hopkins, Jones, Hoguet, and I decided to apply for entry either to Dunster House or Elliot House. First we met with Gale Noyes, the Senior Tutor of Dunster House, who made a great impression on us, perhaps mainly owing to his lively sense of humor. Then we arranged to have a talk with Professor R.B. Merriman of History-I fame and the Master of Elliot House. While this impressive man was a brilliant and entertaining lecturer, he failed to sell us on his "House". We all decided to list Dunster as our first choice, partly because Mr. Merriman, on being informed by us that Dunster was also being considered, made disparaging comments about Mr. Noyes.

I mentioned above that about halfway through the football season, I decided to give up football and begin rowing with one of the freshman fall rowing crews. So I moved my athletic clothes from Dillon Field House to Weld Boat House. There was no special boating in the fall and the oarsmen were divided at random. The two classmates I remember having rowed in my boat were Tom Whitney at stroke and Dick Thorndike at number five. In the big race that brought the fall crew season to an end, our crew came in first, mainly owing to Tom's skill as our stroke oar.

As soon as the ice broke up in the early spring of 1932, Bert Haines, our English trained coach, selected two crews for our organized rowing. Bob Cutler rowed stroke in the first boat and I stroked the second crew. Tom Whitney, mentioned above, decided to go out for the 150-pound crew, as he was quite a bit smaller than the rest of us. During that Easter holiday, our first two freshman crews remained in Cambridge to train for the upcoming races. It was exactly during that two-week period that both Claire and Grace were to be married – Grace to Manoel Bon de Sousa Pernes and Claire to Dr. Fuller Albright. Claire's wedding was scheduled a week after Grace's. I asked Bert's permission to let me off the Saturday of Grace's marriage, but as at that time early in the season I thought I had a chance of rowing on the first boat, I did not dare to ask him again to let me off one week later for Claire's wedding. Hence, I missed seeing Claire married to Fuller. I do not believe that I was sorely missed, but later I never quite forgave myself for my mixed-up sense of values.

Before long that spring, Tom Whitney was promoted to stroke of the first freshman heavyweight crew and Cutler and I were moved to number two on the first and second heavyweights, respectively. And again I went out to Groton – this time to race against their first crew, which was stroked by Frank Roosevelt, Jr., and was an outstanding outfit, which crossed the finish line a length ahead of us.

Shortly after the beginning of summer vacation at the end of my freshman year, I asked father if he had any ideas as to how I might land a summer job. In that depression year that was not easy; in fact, there were no jobs to be had. Father, however, had a suggestion, namely a position as a "work away" on one of the freight boats owned by a good friend of his, Clifford Mallory. The next day, he approached Mr. Mallory and the day after that I called at the offices of the Mallory Line and the arrangements were made.

That same week, one of the Mallory Line boats was due to sail for Jacksonville and Porto Rico (they spelled it that way then). The next stops were as yet unknown, for so-called tramp freighters usually had ports of call arranged by the head office while they were at sea. Needless to add, a "work away" did not receive any pay, but I was not a great deal worse off than the seamen for at that time an ordinary seaman received $40 a month and an able seaman, about $60 – not exactly the road to riches.

In view of Mr. Mallory's relationship with father, I took meals in the very small dining room with the captain and mates. The duties I was slated to perform were not exactly thrilling, nor were they fraught with difficulty, for most of my time was spent scraping rust from the iron decks – also scraping rust from the iron sides of the ship below decks. That, of course, turned out to be pretty warm work in June and increasingly so as we steamed south.

As mentioned above, our first port of call was Jacksonville and we arrived on a very hot Sunday morning. I decided to take a look around and walked along the road that skirted the docks until I came to a small seamen's missionary church by the side of the narrow road. Standing just outside this edifice of rickety construction was the minister whose immediate purpose just at that time was to urge passersby to come in to the service. I stopped beside this servant of the Lord who at once went to work on me. "Step right in, son, and join us in praising the Lord. Where are you from?" For some reason I replied that I had just very recently left Harvard. Of course there was no reason why I should not accept this invitation to attend the revival service, so in I went, albeit very informally dressed with old trousers and a t-shirt, owing to the hot weather. What I best remember about this service was that during the singing of one of the revival-type hymns, the minister, after each verse, stepped forward and exhorted anyone wishing to be saved to please step forward. He repeated this at least four times, but nary a person stepped forward. Then, somewhat to my embarrassment, he announced that when the congregation left the church he hope that they would shake hands with a young man from Harvard who had joined them on that day. Of course, this did not really bother me and I shook hands with a lot of people on that Sunday morning and they all treated me like a visiting dignitary.

Perhaps my best newfound friend on board ship was the Third engineer, an Italian-American by the name of Franzini. When we docked at Jacksonville, this worthy son of Italy asked if I would like to "get laid." In spite of my extreme innocence, I knew what that meant. I explained to Franzini that I was totally inexperienced in the activity he had in mind and did not think I wanted to do what he suggested. "What have you got it for?" he asked incredulously. I finally agreed to accompany my friend to the *cathouse* he apparently knew well from previous visits. So on the day following our arrival in that port – in the late afternoon after chores, we set out together and with us came also Mr. Gelschleiger, the German-American cook, an old timer in the seafaring business who seemed to be about sixty.

When we arrived at our destination the *Madame* greeted Franzini like a long-lost relative and she at once agreed to supply me with "a real nice young girl." I was ushered into a rather shabby, but I presumed adequate, room where I sat down on the bed, there being no chair that I could see. Presently a rather nondescript, but fairly pretty, though heavily made-up and hard looking girl stepped into the room and sat down on the bed beside me. I at once launched into a meaningless conversation in hopes that Ruby (for that, she had informed me, was her name) would somehow forget the purpose which had impelled me to come there. After an interminable two or three minutes of this embarrassing situation and while I was momentarily at a loss as to what to say next, Ruby ventured, "Do you want to do some business, or not?" I must have given her a startled look and in any case, I made no move to take off any clothing. So this apparently good natured but business-minded soldier of that *house* added "You don't have to do anything if you don't want to, honey." "Thanks a lot," I replied, "but how much do I owe you for your time?" The price was two dollars. I extracted two one-dollar bills from my pocket and pressed them into her rather grubby looking hand. She then, with what I am sure was a practiced motion, lowered one stocking, slipped the bills inside, raised the stocking again and seemed rather pleased with herself that she had done nothing – well, very little anyway – to earn this sum which in that dismal year of 1932 was a tidy amount.

Within a few minutes my friends, Third Engineer Franzini and Cook Gelschleiger, were ready to move on. Our next stop was the dwelling of a couple, who had been recommended to these two as reputable makers of home-brew, i.e., beer.

We spent about an hour in that make-shift brewery and by the time we bent our steps in the direction of the Mallory Line freighter we were all pretty tight; Gelschleiger in particular was really stinking – the adjective most frequently used in those days to describe one who could hardly walk owing to previous heavy intake of an alcoholic beverage. That home brew must have been very strong indeed, for despite Franzini's and my own parlous condition, we almost had to carry that old German back to the ship. I felt terrible. "No more home brew for me," I vowed.

During our voyage down to Trinidad, I was asked to take the twelve to four watch along with the crew's most experience helmsman, Gilboy. He was quite a guy, entertaining me with a series of amusing stories and cheerfully answering any questions I asked with regard to navigation and keeping a vessel on course. His favorite expression was, "They broke the mold when they made Trinidad," and he promised to show me all its charms.

Much to my new friend's chagrin, we had just come in sight of that fabled island and were preparing to enter the harbor when "Sparks", the operator of our wireless, reported to the captain that we were not to land at Trinidad after all and should proceed to San Juan. There was keen disappointment throughout the ship, but when an order was received signed "C.D.Mallory", it was obeyed.

When we docked at San Juan the following day there was a horde of women on hand to meet us. Mother, in her own way, had warned me about "bad women", admonishing that they should be avoided. Even without this somewhat embarrassed warning, I would hardly have been tempted to get to know any of that troop. There was no Helen of Troy among them; nor would Aeneas, had he been on our ship, have seen his Dido among that eager group.

Three things I recall in connection with that visit to San Juan: first, I took a long walk and almost passed out from the sun and heat; second, I spent a lot of time, even while in port, scraping that seemingly ever present rust from the hot iron decks; third, I again accompanied Franzini on a visit to a female acquaintance of his – an eighteen year old he had met on his last trip to Puerto Rico. That girl had a younger sister who started to climb all over me, but finally ended on my lap, probably with lascivious intent on her part, but with innocuous result for me. On that trip, Puerto Rico did not impress me but on a visit made some forty years later, I revised my opinion and now see it as an increasingly attractive pearl in America's crown.

Our next stop was Tampa. It was as hot as blazes and the first thing I wanted to do after docking was to rush to a drug store to eat a peach sundae. Apart from that welcome refreshment, there did not seem to be anything interesting to do or see there, and most of us were relieved when we pulled out en route to Norfolk, Virginia. On the way several men tried to borrow money from me, having first been unsuccessful in getting loans from others. By this time, however, I had learned that a promise to repay money owed on that ship was an empty promissory gesture, so I was able to withstand the "Gee, Walt, I'll pay you back double tomorrow, - payday."

The steaming south and then north to Norfolk took two days and by that time I had made up my mind to leave the ship and head north to the Adirondacks. First, after bidding cordial farewell to the captain and other new friends – notably, Franzini, I took a ferry to the southern tip of Maryland, then a bus to New York and finally the train to the Little Moose railway station at Thendara. In those days, all fares were almost unbelievably inexpensive, so the money I had brought with me at the outset of this adventure was sufficient. And thus ended my first and final experience as a *work away seaman*.

In the fall of 1932, we began our sophomore year in Dunster. Burke continued to room with Roger, Joe roomed with a classmate whom he known at Middlesex, and Bobby Jones and I shared G-33, a room facing the courtyard. When I refer to a room I mean a fairly large sitting room, two bedrooms and a bathroom; and I must add that, compared to the quarters I saw at other colleges, then and since, our suite was palatial. On the other side of the fire door, which separated our place from another room there lived a perennial graduate student, Lambert Ennis, whose 6'6"frame seemed perpetually stooped. Fire doors were normally locked so as to keep the rooms on either side completely separate. Both Jones and I took a special liking to Lambert, however, so we soon unlocked the fire door, and Ennis was always welcome to stoop his way into our quarters. Lambert had been working for four years on his PhD thesis entitled, "The Influence of Burne Jones on the Poetry of Christina Rosetti," or a title very similar to that. A year or so after we met him and after more than five years of assiduous work on that thesis, Lambert was informed by the English Department that the subject he had selected was too obscure to be acceptable for a PhD thesis. When we were told about this, it seemed odd to us, as presumably Ennis had discussed what he intended to write about before he launched on this arduous work. After a few days of seeming despondency, Lambert started all over again to do research on an entirely different subject, and two years after my graduation, he was still at work on this second try.

During that sophomore year it was always a pleasure to see that stooping figure make his way into our living room. "Hello, Bish," he would greet me – I was still known by my Groton sobriquet – "Is Bones up yet? Was he tight last night?" I had bestowed Bobby Jones with that nickname for no particular reason and Ennis also thought it suited him and perhaps it did. Lambert's question as to whether Bobby might have been tight the night before had some logic, for he used to drink a lot on weekends, and the predictable hangovers would invariably incapacitate him for all the following morning.

Bobby had an excellent mind, wrote well, was articulate and always enjoyed a good story or joke. Actually, we did not have much in common but we got on very well. Toward the end of that year, he made several new friends whom he had met in the final club which he joined that winter, so his last two years in Harvard, he lived in a private apartment separate from the college. The same upper-classmen who approached Bobby in connection with his becoming a member of the Fox, their final club, also suggested that I also join that club. I informed them, however, that as my brother had been a member of the Spee Club, I preferred to join that club, if asked. .

Burke Wilkinson was undoubtedly the brightest man I knew well at Harvard. He was not only a fine scholar but also a fast learner who could cut classes and then rapidly go over whatever text was involved and get an A in the exam. Incidentally, he was also a fine tennis player, especially in doubles, and played on the varsity tennis team. Later, he was very successful at Wimbledon, playing there twice, in 1946 and 1948.

In those days, when Radcliffe was almost completely separate from Harvard, the only contact with girls was via invitations we had received as freshmen to attend Boston *sub-deb* parties. These girls were now full-fledged debutantes and most of them were in college. Burke was the only one of our group who owned a car during our sophomore and junior years – a Ford two-seater with a *rumble seat*. A *rumble seat* was a small pullout double seat in the back of a car where a trunk would be nowadays. It was accessible only by climbing into it from the rear end of a car and was separate from the inside seats. As it had no roof, it was entirely open to the elements. They were awfully cold in winter, but if your companion back there was a girl, the cold winds were more easily borne.

It was during our freshman year that I introduced Burke to Frances Proctor, a tall, very attractive and proper Bostonian whom he married in 1938. Well do I remember driving with

Burke in that small Ford out to Smith College to attend a Gillette House dance to which we had been invited by Franny Proctor and Eleanor Leith, our respective girlfriends. Elly Leith, whom I had met at one of those sub-deb parties the previous year, was an unusually attractive, intelligent and somewhat unconventional nineteen-year-old charmer. Her parents were not old-line as were such families as those whose names were Cabot, Lowell, Forbes, Lodge, Adams and selected others. In any case, in those days I hardly knew the difference between the elite Bostonians, the so-called *Brahmans,* and the *wannabes.* While I was not in love with Elly – at least not in love the way I later came to understand and appreciate the meaning of that term – I was beguiled by her.

On that trip to Northampton with Burke, we drove over the icy, narrow roads that were eventually replaced by the Mass Turnpike. Prohibition was still in effect so we brought with us two small bottles of Scotch in small and flat silver flasks which fitted into our hip-pockets. I quickly learned that according to the customary procedure at Smith dances, you would take your girl out to your car; each would take a swift drink and you would return to the dance floor. But then, what were you meant to do the rest of the short weekend? Many, if not most, of the visiting college men took their girls to their hotel rooms on Sunday. As for Elly and me, we spent a few minutes in my room, but then took a long walk. I was an innocent in those days, as was Burke, I am sure. Elly and I went through some of the pre-consummation moves but stopped well short of the act.

One character from St. George's School who entered Harvard as a member of our class was George Cary of Buffalo. How he managed to pass the entrance exams I cannot imagine, for while he was imaginative, flamboyant, good natured and energetic, he was unorganized. After the "November Hours" autumn exams, he received a communication from Dean Hanford informing him that he was expelled for academic shortcomings and suggesting that he seek entrance into a university where he might receive more individual attention. George answered the Dean's message in writing, on his fine monogrammed stationery, asking whether he might be allowed to remain in Harvard until the Christmas holidays as he had made several important social commitments, which could only be fulfilled if he were still a Harvard student. It need hardly be added that the Dean turned a blind eye to George's request, so my friend betook himself to New York where he rented a penthouse apartment belonging to Mr. Arthur Brisbane, a prominent editor of the New York Herald Tribune who was married to George's aunt. As George had just reached the age of twenty-one, he had inherited over $300,000 from his grandmother whose maiden name was Birge. This estimable wall-paper heiress – a distant relative of mine – had, quite a few years previous to the time of our entry into Harvard, sailed for France, but unfortunately the sea had been so rough and George's grandmother had become so seasick that she had vowed never to sail on an ocean liner again and thus was never more to see her native country and lived the rest of her life in France.

In 1932, $300,000 was a lot of money – perhaps the present day equivalent of at least $3,000,000, or maybe even $6,000,000. The first thing my young friend did was to buy a forest-green colored Duesenberg touring car. He remained in his penthouse for two or three years, so I saw him occasionally during Christmas and Easter holidays. As soon as he came into his grandmother's bequest, George let it be known in the big city that he was interested in making investments in fledgling enterprises. At once, as can be imagined, all manner of opportunities came his way, so he began to lose some of his newly acquired wealth. Father pointed out to him that all he needed to do in order eventually to increase his capital was buy almost any reputable stock listed on the New York Stock Exchange and he would sooner or later make a killing. George listened but did not take father's advice. (I often thought George was very like Bertie Wooster in the *Jeeves* stories). At that time the market was near its all-time low in the big depression.

George had two sisters: Althea and Maria, and a younger brother, Charles. Maria had a *coming out* dinner-dance in Buffalo in the early summer of 1933 and I drove out to the Cary place with George in his Duesenberg. We seemed to fly over those winding roads that pre-dated the New York Thruway; often, George pushed his car up to 100 miles an hour. Fortunately he was a skilful driver.

At the dinner party I was seated next to Maria – an unexpected honor – and I was expected to offer a toast to that attractive girl. All I could think of to say was that the younger the Carys were, the saner they seemed to be, a toast that was received with mixed expressions of approval and the opposite.

After the midyear examinations of my sophomore year, I was put on probation as I had missed a few laboratory periods in biology and had also failed adequately to master the finer points of one of Dostoyevsky's novels, a book which, owing to lack of time and paucity of intellectual curiosity on my part, I had only skimmed through. Needless to add, I deserved the letter from Dean Hanford, which was anticipated and right on time. In short, it informed me that I was not to take part in any activity that involved representing Harvard in any field – that admonition to be effective until the final examinations in late spring. If I received the equivalent of four C's in those exams, I would again be in good standing. If I did not achieve those grades I would be expelled. The winter of my sophomore year was the nadir of my time at Harvard, not only because of the poor academic work but also owing to a general apathy as far as life in Cambridge was concerned. I began to entertain the idea of transferring over to Heidelberg – of all places that - just before Hitler's seizure of power in Germany. Then, in that early spring earthshaking events took place and impelled my coming to my senses: Franklin D. Roosevelt was inaugurated president in March and Adolph Hitler almost simultaneously became Chancellor of Germany. At that time also my first priority became my determination to get off probation – which I did with no great trouble in late May.

As for rowing, had I been in good standing academically, I would have gone out for the heavyweight crew, not that I would have had the remotest chance of rowing even on the junior varsity; however, owing to the probation problem, I began to row on what coach Whiteside called the *pro crew,* which oddly enough turned out to be the strongest crew I rowed on during my years at Harvard. This boat was made up of men all of whom were also on probation and a few of whom were outstanding oarsmen. We often practiced with the great varsity crew of that year, which at New London that June defeated Yale for the third straight year.

As already mentioned, the spring of 1933 marked the time of year when the final clubs began to seek out potential future club members from the sophomore class. As expected, two members of the Spee Club called on me at Dunster, reminded me of my brother's past affiliation and enquired as to whether I might be interested in also becoming a member. One of my callers, Oakley Brooks, was a Groton graduate and I remembered him as being a very decent individual. When I informed Brooks that indeed I would be interested in becoming a member of his club, he asked who were my friends in the sophomore class. I mentioned Burke Wilkinson, Roger Hopkins and Joe Hoguet. Then, before long, two things took place that effectively stifled that Spee-bound progress. First, there was the trip to Northampton and the already mentioned Gillette House dance. It so happened that Nelson Aldrich, a very personable Spee Club member, was also at that dance. I had already met Aldrich, but did not know him well. When I saw him across the dance floor I called out, "Hi, Nelly." That was not done. Of course, had I not had a fairly stiff drink a few minutes before I probably would not have greeted him so informally and from the distance of half the length of the dance floor. I was told later that Aldrich, who was not only very affluent but also an influential Spee Club member, began to interpose objections to my candidacy. Perhaps if I had been in his position and a candidate I barely knew had called to me from thirty feet away, I might well have reacted as had Aldrich.

Then there was the question of wearing a hat. I those days, every gentleman wore a hat from the instant he set foot outside his dwelling. I well remember my father insisting that on no account should I ever venture outside our New York apartment without a hat. A day or two following my above mentioned trip to Smith College, Grayson Murphy, a student at Harvard Law School, one of Julius' closest friends at Harvard and a fellow Spee Club member, called me up to ask if I could drop in to his apartment for a few minutes. Grayson had become engaged to Mary, his wife, while they were both guests at our place in the Adirondacks, so I knew him very well The minute I entered his apartment, he asked why I didn't wear a hat. For some reason I had the idea that going without a hat would prevent premature baldness and I explained this to Grayson. "How about breaking this custom for a few weeks until the club votes on the new members," he said. That made sense and for a while I did wear the customary brown felt fedora that most of my friends wore, but to no avail, as the horse had already fled the barn.

Mention has already been made about Jones becoming a member of the Fox Club. Another of my by-that-time very good friends was Larry Nichols and he joined Bobby in that club. At

Groton, I had not known Larry very well, as at school he had been pretty much a loner, mainly because in our fifth form year he had developed a bad case of acne. This handicap had become a millstone around his neck. But at Harvard, he recovered from this down cycle of his life, made many new friends, moved into Dunster House and took an active part in house activities, of which more later.

At the outset, it had not been my intention even to mention the final club episode, but in those days this was, at least for many, an important facet of life at Harvard and as all my best friends did enter a club, it seemed logical to write that Burke, Roger, and Joe entered one and Bobby and Larry entered another. At first, this situation was disappointing, but not for long, for I became active in Dunster theatricals, rowed stroke my last two years on the Dunster crew and played leading parts in two Hasty Pudding plays, inter alia.

As far as rowing was concerned, at the start of spring training for the varsity heavyweight crew my junior year, I was a member of the varsity squad. In retrospect, I doubt that I would have done better than row in the third boat, mainly owing to my light weight of about 160 pounds, but I seemed to be doing better than I had expected at the start of the training time. Then along came Bobby Jones. He had written the Hasty Pudding show and informed me that he had written a part made to order for what he termed my "unique histrionic talents." I had a difficult choice to make; keep rowing with only a slight chance of winning a major H in crew, or accepting a leading part in the Hasty Pudding Show. I chose the latter and I often regretted that decision. I made many new friends in the Hasty Pudding, but so would I have done had I continued varsity rowing. A few days after I had started rehearsals for the up-coming Easter holiday performances, I encountered Charles Whiteside, the varsity crew coach, near Harvard Square. He stopped and asked, "Weren't you one of my crewmen? What happened to you?" When I feebly explained the reason for my disappearance from Newell Boat House, he just cast a disgusted look in my direction and walked on. I was complimented that he had noted my absence. That Easter vacation of 1934, we put on our Hasty Pudding show, not only in Cambridge, but in Providence and Hot Springs, Virginia as well. In my senior year, when I also had a Jones-designed part, we traveled to New York and

Washington where we were all invited to the White House. There, Mrs. Roosevelt served tea at one end of a long table and her daughter, Mrs. Dall, offered hot chocolate at the opposite end.

The Hot Springs visit was memorable because there I met a very dear girl, June Rossbach, who was spending the Easter holidays with her parents, a distinguished, attractive couple. Mrs. Rossbach was the niece of Governor Lehman of New York. Max, the father, who had come to this country from Frankfurt just before the First World War, was a typical German of the old school. June was already a beauty of, as I thought then, seventeen (much later I found out that she was only fifteen), who gave promise of becoming a fascinating woman in a few years.

I visited the Rossbachs twice for brief stays before leaving Harvard. Had I been more mature and perceptive at the age of twenty and had June been a little older, perhaps a Birge-Rossbach romantic merger might have eventually come to pass. A few years later June, who became a successful writer and playwright, married Jack Bingham, a brilliant scholar who was a year behind me at Groton. Jack also had a distinguished career, first as an administrator in the government and then as a congressman from New York.

During the ensuing half century I saw June again periodically at receptions and at the Bingham's Washington apartment; we also occasionally exchanged Christmas cards. In 1986, Jack Bingham died and a year or two later, June telephoned me to announce that, believe it or not, she would soon be marrying Robert Birge. As there is only one Birge family that ever came over to America, I ventured the guess that he was about a fourth cousin. When I arrived in Turkey in 1942 for my Istanbul assignment, Kingsley Birge, Robert's father, had just left to return to the United States after having served for several years in an important capacity at Robert College in Istanbul. His son, Robert was a distinguished theologian and professor. In the fall of 1989, my wife and I met June and Bob for lunch in Sandwich. As we were leaving, Bob drew me aside and said, "You know, Walter, June told me that you were her first love." What a wonderful compliment from that adorable young girl and the beautiful woman she had become.

This account of my Harvard years would be incomplete without comments on my close friendship with an unusually interesting and attractive character who was already in Dunster House when I came there. This was Valentin Edouard Blacque, known as Teddie. His father, who had died many years before, had been a Turkish diplomat though he was descended from a French emigré family, which had fled France during the French Revolution and settled in Constantinople. Teddie's mother, née Kalman, was from St.Paul, and had met Teddie's father when he was Minister from Turkey to Austria, where she was being presented at court. She was from a rich family, of Jewish background, a fact never mentioned by Teddie, who indeed, often made anti-Semitic remarks! Pasha, as I called him, was exactly my size, both in height and in weight, of dark complexion, with a rather prominent nose, and above all, he was known as a lady-killer. His infectious *joie de vivre* had a salubrious effect on me and I learned to take myself less seriously.

I made his acquaintance in the *Cercle Français*, a Harvard group which put on French plays, As he and I were about the only members whose knowledge of French was very good – actually his was perfect – we naturally hit it off while acting in Molière's *Le Médecin Malgré Lui*. Pasha was very different from anyone I had met up to that time – a sophisticated man of the world and suave and knowledgeable in matters of the heart. Pasha was one year ahead of me, but as he was going through Harvard in three years he graduated at the end of my own sophomore year. He had no problem achieving this three-year term, as his field of concentration was German literature, a logical choice in view of his having been brought up in Vienna.

On May 19, 1933 Pasha celebrated his twenty-first birthday, and since my twentieth was on May 21, we decided to buy three hundred shares - one hundred-fifty each – of a one-dollar stock called Seneca Copper. Because I was not twenty-one, the shares had to be bought in Pasha's name – an unfortunate necessity, as that summer father advised me to sell my shares of this nearly worthless stock, but as I did not know Pasha's address, I was unable to ask him to unload them and my investment went by the board. The one good thing, which came of this is that since that time I have avoided one-dollar stocks.

Upon graduation, Pasha moved to New York where he rented a one-room garret apartment on Park Avenue for $28 a month, not especially cheap, remembering that this was the pit of the depression. His mother was sending him an allowance of $100 a month and he was managing to live on this without too much difficulty. He naturally gravitated to an international set of Germans, White Russians, Italians and Austrians, and he also met my sister Grace, by now married to Manuel Bon de Souza. When mother and father gave me a twenty-first birthday party in their apartment at 580 Park Avenue, Pasha brought what looked like a cake, but when he removed the icing on top with a deft motion, he revealed inside the hidden case of champagne. Such a costly gift was possible because Pasha was then a salesman for a French champagne firm.

So far I have only mentioned Gale Noyes in passing. It was he who gave Dunster House its unique flavor. Most evenings after dinner he would play the piano in the common room – usually popular songs of the time, such as *Isn't It romantic* or *All of Me* or *Smoke Gets in Your Eyes* and occasionally I and a couple of others would sing, reading the words over his shoulder. At least once a year, Gale would also put on a house play and I can remember three of these: "The Fire in the Apartment House" – a three-character comedy set to the tunes of Italian operas – "The Importance of Being Ernest", and a medieval play about "Summer is A Comin' In". In all three, Larry Nichols acted with me. We would also often meet with Gale in his attractive apartment where he might give us his special rendition of *Cats On the House Tops*, sung to the tune of "Do You Ken John Peel at the Break of the Day". It went like this:

> Cats on the housetops, cats on the tiles,
> Cats with the syphilis, cats with piles,
> Cats with their assholes wreathed in smiles,
> *As they revel in the joys of fornication.*

Unfortunately, Gale took a sabbatical my senior year and for that interim was replaced by Seymour Harris, a very able economist, but otherwise rather dull.

Gale Noyes' last official act as far as I was concerned, was arranging for Larry Nichols and me to occupy G-53, a fifth floor room, facing the back alley behind Dunster House, a slight inconvenience but well worth it at a price of $120 a year. We all greatly missed Gale our last year at Dunster and, looking back on the house experience, at least as far as I was concerned, he was the high-light of that time.*

The other member of the faculty, living in Dunster House who will always be specially remembered, was professor Crane Brinton, my tutor in modern European history. Occasionally, he would give me a special assignment – this in connection with my being a candidate for an honors degree – and they were always interesting, requiring as they did a lot of research. The one I remember best was entitled "The Influence of Protestantism on the Rise of Capitalism." I do not know whether Crane coined the aphorism, but it was he who insisted that I never forget it, namely, that the Catholic Church believed in good works, while Protestants – especially those influenced by Calvin – believed in good work. "Think about it, Walter", said Professor Brinton, "The great cathedrals, most of the great art of the Renaissance period, Europe's and England's great universities were the result of the Catholic faith. On the other hand, the industries of northern Europe, America's proclivity for work, the industrial revolution – these sprang from Calvin's belief that good work was for the glory of God, that work would displace evil doings, etc.".

At the beginning of my senior year, Crane Brinton told me that as he was slated to be one of the oral examiners to determine who would receive honors in history, he could no longer be my tutor for such a double arrangement would be a conflict of interest in his relation to candidacy. His successor as my tutor was a relatively young assistant professor whose name, I regret to say, has been forgotten. He was of great help, especially in aiding my choosing of a subject for my honors thesis.

As it happened, in October of 1934, King Alexander of Yugoslavia and Louis Barthou, the French Foreign Minister, were assassinated while in Marseille. In view of the part Barthou had played in building a system of alliances to prevent the resurgence of Germany to a position of menacing power in Europe and in view of my interest in Germany during that period between the two wars, which coincided with my Groton and Harvard days and owing also to my knowledge of French, my tutor and I (he was the first to suggest it) decided that I should write a life of Louis Barthou as my honors thesis. In connection with this enterprise I ran into an almost unbelievable stroke of

* Noyes (1898-1961), after receiving his PhD from Harvard, returned to Brown University (where he had earned his B.A. and M.A. degrees) in 1938, where he had a distinguished career as a professor of English, and was known for "his erudition, his sense of humor, and his vast humanity."

luck. One Sunday afternoon, after having had lunch with Claire and her husband, Fuller Albright in their apartment in Joy Street on Beacon Hill, I was on my way to the Dunster House library and as I was passing by the door to someone's room, I noticed an attractive-looking French newspaper with a lot of pictures on the front page lying on the floor in front of that door. I picked up this interesting periodical and what did I see on the front page but the first part of a long article on the life of the recently assassinated French Foreign Minister. I doubted that the rightful owner of that paper needed it nearly as much as I did, so I filched this valuable source material and I must confess that I suffered no qualms of conscience afterward. This, together with many sources found in Harvard's Widener Library, provided invaluable help in my work that fall and winter of my senior year. How well I remember leaving Widener late in November and in early December of that year, into a pitch-black Cambridge and then the quarter mile or so walk down to Dunster House.

In connection with preparing that thesis, there was another fortuitous circumstance. One day Crane Brinton, who almost always had lunch in the House, came to where I was eating and said he had an interesting suggestion for me. It appeared that a very well known professor, a Frenchman named Bernard Faÿ (pronounced Fah-ee), who had been staying with him for a few days, was scheduled to take a train to Buffalo from Back Bay station at ten o'clock the next day. Mr. Brinton went on to explain that professor Fay had been a long-time friend of Mr. Louis Barthou and would be in a position to answer any questions that might come to mind during the drive to the station. Needless to add, I accepted Mr. Brinton's proposal with antelopean alacrity. Professor Faÿ turned out to be a charming individual and was a valuable mine of information during that all-too-short Sunday morning trip.*

Aside from my first of two Hasty Pudding theatrical performance experiences, the junior year brought other rather special facets of interest. First, that was the coldest winter on record for the Boston area. The temperature, which on most days was near zero degrees Fahrenheit, brought solid ice over a

---

* This is undoubtedly Bernard Fay, of the Collège de France and director of the National Library, author of books with titles such as *Revolution and Freemasonry* and *Franklin,* who was tried and convicted as a collaborator responsible for the death of 549 Freemasons during World War Two. He was sentenced to imprisonment at hard labor for life, the confiscation of all his property, and "national degradation".

foot thick to the Charles river all the way to the dam, which was about two miles down stream from Dunster House; and as there was not much snow, one could skate all the way to Boston.

That smooth, black ice brought hundreds of people out to skate. Almost every day, I joined the throng on the river, partly in hopes of meeting a pretty girl. It so happened that one bright January day when the temperature had relented and was back to about fifteen degrees, I caught sight of a devastatingly beautiful young woman who was skating all by herself. Dressed in bright red and gold, and wearing a jaunty toque, she was a sight for sore eyes, as they used to say in the 1930's. How could I introduce myself to this beauty?

At boarding school, there had been no girls and during the holidays, at the organized dances, you were always introduced to all the girls. The same applied to the sub-deb dances that I attended during freshman year. And even at the large Boston and New York debutante parties, there were always ushers to introduce you to any girl you wanted to meet. Very rarely had I ever introduced myself to any girl. So – what was I to do about getting to know this skating Helen of Troy?

While I skated in wide circles around and then away from the object of this dilemma, a young man, who was presumably also a Harvard student, made an appearance, took a look at this beautiful girl, hesitated a few seconds and then, to my consternation, skated up to her. I heard him ask, "Do you mind if I talk to you?" Any move I might now make would be too late. The only positive result of this experience was that it taught me a lesson: i.e., shake off the Groton-related syndrome having to do with the opposite sex. And this leads directly to a somewhat similar situation.

That spring of 1934, I took up rowing in a single skiff. One afternoon, just after rowing down stream past the Lars Anderson Bridge, I saw a young woman sitting on the south bank, a sports car parked by the side of the road behind her – that is, in front of the Business School. I stopped rowing and floated slowly past this female who, from the distance of some fifty to seventy-five feet, looked very attractive. Then, miracle of miracles, she actually waved to me. Of course, I momentarily grabbed both oars with my left hand and waved back; then I took a few short strokes toward the bank and came close enough to talk to this friendly soul. After a minute or so of meaningless chatter, I asked her to wait for me while I put my skiff away in Weld Boat House. She said she would gladly wait.

There ensued the fastest shower and getting dressed ever and I ran most of the distance back to that sports car and its owner. As I remember it, we took a short ride and then agreed to meet the following afternoon for an excursion to the Singing Sands Beach near Manchester on the North Shore. This was just before the final exam time, and I could ill afford taking too much time away from the books, but this was something special.

I met my new friend in front of Dunster House and I came prepared for intimacy. Her sports car was a spiffy MG. During our ride to the North Shore I learned that her name was Zozia, that she was Polish-born and that her husband, a member of a prominent Boston family, was much older than she, and the class of '15 at Harvard. I guessed her age at about twenty-three or four.

When we got to Singing Sands, there was no one else there. It was nearly high tide and the only sound was that of the gentle waves coming onto the beach and then receding. We removed our shoes and lay down on the warm sand. Gradually there ensued love-play, which would logically lead to the consummation I knew so little about how to achieve.

I was too embarrassed to take the prophylactic precaution, which I had been warned was always advisable, right there next to Zozia, so I got up, whispered, "I'll be right back," and ran to a large nearby rock behind which I donned the contraption. I then sprinted back to my puzzled companion.

The outcome of this, my first near-intimate experience, could only be described as a fiasco as far as my premature performance was concerned. Zozia, however, must have understood for she said nothing. During our seemingly long drive back to Cambridge, we talked very little. Zozia did, however, mention again that she was married. When I asked what her last name was, I learned that her husband was W.S.F., a Harvard graduate.

When Zozia dropped me off at Dunster House I took her hand and managed to say, "You are a beautiful, very special woman." She smiled an enigmatic smile as she replied, "I hope to see you soon again, Walter." Three days later, she telephoned to say, "I have two tickets to the symphony for tomorrow evening. Would you like to take me?" My final exam in art history was scheduled for the morning immediately following the evening of the concert and I knew that I would have to put in many hours of study before that exam in order to get a B for the course, a requisite if I was to graduate with honors the next year. The thought also crossed my mind in those few seconds that attending a symphony concert with a married woman – even a very attractive one – at the end of the school year did not make sense. I explained about the pressing need for study immediately before the exam – not too convincingly, I fear. "I am sorry you can't make it," Zozia retorted rather coldly, and hung up. I never heard from her again. There is a post-script to this brief saga: fifty-six years after saying good-by to Zozia, I read on the obituary page of the Boston Globe that Mr. W.S.F. had died and that his wife, Zozia, had predeceased him many years before.*

As already mentioned, both Adolph Hitler and Franklin D. Roosevelt came to power in the winter of my sophomore year. Many of us had actually believed that Herbert Hoover might win the presidential election of 1932, and this might logically be explained by our having been fairly well insulated from the country's widespread misery including that of the poor men who during that parlous time sold apples at a nickel apiece on Park Avenue in New York. People were losing jobs everywhere. Men who had been prosperous stockbrokers or important business executives became peddlers of Fuller brushes door-to-door, and destitute couples moved in with relatives even though the latter could often ill afford to take care of them. Gasoline was ten cents a gallon and a pack of cigarettes – if you bought a carton, cost ten cents also. That same sum, one thin dime, also bought a simple but usually adequate breakfast in Harvard Square – that is, a good sized Danish pastry and a half pint of milk. "Jim's Place", near Adams House, advertised a dinner for thirty-five cents, a three-course, plain, but filling meal.

I have already mentioned Ellie Leith, the very attractive girl I had met at organized dances during freshman year. We continued to see each other fairly often even after she went out to Smith College; and during the summer of 1933, that is, after sophomore year, I invited her for a visit at Little Moose. I had, of course, told mother and father about her, and father had

---

* This lady's identity was not divulged, although in the manuscript, Birge mentions that her husband was in the class of 1915. He also calls her Olga in the manuscript. The only man in the class of 1915 with those initials who died in the early 90's was W. Sidney Felton, of Beverly (on the North Shore), who died in July of 1990 at age 95.

made a few enquiries about her family during one of his business trips to Boston. Mother decided, even before Ellie's arrival, that this girl was not good enough for her youngest offspring, and she planned her behavior and degree of welcome accordingly.

Ellie stayed with us for about a week. Mother was always polite, but never turned on the charm of which she was eminently capable. An old female friend of the family from St. Louis was spending the summer with us that year, and she and Ellie got on very well. That summer visit of Ellie's, however, was in effect the swan song of our romance. Instead of a bread-and-butter letter following her visit, Ellie sent a box of chocolates to mother and she told me later that, having been well aware of mother's freezing technique, she could not bring herself to write something she did not feel. For that honesty, I gave Ellie high marks, but our situation cooled down during my junior year and other less binding relationships came to the fore my last year.

As I write this account well over half a century later it all looks very dull in my mind's eye, but of course, at the time such was not the case.

In most ways my senior year was the best. While the absence of Gale Noyes was a big loss to all of us, the positive factors included having Larry Nichols as a room-mate, writing the honors thesis, the visit of professor Welbourne of Cambridge who coached our Dunster crew and the anticipation of an upcoming job in Argentina, of which more later.

In the spring of our senior year and on the occasion of the annual Dunster costume dance, Larry Nichols and I cooked up the idea of assembling a group of friends, all dressed as admirals or other seafaring men, and hiring a sight-seeing boat in Boston, which we would then cruise up river and moor to the bank exactly in front of Dunster. Wilkinson, Hopkins, Hoguet, and two or three others joined us. First we proceeded to Claire and Fuller's Joy Street apartment, where we had cocktails and then we cruised up to Dunster. The idea was to serve drinks on board with guests boarding our craft by means of a narrow gangplank. We foresaw that this exercise might lead to trouble, so I arranged with Garrow Geer, a big, powerful classmate, to act as bouncer for the boat. There were no big problems other than a couple of our guests falling into the river and this was a fitting sort of swan song to our Dunster House years.

I have to mention one instance of Larry's not-so astute advice as to how to handle an attractive girl I met that year. Professor Samuel Elliot Morrison had a beautiful daughter, Wendy, whom I had met at one of the Boston deb parties. She was a Nordic beauty. On our first date, I came to her parents' Brimmer Street house to listen to classical music. I recall that while seated together on a sofa, I started to hold her hand which she at once withdrew, having no doubt been warned by someone that this ploy was the first step leading eventually to perdition. At the time, I did not give this special thought, but I was determined to see her again.

I week or so later, I invited Wendy to go out with me for an evening's entertainment which was to entail taking her to Claire's apartment and then out for a simple dinner – simple because my finances were perennially weak. When I drove to the Morrison's house and rang the bell, a maid came to the door and immediately informed me that Wendy could not go out with me because she had a "fearful cold", leaving me irritated as I doubted this was the case. When I related this episode to Larry upon my ignominious return to G-53, he at once said that I should get back at Wendy by standing her up just as I had been stood up by her. I hesitated a moment but then fell in with this plan. I called Wendy and invited her to go swimming the following Saturday. I did not show up, however, and that was the last I saw of this super girl until a few years later, by which time all the waters of opportunity had long since flowed by. In retrospect, Wendy was without doubt the most attractive girl I had met up to that time, and indeed this would hold true for many years into the future as well. O course, one can never be sure that we would have hit it off had I called for her on that Saturday; the chances and theory of averages would have militated against it. The fact remained, however, that I should not have followed Larry's advice.

Aside from the Wendy episode, which at the time seemed like a proverbial tempest in a teapot, only good things came from my friendship with Larry. Though we saw each other only infrequently after graduation, (he was living in California) we remained in contact until the day in 1976 his wife, Moira, wrote to inform me that he had been killed in a car accident.

During that senior year, Mr. Welbourne, a professor of history from Jesus College, Cambridge, England, came to Harvard as a visiting professor. At that time Jesus College was known as a rowing power in England, and through Crane Brinton, who was working with Mr. Welbourne, I arranged for the latter to coach our Dunster crew and in doing so to teach us the "Jesus stroke". As it turned out, our crew met with only moderate success owing to the paucity of effective oarsmen in Dunster House, - Larry and I being the only experienced crewmen in our boat, - that, plus the fact that Welbourne, notwithstanding his brilliance in history and engaging personality, was not a very good coach. Nevertheless, we enjoyed his company and the hours we spent on the river under his tutelage were always fun and provided a fitting end to our days in Cambridge.

Early in my senior year, there emerged the keen anticipation of an up-coming job in Argentina. During the previous year, I began to think that it would be a great idea to enter one of the Oxford colleges for post-graduate studies, thus to broaden my horizons and better to prepare me for the hiatus when I would choose a career. At Little Moose, I had become a close friend of Julius Byles, a scholar-athlete at Princeton, who, after graduation entered Magdalen College at Oxford as a Rhodes Scholar. That led me to write to Magdalen, and in connection with that application for admission, I wrote to a close friend of my parents, Alexander Weddell, who at that time was ambassador to Argentina, asking if he would write to Magdalen a letter on my behalf. I mentioned that I was thinking seriously of eventually applying for entry into the U.S. Foreign Service.

What Mr. Weddell wrote in reply came as a total surprise. He suggested that instead of studying at Oxford, I might consider serving in Buenos Aires for a year as his unpaid private secretary. At the age of twenty-one, an offer such as this was exciting, to say the least, and I lost no time in replying to the ambassador that I accepted his suggestion and looked forward to further word from him as to details.

It so happened that the Weddells came to the United States not long after this exchange and called father to arrange for a meeting of our two families. Of course, what they really had in mind was to give me a once-over. The last and only occasion they had laid eyes on me had been in about 1923 when I was ten. Father invited the Weddells to have dinner with us at the St. Regis Roof restaurant. (a complete *table d'hôte* dinner there at that time cost about $40 for the five of us!) I suppose that I must have avoided making a bad impression, for the ambassador repeated his invitation to come to Buenos Aires as soon as possible after leaving Harvard. There was to be no salary and I was to bring down my own automobile in which I was to drive the ambassador to the office each workday morning.

After receiving Mr. Weddell's first letter about that job, I had immediately made arrangements to study Spanish with a well-known tutor in Harvard Square. As I had already signed up for my four regular Harvard courses, this was the only way I could adequately prepare myself. I also took a typing course at the same tutoring establishment.

That senior year included what might be termed a milestone in a rather special phase of my development; that is, I ceased to be a "virgin" – untrammeled – as the Rector might have termed it. There were two girls involved, one from Providence and the other, a Radcliffe student, the first from that sister college I met during those Harvard years. I was very fond of both girls, but there was no serious involvement. The intimate contacts were short lived and the acts of seduction – though technically speaking they were not really seductions – took place in Claire's Joy Street apartment while she and Fuller were away for a few days.

I also met two other much more interesting girls – that is, aside from Wendy Morrison – that senior year: Louise Morgan and Pamela Prime, both from New York. I met Louise at a Boston debutante party introduced by George Eyer, who had been two years behind me at Groton and who was also from the "big apple". I did not make any connection between her name and that of the famous Morgan banking family, for after all, Morgan was a fairly common Anglo-Saxon name. I invited Louise for dinner and then, as there did not seem to be anywhere else special to go, I suggested that we go to my sister's apartment for a while.

I remember sitting beside her on Claire's sofa and also I recall Louise saying something about preparing herself for marriage. I did not understand exactly what she meant by that but assumed it had something to do with learning how to do certain household things, how to relate to people and men in particular and, in general, how to become more mature. There was no kissing or other unseemly behavior on that couch. I had a gut feeling that this girl, who by that time I knew came from that very prominent family, had undoubtedly been lectured and warned about how properly to behave with boys.

That year I also met, as mentioned above, Pamela Prime, a tall, very distinguished looking debutante who lived in New York with her younger sister –who died later that year of leukemia – and her divorced mother. With Pamela I fell in love, or I should say I became obsessed with this glamorous creature who was far more sophisticated than I and I am sure, much more worldly.

That Easter vacation I was scheduled to act in the Hasty Pudding show in New York. I wrote to Pamela inviting her to come to the show and then to join me at the dance that was to be held immediately after. About three days after issuing this invitation, Louise Morgan wrote asking whether I would join her and her parents at their table following the performance.

This did not exactly place me in a quandary, as Pamela was then the girl I was really interested in. Pamela almost cancelled our date because of her sister's deteriorating condition and in retrospect, it was too bad she did not choose to remain with the invalid, for in every way Louise was not only a far more logical best girl, but seemed to be quite interested in me, - at least more so than was Pamela.

For me, my senior year in effect came to an end in mid to late May of 1935. In those days – and it may still be the case – candidates for honors did not take final exams just prior to graduation. They did, however, have to undergo a tough oral going-over by the board, which was charged with making the final decision as to whether a candidate was to graduate with honors. Crane Brinton was the chairman of that oral board and he called me to appear before his committee one day in early May.

Professor Brinton started my hearing with the question, "Mr. Birge, do you think there is a chance that France might go communist in the fairly near future?" This was perhaps a logical question in those days when Leon Blum, a socialist, had recently become prime minister and there were many who expressed concern about the future status of the capitalistic system in that country. My answer to Mr. Brinton's question posed no problem. I stressed the importance to Frenchmen of the private ownership of land and of the strong position held by farmers – a situation which had been ensured by the Napoleonic reforms in the very early nineteenth century by which land had to be divided equally between surviving children. Indeed, the idea of a communist collectivization of land would be anathema to any

Frenchman. The other questions involved the French Revolution, the career of Louis Barthou, the future of Austria, and economic questions having to do mostly with principal products of some of the European countries.

The question now arose as to how soon I could leave for Buenos Aires. Mr. Weddell, in a recent letter to father, had urged that I come just as soon as possible. There was nothing to prevent me from leaving as soon as the lectures in my four courses were over. There was, of course, Harvard graduation looming ahead in mid-June. At that time, however, getting off to Buenos Aires seemed much more important that taking part in the gradation exercises. So I packed my relatively few possessions and set off for New York in my old Studebaker, the fifty-dollar car which had served me so well during that last year in college.

The day before my departure, I drove to 9 Joy Street in Boston to bid farewell to Claire and Fuller Albright. I can say, without doubt, that these two played a most important part in my life during my last three years at Harvard. When I felt like having a Sunday dinner with family members they were there. I was always welcome, whether alone or with a friend or two – or even more. I have already gone into some detail about how important a role Claire played in my life from my early childhood. As for Fuller, it might suffice to say that he was a truly great man. Even a quarter century or so after his death, staff members in the Massachusetts General Hospital speak his name with awe.

During the summers, he and Claire visited us at Little Moose. In the Labor Day tennis tournaments he and I played doubles together. He was an excellent player and could have played with much better performers than me, but for him that would have been out of the question. He loved the woods and fishing and we often hiked together and he taught me how to cast for trout. He also loved to play bridge, as did father and I. We usually played every evening after dinner and he played that game well as, indeed, he did everything well that he undertook to do.

One evening, while we were playing bridge in front of the open fire which could take logs five feet long, Fuller noted that his right hand had ever so slight a tremor and he periodically held it with his left hand. During that three-week visit, this hitherto unnoticed affliction, if one could call it that, seemed to grow worse. He commented that maybe he should cut out his usual before-dinner drink, as he could not imagine why he had this peculiar tremor. When he returned to Boston, he consulted two physician friends in Mass General Hospital. Within a few days following a series of tests, he learned the bad news: Parkinson's syndrome.

Here was a doctor with a brilliant future who, even at that age, had already established himself as one of the leading clinical scientists in the world. But little did I realize how devastating this disease was to prove. For within five years Fuller could no longer write; ten years later his speech was difficult to understand. At Harvard commencement in 1955, Harvard bestowed on him an honorary degree, one of the youngest men ever to be so recognized. (Conrad Adenauer and Helen Keller were two of the other recipients) He managed somehow to reach the stage and as he slowly made his way to the platform, every one of the ten thousand people there rose and cheered.

In 1955, he was hospitalized following a seemingly successful operation on his brain. He was free of tremor, could walk more easily and could use his left hand. Then, he suffered a stroke from which he would never recover. He never spoke again and finally passed away in 1969.

But this in 1935 was still in the far unknown future, and right then, all my thoughts were concentrated on my exciting sojourn in Argentina.

Chapter Four

Argentina

On a day in late May, 1935, following my goodbye visit with Claire and Fuller, I drove to New York on the first leg of the long trip to Buenos Aires. The Furness Prince Line ship, *Western Prince,* was scheduled to sail on June first, but as mother had prepared everything for my departure very efficiently there remained little for me to do that last week.

The voyage to Buenos Aires lasted eighteen days, including a one-day stop at Santos, Brazil the port for São Paulo. I remember well two of my fellow passengers: Philip Deronde, a Union League Club acquaintance of father's and Alice Claghorn, a young woman who was traveling with her three year-old boy to rejoin her husband in Buenos Aires.

Deronde was what might aptly be described as an old Argentina expert who had spent probably half his life in that country and in Paraguay. I learned a lot from him for he identified with the countries in which he had lived so long, spoke Spanish fluently, without an American accent, and always kept his sense of humor. He also liked women. Alice Claghorn was very good-looking and doubly so in the eyes of an almost totally inexperienced twenty-two year old just out of college.

I quickly gained the impression that this beguiling blond was not too happy in her marriage. It was not that she said anything leading to that conclusion; it was just that she did not act the part of a happy wife traveling to rejoin a husband. What I quickly understood was that Alice wanted to take me in hand, which she did. Deronde was also interested in Alice but, as far as I know, he did not make much headway, that is, until the last two or three days of the voyage. For by that time, Alice had come to the correct conclusion that this somewhat saturnine and amusing international businessman had far more to offer than I.

After we landed in Buenos Aires, I saw Alice twice – once for a late tea and the second and last time, at a sort of love-nest rendezvous of her arranging. Somehow, Mr. Weddell learned of my interest in Alice. It seems that someone on board the *Western*

Prince, who knew him well and who also was aware of my connection with him, had regaled him with a few details of his shipboard observations. When the ambassador questioned me as to exactly what was, or rather what had been my relationship with Alice, I informed Mr. Weddell as to the salient facts. After all, he was an old friend of the family and a Virginian – not a puritan. At the end of our conversation, Mr. Weddell asked me to promise not to see Alice again. I could understand that, but in any case, Deronde, when I met up with him again, as I did on several occasions, made it clear that he had gotten to know Alice quite well indeed.

When I met Deronde again in New York the following year, he informed me that Alice had left her husband, that she had then looked up Deronde in New York and that he had lent her his car to enable her to drive to California. This vehicle was never returned.

The pattern of my life in Buenos Aires was rather uneventful. In the morning, I would drive Mr. Weddell from 4402 avenida Alvear, the address of the ambassador's residence (where I also lived), to 1419 avenida Alvear, the address of the chancellery office. I was given very little to do and I fault the ambassador on that. On the other hand, I should have made a greater effort to be useful to him. My bedroom was a spacious one facing the garden in back of the large and impressive residence. The ambassador had a Czech valet, Miroslav Sauer, whose wife, Sonia, was Mrs. Weddell's maid. Every morning Miro would come into my room, pull back the curtains and bring in my shoes, which had been shined earlier that day. That was the first and last time in my life that I had a valet and little did I know that almost exactly ten years later I would be posted in the land of Miro's origin

The Weddells – I should say, Mrs. Weddell – had a secretary, Señora Suárez, who guided Mrs. Weddell through the maze of Buenos Aires society in the *Libro Azul*. The *Libro Azul* was a sort of Buenos Aires equivalent of the New York Social Register, albeit far more important than its northern counterpart. In short, any person who was not included in the *Libro Azul* was, ipso facto, of little consequence and had small hope of attaining any post of importance in either business or the government – and certainly that applied to Buenos Aires society. I had lunch every day at the Embassy. Usually the Weddells lunched there too;

and always, except on weekends, la Señora de Suárez ate with us. When the Weddells were invited out, I had a good opportunity to practice my Spanish on this Social Secretary. When I mentioned the name of an Argentine girl I might have met at a reception, the Señora would invariably offer a comment as to that young lady's social position and sometimes she would turn up her aquiline nose at the mention of someone of whose antecedents she did not approve. But of course, all that made no difference anyway as it was out of the question that I would ever invite any of the prominent girls out on a date. The same pattern of activity did not hold with girls of non-Argentine origin whom I met: there were Heidi, the pretty Swiss girl, and Rosie Dickinson and Molly Beak, the English beauties – the last two whom I had met at the British Hurlingham Club. However, as I lived with the Weddells and had comparatively little money to spend, no serious involvement with any girls I met down there ensued. And Mrs. Weddell, as it will be discovered, was at least partly responsible for this.

Shortly after my arrival, I received a letter from Cambridge. On the upper left corner of the envelope was written the name of Crane Brinton, so I was almost certain as to the subject of the letter: had I or had I not received honors in history at graduation? I knew that this verdict depended on how the board had viewed my thesis on the life of Louis Barthou. Crane Brinton's terse remarks were: "One reader graded you with *honors*; one reader awarded you *honors plus*"; so that wrapped up the only loose ends of my Harvard years.

Two American visitors then arrived within a week of each other: the first was Professor Haring, the Master of Dunster House and an authority on Latin American history. When I informed the ambassador as to my former connection with this distinguished scholar, the latter was invited to lunch at the embassy and during the course of that meal, the ambassador learned more about the early history of Argentina and Chile than he had gathered during the series of briefings he had undergone in the State Department immediately following the appointment to his post – at least, so he told me that same afternoon. Indeed, it should have been Professor Haring conducting the Department briefing. What fabulous history professors Harvard had in those years: Brinton, Faÿ, Langer, Haring, to mention but a few.

The second visitor was none other than Clark Gable, who just at that time was approaching the zenith of his colorful and fabulously successful Hollywood career. Just why Gable was paying a visit to Buenos Aires, I never learned; it may have been in connection with MGM's effort to sell more moving pictures to Latin America. If that was the case, Buenos Aires was the logical country in which to make an effort, for at that time Argentina was the most important country in Latin American, economically and culturally; yet despite its importance, Argentina was certainly not a tourist center; nor is it now.

As soon as word reached the embassy of Gable's arrival, he, too, was invited for an informal luncheon at the embassy. He was not a brilliant conversationalist, his remarks being restricted mostly to one syllable replies to such questions as Mr. Weddell asked in an effort to keep some measure of interchange going. Afterward, the ambassador asked me to accompany Gable on any occasion when I could be of assistance – a sort of *aide-de-camp*. Gable was very pleasant, rough-cut, and could seemingly down bumpers of Bourbon without showing any effect.

In early August, the Weddells decided to travel by rail to Rosario de la Frontera, a small resort of sorts situated in the foothills of the Andes, not far from the Bolivian border. At that time the Argentine railways were owned by a British company and they were very well run indeed. A private car was made available for the Weddells, Miro, the valet, Sonia, the maid, and for me, and the five of us had plenty of room. As there was a dining car on that train, no cook was necessary. We stopped first at Tucuman, where we visited a sugar plantation and were entertained by the attractive owners who had a daughter, aged eighteen or so. So there ensued more practice in the Spanish language. Doubtless life at that *estancia* (the name for a large, self-contained ranch – often owned by rich absentee landlords) was just about the same as it had been a century before our stay there. There was an impressive Bentley automobile parked in front of the main house; but otherwise, horses predominated, for the overseers all rode horseback and horse-drawn conveyances were much in evidence.

The day following our arrival in Tucuman we continued our journey into the northwestern part of Argentina and at the end of that third day, we arrived at Salta, where a guide took us around that town where we were put up at another *estancia*.

When we were about to pull out of the station of that town, a large crowd gathered around our private car and I well remember Miro trying to shoo the people away with the words *"Vámanos. No es un cine."* ("Beat it! This isn't a movie")

On the fourth day, we traveled to Jujuy which is very close to the border of Bolivia; and there we left our train, found two autos awaiting us and proceeded to drive further up into the lower Andes – the Weddells and I in one car and Miro and Sonia in the other with all the luggage. And so we finally arrived at the very fashionable spa of Rosario de la Frontera, where there was a six-hole golf course, a small gambling casino in the hotel, and plenty of horses for hire.

Mr. Weddell was a pretty good golfer and he wanted to play every day. He had suggested that I bring clubs with me but the only ones I had to bring were a putter and a number five mashie. We played together each day, as naturally the ambassador did not want to walk over that course alone. As it turned out, my number five was made for that course as there were several hills between holes three, four, and five. So not withstanding my paucity of clubs and proficiency, the ambassador did not beat me by very much. Near the last day of our sojourn at Rosario, they held a *Canadian* tournament for mixed doubles; that is, each team of a man and a woman alternated shots. I drew an attractive widow who was in her early thirties – *la Viuda Alegre* (the Merry Widow) - I called her. Even with that mashie I drove about two hundred yards as the ball rolled quite a long way and that shot started us off. Despite my miserable putting, we won the tournament and on that evening each of us, "The Merry Widow" and I, received a small silver cup at the hands of the Minister of Foreign Affairs, Señor Savedra-Lamas, who, being the highest ranking hotel guest, was asked to make the presentations.

The ambassador and I also went riding almost every day and as Argentina is known for its fine horses, our mounts were superb.

In those days, no Argentine girl would every go out on a date with a man, if she was of *Libro Azul* society, but at Rosario, I soon found out that the young men of my age and a bit older got around this inconvenience by quietly suggesting to a girl that she meet him on horseback at such and such a spot in the surrounding countryside. Those guys did not waste time and I was told that they would politely greet the girl, suggest that she dismount and then they would speedily make love.

I spent several evenings trying my luck with small sums at the roulette table. *"Negro – el ocho"* or *"Colorado - el diez y nueve"* would call out the croupier. I guess I came out about even.

On the way back to Buenos Aires, we made no stops. During that trip, I ventured into the dining car at teatime and when I stopped to watch two men playing a strange card game, they invited me to sit with them and explained that the game was called *truco*. After a few minutes, I joined in their game and learned not only *truco*, but also some more Spanish. One of the men was a Dr. Beretervide, a name I remembered because it had five syllables and I determined to remember it. And indeed, not long after our arrival back in the capital, I met him again at a reception held by the British.

Perhaps the most important event in the diplomatic field that took place during the last half of that year of 1935 was the Chaco Peace Conference, which was held to bring to a close the war between Paraguay and Bolivia and to settle the boundary dispute, which had been the cause of that war. In those days, the State Department used the so-called Brown and Grey codes, very primitive and, I am sure, easy to break, to transmit messages to Washington. I was drafted as an extra code clerk and almost every day I laboriously encoded messages to the State Department. The United States delegate to that conference was Mr. Hugh Gibson, one of the ablest career officers we had in the Foreign Service of those days, who, during World War One and immediately following that conflict had been our ambassador to Belgium. In the Brown Code book his name was Gumli. As a result of that peace conference, Paraguay, whose armies had pretty soundly defeated the Bolivians, gained territory, which increased the size of their country by at least a third. The main reason for the success of the Paraguayans was that the territory where the fighting took place was in low-lying, hot and jungle-like areas, where a climate prevailed to which they were well accustomed. The Bolivians, on the other hand, who were upland, high altitude people, could not cope with the hot and humid climate. This leads one to come to the conclusion that the disputed territory should have been part of Paraguay to begin with. My friend, Philip Deronde, who had spent years in Paraguay, had remarked that the Guarani Indians, who made up most of the Paraguayan population, were fine people and great fighters. He also told me about how terrible the loss of life had been many years before when the Guarani-Paraguayans had fought the Argentines. So many men had lost their lives that, after the fighting, it became the custom for a few years for each surviving male to impregnate four or five unmarried girls with a view to restoring the annual birth rate. Apparently this worked out well.

My situation in Buenos Aires was an unusual one, for living with the Weddells was almost the same as life with my parents would have been. When I left New York, father arranged with his bank that I have joint access to his account, but he asked that I restrict my monthly drawings to $100. In those days that was roughly the equivalent of about $2000. As I had no rent to pay and as I was fed, I had no financial problems. That half-year spent with the Weddells, despite the fact that I did not seem to be headed directly toward a career, was valuable: first, I came to know the fine qualities of a true Virginia gentleman, and second, that the phrase – *This is just a suggestion* could be substituted for a direct criticism. I also noted that when Mr. Weddell and I approached an elevator or a door together, he always made a move as though to defer to me, that I enter the elevator or pass through the door ahead of him. Of course, he did not expect that I would do so, but his polite gesture was typical. After several months of close association with a man such as Weddell, at least a few of his perceived qualities were apt to rub off on one.

The time spent in Buenos Aires was also valuable relative to my speaking ability in the Spanish language. When I first arrived, I could understand very little of what was said around me – at a dinner party or a reception, for example. What I had learned of Spanish grammar was a big help, however, for soon the words rattled off near me began to fall into place, and by the time I left I could carry on a conversation in the language of the Porteños with fair fluency. Lastly, I came to know what life was like in a typical oligarchy – for, indeed, that was Argentina in the 1930's: namely, rule by a few hundred leading families, many of which owned vast tracts of fertile land (as a rule, used for raising cattle, but also for wheat or corn). Many families owning tens of thousands of acres lived in Paris and only very occasionally visited their estancias - perhaps once in five or ten or even twenty years. I visited one of these country places, which had not seen its owner since 1921. In the attractive house was a large ballroom. The library contained what seemed like a thousand leather-bound volumes; the caretaker kept everything in perfect order and readiness in case the *estanciero* should make a sudden appearance.

Of course, Argentina is not typical of Spanish America; and this was especially so in the early twentieth century. When I visited that country in 1935, I was told by a boastful Argentine that the city of Buenos Aires had more telephones than all of Latin America put together. What set Argentina apart from the rest of the lands south of the Rio Grande was that its population was about eighty-five percent of European stock. About sixty-five percent of that population was of Spanish origin; about twenty-five percent was of north Italian origin and the remaining ten percent were mainly British, Irish, German, Austrian, French, and Portuguese. Those not of pure European descent were generally *mestizos*, that is, mixed European and native Indian. Perhaps only 50,000 pure Indians inhabit Argentina today, of an estimated 250,000 when the Spaniards and other Europeans arrived in the 1500's. Many of those were killed by the newcomers, but most died of European diseases.

The pampas, which cover perhaps half the area of the country, have probably the most fertile soil in the world - vast hectares with forty feet of pure loam. There was little industry in 1935, and there was no pressing need for factories. The English owned most of the *frigorificos* (meat packing plants) and most of the beef that the Argentines did not eat themselves was shipped to the United Kingdom. As the population in the 1930's was only about thirteen million, there was practically no unemployment problem. The people lived reasonably well, for beef, considered by many the best in the world, was relatively inexpensive, as was the good red wine (of which there was no surplus for export as it was rapidly consumed locally). American tourists who ordered roast beef at Simpsons-in-the Strand in London in those days probably did not know that those succulent morsels had probably come from the Argentine pampas.

The one foreign group that did not assimilate was the British. They usually sent their sons to school in England, and occasionally their daughters as well. The Germans also retained their customs and language; and when the European wars came, those two nationalities, especially the British, went to the old country to enlist. While the upper class of the Argentines – the *Libro Azul* group – admired the British, that feeling did not apply in the lower classes. When Italy embarked on its Ethiopian venture, despite the trade sanctions imposed by England and other European powers, Anglo-Italian relations worsened, and the Argentine press cheered on the Italians with such statements as, "The English bring us trade, but Italy has given us sons." Interestingly enough, the sons of north Italy who settled in Argentina were unusually capable and many were well educated. These were not Neapolitans and Sicilians; they were from Milan and Turin and Genoa. Skilled workers these, many of whom, having made a fortune in the great port city returned to the country of their birth, but all left their mark, and the same was so in the São Paulo area of Brazil.

Revenons à nos moutons, as my French friends might comment. To get back to the subject of my own situation, I began to sense in November that the time of my usefulness to the ambassador and advantage for myself was drawing to a close; and it came to a head the day I received a letter from father suggesting that I return to the United States with a view to embarking on a career, probably in business.

Many years later, I came across a letter from Mrs. Weddell to my parents in which she wrote some complimentary things about me, but expressed concern about my relationship with an Anglo-Argentine girl whom she considered unworthy of any serious intentions I might have in her regard. Mrs. Weddell then suggested that perhaps the wisest thing to do in that situation would be for father to suggest that I return to the United States, but without mentioning anything about the girl (whose name was Rosie Dickinson).

In view of the above, a few comments about Rosie are in order. She was the nineteen year old daughter of undistinguished British parents who were separated because the father held a clerical job in Santos, Brazil, and the mother thought it advisable to remain in Buenos Aires, believing that that city was a better place in which to bring up her two daughters, which it was. Rosie and I saw one another frequently, but I did not get to know her in the biblical sense. I was not in love with her but, of course, another half-year or so of frequent proximity might have changed that. There was another Anglo-

Argentine girl, Molly Beak, who, toward the end of my stay in Buenos Aires, I was getting to know about as well as Rosie. Her father had an important position as the head of one of the British-owned *frigorificos*. I venture the guess that the safety of that dual number would probably have prevented an overly close relationship with either girl. Actually, Molly might have achieved a borderline acceptance by Mrs. Weddell though even that is doubtful. In any case, the die was cast and I began my preparations to leave on the next Furness Line ship sailing for New York in the last week of November.

Looking back on that time, I think that Mrs. Weddell's oblique intervention was fortuitous. I was ready to move on. Who can say whether that period of time might have been better spent in Oxford. The immersion in the Spanish language was a big plus and the close contact with the Weddells was an equally big advantage.

Before leaving my draft of this chapter of my life – a few additional comments about the Weddells. They were very different, one from the other. As mentioned a few pages back, Alex Weddell was the quintessential Virginia gentleman. He was able, though not brilliant. He was dedicated, decent, straightforward and a man of ideals. I always had the impression that he was a moral rock who believed that any sexual involvement should take place only with a marriage partner. He and the Rector might have been good friends. (As a matter of fact, Weddell's father was the Episcopal rector of St. John's Church in Richmond). Alexander Weddell's manners were exemplary and set an attractive albeit formidable example for any young associate. This was indeed the opposite of what was much later described as the *ugly American*. Mrs. Weddell was different. She would not hesitate to contradict you. She was gracious, but she never hid the force of her convictions under a bushel.

I saw the Weddells once more after leaving them that November, and that was on the occasion of the christening of my son, Walter III, when Mr. Weddell, along with Bill Kilborne, was a godfather. That was in December 1938, at the end of Weddell's five years in Argentina, when the storm clouds of World War Two were darkening the skies of the western world. (From 1939 to 1943, he served as ambassador to Spain). In January 1948, when I was serving in Prague, father wrote that Alex and

Virginia Weddell had been killed in a railway accident when en route to Arizona. Thus perished my good friends who, despite my many shortcomings of youth, gave me their loyalty. For when I took the Foreign Service exams in the fall of 1940, Mr. Weddell wrote a strong letter of recommendation on my behalf. In Richmond, there stands beautiful *Virginia House* which the Weddells had brought over stone by stone from England and had rebuilt for their home in 1929, but willed to the state of Virginia. It is now opened as a museum.

Chapter Five

The In-Between Years

Father was there at the Furness Line pier to meet me at the *Eastern Prince* as it docked on that mid-December noon, 1935. He was in a good mood for his financial situation had markedly improved; and a few lines on that subject might be of interest.

Just before the big depression hit the United States with the full force of its staggering problems of unemployment, devastating stock decline, and widespread despair, father had invested several hundred thousand dollars in the common stock of Certainteed Products Company, a roofing manufacturer of which the president was George Brown, the West Point trained close friend of father. The fall in value of those shares brought gloom to the Birge household and father came close to being wiped out. That same company had a convertible preferred stock with a $7.00 coupon and father decided to switch gradually from the common stock, when priced at one or two dollars a share, to that preferred stock which was quoted at about three times the price of the common shares. So dad ended up with about four thousand shares of that convertible preferred. As those shares had not paid a dividend for several years their accumulated dividends were worth many times what their annual dividends amounted to.

At just about the time I returned, Mr. Brown informed dad that a large company was about to offer $100 a share for the preferred stock. Before this news reached the market dad began buying preferred shares on the open market and then tendering them for the $100 a share – that is, for far more than the price he had paid for the shares in the market. Of course, what dad was doing was arbitraging and he was doing very well.

Along about mid-January of 1936, dad received a special delivery letter from Grace's husband, Manoel, (then working in Geneva for Aluminium Ltd.), to the effect that Grace was apparently planning to leave him for an Indian Moslem by the name of Mir Khan, a young man from the State of Hyderabad who was an *Observer* for the Nizam at the League of Nations. Father at once suggested that I go to Geneva to ascertain what the situation was and to do what I could to deal with it until father and mother could join me. Just at that time, as father was in the midst of his arbitraging maneuvers, he did not want to take even a day off from that (so far) profitable activity. On the day following receipt of Manoel's letter, the North German Lloyd liner, *Europa*, was due to sail for Cherbourg and Bremen. At that time of year, February first, the tourist season was at its nadir, and all we had to do was first buy express checks at the Irving Trust and then take a taxi to the pier, walk up the gangplank and pay the fare to the purser who was standing there.

The *Europa* and its sister ship, the *Bremen*, were the fastest ocean liners afloat at that time and it took us just under five days to reach Cherbourg. My partner at a small table in the dining saloon was Freiherr (Baron) von Salsa from Breslau whose English was almost perfect. We got on very well, and I learned a lot about Germany under the first years of the Hitler régime. Dining with von Salsa brought still another advantage as the steward, aware that this upper class nobleman was important, treated him – and me to an extent – with marked respect. *"Ja wohl, Freiherr; Natürlich, Freiherr"*, I heard three times a day.

In Paris, where I stayed three days, I took a room at *l'Hôtel de l'Université*, which cost $2.00 a day. It so happened that Phoebe Davis, a very attractive girl from New York I had known well during the Harvard years and who had graduated from Smith the previous spring, was then taking a post-graduate course at the Sorbonne. I obtained her address from that university and we spent an evening together during the course of which I quickly realized what a fascinating woman she had become since I had last seen her two years before. I also at once came to the conclusion that the callow youth seemingly without notable prospects was of little more than passing interest for her. By way of mention, Phoebe soon married Frank Eshelman, who had been a year ahead of me at Groton but had been expelled as a "trouble maker". I had liked Frank. We were both in the choir during our respective first and second form years and I still have a picture of us standing beside one another when the choir photo was taken in May 1926. Frank had turned out very well indeed, despite the headmaster's rule-of-thumb decision to "get rid of the bad boy." I never saw Phoebe again perhaps owing to the vicissitudes of my ensuing *vie mouvemonté*.

On the morning of my fourth day in Paris, I took a train for Geneva and upon my arrival that afternoon took a taxi to the de Sousa apartment. Manoel at once recommended a nearby hotel where I took a room costing $3.00 a day at the exchange rate of about 4.25 francs to the dollar. I took most of my meals with Manoel and Grace, and it was obvious that the atmosphere in that apartment was charged with tension. It also became clear that I was not the one who could do much, if anything, to improve the situation. On the second day, after Manoel left for his office, Grace telephoned Mir Khan to come over to meet me. Immediately upon his arrival, I saw him to be very attractive indeed; slender, regular features, café-au-lait complexion, charming manners. His accent in English was typically Indian, as though spoken with his tongue kept on the roof of his mouth. He was articulate, affectionate with Grace's two little girls, and he went out of his way to ingratiate himself with me – not at all obsequiously but just to ensure that we become friends.

About four days after my arrival and in hopes of alleviating the parlous situation, I suggested that Grace accompany me to Villars-sur-Olon, a ski resort not far from Montreux. The very next day, the two small children, Pepita and Manuela, Pensie, their nanny, Grace and I, left for Villars where I, at least – and Grace too, I think – had an enjoyable time. While my skiing skills left much to be desired, I did manage to win a race for novices. There were many attractive British and French girls at that resort, of whom two I remember well. The French girl was Ghislaine de Chaligny from Paris and the English girl, Gwen Frampton, who was attending a nearby boarding school, and with whom I often skied, came from Somerset. Both were good looking and charming.

Mir showed up near the end of our stay, and just about in time, as the *animateur,* i.e., the entertainer and activities organizer, had been pursuing Grace and was getting out of hand. We arrived back in Geneva just in time to meet mother who was arriving from New York unaccompanied by father who was not yet able to get away. Then, after three days, Grace announced that she and Mir wanted to go to Berlin where Mir was to purchase a Horsch sports car. Mother at once insisted that I accompany them as a chaperon of sorts. "Me! A chaperon?" I said to myself. So off to Berlin the three of us went and in that city of marching men, *Sieg heils* and straight-arm salutes, we took two rooms at the Adlon Hotel. Especially noticeable just three years after Hitler's accession to power were hundreds of newly recruited Luftwaffe cadets. And what a role they were soon to play!

As every student of the history of those days now knows, that spring of 1936 was crucial with regard to stopping Hitler from his policy of adventurism and expansion and the flouting of the Treaty of Versailles. Having completed my honors thesis about Louis Barthou and his determination to prevent Germany from again menacing Europe and not then realizing the horror that awaited the German Jews, I tended to be mildly pro-German, certainly not pro-French and pro-Versailles. It is an American tendency to be for the underdog, as Germany had been for the past eighteen years of my boyhood and youth; so the sight of all those Nordic cadets on the streets of Berlin did not upset me at all; nor were any but a handful of my fellow Americans concerned that the re-emergence of a German army – at that time still miniscule in size – could conceivably, and in the then foreseeable future, be a match for the French army, which was considered the most powerful in Europe.

On the seventh of March of that year, I boarded the *Schnellzug* (express train) bound for Aachen, Dunkirk, and London via the train ferry. On my way to the station on that day, one could sense tenseness in the city. Lorries bearing troops were leaving the city, headed westward. My train passed through Magdeburg, Kassel, and Köln (then known as Cologne). As we slowly crossed the bridge over the Rhein in that great cathedral city of Köln, our crossing of that strategic river coincided with the passage of the German cavalry and infantry units, cheered on by thousand of their countrymen and women, throwing flowers. All this looked very exciting to me, friendly as I then was to the Germany of Wagnerian folklore, of Heidelberg, of the songs of Schubert and of the just re-arming to right the wrongs of Versailles. Little did I realize that that fateful day, the seventh of March, marked the best opportunity France and England would have to stop Hitler in his tracks and thus to prevent the horrors which would ensue.

Much later it was learned that the German minister of defense, fearful of the large French army, had given orders to his troops to withdraw back across the Rhine should the French make a move to oppose them. Hitler, himself, later admitted that the two days following his army's march into the Rhineland were the most nerve-racking in his life. He also said that his troops would have had to withdraw with their tails between their legs in view of the totally inadequate resources at Germany's disposal for even a moderate resistance. For France, historians generally agree, March seventh was the beginning of the end.

Mir Khan took Grace back to Geneva and then came to London, where he joined me at the Mount Royal Hotel, thus giving me an opportunity to get to know him better, and I found him to be highly intelligent and a good companion. Nothing, however, was going to change the fact that, as Kipling wrote, "East is East, and West is West, and never the twain shall meet".

While skiing in Villars-sur-Olan in late February, I had met an unusually attractive English couple from Worcester, Freddie and Jean MacConnel. As previously reported, I had also met two very attractive girls, each three or four years younger than I. As soon as I arrived at the Mount Royal, I wrote to Gwen Frampton at her boarding school to let me know when she would be arriving in London en route to her family's home in Somerset. In the interim, the MacConnels invited me for a visit to their house near Worcester. So there I went with the intention of taking a short bicycle trip in that vicinity. They talked me out of this plan, however, and I had a much more pleasant time with them than I could have had on my own. While I was with them, they introduced me to a rather plain, but very likeable girl of about my age, Mary Lea, whose family owned Lea & Perrins of Worcestershire Sauce fame. All that was fifty-five years ago at this writing but still remains quite vivid in my mind's eye. Spring had arrived and all was green in England, which at that time of year is a beauty to behold. No war clouds yet had come over the land; the Empire was intact and powerful; Hitler was not yet taken seriously; Mussolini was a nuisance and Spain had problems, but the frightful civil war in that country had not yet broken out. In short, early 1936 was a pretty good time.

When I returned to the Mount Royal following a few days visit with the MacConnels, I found a letter awaiting me, postmarked "Villars", which was from Gwen, suggesting that I meet her at Victoria Station, where she expected to arrive at 9:30 a.m. en route to Somerset. From Victoria she was to board the train, which would take her west later that morning, but we would have an opportunity to see one another in the interim. I quickly looked at the date on her letter, then at the date she had indicated as that of the arrival of her train at Victoria Station, then at my calendar, and I realized that she had arrived the day before, that I did not know her home address and that I had no way of explaining why I had failed to show up. I was crestfallen that I had no way of explaining why I had failed to meet her. In retrospect, I could have ascertained her exact address by requesting the telephone operator to find out the number of her school in Villars to call and find her address, but this solution never occurred to me. While I had no special feeling for Gwen, I had grown quite fond of her. Had I met her at Victoria I would probably have accompanied her to Somerset as at that time I had nothing special to do or prevent my taking that additional trip and who knows; had the fates intervened in a different way and as I was at loose ends and adventuresome, my life might well have taken a completely different course, especially in view of the fluid and menacing world situation during the late 1930's.

On the second morning following my return to London, I telephoned Burke Wilkinson in Cambridge where, it will be recalled, he was spending a year as a Lionel de Jersey scholar. I had written to him suggesting that I pay him a short visit and he immediately invited me to come that very day, which we spent pleasantly, touring Cambridge. Burke showed me his room where John Harvard had lived early in the seventeenth century. We visited a favorite pub of Burke's and we walked along the Cam River where the Cambridge college crews trained. Burke, who, as I have already mentioned, had played doubles on the Harvard varsity tennis team, was now a member of the light blue team in that sport. That year had clearly been an enjoyable and successful one for him and he was taking the first post-Harvard steps in what would become a life of many faceted successes.

A few days after my return from Cambridge, father wrote to announce his impending arrival in Geneva at long last, with the suggestion that I join him there. So off I went again, by train of course. I stopped for a couple of days in Paris and seized the opportunity to call Ghislaine de Chaligny, the French beauty of Villars acquaintance. When I reached her home by phone and asked to speak with her, a voice in French, of course, replied that Ghislaine was unable to come to the phone as she was in bed with a high fever. *"Elle est gravement malade, monsieur; elle a une fièvre de quarante degrées."* That translated into a temperature of a hundred and four. There was nothing I could do except express the hope that she would soon recover. Was this another stroke of fate? So, owing to the receipt of a letter a day too late and owing to an intervening illness, which for all I knew might have been fatal, I never did see again those two young girls. What did it really matter? - Not at all, probably. But over the years I have often wondered what ever became of those two lovely creatures.

The saga of Grace and her marriage finally reached its conclusion when she in effect abandoned her two daughters and returned to the United States. In the following year, 1937, father and mother accompanied her to India where she married Mir, - Manoel, in the interim having obtained a divorce. I have always felt that Manoel was a fine husband and he certainly became very successful, finally ending up as the European manager of Aluminium, Ltd. Of course, Mir also made his mark, moved to Pakistan and was appointed ambassador for that country to the United Nations and later to France. Grace left Mir at the end of World War II and married an Anglo-Irish officer, but that is another rather long story not very germane to this account.

After spending a few days in Geneva, I returned to London and moved into a hotel where Molly Beak, whom, it will be recalled, I had met in Buenos Aires, had come with her parents. A mild romance of sorts ensued but nothing came of that. Father joined me there and took all of us, including the three Beaks, out to dinner and then he returned to the United States.

He had been gone two weeks when he cabled suggesting that I come back to New York as he had some suggestions in regards to my entering business. As there was nothing pressing to keep me in the U.K., I said goodbye to Molly – for good as it turned out – and a week later was in New York.

On the boat going over, I met a man who was active in the securities business and when I told him that on arrival back in New York I would be looking for a permanent job, he suggested that I apply at Vick Chemical Company, the famous firm which produced Vicks Vapor Rub, the product well known to every child suffering from a chest cold. Soon after arrival back at 580 Park Avenue, father took me to meet (re-meet, actually, as he had been an occasional guest in our house in Greenwich) Elon Hooker, the president of Hooker Chemical Company, whom he had already approached with the idea of my working for his firm. Soon after we were ushered into that executive's office father left and I remained with Mr. Hooker for ten minutes or so. The first thing he said was that if I was anything like my father, he knew I would be an asset to his company. After a few more remarks of a general nature, he said that he would talk to some of his colleagues to see where I might best make a start, and he said he would soon let me know how things stood.

Two days later, I went to see the Vick Chemical Company and I was taken to meet a Mr. O.L. Tinklepaugh, the chief of personnel. He was a thin bespectacled man of medium height with a nasal, mid-western accent. After a few minutes conversation during which he enquired as to my education and interests, he handed me a sort of intelligence test, led me to an adjoining small room and instructed me to finish it within an hour. This I did without any problem and I was then told that I would hear from him within a few days as to whether I would be hired or not.

So I went back home and that evening told my parents what had transpired. I knew with almost complete certainty that the job with Hooker Chemical was mine – and probably would be in Buffalo, where the operating offices and factory were located. The big question was what to do if Vick Chemical came through.

Less than a week following my interview at Vick, I received a phone call from Mr. Tinklepaugh, who informed me in a tone he might have used to make a weather report that he would like to have me return for a second interview, that same day if possible. So that afternoon at two o'clock, I went again down to the Grand Central Building and following a five minute wait next to the receptionist, found myself again sitting opposite Mr.O.L.Tinklepaugh.

I was almost certain at that juncture that I was going to be offered the job, so what was I going to do? Would it be Hooker or Vicks? I hardly hesitated. I knew father had gone out of his way to arrange things with Mr. Hooker and I liked the latter. However, in principle, I really wanted to get my own job without help from anyone, even from dad. Moreover, I felt that there would probably be more scope at Vick Chemical Company. Then there was the idea that Vicks was headquartered in New York, whereas Hooker, with the exception of the president's office, had its operating center in Buffalo, a city which had no special charm for me. So I accepted Mr. O.L.'s offer of the job and was instructed to report back to his office for a month's training on August 1st, it then being mid-June.

This situation was still another case of two roads of destiny, one of which I had to choose. On other occasions I had had no choice as to which road to choose. But now I had elected to take one of those roads. Looking back, it is almost certain that my life would have taken many different turns had I gone to Buffalo. First of all, I would not have married my first wife, Madeleine, and secondly I probably would not have studied for the Foreign Service. But then again, I might eventually have ended up in that service anyway.

Father was not too pleased that I had decided not to work for Elon Hooker and he urged me to go at once to see Mr. Hooker to inform him that I would not be accepting his kind offer. That was not easy but somehow it gave me some additional self-confidence, which at that stage of my life was welcome.*

How was I to spend the intervening six or more weeks until the August checking in at Vicks? I accompanied my parents to Little Moose where I had spent the summers of my last two school and first three college years, and there I stayed until my return to New York.

It so happened that the summer of 1936 marked the time between Julius' second and third years at the University of Virginia Law School. Both he and his best friend at that school, Charlie Woltz, had arranged to rent an apartment in New York (at father's expense) so that they could take on summer jobs with New York law firms. Just before moving in, another student, Jack Elliot, also studying in Charlottesville, and his bride arranged to join them in that apartment. As I was due to start my month's training at Vicks in the beginning of August, I was to join that foursome on the first of August. Meanwhile, I had a quiet time at our camp at Little Moose, where I met an adorable girl, Virginia Slade, who was only fifteen, but seemed older. It was my respect for her entreaty that I allow her to remain intact that prevented our relationship from moving into what might have been an embarrassing and possibly very difficult situation. We called each other *Paul et Virginie* and it was all very touching.

---

* This is undoubtedly the same Hooker Company that had to pay millions of dollars in reparations for the *Love Canal* pollutions scandal many years later, most of the money going to the lawyers, not the victims.

As I never really forgot this girl, so poignant and affectionate had been our friendship, I can assume that had she been a few years older many future developments might well have taken very different turns.

On the first, I moved into the New York apartment mentioned above, where I found Julius and his University of Virginia classmates comfortably settled. Jack Elliot's wife was the housekeeper of sorts to keep things in order.

About ten other neophytes reported along with me to Vicks in that first week of August. My salary was $100 a month – not too bad for those days when a table d'hôte dinner at the St. Regis Roof restaurant cost $3.50 and a carton of cigarettes, $1.00

One evening the five of us - that is, Julius, Charlie Woltz, the Elliots and I – went to the St. Regis for drinks after dinner. That evening was important as it was a milestone in my life; namely, the occasion when I met Madeleine Black of Baltimore, who a few months later became my first wife.

Seated at a small table next to ours were a middle aged man and a young woman aged about twenty with whom I soon struck up a conversation as only about eighteen inches separated our tables, so in effect she was seated right next to me. It soon became clear that this girl's companion was not a boyfriend in the accepted meaning of that term, as he was much older than she and obviously welcomed the interchange of small talk which ensued between him, the girl, and me. George Bender, the gentlemanly table neighbor, introduced himself and then Madeleine Black as an old friend visiting from Baltimore. I danced at least twice with Madeleine and we got on so well that I suggested that we meet in the St. Regis lobby the following afternoon at five-thirty. The die was cast.

During that week of mid-September I saw Madeleine Black every day. Notwithstanding her being somewhat overweight, she was handsome with distinguished features, expressive eyes and a winning smile. She was also good company with a laid-back sense of humor. She lost little time in mentioning that her family controlled the *Baltimore Sun* newspaper. She then took me into her confidence by letting me know that her father, who had died several years before, having fallen overboard from his yacht and his body never recovered, had left her considerably more than a fair share of his estate. Apparently she wished to establish her financial credentials. As it turned out, her future prospects, as she described them, were almost totally fabricated. At her twenty-first birthday, she did come into a modest income, but that was all she was to receive until her mother was to die.

About a week following my encounter with Madeleine, I left on my first field assignment with Vicks. I took a train to Knoxville, Tennessee where a company Ford van was awaiting me, loaded with samples of the three products manufactured by that company, namely: Vicks Vaporub, Vicks nose drops, and Vicks cough drops. I was to load the van at the wholesalers and then drive to the retail outlets in a county and attempt to sell as large a volume as possible to each of these stores. I was also to try to nail Vicks posters to barns that I passed along these country roads. Naturally, I was instructed to ask permission of the barn owners and was to distribute samples in payment. When I had covered one county in that way, I would travel to the next county and re-load with products at the wholesaler for that area.

Each week I mailed an expense account to New York and, as the company knew exactly what my route was to be, my checks for salary and reimbursement reached me promptly. During that autumn of 1936 everyone was obsessed as to what would be the outcome in the election between Franklin Delano Roosevelt and Alf Landon of Kansas. No one had the slightest idea as to how crushing Roosevelt's victory was to be. Every time I made a call on a retailer or wholesaler, I made a point of asking how the owner felt about the coming election and almost invariably Roosevelt was the favorite. Notwithstanding the Groton factor and my warm feelings for Frank Roosevelt Jr., who had rowed in the first crew with me at school, and despite FDR's gentlemanly roots, my bias against this Democratic president, fostered as it had been by father's ideas, ran deep. Actually, the area I was traveling in - northeast Tennessee and West Virginia - was normally Republican country, but not then in the fall of 1936.

On two occasions the Vick Company sent a supervisor to spend a day traveling with me. As I later found out, one of these men was not at all impressed with me, while the other, for some reason, reported that I was competent. The latter might have been unduly impressed by the rapidity with which I changed my left rear tire when it went flat. There was no problem. I had a jack, a readily available spare and a circular wrench; so I could change a tire in about five minutes – no sweat.

While I often looked back on the recent experience in Buenos Aires with nostalgia, especially when I failed to make a sale, I must confess that the six or seven week experience in those Appalachian hills was well worth it. Obvious poverty was ubiquitous. Most of the children went barefoot and it was clear that money was scarce - but not always, as I found out. On one occasion the owner of a small retail outlet – a sort of general store – was a woman of about thirty-five or forty. I launched into my customary spiel about the efficacy of the three products I was peddling and she was giving me her full attention. I noted that she had a head cold and suggested that she allow me to place a few drops of the Vick preparation I could dispense with a small dropper. She agreed that this was a fine idea. I had no sooner deposited two drops in each nostril than she let out a howl of pain. I stepped back and quickly offered apologies. She looked me in the eye and said, "Young man, I'll take a gross of them there nose drops, and throw in a gross of Vicks Salve, too. When I thanked her for this unusually large order – the largest I was to receive from any retailer on that trip – the female proprietor offered the following explanation: "Do you know why I just ordered a gross of nose drops and salve? Remember, young man! You just hurt me bad when you gave me them there drops in my nose; and when a man hurts a woman he can get anything he wants out of her." I wrote out the large order and bid her a quick farewell, fearful lest she change her mind.

During those weeks of working in the mountains for the Vick Company, I remained in continuing contact with Madeleine Black. Indeed, each Friday evening on three or four of the weekends I boarded the B. & O. night train for Baltimore. I got on well with Mrs. Black and also with Madeleine's brother, Gary, the powerful ex-Gilman School fullback. At some time during one of those visits Madeleine and I became informally engaged but as yet we did not discuss formal wedding plans. What about Madeleine? What was she like? As reported above, she had a sense of humor and was intelligent, albeit not very well educated, notwithstanding her ability to recite some of Verlaine's poem, *Il Pleure Dans Mon Coeur*. While she drank too much, she was not an alcoholic, and I do not recall ever seeing her drunk. She was affectionate and fun to be with. At that time I was too immature to understand that, while not immoral, she was basically amoral.

During those weeks of tacking signs on barns and calling on the country stores, Madeleine and I often exchanged not only letters but an occasional telegram as well. One message from her is well remembered, even after fifty-five years. Her telegram read as follows:

There was once a young man called Birge
Who had a strong and terrific urge.
He met a young lady
Whose past was quite shady
But nevertheless said, "Let's merge."

Before resuming the saga involving Madeleine, a few additional comments on my activities on behalf of the company might be of interest; for in those pre-World War II times Appalachia was a region apart and very different from the rest of the country. As is the case in many mountainous areas the people and their mode of life and habits were primitive. This changed a great deal during and after the war when so many young men entered the army, saw other parts of the world and never returned to their former simple way of life.

As mentioned above, one of my principal duties was to tack as many advertising signs as possible on barns which stood close to the roads. I had been instructed never to affix a sign without first getting permission from the owner, so when I spied a likely barn not far from the road, I would stop my panel truck and seek out the owner who might be out in the fields or in his house or, on some occasions, nowhere to be found. Almost always the barn owner was happy to have a Vicks sign on his barn. "It helps keep the cold air out in winter," was a frequent comment. I had been supplied with a bow stitch which, when struck against the edge of the sign would leave a U-shape tack imbedded in the wood. Of course, I had a ladder that I would climb, carrying the sign (Usually a rather large one measuring about 4' by 3') and the bow stitch. On one occasion there was a pigsty fenced off at one end of the barn. Unfortunately, I lost my footing when I was half way up the ladder and landed down in the midst of some large porkers. I beat a hasty retreat over that fence as those pigs were very large and seemed hungry. If I spied a likely barn near lunchtime the farmer might invite me in for the mid-day meal, and, according to custom in such cases,

I would always insist on leaving fifty cents – the equivalent of several dollars in those depression days.

When I would walk into a small general store – for example, in a place called Crum, West Virginia, I noted all around me the unmistakable signs of poverty – few items on the shelves, the barefoot kids, the wreck of a rusting car in the yard, a few old tires lying around, weeds and an unrepaired, broken fence outside. I would ask myself how I could try to sell a lot of products to the store-owner when it was obvious that his (or her) children did not have enough to eat and insufficient clothing on the chilly, fall day. This was a part of my country that few Americans knew. It was depressing and a frightful contrast to the worlds I had known – even in the world of my family's somewhat reduced circumstances of that time – and what a contrast to the environment of a U.S. Embassy or that of dinner at the Savoy in London, where black tie was informal dress. I was destined to return very briefly to Appalachia four years later, but by then my future was more assured.

In mid-November of that momentous year during which Edward VIII became king for a short time, before Prime Minister Baldwin brought about his abdication, the Vick Company informed me that I should drive my little van back to New York and prepare for a new assignment in the city of Philadelphia. I received this message in the one-horse town of Waynesburg, Pennsylvania, where I had been working for three days and where the only tune I could ever get on my car radio was the hillbilly ditty, *"I went to a dance with my mother-in-law. I stepped on her foot and that woman got sore."*

The Pennsylvania Turnpike had recently been constructed and the going was easy. Upon arrival in the city I called *Little Mads*, my special name for my fiancée, who informed me that she was at loggerheads with her mother, who, it appeared, was taking a stand against her daughter marrying me. According to Madeleine, her mother insisted that any prospective husband should have an income of at least $25,000. In retrospect, I am inclined to doubt the veracity of that statement, but at the time Madeleine and I decided that our only alternative to that impasse was to elope to Elkton, Maryland, then known as the best-known elope-city around. So we laid our plans and Madeleine even arranged for Hulton, her mother's chauffeur, to drive us to Elkton. And that was how I married my first wife and entered the third phase of my "In-between Years."

Just about the time Madeleine and I were married, father completed his financial recovery from the nadir of his situation of the depression years. While he was no longer in active business and thus not earning salary, his capital was again substantial; so, as he explained, partly for tax reasons, he gave each of us four children $50,000, thus enabling Claire to build a house in Brookline, Massachusetts, and me to keep financially afloat following my marriage in November.

In 1936, interest rates were far lower than these days of the early 1990's. I could thus count on $200 a month. However, paying for living with a wife accustomed to living high on the hog (as was the saying in Missouri) was going to take a lot more than $200 a month. It is not my intention to dwell on this subject. Suffice it to conclude that my naïveté and Madeleine's proclivity for untruthful pronouncements resulted in the gradual disappearance of the money I had received from father by the time Madeleine and I separated less than three years later.

I was not at all reluctant to resign from the Vick Company and I then, at the beginning of 1937, began seriously to consider several different careers to follow: first, in view of Madeleine's supposed future interest in the newspaper business, an activity in that field; second, graduate study in economics preparatory to entry into one of several fields; third, law; last, the Foreign Service.

It so happened that father was acquainted with Mr. Tom Gannett, a prominent newspaperman, who suggested that I attend the Empire State School of Printing, a small establishment he had been instrumental in founding in Ithaca to train typesetters. Mr. Gannett explained that learning the typesetting rudiments of the business would be valuable later on. Without more ado, we rented a house on Hanshaw Road, not far from Cornell University, and hired a cook-butler, whose appropriate name was Rolls.

It was cold up there above Cayuga's waters, but we made a few friends and that first winter of our marriage passed quite pleasantly. Madeleine cut down on her drinking, lost some excess pounds and by the time we left that place late in May she had taken on the very good looks that were her birthright.

By the time the printing school course was over, I had decided to spend a year in graduate school. As I was married, the London School of Economics seemed more logical than Oxford or

Cambridge. Moreover, Madeleine had never been in Europe so, in a way, that sojourn would be a sort of equivalent to a delayed honeymoon. Another reason for choosing L.S.E. was that Harold Lasky was teaching there, following a somewhat stormy few years as a visiting professor at Harvard. While I knew Professor Lasky was very much to the left of my views, I had heard that he was a scintillating lecturer. In retrospect, that year in London was very well spent, for England's great capital city was an especially interesting place just at the beginning of the reign of King George VI and about two years before the war.

We sailed for England on the R.M.S. *Queen Mary* in mid-June of that year of 1937. It was the time when Italy was crushing Ethiopia, when the Spanish Civil War was raging, when Hitler was consolidating his power, when the French Third Republic was sinking into ineptitude which led to her eventual crushing defeat, when England was still clothed in the trappings of a great Empire but was led by mediocre men; for those who should have been her leaders were dead beneath Flanders Fields, their proud names chiseled on countless blocks of stone in the naves of their country's public school chapels.

During that trip on England's great liner we met two unusually attractive British army officers: Lt. Colonel Hamilton and Major Roy Urquhart, the latter an impressive Scot who became a hero in the war, during which, in 1944 he commanded the parachute invasion at Arnhem behind the German lines – the exploit which was made famous by the moving picture, "A Bridge Too Far". On the *Queen Mary* we also met Jack and Betty MacTaggart with their three boys, ranging in age from seven to twelve. We saw a lot of these people during our year in London and indeed over the ensuing more than half a century, none of them was forgotten.

Prior to our departure from the U.S., Madeleine had persuaded her old nurse of childhood days to accompany us. I questioned the logic of this arrangement but very soon was glad to have Mamie with us, for she was always pleasant and helpful as most Irish-Americans I have known usually are.

The first thing we did upon arrival in London was to look for a place to rent for the ensuring year. We finally settled on a rather small but beguiling two-story house at 8 Mount row just off Berkeley Square. It was owned by Commander (Royal Navy Ret.) Frampton and his wife, Peggy, who ran a social club adjoining and which had access to our house by a door leading from our living room. The rent was, as I recall, twenty guineas a week. The English had a habit of tacking on an extra shilling when they were selling or renting something. Thus a guinea was twenty-one shillings, instead of the twenty shillings, to a pound. Thus, in U.S. dollars of that time this weekly rent came to about $100 a week, or about $5200 a year – a great deal of money, even now. In today's dollars that sum came to approximately $4,350 a month. Half the rent was payable in advance, which saved my having to worry each month about coming up with rent money.

As we had no summer plans, Jack MacTaggart suggested that we join them in France in a small beachside hotel, which was situated in a village between Saint Raphaël and Saint Tropez. The place was called Val d'Esquières. We had brought our Ford convertible with us and decided to follow to an extent the same route Claire and Fuller had taken on their wedding trip.

Everything went fine and we drove down to the Pyrenees to Gavarnie, which was only a mile or so from Spain, and the place was filled with refugees and talk of the atrocities being committed by both sides. We had a serious mishap, however. As we were driving through Aix-en-Provence, I momentarily forgot that in France one must always remember the rule of *la priorité à droite.* A car banged into us and our car tipped over onto the canvas roof. Fortunately neither of us was injured, as we had not been driving fast. It was a bit disquieting, however, to hear some of the onlookers who had gathered around, exclaiming, "Où sont les morts?"

We proceeded to Val d'Esquières by taxi and almost at once decided to take a train to Paris with the idea of getting a new car. At this juncture, it must be added that I was just at the age when I had not yet outgrown a fascination for certain European automobiles, especially Bentleys and Mercedes sports cars. While we were in London, I had priced the Rolls-Bentleys and ascertained that they cost about £3,000 ($15,000) in the money of that day.

The first auto show room we visited in Paris was that of the Mercedes-Benz establishment on the Champs Elysées. As the German government in that fourth year of Nazi rule sought to obtain as much foreign exchange as possible, the prices of those elegant Mercedes sports cars were significantly lower than those

I had noted in London for roughly equivalent Bentleys. The effusive salesman hastened also to point out that if a car were to be imported into England there would be an additional rebate as the British import duty on imported cars was twenty-five per cent. Hence, the *Cabriolet A* that I fancied was priced at about £1500 or $7500. That made more sense than paying twice that sum for the British Bentley.

I asked the salesman whether the factory in Stuttgart had a *Cabriolet A* available. The impeccably garbed car-monger at once telephoned Stuttgart and within two minutes informed me that there was indeed a *Cabriolet A* available. It had been spoken for by an Englishman, but as the sale had not yet been consummated, I could probably get the car if I went to Stuttgart at once where a certain Herr Doerschel would meet me at the station the following morning.

As I look back on that episode, I wonder how I could have been so extravagant and foolish. My little Ford had been damaged in that accident at Aix, but it was certainly reparable.

Sure enough, the following morning, Mr. Doerschell was waiting for us as we alighted from the *wagon lit* in the Stuttgart of Hitler's new Germany. His English was that of the stage comedian, Baron Munchausen. He guided us first to our elegant hotel. None but the best for a prospective Mercedes owner! After checking in at that hotel, he accompanied us to the Mercedes offices from which we were taken on a tour to see all the models that had been produced since about 1900. Not a word about whether our *Cabriolet A* had already been snatched up by the Englishman or not. Then we came to that beautiful forest-green convertible, a 5.4-liter, supercharged straight eight. What a car! Of course, we could not really afford it, but I did not realize this, owing to the truth stretching statements Madeleine had made relative to her financial expectations. It had not occurred to me in those days of my youth that sometimes even attractive people of impeccable background did sometimes say things that were not true.

Be all that as it may, Madeleine and I drove away from Stuttgart in that forest green powerhouse with its twin chrome exhaust outlets protruding from the right side of the hood. En route back to the Côte d'Azur, we drove through Munich and along the same road Charlie Butler and I had bicycled on back in 1931. There was the hotel on the Walchensee and there, the steep highway over the Tyrol and down to Innsbruck. From the latter, down we drove through the Italian Tyrol, which had been taken from Austria-Hungary in 1918, through Bolzano and along Lago Garda, then down to the Italian Riviera where we spent the night following the long drive from Innsbruck. Finally on the third day we rejoined the MacTaggarts at the little hotel just across the road that separated us from the beach.

That was the first of two holidays we spent with Betty, Jack and the three young boys. The second was the New Year holiday at the end of that year, 1937. At the beginning of the Second World War, Betty took her three boys to Canada and the United States and in those perilous years the boys attended school in our country. Sandy, the youngest and perhaps the most attractive, finally settled in Edmonton, Canada, having graduated from Harvard in 1950. A few years ago I re-established contact with him by mail but have yet to see him again in person.

When Madeleine and I finally arrived back in London all we had to do was move back into our already rented house on Mount Row where Mamie was awaiting us. The first thing I did was to enroll at the London School of Economics. The next move was to enquire whether LSE had a rowing program. Upon being assured that they did in fact have two crews, I reported to their boathouse near Putney Bridge. After the second outing which convinced me as to the mediocrity of LSE's efforts on the Thames, I got to talking with Willi Geer, a fellow student from Switzerland, who seemed to know a lot about rowing and who had also expressed disappointment with both the coaching and the caliber of the oarsmen we had rowed with.

This personable crewman from Zurich then suggested that we both join the Thames Rowing Club, which, he assured me, enjoyed a fine reputation for turning out good crews and which, in fact, competed every year in the Grand Challenge Cup race at Henley.

The very next day, Willi and I met the Thames Rowing club people and joined up. Somehow I managed to make the first boat in which I rowed at number six all that autumn of 1937. I guess Willi may not have been as good an oar as I had thought, for he ended up on the second crew. Now comes the interesting part of this chronicle. At that time – that is, in late 1937 – MGM was working on a movie called "A Yank at Oxford", starring Robert Taylor (a heart throb of that era), Lionel Barrymore,

Maureen O'Sullivan, and Vivien Leigh. In this picture Robert Taylor played the part of a great athlete from the U.S.A. and at the very end of the story, he rowed stroke on the Oxford crew in a come-from-behind victory over Cambridge.

One day, an MGM agent approached the Thames rowing Club captain and coach, Mr. Alanson-Wynn, with the suggestion that Thames Rowing Club agree to supply two crews for the picture; the first boat to impersonate Oxford and the second boat to row the part of the Cambridge crew. The oars of the first and second crews were, of course, to be painted dark blue and light blue, respectively. For this service, Hollywood MGM was to pay Thames Rowing Club £1 sterling (then over $5.00) per man, per day. As the filming was to be carried out from the bank, from Putney Bridge and even from the cox's seat, these workouts, as I recall them, lasted three days. Hence the club earned £57 sterling, the extra pounds representing the continuing presence of our captain. The money earned all went to the club for the upkeep of the shells.

When the cameraman was occupying our cox's seat for close-up shots of the hero, Taylor replaced Eric Beresford, our stroke, and an English actor – then unknown – who was rowing at number seven in the film, sat just astern of me. Hence, in two sequences, I appeared briefly.

Taylor was a pleasant enough guy, but an inferior oar, despite some hurried coaching. When our two crews were filmed from a distance, however, with our "Oxford" boat overtaking "Cambridge", Beresford and our regular number seven were in their regular seats and it was not too difficult to overtake "Cambridge", especially as Alanson-Wynn was admonishing our second crew through his megaphone not to pull hard.

At the end of the race, with the cameraman again occupying the cox's seat, there was a close-up of Taylor fainting away from exhaustion just after our crew crossed the finish line.

Eric Beresford, whose father was alleged to have stroked a winning Henley crew at the age of fifty and whose brother, Jack, had rowed stroke on England's 1928 Olympic crew, was himself an outstanding oar in that number eight seat. He weighed only about 140-145, but his rhythm, flawless recovery and perfect blade-work were as good as I had ever seen. Moreover, he was unusually strong for his weight.

At Harvard, my effectiveness as an oarsman had left much to be desired, but since 1935 I had gained about fourteen pounds and, under Alanson-Wynn's tutelage, I had gotten rid of a couple of bad habits on the water. Anyhow, as I mentioned above, I managed to make that first boat. On one occasion, the captain asked whether he was correct in estimating my weight at just under thirteen stone (i.e., just under 182) "That is about right, sir," I replied, though that was a bit of an exaggeration as I then tipped the scale at 173 or 174. But Alanson-Wynn had the right idea, for in view of Beresford's light weight in the stroke seat, a heavier man was needed at number six, so Brown, our number four, who weighed about thirteen-six stone (188lbs) and I exchanged seats.

With regard to "A Yank at Oxford", I never saw this picture until almost a half century later when it was shown on television. Shortly before World War Two, when I was spending an evening with Bill Kilborne with whom I had rowed at Groton, and who had subsequently rowed three years on the Yale varsity crew, he commented, "Say, I recently saw a movie called "A Yank at Oxford" and I could have sworn that was you rowing six in the Oxford boat."

That was a fine group of men at the Thames Rowing Club. We trained on an occasional beer mixed with a soft drink, and well do I remember our loquacious bowman commenting, as we were headed back to Putney following a time-trial to Mortlake, " I could do with a Cold Spring beer and ginger. How about you chaps?" It was a very refreshing drink also known as a shandy gaff.

The annual Thames Rowing Club formal dinner held during the Christmas holidays comes to mind. All of us, including guests, were in white tie and tails. One elderly gentleman who, I was told, had rowed for Thames in the *Grand* some forty years before, came up to me and said, after first taking a swallow from his iceless scotch and soda, "I say, Birge – you <u>are</u> Birge, aren't you?" "Yes, sir," I replied. "I see you have been moved back to four. I liked the look of you at six but I suppose our captain knows what he is doing – what? Well, good luck, old chap." Then we all sat at our appointed seats and some sort of major-domo came to the head of the table, motioned for silence and in a stentorian voice, commanded, "Gentlemen, the King!" And we all rose and drank to George VI.

In the early spring of 1938, the Cambridge crew used our boathouse for two weeks while training for the up-coming Oxford-Cambridge race. And whom did I see at cox of that boat but Tommy Hunter - who had occupied that seat on the Harvard varsity crews of 1934 and 1935 – and also Gordon Keppel, a former Groton fellow crewman, rowing seven, who had been captain of his Princeton crew. Sad to relate, Gordon died a premature death caused by a serious wound sustained in the war.

That spring, our Thames Rowing Club crew was headed for the Grand Challenge Cup race at Henley. For me, however, that great experience was not to be, as will be explained below.

Now, more observations about London of that time. There were some excellent nightclubs: Quaglino's, Café de Paris, and many others. The former had a slowly revolving copper dance-floor, and in the latter, a black man, known as "Snake Hips Johnson" presided with his great West Indian swing orchestra. (The leader and all the members of the band were killed on stage when the Café de Paris burnt to the ground during the blitz in 1941.) If you dined out with guests – indeed, any time you were invited to dinner, white tie and tails were *de rigueur*. If the occasion was informal, black tie was all right. Our best friends were the MacTaggarts and the two army officers, Hamilton and Urquhart, whom we had met coming over on the *Queen Mary*. We also met a German, Herr von Stubnitz, who was head of the London office of the *Nachrichten Dienst* (Information Office). When we were in London, the Germans began their moves leading to the virtual conquest of Europe – that is, preliminary to the first stage of the war that was to come.

During that winter and early spring it became obvious that Hitler, having re-occupied the Rhineland early in 1936 with no French counter-moves, would probably next annex Austria. Well do I remember Herr von Stubnitz commenting: "Remember, Walter, Austria will be Hitler's soup course; Czechoslovakia will be the fish course, and Poland will be the *pièce de résistance*." And thus it happened exactly as predicted by our German acquaintance.

In 1937 and early 1938, the period of which I write, England had in many ways not recovered from the "Great War". The men who should have been providing leadership had been killed at the Somme and Yprès and many other bloody fields. Had Winston Churchill been a few years younger, his name too, might have joined the vast honor role. The England of those months when I studied at LSE, rowed at the Thames Rowing Club, and spent evenings at the Savoy and Quaglino's and the Café de Paris was not yet concerned with what was taking place in Europe. Czechoslovakia was far off. A mere score of years before that it had not even existed. People heard of Hitler's hatred of the Jews and of deplorable events such as *Kristall Nacht*, but a great many Englishmen, along with Americans, were anti-Semitic in any case. Had not many of the English administrators in Palestine been working against the mandates of the Balfour Declaration and League of Nations, which had bestowed the Palestine Mandate on Britain on the condition that the latter promise to provide the Jewish homeland in Palestine? And so, indeed, England slept until a year and a half following my departure for New York, when

Hitler devoured his *"pièce de résistance"*.

That early spring of 1938 our Thames Rowing Club began seriously to train for the Grand Challenge Cup race scheduled for early summer at Henley. But Madeleine, for some reason, began to be restive. In March she was two months pregnant and she began to talk of wanting to go back to New York to visit Dr. Halsted, her obstetrician in that city. She spoke of returning to London after a short stay in the U.S., but as things unfolded it is obvious that she had no such intention. Finally, in late March, she took off, accompanied by Mamie.

Not long before her departure a Harvard acquaintance, Walter Cline, who had been an instructor in anthropology, turned up out of nowhere. We invited him to stay a while and that *while* lasted a couple of months. Walter had left Harvard mainly owing to recurring cancer in his right hand and he had already lost two fingers to the disease. He told me that he was living on an income of $50 a month – very little even in those days. So when Madeleine left for New York on the *Queen Mary*, I had company and I was glad to be in a position to help Walter by putting him up.

Each day, I was attending the LSE lectures and rowing on the Thames, so life was quite pleasant; then a sort of bombshell dropped in the form of a cable from Madeleine, who was still a day from her New York landing. As I remember her message, it read, "Cannot stand separation. Please come to New York." That really put me in a difficult position. Was I to leave LSE and relinquish my number four seat in the boat to a big oarsman who had recently arrived from Germany as a refugee? I am pretty sure – at least according to assurances received from Alanson-Wynn at that time – that I would have been kept in the first boat. In any case, what it really boiled down to was whether I was to risk a serious crisis in my marriage or stay on in London in the hope that Madeleine would soon return. I managed to reach the *Queen Mary* by radiotelephone but all I could hear, in addition to all manner of static, was a brief, hardly audible plea from Madeleine to join her in New York.

I think I made a mistake when I decided to leave London, in light of what was to unfold during the next year. It should also be mentioned that a few years later, after the Madeleine chapter of my life had come to an end, I came across a letter in the midst of papers I was examining prior to discarding them; this letter had been written to Madeleine by our London acquaintance, Herr von Stubnitz, in which he mentioned, inter alia, that "you are going to America to get a divorce". As I look back on that, I do not believe that Madeleine at that time was thinking at all seriously of leaving me, though obviously that possibility had entered her mind. She might have mentioned divorce to von Stubnitz just to intrigue him.

Be that as it was, I told Walter Cline to stay in our house for as long as he wished up to the closing date of our year's rental and to give our servant a week's notice. I also left some money with Walter to pay a few outstanding bills. I regret to say that I never saw Walter again. His friendship was another worthy dividend of the Harvard years.

When I boarded that same RMS *Queen Mary* at Southampton at the end of March of that eventful year of 1938, I left behind a graduation from LSE and participation in the *"Grand"* and I was headed for what became in many ways the worst year of my life. By way of mention, I sold the Mercedes at a good price two weeks following my arrival in New York.

Really the one and only good gift of that year was the birth on October 12 of Walter, III, who was to turn out to be a truly outstanding son, and who seems to have inherited the good qualities and genes of his mother's forebears along with some bestowed by my parents.

Once settled in an East 57th Street apartment, I began soul-searching for a future career; in each instance, when a positive result seemed to be in the offing, I had to cope with a negative reaction from Madeleine. Then, I applied to and was accepted by the University of Virginia law school. Madeleine at once adamantly refused to move to Virginia because that would bring us closer to her mother, whom she wanted to keep at a manageable distance. Finally, in May of 1939, came the denouement of our marriage. Madeleine suddenly announced one evening that she intended from then on to lead her own life, to come and go as she wished. Our life together to all intents was over. Within a day, it came to light that she had some time before entered into a liaison with Alexandre (Sasha) Tarsaïdse, a White Russian émigré from Tiflis, who had been living in New York since the mid-1920's. Sasha had been an occasional guest in our apartment, but I had not looked upon him as anyone but a pleasant acquaintance.

The upshot of this development was that Madeleine left the apartment almost every evening at about eight o'clock and did not return until four or five the following morning. In June, Madeleine, Mamie, and Walter, aged eight months, left for Bass Rocks, a sea-side resort north-east of Boston, where they remained that summer, periodically visited by Tarsaïdse. As for me, I spent the summer with my parents in the Adirondacks. When World War Two broke out on September 1st, I thought of enlisting in the Canadian Army, but then made what was probably the more logical decision, namely that of studying in Washington for the United States Foreign Service examinations. I bid my supportive parents farewell and took a train to New York where I bought a two-year old Mercury auto, which was to carry me to the nation's capital. Naïvely, I thought the marriage could still be salvaged, but my innocence came to an abrupt end when I went to the apartment I had left two and a half months before and found that it had been stripped of everything except a few of my personal belongings such as clothing. The building manager informed me that Madeleine had moved every piece of beautiful antique furniture, works of art, china, and silver (that *I* had collected in England and Europe the year before) to another apartment. And that spelled the end of our life together.

So I set out for Washington and picked up the pieces of a life that seemed to be in shambles and eventually brought purpose and order to it again.

Chapter Six

Washington, 1939-1940

I arrived in the nation's capital during the Labor Day weekend of that fateful year of 1939 to enter one of the special tutoring schools that prepared applicants for the annual Foreign Service examinations. First, I checked in at the Shoreham Hotel where a single room cost five dollars a day, and the following day called on a real estate agent to enquire as to the availability of a small apartment. I was fortunate, for the agent showed me a place on California Street, which was exactly what I had hoped to find: two small rooms, tastefully furnished with an adequate kitchenette, at a monthly rent of $84; and especially convenient was the arrangement I made with the wife of the janitor of the building who agreed to cook my evening meals and keep the apartment clean. My year's lease was to begin in a week's time.

That same day the hotel photographer, a most friendly middle-aged woman, took a photograph of me, which I promptly mailed to mother, and then suggested that I allow her to introduce me to a charming young woman who was the manager of a small gift shop in the hotel lobby. We at once walked over to the shop and I met Dorothy Mayo, who indeed was attractive, but more important, she asked whether I might like to take her to a cocktail party the following evening. I had arrived in that city knowing not a soul and Dorothy provided an entrée. She also suggested that I take her to a few of the Chevy Chase Country Club dances held each Saturday, so I gradually increased the circle of my acquaintances. I met several unattached girls but, of course, word rapidly got around that I was married, for Madeleine and I were just separated and not yet divorced, so until my divorce the following April, I was not considered a suitable escort for eligible young ladies. And that was especially true in the Washington of that time; for when I first moved there, it was almost like a small town and a very gossipy town at that.

There were at least fifty or so young men studying in Washington for the Foreign Service exams and it was common knowledge among all of us and among many others too, that any publicity in the press about any of these aspirants – if the publicity were unfavorable – would probably spell finis to his hopes of passing the feared oral exam.

At that time, one of the Washington newspapers had a social-gossip columnist, Igor Cassini, an equivalent of Cholly Knickerbocker in New York. I knew Igor quite well. He frequented most of the parties and when he was not present he always had a co-worker or spy present who could report what went on. At one point, Igor reported in his daily column that I had been in a fight at an evening reception, which was not true. I at once went round to his apartment and rang the bell. He came to the door and in a friendly way asked what he could do for me. I pointed out that I had not been engaged in any fracas and had carefully avoided trouble. I also reminded Igor that his report could have damaging results for me. The very next day, Cassini apologized in his column for the erroneous report involving me. And that was that.

But let me return to my narrative. When the time came to check out of the hotel, the credit manager apparently suspected me of intending to leave without paying my bill, as he had detected me going in and out with suitcases in which I had been carrying clothes and odds and ends destined for the apartment. I was told that I would have to present a cashier's cheque for an amount sufficient to settle my account, which amounted to a little over $100. So I immediately telephoned John Betts, my New York broker, to liquidate my account, which at that time had dwindled to $1700, and cable me that sum in care of the Shoreham. As that amount had the purchasing power of about $20,000 in the early 1990's, the credit manager abruptly changed his tune and apologized for "any misunderstanding", and I drove off to California Street.

There were two well-known tutoring schools in Washington where one could prepare for the Foreign Service exams: The Mannix Walker School and Turner's Diplomatic School. The former was a one-man operation with all subjects taught by Mr. Walker. The Turner School was owned by Turner, who taught International Law himself, and employed two professors from the faculty of George Washington University – one to lecture on history, and the other, on economics. I decided to study for the exams at the Turner School, but as his classes did not begin until January 1940, he suggested that I attend those courses at

George Washington University which were to be taught by the same men who would later be lecturing at his school. I therefore arranged with G.W.U. to audit the courses taught by professors Ted Acheson and Howard Merriman of the departments of economics and history, respectively. Ted Acheson's older brother was Dean Acheson, a former Grotonian who served as Secretary of State in Harry Truman's administration, and was, to my mind, perhaps the ablest Secretary of State our country ever had. Ted introduced me to his sister, Margo Acheson Platt, who became a good friend and often invited me to dinner. On the first of those occasions, I brought her a bouquet of flowers. When she invited me a second time, she suggested that if I intended to bring a similar token of our friendship, a side of beef would be more practical and not any more expensive than flowers. It should be mentioned there that during the autumn and thus before the opening of the Turner School, I accepted more readily invitations such as those to Margo Platt's house, for after January, my studies were more purposeful and intense, thus demanding disciplined study every evening.

It will be recalled that following the defeat of Poland in mid-September, the so called "phony war" between Germany and the French-British allies lasted until April 9, 1940, on which date the Germans unleashed their attack against Norway and Denmark. On November 30 of '39, however, the Germans for once were caught by surprise when the Soviet Union attacked Finland. At first this war was seen as a David-against-Goliath struggle, but not for long. The rapt attention of everyone in Washington was riveted on the gallant Finns defending their country brilliantly, though greatly outnumbered. Then came one of the coldest North-European winters on record – even in early December, detachments of skillfully led Finnish troops, on several occasions surrounded and annihilated inadequately clad and poorly led Russian soldiers. Soviet sentries froze to death as they stood watch; many of their horses met the same fate in that minus forty degree cold. But finally, vastly superior numbers overcame the Finns, the Mannerheim Line was captured and parts of eastern Finland were annexed by the U.S.S.R. The most popular diplomat during those winter months was ambassador Procope of Finland. Everyone greeted him as a hero. Many Americans spoke of possibly getting over to Finland somehow to enlist in the army of that intrepid country. I, too, thought of that possibility.

Then on April 9 came the above-mentioned invasion of Norway, then the crushing defeat of France, executed in just five weeks – May 10 to June 15. Germany had now won what many later called the "first war" of the Second World War. During that fall, winter, spring and even summer of 1939-40, few Americans expected that we would become a belligerent. I spent the Christmas of l939 with the Ted Pratt family on Long Island. They and their friends said they expected an ultimate German victory. And they were not alone in that opinion.

During the year and a few months I spent in Washington, especially after Winston Churchill became British Prime Minister, most Americans came to believe in a final British victory. At Turner's School, however, we were immersed in studies and had little time to speculate on the final outcome.

The routine at Turner's Diplomatic School was as follows: lectures began at 3:30 pm and continued until 5:30, thus making it possible for the professors from G.W.U. to finish their day's work at the university before starting their lectures at Turner's. During the winter of 1940, we studied economics with Ted Acheson; in the spring we listened to Howard Merriman's lectures in U.S. and world history, and that summer, we studied international law. This routine gave us plenty of time to do the necessary homework. Every Friday we took a test at school.

We had fifteen students at Turner's of whom two had been my classmates at Harvard: Fisher Howe, and Dorilio Braggiotti (Drib for short, but also known as Chad). Of those students, six passed the September written exams. Interesting – and fortunately – to note: although both Howe and Braggiotti failed the written exams, they later entered the Foreign Service *laterally*, and both, especially Howe, did very well during the ensuing years.

By that January 1940, I had reached a low point financially, so I sold my car and purchased a three-speed Raleigh bicycle, which was all the transport I needed to get me to and from school, and it tended to keep me close to home.

Now, a brief note about my marriage. In April 1940, Madeleine telephoned me from Reno, Nevada, to which divorce-mill she had gone with her mother and where she would soon be joined by Sasha Tarsaïdse, the diminutive White Russian with whom she had been living for most of the past year. She had called to ask that I sign a paper to the effect that I was not contesting her action. Until that still-married situation was thus eliminated, my off-and-on relationships with female acquaintances had been somewhat difficult, as I already mentioned. Even when Madeleine's divorce became final, however, and my own eligibility thus clarified, I was too busy with Turner School homework to engage in much socializing.

In mid-June, mother and father came to Washington for a few days and I arranged for them to stay at a small hotel, which was only a short distance from my apartment. It so happened that the annual June horse show was being held two days after their arrival at which *le tout Washington* came together, including the entire diplomatic corps. I mention this for two reasons: first, because I had an opportunity to introduce my parents to one of my female acquaintances, whom I did not know well, but liked very much – Sylvia Szechenyi. Sylvia was the daughter of a Hungarian diplomat, Count Szechenyi, deceased, and Gladys Vanderbilt. She was an attractive, decent, intelligent girl, then about twenty years old. The second reason I mention the horse show is that we noted that no one – not even any of the State Department officers – spoke to any of the many German diplomats who attended – no one, that is, except fellow diplomats from the Italian and Japanese embassies. Those Germans all seemed to be in a jovial frame of mind; their conquest of France having taken place just two weeks previous.

The main reason for my parents' trip South was father's wish to drive to East Tennessee where he held tenuous title to half a million acres of land in the Appalachian part of that state. Father had acquired those titles as security for a loan he had made to a man he had hardly known. Apparently father had looked favorably on the man seeking the loan, as the latter was the nephew of an Episcopal bishop. What happened was that the recipient of father's money just disappeared, leaving father the holder of land titles which in that part of the country meant very little despite their having been verified by the Supreme Court of Tennessee. Unfortunately, father spent good money after bad, paying a fast-talking Tennessean from Jamestown who had a thin veneer of culture, to build so-called "possession houses" on his land – in addition to hiring a few unofficial deputies to try to drive squatters off his land.

After a five-day visit, my parents set forth the first week of July 1940, in the large Packard roadster that father had bought the year before. They planned to cross Virginia and then drive southwest and into East Tennessee. That trip, however, did not come to pass.

Two hours after their departure, my phone rang and when I lifted the receiver, a lugubrious male voice asked whether he was speaking to Mr. Walter Birge, Jr. Immediately after I identified myself as being that person, he informed me that he was the proprietor of the Culpepper Funeral Parlor, that my parents had been seriously injured in an automobile accident and were at that moment being transported in one of the funeral parlor vehicles to the nearest hospital which was in Charlottesville. I later learned that father had fallen asleep at the wheel and that the car had crashed into a concrete culvert.

As I no longer had a car, I at once hired a taxi (rental cars being almost unknown then) to drive me the one hundred miles to Charlottesville, where I arrived late that afternoon to find that mother had lost her right eye and that her beautiful face had been crushed in from just above her mouth to a fraction of an inch below her left eye. Good luck and the intervention of the Almighty saved her left eye. Father had suffered a compound fracture of his left leg. Worst of all, however, mother was in shock and her life in serious danger. I immediately telephoned Claire in Boston who was able within two minutes to ascertain from Fuller that one of the ablest specialists in the country on the treatment of that kind of trauma was on the staff of the Charlottesville Hospital. That was the only positive news.

Claire then lost no time in arranging for a nurse to live in her house to take care of her boys, Birge and Read, aged five and two, and then she took a train to Charlottesville where she remained for a month to bring the comfort of her continuing presence, to write letters to mother's many friends and to read aloud to her. As for me, almost every weekend until my parents left the hospital, I spent near them. It so happened that the parents of a fellow student, "Cue Ball" (owing to his paucity of hair) McCabe, lived in a house not far from the University of Virginia; so I drove down and back with my friend every weekend. Cue ball's father was a retired colonel and former Chief of G-2 (Military Intelligence).

How well I remember mother's courage. Despite the intense discomfort she must have suffered owing to a sort of iron mask, which had been attached to her head in such a way as to bring her facial bones back into place, she never complained. As soon as I would enter her room upon arrival from Washington, the first words she spoke might be, "Aren't you uncomfortable in this heat?" with no complaint about what she had been going through. (After her death, we came across a manuscript of inspirational poems she had written during this ordeal).

On those weekend visits I stayed at the Charlottesville Country Club, which was both convenient and comfortable. Unfortunately, however, I was not learning as much about international law as would have been the case had I been following my customary routine of studying all weekend.

After my parents had been in the hospital for a month, they moved into a comfortable house which father rented for a year, a logical arrangement as he had leased the New York apartment; moreover, mother was able periodically to receive treatments by her doctors. A live-in colored couple took good care of them.

When one recalls what happened during the summer of 1940, it seems incredible that we were able to concentrate on our studies at Turners. First, the Germans captured Paris, then the British recognized Charles de Gaulle on June 28 as leader of the Free French. Five days later, British warships destroyed three French battleships and an aircraft carrier at Oran; on July 10, the Luftwaffe launched the battle of Britain; the Soviet Union annexed the Baltic states; on August 20, Churchill saluted the R.A.F. thus: "Never in the field of human conflict was so much owed by so many to so few." Then, on September 3, President Roosevelt presented England with fifty overage destroyers in return for bases in Newfoundland and the West Indies. Yet few, if any of us, preparing for those exams believed that the United States would go to war. And all that summer we heard over and over again those songs, *The White Cliffs of Dover* and *The Last Time I saw Paris.* No one could doubt where the president's sympathies lay; but while running for a third term against Wendell Willkie, he assured his listeners, in a campaign speech, that he was not going to send "your sons" to fight overseas.

Finally in mid-September came the proverbial day of reckoning and over nine hundred candidates for entry into the Foreign Service sat for the State Department written examinations. These exams, which lasted for two and a half days, involved not only three-hour tests in economics, history, and international law, but also a three-hour exam to test the candidate's general knowledge. In addition, a candidate took an exam in at least one modern language. He could also be tested in a second language for extra credit, and if he did not do well in the second language it did not count against him. During the summer I brushed up on my first language choice, French, and also on Spanish, with teachers recommended by Mr. Turner.

When those examinations were over, I knew that I had done well in history and economics, but I was also fairly certain that I would probably receive a failing grade in international law. I was not worried about the general knowledge test; nor did I doubt that I had passed in French. As for Spanish, it was academic. All things considered, I was optimistic.

By the time the examinations were over I had occupied my California Street apartment exactly a year, so I cancelled my lease, purchased an old Packard for $75, in which I loaded my relatively few belongings, and drove down to Charlottesville, where I moved in with father and mother.

After I had been there for a week, I decided to cast an anchor or two to windward with regard to future employment in case I failed either the written exam or the oral test which would be scheduled for either mid-December or early January, if I passed the written exam. I would be informed later that autumn exactly on what day and at what time it would take place. First, I had a talk with Colonel McCabe, who, it will be recalled, was the father of my friend, Cue Ball. I explained my situation to the Colonel and asked whether he would be good enough to write a letter of recommendation to Naval Intelligence, which agency, I had learned, was beginning to recruit people, presumably in anticipation of an increasingly probable involvement in the war. So I mailed an application to Naval Intelligence. Second, I drove to Washington where I made an appointment to see Major Quesada, later to become famous, and at that time in the fall of 1940, the person to see if you wanted to train to become an officer in the Army Air Corps. The major was an attractive, no-nonsense individual. The first question he asked was my age. When I informed him that on May 21 of that year I had entered into my twenty-seventh year, he stated that no one who had passed his twenty-seventh birthday could be accepted. So that was that. In view of my situation, it did not seem advisable that I lie about my age.

On the day following my brief meeting with Major Quesada, I bid farewell to my Washington friends: Mr. Turner, Margo Platt, the Mayo family, and Sylvia Szechenyi, among others. The last was the most worthwhile young woman I had met during the past year. I then drove back to Charlottesville, and then came the waiting time when only those white cliffs of Dover and the Spitfires were preventing a Nazi victory over Western Civilization as we knew it.

Chapter Seven

The Waiting Time

When I arrived back in Charlottesville again, I found mother and father already well-settled in their rented house and well cared for by the already mentioned colored couple, John and Selma, who had obviously been expertly trained by previous employers and, in view of mother's slow recuperation, were invaluable. There was plenty of room for me in the large guest room, but on the occasion of that visit I remained only three days, for father wanted me to try to accomplish what he had set out to do when he and mother had left Washington in early July: namely, to drive to Jamestown, Tennessee, look over some of the property to which he was meant to hold title, consult with his representative, Mr. McNeil, and then decide what to do next. Two years before, Julius had urged father to cut his losses and get out. To an extent, father had done that and the arrangement with McNeil was a compromise.

It took me two days to reach "Jimtown", where I made an arrangement for room and board at the rather primitive, but adequate hotel where Mr. McNeil was staying. That cost me all of $1.50 a day, so I figured that grubstaking McNeil was not costing dad very much.

A short time before I left Washington, on September 14 the Selective Service Act was passed in Congress by one vote and the registration day happened to fall the second day after my arrival in Jamestown. Hence, that was where I registered. Had that draft bill - the first peacetime military draft in U.S. history - received one vote less, America would have been almost totally unprepared for what lay in store a year and two months later. When I left the Jamestown town hall following my registration, I wondered where I would end up: in the Foreign Service, in Naval Intelligence, or in the army.

What a dismal town that county seat turned out to be. There was one dilapidated moving picture theatre and every time I entered, half the people would turn around in their seats to give me a distrustful once-over. Every day I explored part of father's land - that is, presumably his land - via narrow woodland trails.

On one occasion, quite by accident, I came upon an illegal whisky still that was being operated by three tough looking mountaineers. I beat a hasty retreat in what I hoped looked like a non-purposeful manner, for I was reasonably sure that three rifles were pointed at my back, just in case I might be a revenue agent.

When I had been in Jamestown ten days, I concluded that no useful purpose involving the protection of father's interests in that area could be served by remaining longer, so I headed back East via a northern route. I drove up through northeast Tennessee, through Kentucky and up to Seymour, Indiana where father's older brother, Ernest, was manager of a small family-controlled company that manufactured agricultural hand-tools. Unfortunately, I had a slight mishap en route. Attempting to avoid hitting a dog, I ran over a rock that was just large enough to strike and bend slightly the connecting rod which transmitted power from the engine to the rear wheels. This soon resulted in a vibration, which steadily worsened.

I spent that evening and night with Uncle Ernest and Aunt Mary whom I had not seen since 1923 at Charlevoix on the occasion of my grandparents' fiftieth wedding anniversary, and neither of them was I destined to see again.

The following morning I drove east, passed through Columbus, Ohio - where I was destined to spend eighteen years from 1957 to 1975 - and stopped overnight in Zanesville. And all along that way the connecting rod vibration became steadily worse. What I wanted to do first on that Indiana to New York journey was stop by to see Mary Markle Rockwell, whom I had met while my parents were in the Charlottesville hospital. Mary was a twenty-one year old divorcee who had returned to Mauch Chunk (name changed to Jim Thorpe in 1953), Pennsylvania to live with her parents in what I found to be an impressive hilltop house in the anthracite mining area. I had become very much interested in this charming, affectionate young woman and in each of us there even lurked the idea that an eventual marriage was possible. At that particular time, however, the priority of my concern remained: had I passed the written examination?

On the morning following a half-day and one night's visit, during which we had the house to ourselves, I left for New York. While driving through northern New Jersey, my car finally broke down and I had to leave it in a garage to be repaired; and I continued by bus. I spent three days with Teddy Blacque, now married to June Blossom, returned to New Jersey to retrieve my old car, and then drove up to Boston for a short visit with Claire and Fuller. En route back to Washington I stopped in New York again, long enough to see my by-then two-year old son of whom I was destined to see very little during the six years to come.

It was now mid-November and word as to whether I had passed the Foreign Service written exams could be expected any day. The first decision I made immediately upon arrival in the nation's capital was to find an inexpensive temporary apartment conveniently situated. I checked in at the Hay-Adams and carefully read the *apartment-for-rent* ads. I could hardly believe my good fortune upon noting that there was a furnished basement room for rent by the month for $25. I at once phoned father to let him know about the arrangement, had a telephone installed and walked over to the old State Department Building, which was next door to the White House, to ensure that the competent authorities be informed as to my new address, thus leaving no doubt that news about the exam result would reach me without delay.

I spent that weekend with father and mother and reported to dad as to my opinion on his Tennessee land claim: namely, that he should not spend any more than the small outlays he was then making to clear up his titles. Upon my return to Washington, I called on my old friends, Margo Acheson Platt, Sylvia Szechenyi and Dorothy Mayo. A week later, the long awaited official letter from the State Department arrived. I had passed the written exams with a 76% (out of 100%) – not bad, considering the 62% grade in International Law. Economics and history saved me, with grades of 88% and 89% respectively. In order to qualify for the oral exam one had to obtain at least an average of 70% in the written test, so in that same communication I was informed that I should report at 10:30 am on January 4th at a certain State Department office in connection with the obligatory oral exam. That crucial test was one month away and the best way to prepare myself was to read carefully *The New York Times* as well as issues of *Time Magazine*, for current events were almost surely to be involved in questions I would have to answer.

Momentous events were taking place across the Atlantic during that time of late fall, 1940: the Luftwaffe hit Coventry with a terror-bombing attack; Hungary and Rumania joined the Axis; the Greeks, having been attacked by Italy in late October, routed the invaders and took 5,000 prisoners on the Albanian front; in Paris, Latin Quarter students began organizing the first resistance cells; the Royal Navy gained almost complete domination of the Mediterranean after aircraft from Malta inflicted serious damage to the Italian fleet anchored in the harbor of Taranto. Then, early in December the British Army under General Wavell was inflicting defeats on the Italian forces in North Africa. In early November, President Roosevelt had won a decisive victory over Willkie and an unprecedented third term in office began. Perhaps most significant of all, over sixteen million young Americans had registered the month before under Selective Service.

It was during those days that I received an impressive looking envelope from the White House, which contained an invitation to attend the coming-out ball of the daughter of Mr. Morganthau, Secretary of the Treasury, which was to be given by President and Mrs. Roosevelt in the White House. The evening of that event, as I recall, was during the second week of December.

In those days, my full dress and white tie were ready for instant use, for in that time of fifty to sixty years ago, one did not attend a formal ball – certainly not one held in the White House – in any attire other than white tie and tails.

I arrived at the White House at the appointed hour, but when I searched for my invitation to hand to the security official, I found that I had left it in my room, so I retraced my way back to my basement lodging, retrieved the invitation and returned at a swift pace.

Upon entering the great and beautiful White House, the first person to whom my attention was especially drawn was J. Edgar Hoover, the often fearsome head of the F.B.I., standing, with the pugnacious mien of a pit bull, on the staircase landing which was half way up to the ballroom. His feet were planted wide apart, as his eyes, ever alert, roved from side to side as though seeking to identify a potential assassin. The receiving line was already quite long and as I moved forward slowly, preparatory to shaking hands with the Secretary of the Treasury, his wife, his daughter, and Mrs. Roosevelt, I noted several men standing around, part of the company, but obviously not of the company. They were dressed in dinner jackets – i.e., tuxedos – which seemed to be ill fitting. These, of course, were obviously F.B.I. henchmen; and I thought back to the time of my junior year at Harvard and the fine arts course of Dr. Edgell, when we studied the painting of the *Adoration of the Magi* by Dierick Bouts, who had obviously used peasants as models and dressed them up in royal garb.

As was to be expected, the orchestra occasionally played Viennese waltzes and as at that time I fancied myself as an accomplished dancer of that graceful, elegant dance, I walked up to Mrs. Roosevelt, who was seated beside a few friends on the edge of the dance floor, and asked her to dance, - this with what I hoped was a proper bow. "Would you like to dance, Mrs. Roosevelt?" – "Why, I would love to," she replied, as she rose effortlessly and majestically to her feet. As soon as we started to whirl around, reversing these whirls every eight measures or so, I at once knew that this First Lady was perhaps the most graceful dancer I had ever met. She moved as lightly as a feather, for indeed, during the time of her girlhood, every young lady went to dancing school year after year. When I escorted her back to her seat, I seized the opportunity to say that Jimmie, her oldest son, had been my dormitory prefect during my first form year and that Frank and I had rowed together back in the Groton days.

I never saw Mrs. Roosevelt again – to speak to, that is. I would like to have had the opportunity to know this outstanding woman – perhaps the greatest of her time. Her only shortcoming, to my thinking, was her naïveté with regard to the intentions of fellow travelers and apologists for the USSR.

Aside from my waltz with the First Lady, the very special and noteworthy event of that evening for me was the meeting of Hélène-Marie (called HM) de Limur, a tall, distinguished, and sophisticated Franco-American girl to whom I had been introduced several months before, but had not seen again since. This encounter nearly had a lasting impact on my life.

After two dances with HM, I was convinced that she was, without doubt, one of the most attractive – if not *the* most attractive – young women I had ever met. And during the ensuing months of that winter and spring of 1941, that impression and captivation became ever stronger.

As far as looks were concerned, HM was tall, athletic, and slender. She was not beautiful, but she was distinguished, with an aquiline, aristocratic nose, expressive blue eyes, fair hair and graceful movements. As to personality, she had charm, a lively wit, and obviously a romantic nature.

One could see at once that she was to the manner born and that was understandable as her father, Count André de Limur, was a former French diplomat and her mother, née Ethel Crocker, was a member of one of San Francisco's "big four" families. This – then twenty-year old – young woman re-enters this narrative later on.

After spending that Christmas with mother and father in Charlottesville, I returned to Washington preparatory to reporting to the State Department for my crucial oral examination. In the interim, I had carefully read every issue of *Time Magazine* and *The New York Times,* especially the sections having to do with foreign affairs.

On the appointed day of January 4th, I donned my best blue suit and set out on foot for that old State Department Building, and during the ten-minute walk I thought only about what was in store. I had been informed by a friend who had entered the Foreign Service the year before that immediately following the oral exam, a candidate reported back to the waiting room which he had left twenty or thirty minutes before. Within a minute or so a clerk would enter. If you had passed you would be instructed to report at once for a physical exam at a room situated a short way down the hall; following which you were to report to another office to take a brief oral exam in the language which had been chosen as that of first competence – French, in my case.

Upon arriving at my destination that 4th of January, I was without delay escorted to an anteroom in which were four uncomfortable chairs; no one else was in the room. After about five minutes, a thin, expressionless clerk entered and nodded to me, saying, "Kindly follow me, sir." After a short walk down the hall, we came to a closed door. The clerk knocked, opened the door and motioned me to enter, then left the room and quietly closed the door; and there I stood facing five men ranging in age from about forty to late fifties. Two of these examiners I recognized by name and stalwart reputation: G. Howland Shaw, a Groton graduate and Assistant Secretary of State; and Adolph

Berle, also an Assistant Secretary and known for his brilliance. The other three department officials, I had never heard of. Mr. Berle, who occupied the center seat, was the first to speak. "Mr. Birge, kindly be seated." I sat down gingerly in the only available chair about twelve feet in front of that fearsome five.

After the passage of a half-century, I do not remember all the topics, including recent and long-past events, about which I was asked to comment. Three of the questions I do recall, however. In that January 1941, it was obvious that I would be asked something about the war which had been going on for almost a year and a half. Indeed, that is exactly what the first question was about. Mr. Berle spoke first. "Mr. Birge, do you feel that the United States should enter the war to prevent a German victory and to bring assistance to England?" My reply, in substance, was as follows: "Mr. Berle, I believe that in the immediate future we should do everything possible short of entering the conflict, to ensure that England will remain free. If it becomes necessary for us to enter the war to ensure the safety of Britain, so be it." The next question was asked by Mr. Shaw. "Mr. Birge, would you comment on the political situation in Argentina at the present time as well as during the past few years?" I was prepared for that question and I thought Mr. Shaw had expected that such would be the case. The next query had to do with exports from Bulgaria. That posed no problem as a fairly recent issue of *Time Magazine* had contained an article describing the relative importance of roses which that country was exporting to foreign perfume manufacturers. There were two or three additional questions that, as I recall, did not pose significant problems. That oral test lasted perhaps twenty minutes after which Mr. Berle asked, "Have you anything you would like to add, Mr. Birge?" "No sir, except that I hope to have an opportunity to serve my country."

With that and upon being told that I was excused, I arose, said, "Thank you, gentlemen," and walked out of the room.

I returned to the designated anteroom. Three minutes later, the same clerk who had received me less than a half hour before, entered and instructed me to report at once for my physical exam, and after that, for my oral language test. Both rooms involved were shown to me for they were situated off that same hallway. So I was in. I had passed!

The physical exam posed no problem and I thought that I knew more French than my examiner. Then I walked double time back to my apartment to telephone my parents. When I told father the good news, he said, "We are proud of you." For me, that was all he *had* to say.

For the next five months, HM of the White House ball was the only girl I took out, and she continued to be everything I had sought since leaving college. During that spring my parents' house in Virginia was my headquarters, but of course, I often visited the de Limurs in Washington.

France by then had been conquered by Germany over a half year before and quite a few French people had managed to make their escape to the United States where many had stashed away substantial sums of money over the preceding years. I well remember an occasion at a small family dinner in HM's house in Georgetown when I met a French man who had long been a close friend of André de Limur, HM's father, and a recent escapee from Paris. This refugee had been the chief executive of a factory that had manufactured tanks for the French army. He recounted in detail how he, himself, had helped load *Char-B* tanks onto railway cars for transportation to the rapidly deteriorating front.

It subsequently came to light that the French had possessed more tanks than the Wehrmacht and that the *Char-B* was probably the equal of any tank the Germans had. Of course, the difference was that the Germans had massed their tanks in several armored divisions, whereas the French had scattered their armor along the entire line, with an insufficient number of tanks in any one place. Thus, the effectiveness of the excellent French tanks had been minimized and the swift German victory greatly facilitated.

That winter and spring of 1940-41 was the time of "Bundles for Britain" and almost everyone was strongly pro-British. They were also pro-French to a point, but by then France was out of the war, there was no longer a truly independent France to be for, and the Free French under General Charles de Gaulle were not yet the significant force they were to become two years later.

In early February, HM suggested that I join her and four others, including her older brother, Charles, an Amherst undergraduate, for a long skiing weekend in New Hampshire. It was during those few days that I decided to bend every effort to tie my future to that French-American girl. There was no intimate involvement; that was 1941! I still believed, or one could say, labored under the illusion, that ideally, sexual relations should come only after marriage. HM seemed to believe the same thing. As I look back on the three months that followed, prior to my departure for my first post, I think that had I been less influenced by the ideals taught at Endicott Peabody's Groton, HM and I might have gotten married. However, in view of all that happened in the years to follow, the fates may well have conspired in my favor.

It was just at the time of our skiing adventure that I received a telegram that informed me of the exact grades I had received in the oral and written examinations. They averaged out to 81 and that had been enough to ensure my acceptance into the Foreign Service.

Out of the original 900 plus who had taken the written exam, 450 passed, and of those men, 45 passed the oral exam. I felt proud to be numbered among the five percent.

HM and I considered ourselves unofficially engaged. Of course, I could not know what were the exchanges between HM and her mother on that subject. Several years later I learned that the Countess de Limur, probably doubting the constancy of her daughter – and also mindful of her youth – she was only twenty – was urging her not to rush into marriage; and how can I fault her on that score in light of what ensued. I did not speak to either parent on the subject of my intentions involving HM.

HM had an adorable ten-year old sister, Marie. This minx talked me into setting up her jungle-Jim. As the future unfolded, this sister was to grow up into a far more balanced and happy person than her older sister.

Even in March and April of 1941, it appeared less and less likely that the United States would continue indefinitely to remain neutral, for the Neutrality Act was done away with, thus making it possible for American companies to sell munitions to England, and the fifty "overage" destroyers were given to our island-dweller cousins in exchange for a few British bases in the Caribbean and in Bermuda. Then a U.S. freighter was torpedoed in the south Atlantic. Who could really doubt at that time that before long we would be in the thick of it, side by side with our British friends?

Finally, and at length, the Department of State notified me that my first so-called *trial post* was to be Nuevo Laredo, Mexico, where the United States had a Consulate. In those days, and this probably still holds true, the Americans assigned to that post lived on the American side of the Rio Grande. Hence, I got off the train in Laredo, Texas; and thus was launched my unusually interesting, albeit undistinguished Foreign Service career. There followed many surprises, plenty of excitement, several acts of derring-do and living in places about which, up to that time, I had known next to nothing.

Chapter Eight

Tex-Mex

That post brought my first experience in living among Texans, that very special breed often characterized by tall, lean, rather quiet men and beautiful women. Neither Laredo nor Nuevo Laredo across the Rio Grande would be especially interesting to a tourist or casual visitor. For me, however, now officially embarked on what would presumably be a life's career, there was excitement involved in every encounter, whether these had to do with people, the river, or the ambiance of Texas and Mexico, which I was absorbing with my several senses for the first time.

First of all, there were the Texans and during that year of my assignment I liked everyone I met on *The Streets of Laredo*. As for the climate, it left something to be desired. From May until October it was blazing hot with one hundred degree temperatures not at all unusual. The winters were, of course, mild and had none of the invigorating climate of New England.

The area within a radius of at least fifty miles surrounding Laredo was not horse and cattle and cowboy country. One did occasionally see Stetson hats, but that was farming land, known, at least while I was there, for its onions and oranges, as well as for vegetables for local consumption. On the Mexican side of the river the first thing I noted were the odors – not unpleasant, but characteristic. Then there were the noises and the bars, the loud voices of friends greeting friends, and groups of loiterers seemingly having little to do.

I checked into the Hotel Laredo and for a single room I paid at the rate of $30 per month (the daily rate was $2.00). As my salary and rental allowance came to $244 per month, I felt myself to be quite affluent.

Soon letters and post cards from HM de Limur began to arrive, first from Washington and then from several towns she passed through on her way driving out to San Francisco with a girl friend, Edie Wright, the daughter of a distinguished American diplomat. I began to look for a suitable house where we could live following our marriage that I hoped would take place in the fall. Meanwhile, I settled in and established a routine. As I had brought my Raleigh bicycle from Washington, I had adequate transport. About six weeks following my arrival in Laredo, I rented an unpretentious but comfortable one-story furnished house for $50 a month. Two advantages to this place were a rather rustic, but very serviceable swimming pool, and an orange grove, which supplied me with all the fruit I could use. The owner, a rather plump, but quite pretty widow in her late twenties and with two small boys, lived close by. My house was only a hundred feet or so from the bank of the Rio Grande, then an unpolluted waterway, and, as I look back on it, few if any places I have ever lived in had as pleasant a setting; certainly, none entailed such inexpensive outlays.

The Consulate on the Mexican side of the river was about two to three miles from my house and those daily trips, especially during the cool season, were always agreeable. I enjoyed those months in Texas-Mexico. My boss, Bernard Gottlieb, the Consul General, a thoroughly decent, modest and able officer, was the sort of diplomat who would probably never make a serious mistake. He had good judgment in an emergency and took a keen interest in the welfare of his subordinates. His second in command was a rather odd and I thought ineffectual individual whose first name was Odin. He may have had an ancestor who resembled the great Norse god but such was certainly not the case with this man. About forty-five to fifty years of age, he had been passed over many times for a promotion and these accumulated disappointments showed in his attitude, in his nervous, rather reticent smile, in his hesitation ever to make a decision or to voice a definite opinion which might be contrary to that of his superior. Notwithstanding these drawbacks, Odin was a pleasant person and had a not unattractive way about him.

Next in line was Elias Gonzalez-Garza, the so-called non-career vice consul, who was in charge of the border-crossing and immigration work. This, of course, was logical as Elias was bi-lingual. He was a swarthy, stocky, very Mexican-looking man of about thirty-eight, jealous of his prerogatives and quick to bridle; he seemed to personify what one usually associates with certain types from across the border. He was keenly interested in everything having to do with the LULAC Society (League of United Latin-American Clubs) and as was perhaps understandable, he was convinced that Mexican-Americans were continually being discriminated against and he was going to make sure that this sort of treatment was not going to apply to him. As I had already attained a fair fluency in Spanish, I was assigned to work with Gonzalez-Garza. Although technically I outranked him (in much the same way that a *shave-tail* 2nd lieutenant outranks an experienced top sergeant in the army), I always deferred to him and worked under his instruction. To applicants for a border crossing card, I learned to ask, *¿Jura Usted que todo que ha dicho y escrito en este documento es la verdad, toda la verdad y nada que la verdad?* (Do you swear that everything you have said and written in this document is the truth, the whole truth and nothing but the truth?) By the time I left that post I could speak Spanish about as well as French.

At the start of my immersion in this border crossing work, I learned a lesson which might have been costly, but fortunately turned out all right. I had been instructed by Gonzalez-Garza that when any Mexican applied for a border crossing card, I was to make certain that he or she was actually living within our consular district and if there were any doubts on that score I was to double check on the veracity of the applicant's statements. About a week after beginning to work with Gonzalez-Garza, a man of about thirty-five, non-descript and rather timid, was brought to me by one of the consulate clerks who said, "Mr. Birge, this man wishes to apply for a border crossing card." I gave the applicant the necessary form to fill out and a minute or so later he handed it back. He was then photographed and I asked whether in fact he was living at 23 calle Posada, as indicated in the form, and was he still working as a cook in the Hotel Gloria as he had also written. "How long have you been in Nuevo Laredo," I then asked, "for I see that you are originally from Ciudad Victoria." The young man, looking straight at me and in a respectful tone replied that he had been living in Nuevo Laredo for two months and now would like to see Laredo, Texas and buy a few personal necessities. All seemed to be in order, so I asked the applicant to raise his right hand to swear the customary oath. This he did with impressive solemnity. I then presented him with his border crossing card on which was imprinted a duplicate of the photo we had taken of him and he made a slight bow and walked out the door, armed with the document which enable him to cross over the international bridge and into the United States.

Ten or twelve minutes later there came from the street the loud noise of a powerful motor cycle which abruptly stopped just outside the front entrance to the consulate. Then in walked a large police officer known as a *Federal* – hence not a local policeman but a member of the federal force. "What can we do for you?" fearfully asked our chief clerk. "*Estoy buscando un criminal* (I'm looking for a criminal) suspected of murder and we have reason to believe that he may ask for, or may already have asked for, one of your border crossing cards to enable him to enter the United States." The clerk brought the *Federal* up to me and repeated what the Mexican officer had said. The clerk then asked whether I could show him our duplicates of recently issued border-crossing cards. I pulled out the file of that day's cards and handed them to the officer. The first card he looked at was that of the most recent applicant. "*Caramba, qué barbaridad,*" shouted the *Federal* as he pointed to the photo of the applicant allegedly working as a cook in the hotel Gloria. "¡*Eso sí que es*! *Vamos al Puente*," ("Yes, that's it! Let's go to the bridge") he then commanded. We both at once rushed out the door, the big law enforcer leaping on this motorcycle, while I followed as fast as I could on my Raleigh. As soon as we reached the international bridge, we explained the situation to the U.S. immigration officials who were dressed like Texas Rangers. When the chief Ranger saw the photo of the man we were looking for, he commented, "Well, I'll be damned! That son of a bitch passed through here with his valid card just five minutes ago."

Within fifteen minutes four hastily mobilized *Rangers* and the *Federal* apprehended the alleged murderer, who was at once locked in the Nuevo Laredo jail prior to being transported south to Ciudad Victoria. It took me a while to live down my failure adequately to check on the veracity of the border crossing card applicant's statements.

While Gonzalez-Garza and I got along quite well and I enjoyed his lively humor, I gradually came to the conclusion that he was using his position to enable him to take advantage of some of the good looking girls who wanted border crossing cards. On more than one occasion I overheard him suggest to a young female Mexican applicant that she did not have all her credentials in order and that perhaps a follow-up meeting in one of the local hotels later that afternoon might be helpful. I finally felt it my duty, though reluctantly, to bring this to the attention of

Mr. Gottlieb in order to protect him from embarrassing repercussions. The inevitable upshot was that Gottlieb wrote a confidential dispatch to Washington suggesting that Gonzalez-Garza's undoubted talents could be better made use of in another Mexican post. Hence, there came out of the blue two weeks later instructions for Elias Garza-Gonzalez to report to the U.S. Consulate in Tampico. I was able partially to persuade him that this really constituted a promotion.

I had not been long in Laredo when I met an interesting young man, Charley Prill, a German, temporarily living in the small Grand Hotel of Nuevo Laredo while awaiting his U.S. immigration visa. Charley had been a seaman on a German freighter out of Hamburg. One day at the age of eighteen, he jumped ship in New York and had remained illegally in the United States ever since. Eventually, however, the Immigration and Naturalization Service had caught up with him when he decided he would like to vote. He was told that if he would travel to Mexico and apply there for a visa he should have little difficulty in gaining permanent admittance to the United States, especially as he had by that time married an American woman. For some reason his case dragged on, and then his chances of re-entering the U.S. took a nosedive when U.S. – German relations seriously deteriorated in 1941. Charley had already forgotten a lot of his native German and he thought and acted like an American. But all that was of little help to him and he was stuck there in that small and boring border town. He would periodically come into the Consulate to solicit our help and we became good friends. As I was a bachelor, I had few evening engagements and we often played two-handed poker in his hotel. Charley and I often went on nightlife excursions on the Mexican side of the river. He was about the only good male friend I had during that year and we downed many a *Carta Blanca* and *Dos XX* (Mexican beers) together. Luckily we never pursued the same woman, but once we did spend a rewarding evening with sisters from the U.S. who had to stay in Nuevo Laredo two days in connection with litigation having to do with an auto accident they had had in the vicinity when they were returning to the border from Mexico City.

One hot and cloudless day in early August I received a letter postmarked San Francisco from HM de Limur. There was nothing significant about the day, being hot and cloudless as almost all summer days in Laredo were. I vividly remember that day because of the letter. I had been receiving news from HM about once a week but since around the fourth of July these letters had been arriving less and less frequently. This note, a short one, caused me slowly to sit down, the better to take in its brief message. It was a *Dear John* letter; in short, HM was no longer in love with me. I learned then that absence only sometimes makes the heart grow fonder. Those few lines scribbled in California toppled the romantic world I had been building. What I could not have foreseen that summer day was that five years later HM would try to turn back the clock of our shattered romance and mail to me the opposite of *Dear John*. But that sequel was an eon away.

Perhaps two lessons could have been learned from this experience: the passage of time often provides proof of character, one way or the other, and depth of involvement; so-called gentlemanly behavior, relative to sex, is not always the best way to win a woman.

A good way to make friends in a new community is to join a church. This I did. The Episcopal Church of Laredo was closely knit and its members were among the most prominent of the town. I also joined the choir, partly because of the director of that group, Genevieve Richter. She was an attractive woman of about thirty-eight, the wife of the leading department store head, and had three boys ranging in age from about ten to fifteen. Through the Richters I met several other pillars of Laredo society and, all considered, I spent an enjoyable year on and off the streets of old and new Laredo. About six months after my arrival I did become somewhat involved with an unusually attractive divorcee, a close friend of Genevieve, who was several years older than I and had two small children. I used to bicycle over to her house on my Raleigh – visits which during the fall of 1941 usually took place on Saturday afternoons so that I could listen to Harvard football games over her radio. On occasion, I would pay her a visit in the evening as well and I would conceal my bike in the tall grass adjoining her dwelling, thus shielding her from the town busybodies.

In early December of that year 1941, about the second of that month, mother and father motored down for a visit en route to Mexico for a tour of that country. As I had an extra bedroom and a large living room, there was ample room for the three of us. In preparation for this visit I got rid of the two inefficient and stupid Mexican maids I had had up to that time and hired a competent cook from across the Rio Grande, who brought along a willing an energetic niece to assist her. The weather was pleasantly cool during that season, the war was still a long was off and most things were right with the world. Then came that fateful Sunday morning of December 7th, which was mother's birthday. We listened to the noon radio news broadcast after church and we learned how the world of every American was now turned upside down, for the announcer told of the Japanese attack on Pearl Harbor. Fortunately for the morale of most Americans and unfortunately for the Japanese imperial staff, the full information as to just how devastating to the Pacific Fleet this dawn attack really had been was not made known until much later.

As luck would have it, providence very likely saved the Hawaiian Islands from capture and immeasurably helped our war effort in the Pacific, as the entire U.S. carrier force was at sea on maneuvers at the time of the Japanese attack. Had this not been so, there would probably have been no victories at Coral Sea at Midway in May and June, 1942, respectively. Nor would we have been in a position to capture Guadalcanal and Iwo Jima until much later than was the case.

On December 8th, the days following that *Day of Infamy*, President Roosevelt asked the assembled members of the House of Representatives and Senate to declare war against Japan, and that declaration immediately followed.

Winston Churchill had promised the president that if the United States should declare was against Japan, England would at once do likewise. This pledge was kept without delay and Britain's declaration of war against Japan actually preceded America's declaration.

On December 11, Germany and Italy declared war against the United States, and the U.S. immediately declared war against those countries.

On the day following President Roosevelt's announcement that a state of war now existed between the U.S. and Germany-Italy, the U.S. army at once mounted a machine gun on the U.S. side of the Rio Grande next to the International Bridge and pointing at friendly Mexico. No one could understand the necessity for this belligerent show of force, an act greatly resented by our Mexican friends. In Laredo, we thought this move was ridiculous and even almost hilarious, though across the river no one saw the humor of it.

Following our entry into the war, there was little change in the tenor of my life. At the consulate, however, we all became much more careful in granting border-crossing cards or any other kind of entry visas. One unfortunate repercussion of the state of war was that it precluded any possibility of Charley Prill's obtaining an immigration visa. In a way it worked out all right for him, for not long after my departure in April 1942, the FBI established contact with Charlie and arranged that as an agent for the U.S. he would supply them with any significant information following his internment by the Mexican authorities in a camp for enemy aliens, that is, for German nationals in Mexico. The Mexican government may well have been privy to the FBI's plan. Charlie reported all this to me when I re-met him in New York after the war. Apparently he was reasonably comfortable in the camp, and this useful service to the U.S. government assured his lawful re-entry to the U.S. when it was all over.

In mid-April, the State Department informed me that I was transferred to Istanbul, Turkey, and I was instructed to report to the Department in Washington as soon as possible for consultation.

Bernard Gottlieb promptly notified the mayor of Nuevo Laredo of my imminent departure and the latter invited me to an informal farewell ceremony that took place two days later in the town square. On the appointed morning for the official leave-taking there were gathered together some fifty Mexican civilian and military men and a few curious onlookers. *"Damas y Caballeros,"* intoned the portly *alcalde, "estamos aquí para decir adiós a nuestro amigo, el distinguido Vice Consul, el Señor Birge, quien muy pronto se va a representar su país en las trincheras diplomáticas en Turquía..."* I had not thought of my new post as being in the diplomatic trenches but it sounded impressive. The small crowd cheered and I ventured a short thank you speech in return.

Three days later, mother and father, who had returned to my house from their tour of Mexico, and a few of my new friends, in addition to my colleagues from the Consulate General, saw me off on the morning train bound for San Antonio where I was to make connection with the afternoon train bound for St. Louis and then on to Washington.

Chapter Nine

Turkey – The Neutral German Sandwich

The Washington that greeted me two days later was a city of feverish activity, for it was the capital of a nation at war. Quonset huts were ubiquitous. Everyone seemed to be in uniform; indeed, I felt conspicuous in mufti. During the ten days of this consultation period, which involved practically no consultation at all, I called on the State Department Visa Division and put in a word for Charley Prill, who was still stuck down on the border awaiting his entry permit. As it turned out, my efforts on his behalf were academic in view of what the OSS had in store for him.

During those ten days I re-met Sylvia Szechenyi whom I had known quite well during the time of my exam preparation in Washington; but time was militating against any significant relationship in those hectic days.

When the day of my departure arrived (in early May) I was informed that I was to carry a diplomatic pouch to Cairo. This presented immediate problems, as these pouches were to be with the bearer at all times. I took a train to New York and then took a cab to Bill Kilborne's apartment where I had been invited to spend the night. As we were to go out to dinner, I did not want to carry the very bulky pouch to the restaurant and so carefully shoved it under my bed. Fortunately, for me, it was still in its hiding-place when we returned at about nine-thirty, for the German *Abwehr* (army intelligence unit) had apparently been unaware of its unprotected presence there.

On the following morning I took a cab out to LaGuardia Airport, lugging with me two suitcases and that pouch (my trunk having been sent on ahead). There were about seventy or eighty passengers – all men – on that Pan-Am *Flying Boat* (i.e., seaplane) which was to stop at Miami; San Juan, Puerto Rico; Trinidad; Belém, Brazil; and Fisherman's Lake, Liberia, en route. Not long after this takeoff, all official transport was taken over by the Army Transport command. As the latter organization used only land planes, usually equipped with bucket seats or equally uncomfortable ones, this Pan-Am flight was a sort of swan song of comfort for these long official overseas flights. The main problem with those huge and cumbersome low-flying seaplanes was that they were slow and seemingly took forever to get anywhere; I think our speed was only about 150 miles per hour. That spring of 1942 marked what was perhaps the height of German U-Boat success; moreover, the U-boat captains were especially active along the American east coast, where the shipping traffic, especially that involving oil tankers, was very heavy. Mindful of this situation, a few of us stood voluntary watches, peering out the windows on the slim chance of sighting an unsuspecting German submarine, in the unlikely eventuality of which our Pan-Am captain would radio the U.S. Navy; but the endless ocean remained empty save for two freighters headed north. No subs that day.

Our trip to Miami, then to San Juan and to Trinidad was uneventful. At Trinidad, the last port of refueling, we stopped for the night and I stayed again at the very fine Queens Park Hotel almost exactly seven years after my first visit there. But then we ran into a problem for when we were about half way to Belém, one of our four engines broke down. At the time, I was engaged in a poker game and was about to rake in a few chips won with aces over sevens, when the plane took a sudden drop to what seemed like several hundred feet. It may have been owing to turbulence or maybe the engine breakdown caused it, but drop we did, and the chips suspended in mid-air, as were we and everyone else who was not buckled in.

We were able to continue on three engines and landed on the Baía de Marajó at Belém without mishap. However, we had to spend four days in Belém until a replacement engine was flown down. May on the equator, or indeed any month on the equator at sea level, is not exactly an ideal place for a vacation. And Belém is not a fascinating spa. However, we made the best of the situation by seeking out the most pleasant place to pass the time in the evenings, namely a nightclub called Zizi's. The food was pretty good and the rum drinks were even better. Immediately upon our arrival, I had called at the U.S. Consulate and left my diplomatic pouch in their safekeeping. At Zizi's, each of the three evenings we spent there, the company or group consisted of our own men from the Pan-Am flight plus other Americans, mostly army officers, passing through – either going to or returning from Africa. Well do I recall one of those evenings when I found myself seated opposite a U.S. Colonel Craw, an attractive former West Pointer of about forty. I would probably not remember that particular person were it not for having learned over a half-year later that Colonel Craw, who had been killed during the U.S. Army landing in Morocco, was posthumously awarded the Congressional Medal of Honor.

In the afternoon of the fourth day of our awaiting the installation of the replacement engine, we took off for Africa – some eighteen hundred miles east. Our immediate destination, as previously mentioned was Fisherman's Lake, Liberia, a desolate spot I had never heard of, and indeed, have never heard of since. Obviously the reason we refueled there was that our seaplane had to land on water, preferably on a protected lake or river. The dawn had just come up all of sudden, as it does at the equator, when we alighted on that desolate lake. Ahead we could see a small and rickety dock swarming with scantily clad natives, each bearing two tins of fuel. Directly after tying up at that dock, the procession of fuel-bearing porters began and this process took what seemed like the better part of an hour.

Then began the last leg of our long trip to Lagos, Nigeria. At that time I was thinking that due north of us lay French Africa, and France was now the vassal of Nazi Germany; and northeast of us General Rommel's army was getting the better of the best the British were able to bring to bear against him. In other words, Africa was certainly not an allied controlled continent.

At Lagos, which we reached without incident, we would have to change planes, as a flying boat was hardly a logical carrier to bring us over thousands of miles of desert. The plane to which we were to be transferred was that well-known army workhorse aircraft, a DC-3, which could carry only a fraction of the number of passengers who had arrived on the Pan-Am seaplane. That meant, of course, that some of us would have to be off-loaded. We were told to present ourselves at an office adjoining the shed where we had disembarked. Seated behind a small desk was a young, rather corpulent American army first lieutenant. As each of the passengers from our Pan-Am flight came to the desk, the lieutenant asked for his documents, that is, passport and travel orders. In front of him, this officer had a list of the passengers who were on our flight. The officer would look at the list, examine the man's papers and then curtly inform him either that he was to leave the following morning on a DC-3 for the ultimate destination of Cairo or wait for three days for the arrival of the next DC-3. Right away, this procedure caused consternation, for most of those who were told to wait a few days objected strongly, claiming that they had high priority and demanding to speak to the person in charge. The lieutenant's rejoinder was always the same; "*I* am in charge here. Will you kindly move along?"

I did not think that my own priority was anything special but apparently my diplomatic passport ensured my precedence and I was put on the first departing DC-3, which left the next morning. In that small, but efficient aircraft we occupied bucket seats placed along each side of the plane with our luggage piled in the center. Thus we flew due north to Kano, where we quickly refueled and then almost due East to an outpost called Maiduguri, where we stopped for the night in a small British encampment. At eight o'clock the next morning, we continued our flight to the East, over one of the most desolate areas of the *Dark Continent*. The pilot, with whom I chatted occasionally, announced that the vast, barren, semi-desert land we were now flying over was Chad, otherwise known as *Sweet Fuck-all*. We were glad we didn't have to land there.

Six to eight hours after takeoff we touched down at the oasis of El Fashir, the refueling stop about sixty percent of the way to Khartoum and where the gasoline had to be continually brought in from the Sudan by caravans of camels. From the air, one could see long lines of these plodding creatures, each loaded with two large tins of gasoline, wending their toilsome way from the distant Nile to that far-away oasis.

I have no recollection of Khartoum, that outpost of Empire where *Chinese Gordon* had met his end in January, 1885, except that of sleeping outdoors on one of a long row of cots, protected by that most useful invention for the world of the tropics: the mosquito net.

As already mentioned, in May 1942, the brilliant German, General Erwin Rommel, known as the *Desert Fox*, was in control of the north coast of Africa between Tunis and within 200 miles of the Suez Canal. The British still held the port of Tobruk, but within about a month following my departure Rommel was able to capture that port with the help of an agent he had sent to Cairo – as will be explained later. Hence, the only route we could have taken to reach Cairo was the one we had followed.

Our flight from Khartoum to Cairo, which took about six hours, was uneventful. First, I delivered by diplomatic pouch to the U.S. Embassy, paid my respects to the ambassador, who informed me as to when and exactly how I was to proceed on to Beirut and thence to Turkey, and then I was driven to Shepherd's Hotel, perhaps the best known and certainly the most luxurious and elegant of all hostelries of the years of World War Two. Every afternoon there was tea dancing in the *Palm Court* to passable music offered by an army band. Seated near the dance floor, I watched this sidelight of the desert war and it seemed almost unbelievable that in the early May of 1942, when the fortunes of Britain and its allies were near their nadir, there could be such a carefree atmosphere adjacent to the headquarters of the British army of the Nile. Yet despite the parlous situation of the Empire, of the massive German advances in Russia and of the continuing threat of the *Desert Fox's* forces, then only about seventy-five miles west of Alexandria, there was an air of confidence that Britain and her allies would prevail, come Erwin Rommel or high water. There were good reasons for this state of mind. The Rashid-Ali pro-German rebellion of 1941 in Iraq had been put down by forces organized and under the overall authority of the high command in Cairo; Haile Selassie had been restored to his throne; Somaliland and Eritrea, former Italian colonies, had been taken; and Madagascar had been occupied by the Free French. Most important of all, the powerful United States was now an ally and American tanks were being shipped to Egypt by sea around the Cape of Good Hope.

The Germans and Italians understood the immense strategic importance of Malta, but in spite of heavy daily bombardments by the Axis bombers, that island held firm and the RAF was continually bombing German and Italian supply vessels that were so essential to General Rommel's operations. By way of mention, following the capture of Tobruk by the Germans in mid-June, 1942, the German plan to invade and capture Malta was abandoned; and that decision, perhaps more than any other factor, doomed the German armed forces in North Africa to eventual defeat.

In Shepherds's Palm Court on any May day of that year, 1942, one could see a panoply of Empire: the uniform of officers from Britain, Australia, New Zealand, South Africa, India – and from Britain's allies: Poland, Free France and already a few

Americans. It would not be too long before Mr. Churchill would speak of "the end of the beginning."

Not far from my bedroom on the third floor of the hotel was a lavatory. There, on a hook on the wall, an officer's Burberry trench coat was hanging; that was the first day I used that restroom, and it was still hanging there just prior to my departure four days later. As I was looking at that coat, I noticed that a captain of the Rifle Brigade was drying his hands. I exchanged greetings with the officer of that famous regiment and asked why the owner of a valuable trench coat did not keep it in his room. The captain replied, "Oh, that coat belonged to one of our friends who was killed in the Western Desert last month. We keep it there where he left it – as a sort of remembrance."

During the days of my brief stay in Cairo, I purchased three inexpensive pairs of earrings; for Claire, for Sylvia Szechenyi, and for another girl I had met and seen only once ten days before in Washington. None of those small gifts reached their destination. I also outfitted myself with British army regulation short pants and matching khaki shirt together with gum-soled desert shoes. In light of what took place a day later, this modest outlay proved to be somewhat embarrassing.

On May 18, in accord with the ambassador's instruction, I boarded the train for Suez, dressed in the newly acquired clothing along with by black Basque beret, a practical headgear I have favored for over half a century. While awaiting the ferry which was to transport most of the passengers of our train across the Suez Canal, an imposing and powerfully built sergeant-major marched up to me, brought his heels sharply together and abruptly demanded to see my passport. I fished into the breast pocket of my newly purchased shirt and presented my U.S. diplomatic passport for inspection. The sergeant-major flipped over a few pages, handed the passport back to me, saluted, and as though regretting that my document had been in order, commented, "You see, sir, the clothes you are wearing, while very nearly those which might be worn by one of our officers are not exactly the same; nor are they what I would expect a civilian to wear."

From Port Said, a slow-moving train, closely following the coastline, brought me as far as Haifa; then a bus, passing through ancient Tyre and Sidon, brought me to Beirut where I stayed for three days at the Hotel St. George. There on the shore of the Mediterranean Sea the war seemed far away. At that time Lebanon was controlled by the British. There, I celebrated my twenty-ninth birthday alone on May 21. The short stay in Beirut was necessary, as the *Taurus Express,* the train I was to take into Turkey, left Tripoli, the main Syrian seaport, only twice a week.

As there was little else to do, I went swimming and not realizing how intense the sun could be on the Mediterranean shore at that time of year, I was badly sunburned. On the 23rd of May I took another bus up to Tripoli, where the above-mentioned Taurus Express took me into neutral Turkey and the start of my Turkish adventure.

Just at that period of the war, Germany was reaching the high tide of its success – this, in the minds of most neutrals and even of some belligerents. In retrospect, Germany's high tide came in the summer of 1940 when France lay prostrate and the Soviet Union had not yet been attacked. But in that May of 1942, the German armies were driving the Russians before them in Ukraine, the Crimea and at Krasnodar and Taganrog. The German U-boats were exacting a heavy toll on allied shipping and the Japanese still controlled most of the Pacific. As an American, I was convinced that we would be eventually victorious, but my optimism was not shared by most of those with whom I exchanged views in Lebanon and Turkey in that late spring.

Neutral Turkey, which I saw for the first time in the late afternoon of that day of my departure from Syria and Lebanon, was practically surrounded on three sides by the German armies. General Rommel was about to capture Tobruk and would very soon come close to taking Alexandria. Only the eastern coast of the Black Sea remained in Soviet hands. The salient question asked by many, including competent observers, was whether the Turks would remain neutral or join the Germans as they had done early in the First World War. Most educated Turks, however, remembered what Ataturk *(*born Mustafa Kemal, later called Kemal Ataturk, or *The Ghazi)* had admonished his people shortly before his death in 1938. It will be recalled that this gifted leader had been the president and dictator of Turkey from 1923 and had overseen vast changes. It was he who had overnight altered the spelling of the Turkish language from Arabic to Latin letters based on the phonetic sound of the language. It was he who had forbidden women to wear veils. It was he also who had encouraged the sons of leading families to attend the American Robert College and the French Lycée in Istanbul. What the *Ghazi* had admonished his people was, "Never again fight against the British, for they always win the last battle." It soon became fairly obvious to me that most of the handful of Americans stationed in Turkey shared my view; that, in general, the Turks were pro-German and/or pro-American but definitely anti-soviet and even anti-British. It was assumed by most, perhaps understandably, that Ismet Inonu, the president of Turkey, would try to keep Turkey neutral until he could determine which side would be victorious.

On the *Taurus Express*, I ordered a cup of tea from the Wagon-Lit (sleeping car) conductor with the idea that towels soaked in that liquid and applied to the painful sunburn I had acquired on the St. George Hotel beach would bring the beneficial relief I had heard tannic acid was meant to ensure. This turned out to be true, at least to an extent. However, the conductor was not happy when he noted tannic acid discoloring his towels and, quite rightly, charged me the equivalent of a few dollars to make good the damage.

When the train arrived in Ankara on the afternoon of the next day, I was met at the station by Joe Satterthwaite, an old friend who had been First Secretary of Embassy in Buenos Aires in 1935. Ankara had been the capital of Turkey since shortly following Ataturk's accession to the leadership of his country. Until then and since the capture of Constantinople in 1453 by the Ottoman Turks, that city, to be re-named Istanbul, had been the capital of the Ottoman Empire. .Ataturk declared that the capital of Turkey should be not only near the center of the country, but inhabited by Turks. Istanbul, for centuries, had had large minority populations of Greeks, Armenians, and Jews, the latter having lived there since their expulsion from Spain by the Inquisition in 1492.

Joe Satterthwaite brought instructions from the ambassador, Laurence A. Steinhardt, to the effect that I was to join his staff for a ten-day temporary duty as a code clerk to replace a man who was on leave. The confidential codes then used were more complicated than the old *Brown* and *Grey* codes I had worked with in Argentina. Of course, I had no idea how sophisticated the German code breakers had become and it may well be that the Nazis deciphered many of the messages I worked on during the last week of May, 1942. I do not recall that any of those wireless texts were of an especially confidential or secret nature, so any deciphering would have done them little good.

The most significant result of this ten-day tour of duty in Ankara was getting to know the Steinhardts. Ambassador Steinhardt was a prominent and quite wealthy member of the Jewish upper crust *("Our Crowd")* of New York City. He had entered the Foreign Service at the top when Franklin D. Roosevelt became president in 1933. His posts, in order, had been Stockholm, Lima, and Moscow. A former track star at Columbia, he had an excellent physique and stood about 5'11' with a lean, but strong build, and moved with the grace of a panther. Most women saw him as handsome. He was very articulate, had a sense of humor, and above all, placed great stock in the loyalty of his staff. In most cases, he returned that loyalty. In my opinion, which is based especially on the three years we worked together in Prague, he just missed being an outstanding ambassador mainly because he was emphatically *not* a good listener, fascinated as he was by his own voice and the apparent effect he had on his dutiful audience. I liked him right away and I believe that he liked me in return. Then there was Dulcie, his wife, who in many ways was quite remarkable. Certainly she was talented above all as a gifted linguist. She spoke fluent German, which she had mastered as a child during the pre-World War I era when it had been fashionable for rich New Yorkers to hire a *Fräulein* for their children. Her French was equally good and she was also quite fluent in Swedish and Spanish. She was pretty and she knew it, but extra-marital exchanges were restricted to mild, innocuous flirtations.

Dulcie became a good friend. I think she liked me, inter alia, because she had a passion for bridge and promptly began dragooning me into embassy dinner-bridge parties. I think she also was impressed by my own not inconsiderable linguistic ability. She may also have had it in mind that I just might somehow come to take a romantic interest in her only offspring, Dulcie Ann, then, about fifteen years old. Unfortunately, Dulcie Ann was neither as pretty as her mother, nor as intelligent as her father. Later, she became quite chic, but that was academic.

So the Steinhardts became a factor in my life for the next six years. During the summers of my service in Turkey, they used to come to Istanbul to live in their quarters in the Consulate General.

I reported for duty at the Consulate General in Istanbul on or about June 1st. Sam Honnaker, the Consul General, a career officer in his late fifties or thereabouts, was a decent, obviously dedicated officer who told his subordinates what they were meant to do and then he left them to their own devices and judgment.

It was at once noticeable in Istanbul that there were few cars in the city streets. Even though Turkey was still a neutral in that war, gasoline was hard to obtain. Germany and the countries under its domination had none to spare and the only other logical source involved tankers passing through at least part of the Mediterranean, a U-boat infested waterway. All taxis and buses were powered by ponderous charcoal-burning contraptions.

On the second day following my arrival, looking for possible apartments in the main residential streets, I glanced at the façade of a rather imposing apartment building and there in large letters was emblazoned *Kunt Palace*. I could only assume that the first word was the name of the owner, or perhaps it stood for a suitable assurance that any apartment renter would be happy in that domicile. I decided that amusing as it may have been, an apartment in that edifice was not for me. I then rented a room with a Greek family for about two weeks until I found a small five room furnished flat, also owned by a Greek family, on the third floor of an apartment building overlooking the *Golden Horn*. As the splendid view was out the bedroom windows, I used the second bedroom for a sitting room and rarely used the living room down the hall near the small kitchen and maid's room. I hired a live-in maid to do everything. In that apartment, the owners had a modern refrigerator of which they were so proud that it was prominently displayed near the front door in the entryway!

There was not much consular work in those war days as, of course, tourism had been completely shut off and very few immigration visas were issued. However, some of our work came from unexpected quarters. Many people belonging to a so-called *minorité* – as expressed in French, the *lingua franca* of the educated non-Turks – wanted to get out of Turkey for the understandable reason that those of ethnic Greek, Armenian, or Jewish origin were openly discriminated against by all levels of Turkish officialdom. If a prospective emigrant could obtain any kind of American visa, he or she could gain admittance to almost any country and in many instances the U.S. visa was used simply to facilitate travel elsewhere. Of course, I had had considerable visa experience in Nuevo Laredo but that, such as it was, had provided little logical preparation for what was in store for me. The Turks, emboldened by their advantageous status of neutrality in a war, the outcome of which was still much in doubt, imposed the dreaded *Varlik Vergesi*, a tax ostensibly levied against all owners of any property. This tax, however, was made onerous only for those members of the minorities who had antagonized Turkish officials or were unable to bribe one or more strategically placed officials who were in a position to prevent enforcement of this tax in those special cases.

The sanctions meted out to those unable to pay their Varlik tax was transportation to a remote eastern Turkish town by the name of Atchkali, where one Armenian figured it would take him four hundred years shoveling snow to pay off his tax.

Every day one heard stories, most of them true – though in some cases perhaps exaggerated – of the hardships undergone by a Greek or an Armenian or a Jew who could not pay the tax and was shipped out to the east. Perhaps the most distressing of these tales was that of a Greek widow who supported her two small children by mending clothing with her old sewing machine. One day a couple of tax collectors called on her demanding that she pay several thousand lira, which she did not possess. As she was unable to raise this sum the officials confiscated the Singer sewing machine, her sole means of livelihood. Stories of this kind reached us almost daily.

That summer of 1942, when the Steinhardts moved to our Consulate General from Ankara, Sam Honnaker was instructed by the ambassador to vacate his office on the second floor and to make do with a much smaller office on the ground floor. It should be pointed out that because of the extreme heat, almost all other ambassadors also moved to Istanbul from Ankara for the summer months, but in most cases summer embassies had long since been provided for, usually on the shore of the Bosporus.

There was a motor launch for the use of the ambassador and his family and for no one else. The captain of this vessel was Nagi, a personable Turk with ability and humor. On most

Saturdays, the Steinhardts would invite a few friends – usually diplomats representing Allied countries – out on the *Hiawatha* for a picnic. In view of my very friendly relationship with the ambassador and Mrs. Steinhardt – partly owing to my willingness to play bridge – I was often included. Sometimes this provided a welcome diversion - sometimes less so, especially when I had already made other plans.

I now return to the subject of the Varlik tax. Not long after the ambassador's arrival in Istanbul from Ankara, he was approached by a Jewish merchant, Mr. Levi Soloman, who had a large and profitable shop in the bazaar and who, incidentally, was also an American citizen by virtue of having been born in New York. Mr. Solomon requested the ambassador's intervention with the Turkish authorities to protect him and some of his Jewish friends from ruination by the Turkish tax collectors. Mr. Steinhardt thus found himself in an embarrassing position. He naturally wanted to help Mr. Solomon but he also did not wish to antagonize any Turkish official at a time when it was above all in America's interest at least to keep Turkey neutral and possibly to bring that country into the war on the side of the Allies. "Remember, Mr. Solomon," cautioned Steinhardt, "I am not the Jewish Ambassador." However, in view of Mr. Solomon's claim to U.S. protection, Mr. Steinhardt was able to obtain mitigation in his tax, but some of Mr. Solomon's friends did not fare so well. So the members of the Turkish Jewish minority, and the Turks as well, came to understand that Steinhardt was an American and a pragmatist first – a Jew second.

As the fates were to conspire, I played a very minor role in this situation, but in doing so was able to save about ten Turkish Jews from the cruel effects of the Varlik Vergesi. That is, I was able to assist them in escaping ruin, transportation to Atchkali, and – in the case of two much older relatives, from probable death.

Briefly, this is how it happened. I was sharing a large double desk with a young vice-consul, Charlie MacVicker, who I believe, eventually ended up teaching at Princeton. As I had arrived in Istanbul before Charlie, he was junior to me, which under the circumstances was fortunate. We more or less divided what consular work there was.

One morning, a well-dressed man of about fifty was ushered into our office by Jack Mercieka, the diminutive Maltese jack-of-all-trades, who did a little of everything. "Mr. David," he said, "this is Mr. Birge, the Vice-consul, who will handle your case and that of the members of your family." Jack then turned to me. "Mr. Birge, the Davids wish to visit their relatives in New York and wish to obtain a visitors' visa."

Speaking French, I asked Mr. David to have a seat. "How many members of your family do you wish to have accompany you and are they all here with you?" Mr. David replied, also in that language, "There are six of us: my wife, my three children and my old mother. They await in the adjoining room." I forthwith requested Jack Mercieka to call all members of the David family in and to see that all were provided with chairs. When this had been accomplished, I set about questioning the applicant as to why he wished to visit the U.S., how long he and family intended to remain, how much money he had to ensure that he would be able to finance the return trip and to obviate any chance of their becoming a public charge in the United States.

At once it was obvious that the Davids had no intention of coming back to Turkey and that they could therefore not be considered as temporary visitors. Charlie MacVicker, who had been taking all this in, flashed a look at me as though he had smelled an unpleasant odor and resumed whatever work he had been in process of pretending to do.

During all this conversation, which had lasted much longer than the time it has taken to write it down, the other five members of the David family had sat motionless – the children, ranging in age from about seven to twelve, had been as good as gold. The wife, Rachel, a dark-haired Semitic beauty, looked at me with large and imploring eyes.

What became very quickly obvious was that either I gave visitor visas to this family or they would find themselves enmeshed in the lethal net of the Turkish Varlik – ruined financially and perforce, virtual prisoners of the State. I hesitated only a few seconds and then summoned Jack Mercieka to fingerprint the whole family and then proceed with the preparation of the U.S. Visitors' Visas.

About twenty minutes later the process had been completed and the documents adorned with their red seals had been handed to Mr. David. I then accompanied them to the street to bid them farewell. Before taking his leave, Mr. David took three one hundred lira notes from his wallet and tried to press the bills into my hand. "Please accept this money for your favorite charity," he said in a low tone to lessen the chance of our being overheard by anyone other than his family. Of course, this kind of gesture was normal in Turkey and I was hardly taken aback. I assured Mr. David that I had no intention of taking any money from him, that issuing the visas was in the line of my duty and that I hoped everything would work out for him and his family. "Besides, Mr. David," I added, "You will need a lot of money in seeking a new home. Let me know where you finally settle." Mr. David then decided to hit the iron while he saw it was hot. "Please, Mr. Consul, could you also help my wife's old uncle and aunt who live next to us. They, too, are in a difficult situation and will certainly die from the toils of forced labor if they cannot accompany us." I replied, "Why didn't your relatives accompany you today?" "Please excuse me, Mr. Consul, I did not dare come here with these two additional members of the family, but now your kindness has emboldened me to ask that you receive them as you did us and at your early convenience."

It is too late to make this rather long story short, but the following day I helped the elderly Jewish couple as well, despite the tedious, pretentious lecture of the goody-two-shoes, Charlie MacVicker.

Two months later, I received a letter from Johannesburg, South Africa; it was from Mr. David, who wrote that the U.S. visas had enabled his family and two relatives to reach that sanctuary. "Mr. Consul," wrote David, "You could never know what your understanding action meant to us. Without it, we would be lost souls in a hostile world." Well, that made me feel pretty good. And from that moment I tried to work according to the premise that if you can save one human life, this comes first, with only one exception, namely; the good of the U.S.A.

The reader may agree as this story unfolds, that the saving of a few lives has not harmed America though it might have driven a nail or two into the coffin of my career – but one cannot be certain on that score.

Three months following my arrival in Istanbul, Burton Y. Berry arrived to take over from Sam Honnaker. Mr. Berry was an attractive, dedicated, articulate Foreign Service officer whose arrival immediately brought marked changes in the pattern as well as in the volume of our work. He had been assigned to

Istanbul to create a so-called listening post, the purpose of which, as its name implied, was to obtain as much information as possible from German-occupied Europe. Listening posts similar to ours were in Madrid, Berne, Lisbon, and Stockholm, those capitals of still neutral European countries.

Each one of us junior officers was assigned a country, as follows: Yugoslavia, Bill Fraleigh; Romania, Roy Melbourne; Hungary, myself; Albania, Charlie MacVicker. In addition to our FSO staff, two experts were sent from Washington: Dr. Davis, a former teacher in the American College in Athens, to report on Greece, and Dr. Black, a former teacher from Sofia, to report on Bulgaria.

With the exception of Drs. Davis and Black, none of us had any knowledge of the language of our assigned country. Hence, we hired translator-secretaries to work with us so we were thus enabled to keep Washington informed as to significant press comments in the German-occupied areas. All information was of interest to the Department: editorial comment, economic data, any information as to the occupying army – in short, anything. My assistant was a young married woman, originally from Hungary, who knew no English, but was fluent in French. Hence, she translated excerpts from the Budapest papers into French and these provided the basis for my dispatches to Washington.

As I look back on this assignment, I am appalled at my total inexperience of those days. No one had trained me in the technique of how to draft effective reports. In addition to my duties with regard to Hungary, Mr. Berry assigned me to still another task. One day, a Colonel Radovich of the pre-war Yugoslav army showed up, having been sent from Washington to assist in our reporting on Yugoslavia. The colonel did not know any English beyond the ability to order a meal in a restaurant. But he did know French. As I was the only FSO fluent in that language I was assigned also to work with him, that is, to translate his weekly reports into English for Washington. This two-way task really kept me busy.

The problem relative to Yugoslavia was that Mihailovic, the rightist anti-German leader to whom Col. Radovic was loyal, was bitterly opposed to Tito, the Marxist, anti-German partisan leader. This situation deteriorated further when the British parachuted into the country a few liaison operators who worked closely with Tito, who from time to time fought against Mihailovic's men as well as against the Nazi army.

This situation did not come to a head until after my departure from Turkey in April, 1944, but the rumblings of this Yugoslav civil strife (i.e., rightists versus communist partisans) were already mentally audible as the harbingers of the storm which eventually brought a unity under Tito, the Marxist dictator; the expulsion of the Germans from the country and finally the execution of Mihailovic. Colonel Radovic, whom I came to know well, disappeared from the scene – in what way I never learned, as my theatre of operations was moved to the south and east.

It was Hungary that occupied at least eighty percent of my efforts from that late summer of 1942 to the spring of 1944. The Germans were gradually tightening their hold on Hungary and as that situation became apparent, it was increasingly difficult to find out what was going on in Budapest. Two of my most valuable sources of information on a steady basis were Hungarians. First, and by far the most important, was George Palozi Horvath, known to me and referred to by his British controllers as George Howard. We used to meet at least once a week and I obtained all sorts of interesting intelligence from him – much of it background, which, if it might be important to Washington, was passed on. George came from a well-off, land-owning family. Notwithstanding this very conservative upbringing, he was obsessed with seeking eventually to improve the lot of what he described as the landless peasants. George calls to mind the *limousine liberals* of today – what used to be called *parlor pinks* or *salon communists.* He did not think of himself as a Marxist, but rather as a socialist (with strong Marxist leanings, I might add). Of course it must be borne in mind that in those days of this assignment, the Soviets and the "gallant Soviet army" were our allies and I am sure that messieurs Burgess, MacLean and Philby, albeit Soviet agents, felt no tinge of guilt.

Immediately after the war, George Howard returned to Budapest and made an attempt to work closely with the Communist dominated government. It did not take long, however, for the Soviets to come to the realization that he was a loyal Hungarian and not a Soviet stooge. So when the so-called free elections were held in 1947, he began treading on thin ice and not long after, he was arrested and thrown into prison where for about a year he suffered the acute privation of solitary confinement. He was liberated during the short-lived Hungarian revolution of 1956 and was able to make his way to London. If he still lives, it is fervently hoped that he is now back in the beautiful land of his forefathers.

When I informed George in the early spring of 1944 that I was being transferred to Baghdad, he said he was damned if he was going to collaborate with my successor, which would allow the latter to benefit from what George felt I had done to bring about a close relationship with him and our Consulate General. I partially succeeded in talking him out of this state of mind.

The second, but equally distinguished Hungarian collaborator was Dr. Ferenc Vali, a professor of history on loan to the University of Istanbul. Not only did Dr. Vali supply me with most interesting books (in English) on Hungarian history, but also with

an occasional bottle of *Barás*, that excellent apricot brandy justly famous for its flavor, strength and propensity for mixing well with almost anything else. Dr. Vali ended up teaching in the United States – at Cornell among other universities. He died about 1983, respected in all academic circles with which he had had any contact.

There emerged three other men with whom I worked in close liaison: one Austrian and two Israelis. The Austrian, Dr. Otto Grabschied, a short, *Mr. Five by Five* type with a seemingly ever beaming smile and with sparse but carefully combed hair, appeared out of the blue one day in late 1942. As Austria was more closely connected to Hungary than to any of the other countries we were covering, and, as I was the only officer with at least some knowledge of German, this amiable academic was ushered in to see me. Though Dr. Grabschied's English brought to mind *Baron von Munchausen*, he was able to express himself quite fluently in our language, so my German was not put to a test. When I asked how I could be of service to him, the professor at once assured me, "It is I, Herr Consul, who place myself at your disposal. Is there any way I can assist the Americans to help bring about the freeing of my country from the Nazis?" "Just a minute, Herr Professor," I replied, "Let me think." And I thought for perhaps ten seconds while the professor sat motionless, hands folded, eyes lowered, perhaps as he had sat in class as a schoolboy many years before.

I then addressed Dr. Grabschied. "Would you be able to get me a detailed map of the Austrian railway system? It would be helpful to know which lines, apart from the obvious ones, are the most heavily traveled by the German military." The professor abruptly stood up, made a small bow and proffered his hand. "I will do my best, Herr consul, and I hope to see you soon." About ten days later, *Mr. Five by Five* reappeared, this time with a map showing every railway line within a radius of twenty miles or more of Vienna. The double-track sections were indicated, the bridges pinpointed, the heavily used single-track auxiliary lines were marked. In short, it appeared to be that the U.S. Air Force could use this information. A month after drafting this report, I received a kindly worded commendation from the State Department to the effect that the report under reference was very useful. About two months after my dispatch was sent to Washington, we read on Office of War Information announcement that the U.S. Air Force based in North Africa had heavily bombed the Vienna area. It was an important raid by "Flying Fortresses", but of course, we didn't know how effective the bombing had been.

The two Israelis (we did not refer to them by that name then; they were Jewish Palestinians) with whom it was a special pleasure to work were Teddy Kollek, head of the Jewish Agency in Turkey, and mayor of Jerusalem (1965-1993) after the founding of Israel in 1948. Teddy's assistant was Mr. Uberall, a Viennese, as was Teddy. After 1948, when Uberall entered the Israeli Foreign Service, he changed his name to Ehud Avriel, and lo and behold, his first post was Prague, where he was to live a couple of hundred yards down the road from my own house in the Barrandov section overlooking the Vltava River. He later served in the Israeli Knesset.

One morning in mid-1943, a diminutive and disheveled young man showed up in my office asking to see me – in private. He gave his name as Mr. George. I ushered him into a small room where we would be undisturbed and secure from being overheard. Mr. George drew his chair up closer to mine and said that he wanted to do what he could to assist the Allies, notwithstanding the fact that he was a Gestapo agent. "I am also Jewish," he hastened to add, and that really puzzled me. He went on to explain that the Nazis were holding his family hostage to ensure his prompt and effective compliance with their instructions. I stopped Mr. George right there and immediately telephoned Teddy Kollek to ask that he come over as soon as he could. Very soon he showed up and from then on he was the prime mover of our interesting relationship with Mr. George.

As Teddy Kollek was collaborating closely with the British Intelligence, of which "Gibby" Gibson was at that time chief in the Middle East, this situation was well covered; and very soon a stream of misinformation began to trickle back to Berlin.

One rather interesting and in a way, amusing facet of this collaboration came about when George and Uberall met with me in Cihangir. At that time the Allies had driven the Germans out of North Africa and the Sicilian invasion by Anglo-American forces was under way. George said to us, "I'll bet the Americans will be in Vienna by Christmas. Uberall and I expressed our serious doubts that this would take place that soon. George pressed his point, "I bet each of you five hundred Turkish lira that my projection will turn out to be the correct outcome and that indeed the American and/or British forces will be in Vienna by Christmas, 1943. Uberall and I looked at each other and then agreed to the bet, shaking hands with George to seal the wager.

Of course, the Nazis had instructed George to make this bet to elicit from us what were the ideas of Anglo-Americans as to Allied plans or capabilities. Just before Christmas, Uberall and I each collected the equivalent of about $200. Of course, neither my Jewish Agency friend nor I had any idea whatsoever as to when the Americans might liberate Vienna and we saw no reason why we should not make a little money off the Nazis that Christmas. This sum enabled me to buy a woven silver belt for mother.

Finally, George's situation vis-à-vis the Nazis became so precarious – in fact, he learned reliably that he was slated for liquidation during his next visit to Vienna – that Teddy Kollek arranged with the British to spirit him out to Palestine, hidden under a wagon-lit bunk.

In October, 1943, I received an unexpected phone call from a man whose accent was upper class English but who identified himself as a Hungarian. "You are Mr. Birge?" he enquired. I replied that I was indeed Mr. Birge. "My name is Colonel Andrassi and I would appreciate it very much if you could meet with me at any time convenient for you – preferably in your apartment. I at once suggested that we meet the following day for luncheon at one o'clock. I then instructed Colonel Andrassi:

"Meet me at Taksim Square. I will be wearing a beret. Just follow me at a discrete distance and I will make sure that you are behind me as I walk toward my apartment in Cihangir."

At the appointed time of a few minutes before one, I arrived at the square, waited a minute or two and then started to walk slowly toward my place, which overlooked the Golden Horn. I looked back as though to check my watch with the large Taksim Square clock and was satisfied that a tall, rangy stranger was indeed following me. I stopped at the door leading into my apartment house and my follower approached, put out his hand, bowed ever so slightly and introduced himself. "Colonel Adrassi. I am delighted to meet you, Mr. Birge."

Ireni, my amiable, but not too experienced Greek maid from Mytilene, had had time to prepare a simple but adequate meal. As was sometimes the case, she had neglected to cut off the chicken's head, but the rest was fine. First, we had a glass of sherry, which was obtainable at times, as Spain was a neutral. Then Colonel Andrassi remarked that he had an interesting proposition for me – one that might shorten the war and, he hoped, enable me to play an important part in bringing this about. The Colonel went on as follows: "Mr. Birge, will you accompany me to Budapest by train? I will already have made arrangements for a secret meeting between you and close associates of Admiral Horthy. I have already discussed this plan with these men, who would then escort you to a secret meeting with the Admiral, our president; though we do not use the latter title." The Colonel then went on to explain that he had very good reasons to believe that Hungary – that is, many of that country's leading men – wanted to free herself from Nazi domination as soon as possible and that the envisaged meeting between me, in charge of Hungarian affairs in the consulate General, and the Admiral might well lead to clandestine exchanges between Admiral Horthy and the American Secretary of State.

I listened, dumbfounded and hardly believing that the Colonel could think that I might fall in with the foolhardy plan he had just described. In my boyhood and youth, I had often been gullible and with a tendency to believe what I heard from impressive looking individuals. But this bait was obviously intended to play on what was hoped would be a vain man's desire for fame or perhaps adulation in the inner circles of his government.

It was obvious, of course, that Colonel Andrassi had been instructed to try to lure me into German-controlled territory where the Gestapo would take over, administer drugs and thereby hope to stage a publicized interview – or worse.

My reply to my luncheon guest was somewhat less direct: "Colonel Andrassi, I cannot believe that the German Abwehr would not know at once that I was on that train, for as you must be aware their agents are everywhere in Istanbul. Much as I would like to do anything possible to take your country out of the war as an ally of Germany, I have no intention of playing into the hands of the Nazis."

That subject having been disposed of, I asked my guest how it was that he spoke English so fluently as though he were the product of Eton and Oxford. He explained that during his father's tour of duty in London as a Secretary in the Hungarian Embassy during the 1930's he had in fact gone to a well-known public school and then studied two years at Cambridge. I then asked him to tell me something about himself and his very interesting and almost unbelievable reply unfolded as follows:

"A year and a half ago – that is, in the early spring of 1942, I was assigned to North Africa as a liaison officer on the staff of General Rommel. You may recall that a year before that, near the end of March 1941, Rommel launched his first offensive, drove into Egypt and left an isolated British garrison sealed off in Tobruk, and during the rest of that year the British managed periodically to bring supplies from Malta and Alexandria to the besieged port. Not long after my arrival at his headquarters, General Rommel called me to his GHQ and said he had a special assignment for me. 'What I want you to do, Andrassi, is to go to Cairo, use one of our safe houses, circulate around the night spots frequented by British and allied officers, get to know a few of the British secretaries – your perfect English accent should facilitate this – and endeavor to find out what the exact situation is at Tobruk – in brief – what is the strength in armored vehicles? Are there any shortages such as in ammunition and, most important of all, what is their troop strength and how is their water supply and how is it replenished?' When the General asked for any comments I might wish to make, I asked what kind of clothing I should wear and what kind of work I should claim to be doing in Cairo if asked for this information. 'Wear your regular Hungarian uniform; that will make you less conspicuous and also ensure that, if arrested, you would not be shot as a spy.' The General went on to point out that with so many different kinds of uniforms to be seen in Cairo, my Hungarian dress would not appear at all unusual. He finally convinced me as to the logic of wearing my uniform thus setting my mind at rest as to any danger of being shot as a spy. 'Day after tomorrow,' General Rommel continued, 'I will have you flown to within a few miles of Al Kawra, a town some fifty or sixty miles north of Cairo. One of our Egyptian friends will meet our plane and drive you to the railway station where you will take the next train to Cairo. There you will again be met by one of our men and taken to the safe house. When you think that you have obtained sufficient information for me, so inform our safe-house agent and he will inform you when to take a train back to Al Kawra from which town you will be conveyed back to me, first by car for a few miles and then by plane. In the event that you will not be able to gather the information I require, our man in Cairo will instruct you as to when you should leave, regardless.'"

During our talk in my apartment that early afternoon in October, 1943, Andrassi briefly described what took place in Cairo. No one questioned him as to his uniform. He met several junior officers and at least three English girls. Adequately supplied with money, he bought drinks for his new acquaintances and apparently had little trouble in obtaining most of the data General Rommel needed, notably the number and condition of the British 8th Army tanks and ammunition supply, both of which categories left much to be desired. The day after Andrassi informed Rommel's agent that he was ready to return he retraced his journey back to Al Kawra and thence to the agreed upon meeting place in the desert where a fighter-bomber was awaiting him. Colonel Andrassi pushed his chair back and upon rising, concluded his story: "The net result, Mr. Birge, of this Cairo adventure in a Hungarian uniform was that General Rommel, armed with this new intelligence, was able to capture Tobruk in the late spring of last year. If Hitler had provided half the men and supplies needed, Rommel would have captured all of Egypt."

As an afterthought to this story, it might be added that the key to a Rommel success in North Africa was not the capture of Tobruk, but the capture of Malta, for it was from that strategically located and tenaciously held island that the English were able to sink many of the Italian vessels bringing reinforcement supplies to Rommel. Indeed, it can be said that Rommel's eventual defeat was due just as much to RAF operations based in Malta as General Montgomery's attack at El Alemain.

No report about my assignment in Istanbul could be complete without writing about Archie Walker and Tom Whittemore. I met the latter first because he had a habit of coming to the Consulate to change dollars into lira through Jack Mercieka. Indeed, I also, as well as most of my American colleagues, changed dollars into lira at the prevailing black-market rate through Jack. Before launching into the Tom and Archie saga, another few lines about Jack are appropriate. He was short with a rather large head and with a seemingly perpetually questioning look. When I needed money, he would give me the number of a U.S. bank account into which I would instruct father to pay a given sum and Jack would give me the lira equivalent. This was against Foreign Service regulations, but all the Americans stationed there used this black market, including the ambassador and the consul general. As the cost of living gradually rose, it would have been difficult, indeed, to get by using the official exchange rate.

Back to Tom Whittemore. One day, a slender, distinguished looking gentleman in his early seventies showed up in my office and in a voice reminiscent of that of a Groton master, said, "How are you, Walter Birge? I have heard about you from the Ambassador and Mrs. Steinhardt. What does Jack report today as the exchange rate?" Just then Jack walked in. "What can you do for me today, Jack? How about 2.35?" "I am sorry, Mr. Whittemore, I have heard reports that Tobruk is in danger of capture. The best I can do is 2.25," replied Jack.

At the conclusion of these negotiations, Tom told me that he was staying in a villa on the Bosporus owned by a fellow Bostonian, Archie Walker, the manager of Mobil Oil Company for Turkey and the Balkans. Of course, he went on, the Balkans are no longer under his jurisdiction owing to the war. He went on to invite me on Mr. Walker's behalf, to lunch the following Sunday. As I had no car the only feasible way to get to Yeniköy, where Walker's villa was situated, was by boat, a trip that took about thirty-five minutes, including three stops, up the swiftly flowing Bosporus toward the Black Sea.

Walker's villa was impressive. It overlooked the anciently traveled waterway, and with the Black Sea only four or five miles distant, was cool even on hot summer days. Archie lived high on the hog, supplied, as he was, with a generous Mobil Oil salary, plus, it much later came to light, remuneration from the OSS. Of the latter connection, I knew nothing – nor did anyone else in those days, I am sure. He had four or five servants and the provender was excellent. Though he always served wine with luncheon, cocktails were never in evidence – that is, almost never, as we shall see.

Both Walker and Whittemore were obviously confirmed bachelors, much as a few Groton masters seemed to be. In those days, homosexuality was rarely the subject of loose talk as it is now. Some might have thought of these two men as "fags" (the term used then, now called "gays"), but I never had the impression that they were. Basically, they just did not like women, though of course they were charming and polite to those women who were prominent and influential – notably Mrs. Steinhardt and a handful of other wives of Allied diplomats.

Tom Whittemore of Boston was an archeologist and it was he who had revealed to the world the beautiful mosaics in Santa Sophia, treasures that since 1453 had been covered by plaster following the conquest of Constantinople by the Moslem Turks. One day in the mid 1930's, when Mustafa Kemal, the Ghazi (the latter term means *Conqueror of the Christians*), was still alive, Tom requested an audience with the exceptionally able and far-seeing ruler-dictator. "Your Excellency, based on a lifetime of research and on what I feel absolutely certain to be the case, the mosque which five centuries ago used to be known as Ayas Sophia, contained perhaps the finest mosaics in the world – now, alas, hidden by a cover of plaster. I ask permission to devote myself to bringing the walls of Ayas Sophia back to the radiant glory which they possessed prior to the time of Suleiman the Magnificent." Thus spoke the small, wiry and articulate archeologist from the Bay State.

The Ghazi, who, as already mentioned had already done much to bring his country into a twentieth century European way of life, by taking women out of the seclusion of purdah, by banning use of Arabic characters in favor of the Latin alphabet, by banning the fez as headgear and by numerous other actions which brought Turkey into the post World-War I era, now welcomed Tom's suggestion.

It was very simple; all the Ghazi did was suddenly decree that, as of the coming Friday, Ayas Sophia was no longer a mosque, but was thenceforth to be a museum, and Tom Whittemore was given a free hand to bring the Byzantine mosaics again to the light of day. So Tom went to work.

By the time I met this energetic, archeological ever-busy bee, most of his task had already been done. First, he had had to raise money, mostly in his native Boston, for the project; then the war brought problems. Finally, he returned to Istanbul to which city Archie Walker had recently moved. One day, Tom called on Walker, then about sixty years old, armed with a letter of introduction from a director of Mobil Oil. As Archie recounted the story, "Tom came with a letter. I invited him for tea and he has been in my house ever since."

Archie was an outstanding and enthusiastic bridge player, so it was natural that at least every other Sunday during the summer he would give a luncheon-bridge party to which the Steinhardts, and usually I as well, were invited. These were interesting occasions. Among those very often included in these parties were Mohammed-Bey, a Moslem Turk; Ghalib-Bey, a so-called Dolmei Turk (a Turk descended form a Turkish Jew who many years before had forcibly been converted to Islam), Mavromihailis, a Greek (his name meant *Black Michael*); and Kavafian, an Armenian. There were others including Admiral Kelley, the British Naval Attaché; Bob Kelly, the First Secretary of the U.S. Embassy; and Mr. Sokolnicki, the Polish ambassador and his wife.

During the non-summer seasons, the parties were smaller but were a welcome change from the Monday through Friday pastimes of spending evenings at the Taksim Casino night club, taking out girls, playing poker, etc.

As I look back on those functions held at Walker's villa almost a half century ago, those afternoons provided a welcome respite from the six-day work week of the war years.

Of those usual guests mentioned, Mr. Kavafian, the Armenian, was undoubtedly the finest bridge player I ever met – and an unusually kind, attractive man. Of course, wives accompanied husbands to these parties. Sometimes, we spoke French when playing and this was always the case with Kavafian. Other guests who will always remain vivid in my mind's eye were Ambassador and Mrs. Sokolnicki (pronounced Sokolnitsky), civilized, intelligent, well-educated people, who spoke perfect English and French. (Indeed, that was the case with every Pole I met during those war years). Whenever I think of this couple, a heart-warming episode comes to mind.

It will be recalled that when the Soviet army, in accord with the Molotov-Ribbentrop pact of August, 1939, invaded the eastern half of Poland and annexed that part of the country, they captured and imprisoned every Polish commission officer they were able to get their hands on. When the Germans invaded the USSR in June, 1941, anti-Soviet partisans led the Germans to a mass grave in the Katyn forest where they uncovered the bodies of some ten thousand Polish officers whom the Soviets had slaughtered not long after capturing them. Of course, the Nazis capitalized this and made sure that the whole world was informed about this horrible massacre.

One evening in late 1942, I was included in a large formal dinner given by the Turkish Minister of Foreign Affairs. The only reason for my having been included as one of the guests was that I was spending the days in Ankara and all American Foreign Service Officers at our embassy were invited. As chance would have it, Madame Sokolnicka (I use the feminine form of her last name here) found herself seated directly opposite the Soviet Ambassador. As it sometimes happens at functions of this kind, there came a moment of seemingly complete silence. In the midst of this void of sound, Madame Sokolnicka, in a voice laced with venom and barely-controlled anger that was clearly audible to everyone in that room, addressed the Soviet Ambassador, first in French, then in English: "Monsieur l'Ambassadeur, où sont mes dix mille officiers? - Mr. Ambassador, where are my ten thousand officers?" The Soviet diplomat glared at his country's accuser and said nothing, possibly because he had heard of the French proverb, *Qui s'excuse, s'accuse (he who excuses himself, accuses himself)*. From that day Madame Sokolnicka was our heroine, not only in our embassy, but also in the embassies of every country of the anti-Nazi alliance, save the Soviets.

Outwardly, however, most of the western diplomats seemed to forget about those ten thousand Polish officers who had been slaughtered by Stalin's command because they had been accused of being "socially dangerous and reactionary" – potential future leaders of an anti-Soviet nation, namely Poland.

So we found ourselves in a massive struggle, fighting to destroy the despicable Nazis and at the same time to save from defeat an equally despicable Soviet tyranny. And then came Stalingrad.

During the first half-year of my service in Turkey, the fortunes of the belligerents hung in the balance. For reasons logical to most Americans, we were confident of ultimate victory, but the neutrals - the Turks, the Swedes, the Spaniards, the Swiss, among others - were skeptical. Then came the decisive twin victories of Stalingrad and El Alamein in November, 1942. At that time, we saw the twin lights at the end of that tunnel of frightful war. We put aside thoughts of the Katyn massacre; most of us saw Stalin's ruthless policies as necessary to defeat the Nazis and we saw the soon-to-come train of Red Army successes and the retreat of the "Desert Fox" and his eviction from North Africa as certain portents of our eventual victory.

Some who read this tale of my adventures of so long ago may wonder how I fared relative to female relationships. When I left Laredo, I had no best girl, HM having written her *Dear John* letter. My father had commented that he hoped there would be such a girl, so that I would be less likely to make an unwise attachment abroad. How right his comment was, for there was a State Department rule, in effect during the war years, that any FSO wishing to marry a foreigner was obliged to request the Department's permission, this request to be accompanied by a letter of resignation.

I at first instinctively sought a potential wife, but this state of mind soon gave way to the logical realization that short-lived liaisons had to be the order of the day.

I had been in Istanbul only two or three weeks when I met Moka, a tall, shapely black haired, blue-eyed beauty of Circassian origin. I was attending the graduation ceremony at Robert College when I saw this young woman walking down the aisle of the college theatre to her seat. I lost no time in managing to be introduced to her and learned that she had been married for a year or so but was then divorced. For the next two or three weeks I saw her every day, but it soon became clear that a brief liaison was not what Moka had in mind. I was faced with a tough decision, and in spite of her being unusually attractive, I could not even think of writing the above mentioned letter, and so saw less and less of her. I later met two other Turkish-

Cirsassian beauties during my tour of duty in Turkey - Nevin and Rezan - the former a tall blond, and the latter, a very sexy, dark charmer.

By the time I left the golden Horn for Baghdad, I was able fully to understand what had been in the mind of Mohammed Ali, the Turkish Sultan's Representative in Egypt in the 1840's when he decided that he should *embellir cette race égyptienne* (beautify this Egyptian race) by importing two thousand Circassian girl slaves to be married off to the young men of prominent families. And he succeeded.

Then there was the beautiful White Russian woman of about thirty, Alexandra, who was divorced from a Turk and had a little daughter. Alexandra did not have a lot of sex appeal, as it was called then, but she was elegant, classy and distinguished. We got on well and under other circumstances and at another time I would very likely have come to have serious intentions about a commitment. The main problem of the situation was that the little daughter's Turkish father vowed that he would never allow his child to be taken out of Turkey. Not only that, but he also insisted that she be brought up as a Moslem. It was obvious, therefore, that if Alexandra married a foreigner, she would be faced with a painful dilemma.

One day, an older and gossipy female friend remarked to me that according to her grapevine sources, Alexandra had told one of her White Russian friends in confidence that she expected me to propose marriage. The scenario of getting this mother and child out of Turkey, coupled with the almost certain resignation from the Service, forced me to bow out of this situation before the entanglement became more emotionally charged. The fact was that I was not – quite yet – in love with this outstanding woman; nor was I sure that she was in love with me. Hence, why take on a seemingly unsolvable problem?

Still, at age twenty-nine, I was a romantic, and physically and emotionally in need of the companionship of a woman. Toward the end of my two years in Istanbul, I did narrow down my activity in the romantic field to Rezan, the sexy Circassian. Tom Whittemore met her once and ventured the following one-line comment: "Rezan would have been perfect in the harem of Suleiman the Magnificant, but she is not for you." I agreed with Tom.

We had an interesting group of officers in our Consulate General "listening post". All were bright, attractive and dedicated. First of all, as already mentioned, there was Burton Berry, articulate, charming, very hard working and a born leader. Another was Bill Fraleigh – handsome, with dark hair usually falling over his brow, and rather secretive and quiet. He shared an apartment with Berry. A few whispered that these two had *panzoid* tendencies (i.e., were like *pansies*, an old expression for homosexuals). I never agreed with this rumor, but rather thought that they just got on well and enjoyed each other's company. I do know that just prior to my arrival, Bill had had an unhappy love affair with an English girl who was a secretary in the British Consulate and who had been sent out of Turkey for reasons unknown.

Then there was Roy Melbourne; very serious-minded, rather dull, but always pleasant and cooperative, an assiduous worker, and a decent sympathetic character. He occasionally took a girl out. Lee Metcalf was one of my two favorites. He was lean and about my height (6'1"), almost always in a jovial mood, and an amusing mimic. This Texan loved the girls, but pretty well narrowed his attentions to Yoli, an Italian Levantine. Whenever I went to a nightclub, usually Taksim Casino, it was almost always in Lee's company. At that time he was only a clerk. After the war, however, he was transferred to Bucharest, was promoted to FSO rank and ended up as a Foreign Service Inspector. In retrospect, Lee is one of the finest friends I ever had.

All that has been said about Lee applies pretty much to Herb Cummings. He was married, but had left his wife back in Pittsburgh. To his credit, Herb never once dated any woman during our time in Istanbul. He took his marriage seriously, but did not discuss it. Nevertheless, he almost always accompanied Lee and me to our favorite haunt, the Taksim Casino. Herb had a keen sense of humor and was thoroughly decent. He was very athletic and had been an amateur boxer. One day, an Armenian acquaintance, Vahram Berispek, who worked in the Chilean Consulate, was telling me about what a great boxer he was and to stress his point, he assured me that he would be able to knock me down within one minute. Looking back on the training in boxing that I had received at ages nine to eleven at the hands of Mr. MacIntire in Greenwich, I accepted the challenge. I lost no time in telling Herb about the upcoming match, so he began coaching me in the Consulate basement. Despite by boyhood prowess in fisticuffs, I had a lot to learn and our training sessions were given added impetus by the knowledge that I had a sizeable bet of four hundred lira (close to $200) riding on the outcome of the bout with my Armenian friend.

About a week before the day scheduled for the Berispek-Birge fight, the Chilean Consul General heard about it and forbade his assistant to go through with his plan "to extract several hundred lira from his American colleague by means of flooring him within one minute." And that was that.

It has already been mentioned that we had to work a six-day week in accord with a State Department regulation put into effect late in the summer of 1942. Hence, as can be imagined, Sunday was even more of a special day than it had been prior to the start of the wartime workweek. Every now and then, however, we were allowed to take half of Saturday off and in that connection a memorable day comes to mind.

One of the attractive young women I knew, so far not mentioned, was a Moslem Turk, Hayrieh. Her family was apparently well off for they owned a forty foot two-master schooner. One day in June, 1943, during a rendezvous in my apartment, she suggested that I persuade two of my American colleagues to join her and two girl friends for an afternoon excursion on the Sea of Marmora. Roy and Lee accepted her invitation and planned to meet in my office at exactly noon on that Saturday.

Disaster almost struck, however. As mentioned before, the Steinhardts occasionally invited me to accompany them on Saturday outings on the embassy launch. As the fates conspired that day, my phone rang at about 11:30 am, and Jack Mercieka, whom we referred to as *The Maltese Falcon,* (Tom Whittemore said he was "a pair of eyes without a body") got up to answer the phone. Just as he was about to pick it up, I told him to say to whomever it was that I was out and would return in the early afternoon. As I had feared, the caller was Mrs. Steinhardt, who explained to Jack that she must get hold of me as I was wanted for a picnic on *The Hiawatha.* Jack was scared of this often-imperious woman, but summoned up the convincing voice of which he was capable even when telling a whooper, and told her I was out.

As soon as Jack hung up, I told him to inform Roy and Lee to meet me at the funicular that leads down to the port. And then I tore out of there, fearful lest the bossy ambassadress descend to my office to make sure that I was indeed not there, for to have failed to accept an ambassadorial invitation would have been embarrassing and unwise. And so I went on a memorable cruise on that perfect June day. The luncheon Hayrieh and her friends had prepared was appetizing and the schooner's captain efficiently handled the boat, though I occasionally took the wheel. I can still see the brilliant blue sky and feel the gentle waves of the deep blue Sea of Marmara, where Greek galleys had sped on their appointed ways half a millennium BC, and where the Turkish crescent had swept away the cross of Byzantium in the mid-fifteenth century. And even to this day, and to that day of our excursion, Greek and Turks have periodically been at swords-points – at least in talk and point of view, if not actually in battle.

At the time of my service in Istanbul there remained about a hundred thousand ethnic Greeks in that city, but Asia Minor was almost pure Turk. The Ghazi had seen to that. In the post-war years of the early 1920's, the Greeks were expelled from Smyrna and all 250,000 of them were shipped to Greece or to the Greek islands of the Aegean – this despite the fact that Greece had been an ally of England, the United States, France, and Turkey, one of the Central Powers. But in retrospect, this could be said to have made sense. Some exchanges, even involving the uprooting of peoples, often work out fairly well.

The only members of our "listening post" staff who had a car in those days were Bill Fraleigh and Earl Taylor, the Commercial Attaché, both of whom had arrived before America's entry into the war when it had been far less complicated to ship a vehicle from one neutral country to another. Bill's car was a tiny Fiat two-seater, but Earl Taylor drove around in a chauffeured sedan. The rest of us either took taxis or public transport on ferries or trains. It was in connection with riding a ferry that the following experience took place. About two months after my arrival and following a small luncheon at Archie Walker's, I boarded a ferry bound for the Istanbul docks. There were very few passengers on board that late Sunday afternoon in that parlous summer of 1942 - that time when the fortunes of war seemed to hang in the balance, and we wondered if the Turks would remain neutral.

I was seated on a wooden bench on the upper deck, aft. Across from me was seated a young officer of the Turkish Army. Seeking to make myself a little more comfortable, I placed my feet on the bench directly opposite, but at least six feet away from the officer. The latter apparently felt that this was not allowed or perhaps was a sign of lack of respect for an officer during a time when the country was under martial law. Or perhaps he was just in an officious mood. In any case, he gestured with this hand that I should remove my feet from the bench. I did not obey this implied command, being of the opinion that where I placed my feet was nothing of this officer's business, even though, under that regime of above-mentioned martial law, civilians were required to obey any command uttered by an officer. I had not been suitably indoctrinated, nor had any of my colleagues. When I paid no attention to this officer's gestured command, he knocked my feet off the bench, whereupon I arose, as did the officer and there ensued a verbal exchange in Turkish and English. I then resumed my seat and the officer went below for three or four minutes.

It very soon became apparent that this young officer had communicated by radio with the police at the Istanbul dock, for as soon as I stepped off the gang plank upon our arrival in Istanbul, I was taken into custody by two policemen, who, accompanied by my officer acquaintance, marched me to the district police headquarters. There the chief motioned me to a seat and then patiently listened to the complaint of the irate officer – this, undoubtedly having to do with my lack of respect for a Turkish officer, and failure to obey his order.

The chief, obviously a veteran of many years dating back to the era of Abdul Azziz, asked to see my papers of identification. When he saw my American diplomatic passport, he flashed an understanding and slightly apologetic half-smile in my direction and then proceeded to let the young officer know, firmly, but also tactfully (I knew enough Turkish to gather this), that diplomats were not subject to martial law and had always to be treated with respect. The chief then informed me in French that I was free to go and he offered a dignified apology. I then turned to the by-then chagrined young officer and suggested that I give him a lift in a taxi if he was traveling in my direction. He accepted my proffer of reconciliation and when we were in the cab he not only apologized in French, but also started to weep, so touched, he stammered, that I should extend the hand of friendship under the circumstances. So, I said to myself, I have avoided a contretemps that might have contributed to bringing Turkey into the war on the side of the Nazis – this, of course, in my jocular mind's eye.

One afternoon during the spring of 1942, Burton Berry called me into his office. "Walter, I want you to do me a favor. Archbishop Spellman of New York is coming here for a short visit and I want you to act as his aide while he is here. He is slated to visit the University of Istanbul, the French Lycée, and to have lunch with Monsignor Roncalli, the Papal Delegate."

On the appointed day, Berry and I met the Archbishop at Hyderpasha Station on the Asiatic side of the Bosporus and we took the ferry back to Istanbul. The visit was uneventful except for two interesting events, one of which was to have marked significance many years later. The first day of the visit, we kept the Archbishop's appointment to call at the university. The entire faculty was assembled to meet this important dignitary of the Roman Catholic Church, and the Dean gave a short speech thanking our visitor for having traveled so far and during a frightful war to visit their city. While these remarks were being made, I saw Dr. Grabschied standing in the far end of the room and almost completely obscured by the men standing in front of him. I saw this as an excellent opportunity to do something that might enhance his prestige. After the Archbishop acknowledged the Dean's welcoming words, I raised my hand during the ensuing moment of relative silence. "Dean Menemengoglu," I said, "I am delighted to notice that one of your faculty members is the distinguished Viennese professor, Dr. Grabschied. He is, I am sure, a great credit to your fine university." Dr Grabschied smiled and modestly lowered his head. The next day, he telephoned me to voice his thanks and to report that several of his Turkish colleagues had congratulated him on his well-deserved reputation.

The important and certainly never-forgotten episode of the Archbishop's visit was the luncheon with Monsignor Roncalli, the Papal Delegate. The reader will note that some twenty years later, Monsignor Roncalli became Pope John XXIII. At that luncheon, aside from Archbishop Spellman, the Americans present were Burton Berry, Bill Fraleigh, Jack Seager of the OSS and I. Spellman had studied in Rome with the Monsignor and they had become close friends. I well recall that when we arrived at the Papal Delegate's residence, we noted a bust of Mussolini adorning the outside portico. Monsignor Roncalli came outside to greet his old friend, Francis Spellman, and after the warm expressions of delight, mutually exchanged in Italian, Spellman called attention to the bust of the Italian dictator and in a low voice assured the Papal delegate that Benito was not even half the man that Roncalli was himself, and asked why he had to display a likeness of that pompous leader. In a still more hushed tone, but still audible to me as I was standing just behind the Archbishop, Roncalli replied that his heart did not in this case agree with political dictates.

Before leaving Istanbul for home, Archbishop Spellman asked whether I would like him to call my parents upon his return to New York. I naturally expressed my warm agreement with this thoughtful gesture. A few weeks later, father and mother wrote that they, of course, had been delighted to receive the call assuring them of my good health, but that the Irish maid had answered the phone and upon being informed that the Archbishop, Francis Spellman, was himself on the line, had dropped the instrument. When mother had asked Mary what was wrong and was she ill, Mary had replied, "Faith, Madame, 'tis the Archbishop himself!" From that day forth Mary was a very industrious and devoted helper, for indeed, as she said, she had seen my parents move a step closer to the Lord and his angels.

I suppose that of all the people met in Istanbul, the one who impressed me the most was Archie Walker. We were not at all alike; neither did we share more than one or two interests. He was, however, intelligent and well educated, had a dry sense of humor and gave the impression that he could quickly and accurately judge others. Moreover, he had good taste. Istanbul would have been far less enjoyable had it not been for those many pleasant Sunday afternoons in his villa. I shan't forget his last farewell a few days before I left for Baghdad. "Goodbye, Walter. You are my son." And that was perhaps the finest compliment I have ever received.

The Archie Walker experience that comes especially to mind was the Thanksgiving Day dinner to which Archie had invited the American members of the Consulate General staff. At that time of the year, the Steinhardts were in Ankara, so they were not included. Earl Taylor offered to drive Roy, Lee, Herb and me to Archie's villa in Yeneköy, so there were five of us, plus the Turkish chauffeur. Just before arriving at Walker's villa, Earl told the driver to pull over to the side of the road, right next to the Bosporus, which was on our right. "I have brought along a shaker of martinis," announced Earl. "As you know, Archie never serves cocktails and I'll be damned if I will start a Thanksgiving dinner without first having a festive drink." So we spent the next ten minutes or so polishing off the contents of that shaker.

A few minutes later, when the five of us, feeling very jolly from our roadside cocktails, walked into Walker's large living room, there stood our host with a thin smile of greeting, stirring a huge shaker of martinis held on a silver tray by his head butler. So that got us well started on that memorable Thanksgiving.

At table on that November day, I sat next to Tom Whittemore. The only unfortunate note of that occasion was that instead of having someone carve the enormous turkey in the dining room, the butlers began carrying in our plates, each laden with square chunks of bird – so the traditional and proper carving of that fowl was not to be. "They've massacred that bird," Tom whispered in my ear. Despite that departure from usual practice, all went well, and after dinner, Tom read aloud about Thanksgiving dinners of long ago, not about the first feast of the Pilgrims, but rather about early nineteenth century times. Exiled as we were from home, we enjoyed this reading in Tom's stentorian, Boston Brahmin tones. Such an occasion would have had no great significance in Massachusetts, but in the Turkey of 1943, it was moving.

Few of us, if any, who worked at our Consulate General "listening post" during those years will likely forget Powhatan Baber – called Tan – who was a clerk in our embassy in Ankara. The ambassador as already mentioned spent a good part of each summer in Istanbul, as did almost all the other ambassadors, where the climate during that season was more pleasant than in central Anatolia. Those summer visits were not vacations in the generally accepted sense, for Mr. Steinhardt in effect moved his office to our Consulate General building and he brought a small staff with him. And that was how we came to know Tan Baber, as he was one of the clerks who worked in the Ambassador's summer office for three or four weeks.

Our occasional diversions during summer evenings was to visit the Taksim night club where an orchestra played American jazz, and *artistes,* mostly Hungarian or Bulgarian semi-beauties, would sing and then make themselves available to dance with the male patrons who might be English, American, German, Swedish, Italian, or other nationals stationed in Istanbul.

Tan was an accomplished clarinet player and we lost no time in making this known to the orchestra conductor who very soon asked him to join the orchestra to play the clarinet part to American popular dance tunes he knew. Tan enjoyed doing this and those of us who were with him on those evenings were especially touched to hear our friend bring some of America to us who were four thousand miles from home.

The war seemed to come much closer during that same summer and fall of 1943 when two flights of *Flying Fortresses* took off from their base in Southern Italy in an attempt to destroy, or at least severely damage, the Romanian oil refineries at Ploie°ti.

The first we learned of this raid was when about a dozen American flyers were rescued by Turkish patrol boats near the coast of Asia Minor. Several U.S. planes had been shot down or so severely damaged by anti-aircraft or German fighter plane fire that they had been forced to let down into the Aegean Sea. As Turkey was still a neutral country, these flyers were interned and the wounded boys were hospitalized in Istanbul. I was asked immediately to call at that hospital to ascertain that they were being well taken care of and to enquire whether they were in need of anything special.

Before the end of that year, we managed to smuggle a few of these men, who were by then recovered, to Lebanon. Our OSS men were the prime movers in this action, which involved hiding the internees under berths in the wagon-lit cars of the Taurus Express. Those flyers who did not get out of Turkey in this way were repatriated to their units following Turkey's entry into the war in the summer of 1944.

As can be imagined, chrome was a highly prized, almost necessity for the Germans, relative to the manufacture of stainless steel. Turkey had important mines of chrome ore so one can understand why the OSS sought to find a way to slow down or stop the shipments of the highly prized ore to Germany.

In my capacity of reporting officer for German-occupied Hungary (and sometimes Austria and Yugoslavia as well), I did not become directly involved in the action to slow the output of the chrome ore mines. But two of my friends of the OSS did get involved and succeeded, with the help of a few under-cover Turkish helpers, in cutting the steel cables used to convey the ore out of the deep open-pit mines.

As can be imagined, Turkey was, and had long been, quite an exporter to Germany, not only of chrome ore, but of other products as well, notably cotton waste, which was used in the textile and other industries. Of course, the Germans also bought Turkish tobacco, but we did not worry much about that. The best way to prevent, or at least cut down on, Turkish exports of cotton waste was through our policy of preclusive buying, by which we simply outbid the Germans and either had our purchases warehoused or exported to an allied country.

The member of our staff most directly involved in this operation was Earl Taylor (of the martini shaker). As Commercial Attaché, he was charged with paying exorbitant sums to a few cotton waste producers. And this situation eventually got Earl into trouble.

I had already left Istanbul when I heard what took place. Someone leaked the information that one or more of the cotton waste sellers had for some time been paying under-cover bribes or "commissions" to Taylor to persuade him to ensure that his preclusive buying activity ensured them (the sellers) very high profits. It may well have been that a frustrated German would-be buyer might have leaked the tip off, or it might have been one of the Turkish sellers who was aware of the situation but had refused to pay a commission to the U.S. Commercial Attaché.

At that time, the U.S. Foreign Service had a much-feared inspector, Merle Cochrane. During the summer of 1944, Cochrane made a special trip to Istanbul for the purpose – it was later learned – of investigating the facts of this highly irregular situation. It did not take him long to implicate Earl Taylor. As one of the embassy wits commented at the time, "It takes a Merle to nail an Earl." The Department, however, apparently did not want an open scandal during the war, so Taylor, who had been able to afford a chauffeur as well as a luxuriously appointed apartment on a modest salary, was quietly recalled to Washington and allowed to resign. As far as we knew, based on fairly reliable scuttlebutt, he kept the fruits of his labor, which had been stashed away in a Swiss bank.

More now about Merle Cochrane. He was big, rather fleshy and, at first sight, seemingly jovial; but this was no Falstaff. He was a good listener; indeed, his small, light blue eyes did not wander, but rather bored into you with a hint of menace.

The first visit of Cochrane on a normal tour of inspection took place in the spring of 1943. He arranged for each officer of our Consulate General to invite him for a meal at the officer's apartment. Ireni (my Greek maid) outdid herself for once and Merle enjoyed the luncheon tremendously, devouring two portions of chocolate cake. His reputation as a trencherman did not suffer on that occasion or at any of the other meals he took with my colleagues.

He did not ask too many searching questions of me, but he must have gathered that I would have had a difficult time indeed to have lived on even my modest scale had I changed money at the official rate of exchange. Bit by bit, he extracted information from the local employees as well as from us FSO's. We had an able and very attractive Greek female clerk, Maria Lambros, with whom Cochrane had several lengthy talks. There was little that Maria did not know about our out-of-the-office ways of life. She did not have to know details, but I am sure that she had a good idea as to Lee Metcalf's and my proclivity for taking out quite a variety of unattached young women and that this bit of intelligence was passed on to Merle – not with any idea of causing trouble, but just to make pleasant conversation with this convivial man and possibly to stress the fact that we probably gained useful information through these contacts.

I was not under the impression that Cochrane was trying to find out anything specific about any of us. It was only that he was a ferret by nature. It soon came to light that he was more interested in what was going on in Ankara than in our operations in Istanbul. For he well understood that good or bad influences must inevitably stem from the top – that is, from the Ambassador, and so he spent at least twice as long in Ankara as in our port city.

It eventually became clear that Merle Cochrane was bothered by the currency black market in which all of us FSO's were involved to a greater or lesser extent, and we all assumed that the Ambassador was heavily involved. I, for one, would have had a very thin time and could hardly have gotten along had I not changed money, usually through Jack Mercieka. Of course, the Ambassador changed far larger sums, as did his Counselor of Embassy, Bob Kelly, a very able and attractive Bostonian. I am not sure just what it was that estranged Steinhardt from Cochrane, but by the time the latter left, they were no longer on speaking terms. This was aside from the Earl Taylor business, which did not involve the Ambassador at all, inasmuch as Taylor's operations were entirely in Istanbul.

The ill feeling between the Steinhardt and Cochrane reached such a pass that at his next post (Prague) the Ambassador passed the word to the Department that if Cochrane was sent to his post, he would not receive him, and I was brought into this situation as will be explained in due course. What especially angered Mr. Steinhardt was that Cochrane reported something detrimental about Bob Kelly that prevented his promotion. Indeed, Kelly should have ended his career as an ambassador, but he never attained that rank. When I look back on the Chiefs of Mission with whom I came in contract, none surpassed Robert Kelly in intelligence, imagination, education, or capability.

As is well known, Hitler liquidated some four to six million Jews in his extermination camps of which the most infamous was Auschwitz in Poland. Until near the end of the war, however, only scant information, based mainly on rumors, about his extermination of most of the Jews in Poland and Germany as well as a large percentage of those in Czechoslovakia, Holland, Hungary, and Romania, had reached England and the United States. As chance would have it – that, coupled with the courage, determination and imagination of a young Jewish man, I was among the earliest to hear first-hand about what was going on in possibly the most notorious of these camps – Auschwitz.

As my reporting on German-occupied Hungary often involved less day to day work than that which occupied some of my colleagues, Burton Berry instructed the local clerks to bring all miscellaneous callers to me. One day in mid-1943, Jack Mercieka brought to my office a rather young man seemingly in his early twenties. He had red hair, was about five feet, six in height, and I could not imagine what this person might want with me. I was not long kept in suspense. "What can I do for you?" I asked in English. His reply was in a mixture of French and German. "Est-ce que vous pourriez me parler en français – oder Deutsch?" he asked in a low voice. I replied that I spoke both languages but was much more fluent in French. When I had enquired as to his nationality, where he came from, and why he wanted to see an American official, the following most unusual and hair-raising tale emerged. My visitor's name, as I recall, was Jacob Liebowitz. Jacob grasped the arms of his chair and his eyes scarcely left mine as the tale of his adventures unfolded.

"I landed in Istanbul yesterday having come from the Romanian port of Constanta on a Turkish freighter. My home was in Liberec, Czechoslovakia, where I grew up and lived with my parents and a sister. As Nazi controls in Bohemia were relatively loose, we thought we were relatively safe there. Then, after June, 1941, when the Germans invaded the Soviet Union, our travails began. We were ordered to leave our comfortable home and then were transported to Terezin, where we had to remain, for that town was now a sort of ghetto – not rigidly controlled, but a Jewish internment city nevertheless. Food was less plentiful than had been the case in Liberec, but not a serious problem.

This confining, rather dull, and often frightening existence fraught with uncertainty about our future continued for over a year and a half. Then began the occasional, but obviously well organized deportations to unknown destinations. There had been originally abouot fifty thousand of us Jews in Terezin, but before long our numbers began gradually to dwindle. Our own deportation and that of our neighbors were put off, apparently, because my father, being a skilled accountant, was deemed useful to the German authorities, as he kept neat books containing the names and addresses of everyone living in our section of the town – a list which was continually being either depleted or augmented.

As the deportations continued, some of us naturally sought to find out where they were being taken. "To work in the munitions factories," came the ready replies, "and the living conditions next to those work places are much better than here, so do not worry."

Well, finally our day of reckoning, if you can call it that, came. It was on a cold day last February (1943). That morning there were loud shouts in the streets, "Heraus, heraus, alle heraus." And all families living in our section – that is, about three blocks, were ordered to leave their apartments and to form in orderly ranks outside. "Wohin gehen wir?" my father asked a German *feldwebel* (sergeant). "Arbeitsdienst" (work-detail), was the reply; and we were then marched off to a railway siding about a kilometer from the main gate of the town, where awaiting our arrival was a long train of about forty freight cars, its locomotive with steam up as though impatiently ready to start its journey eastward.

The German detachment in charge of this operation speedily and with efficiency apparently stemming from repeated practice, loaded us about fifty to a car. The heavy bolt on our car door was locked and that train of fearful destiny bearing two thousand souls began to move slowly ahead toward our unknown fate.

Our car, originally intended for non-human freight, had one small partly opened window through which frigid but life-sustaining air entered. There was a primitive latrine beside which stood a fairly large water can. That was all.

While very crowded and frightfully uncomfortable, most of us were not overly worried at the outset of that long, jolting three-day journey eastward. Our progress was painfully slow and several times a day our train came to a stop, presumably on a side track, thus to allow the passage of military trains moving eastward or trains bearing wounded solders back to Germany from the Russian front.

During some of those stops our car door was opened just long enough to have our water can filled and three loaves of black bread thrown in. As almost everyone had brought a little food with him, hunger was not our main problem. Rather, we suffered owing to our confined space which was a fearsome prison of stench, cold, continual discomfort, moaning and increasing fear as to what the future had in store; and as that journey continued, we began to fear the worst as to an ultimate fate. Yet there were a few who indulged in a false bravado when we finally arrived at our destination and slowly pulled into the station at Oswiecem – Auschwitz, as the Germans called the place.

Our car door was unbolted and even that pale late winter sun, which we had not seen in a seeming eon of time, was welcome. "Jedermann aus! (everybody out) This is a labor camp", announced the officer in charge of this detraining operation. We believed him; and to an extent, he was telling the truth. There was indeed plenty of labor – for some.

Our captors then began separating the men from the women, the seemingly strong from the infirm, and the young from the old. During that process, I lost my mother and sister forever. As both my father and I were strongly built and obviously in good health, our temporary fate was that of joining the rock-splitting squads. That was exhausting work, but we were at least alive, though in days which seemed to have no end and nights of rest which were all too short.

Then father was seriously injured when a falling rock crushed his left foot. He was then considered of no further use to the Third Reich and on the third morning following the accident, father's name was called out, along with the name of three others whose health and strength were obviously failing, and ordered to remain behind instead of reporting to the rock-splitting squad. I soon learned from one of our Polish "capos" that my father and the others had been taken to the "showers" or execution chamber. That was when I made up my mind to escape or perish. So I began to plan how I could overcome any obstacles that might lie ahead.

It was clear that the first impediment in the way to freedom was the double barbed wire fence that surrounded the huge camp. My first priority, therefore, was to take advantage of the twenty-minute free time after roll call following the simple evening meal and prior to being marched to our bunkhouses. During that brief interval, we could either sit or stand quietly or walk around in a restricted area.

During that so-called free time, I inspected the section of the inner fence that was closest to our roll-call area and I found that there were four strands of wire which had not yet been electrified, but soon would be, according to one of my fellow prisoners who worked in the camp power-house. I noted that the bottom strand in one section of the fence not far from where we assembled every evening for roll-call was just slightly higher – two inches or so – than the lowest strand in other sections of the fence. I next thought of asking my friend, the electrician, if he might be able to obtain for me a small tool such as a screwdriver that I might use in burrowing under that bottom strand of wire. But then I gave up that idea; the tool might be missed or my friend might talk to the wrong person.

On the very next day after dropping that idea, a fortuitous find led again in the direction of my salvation for partly hidden by a recently split rock, I found a small trowel-like implement used for placing dirt between stones for the road we were building. I quickly hid that tool upon my person.

Then, two days later, the salvation of my escape project and almost surely of my life, came all of a sudden. Every prisoner in our large camp group who was wearing leather shoes was ordered to take them off and throw them on to a pile that providentially was situated about half way between our evening roll-call area and the wire fence. Within about twenty minutes that mound of leather footwear was at least ten feet high. I at once determined to take advantage of this providential situation and during roll call, after calling out my name at the customary time, I quietly slipped out from my place in the rear rank and, with lowered head, I quickly ran on silent bare feet to the pile of shoes. The distance to that welcome mound was perhaps a hundred feet or a bit more, which span I covered while the tower searchlights were pointing away from that area and immediately began to burrow into the sanctuary of all those shoes. Then there was silence for I was now covered by the leather footwear previously worn by some two thousand fellow Jews almost all of whom were destined to perish - a fate which I was determined would not be my own.

I lay perfectly still in my shoe-house for what seemed like at least an hour but was almost surely less. I then very slowly began searching the best I could for footgear which would fit my average size feet. At length I came upon a stout pair that felt about right and then slowly moved back to the edge of the pile so that I could perceive what the situation was. No alarm was sounding and all was quiet. The sooner I started my big move toward freedom, the better. No one was in sight, but the rotating tower searchlights presented ever-present danger. As each full rotation lasted about two minutes, however, I would have little difficulty in reaching the first barbed wire fence during the dark interval. The light shone on my general area and then passed on; and I quietly ran toward the fence section through which I had planned to pass.

The God of Jacob was again with me, for some five meters from the section with the slightly higher bottom strand, there was a small roll of wire about a third of a meter high which had presumably been placed there preparatory to the electrifying process probably scheduled for the following day. For the next fifteen minutes I worked at digging away some of the earth beneath that bottom strand during the intervals of darkness and then crawled back to hide behind the coil of electrification wire just before the searchlight beam returned and until it passed again.

Within about twenty minutes, I managed to slide under that lower wire, an inch at a time, careful to prevent any barbs from catching in my clothes. My newly acquired shoes, I had pushed across ahead of me. My skinny build was a big advantage and owing to the meager meals of the camp, I was even thinner than usual. But now there remained the second barbed wire fence, which I could not yet see except during the brief intervals of light, but which I knew was about fifty meters ahead. Then still another near-miracle occurred. It began to rain while I lay prone waiting for the searchlight to pass. I decided to take full advantage of the storm by waiting to see whether it would rain harder and thus bring a sheet of water between the passing light and possibly vigilant guards and me. Then it did rain much harder as though with a benevolent vengeance directed at my erstwhile captors, but with friendly intent for me. Within two minutes the deluge entirely shielded me from the tower lights and I ran forward carrying my shoes. At the second fence, I found that the bottom strand was so low that burrowing beneath it was out of the question, so I pressed down on that lowest strand and at the same time pushed up on the strand above, thus enabling me to get first one leg and then the other to the other side; then I slowly worked the rest of my body through, again taking care not to become caught fast by the wicked barbs.

Within five minutes, the rain still protecting me but soaking me as well, I was on the other side of the fence, so I now put on the shoes. I could hardly believe my good fortune at having taken the first all-important step to freedom. Had the space between the two lowest strands of wire been less, I might not have been able to pass that barrier. I thanked the careless stringers of that barbed wire. Now, still hidden by the pouring rain. I ran ahead to the perimeter road. What now?

I crossed the road, thus reaching the forest on the far side, sank down to the wet ground beneath a tall fir tree and took stock of my situation. I had managed to bring with me a few pieces of bread which would keep me going for a day or two, but soon I would have to either forage for food in barns where apples, potatoes, or cabbage might be stored or beg for help from a peasant. Travel would have to be mostly by night – not through forests where I would surely lose my way, but along roads where I could hope to be guided by signs and from which I could easily run to safety at the first sight of any approaching vehicle's lights.

During the ensuing two weeks of perilous travel, I was probably saved by my red hair, blue eyes and what many have told me was my non-Jewish look; for, as you may have heard, many of the Polish people are anti-Semitic.

When the weather was clear (fortunately, most of the time), I looked for the North Star and made my way south and east toward what I hoped would be the Romania border. Once I did find some apples in a small storage barn, but I felt that it was more important to forge ahead rather than spend time on future searches for food; but such lengthy searches were not always necessary. On the third day when the sun was sinking in the west and I thought it was about time to resume walking along the road which was leading me more or less south-east, I heard the clip-clopping of a horse just around the bend around which I had walked several hours before. I did not think that I had much if anything to fear from a horse-drawn conveyance which I could now see, so I came out to the road alongside of which I had rested during the day and waved to the man holding the reins of his slowly ambling horse and to the child seated next to him. As the horse and wagon drew closer, I could see that the man was well past middle age and the child, a girl of about ten or eleven.

I stepped up to the wagon as the horse came to a halt. I had learned a few words of Polish at Auschwitz; besides, Czech words and Polish words are sometimes very similar. I greeted them with "Djen dobri" (good day) and they both replied with the same greeting. So I continued, mostly in slowly spoken Czech with a few Polish expressions as well, to the effect that I was fleeing from the Germans, for whom I had been working in a munitions factory against my will, and could these kind people give me a lift and maybe something to eat. The young girl looked beseechingly at the old man and I was able to understand her urging him to help this poor young man. Apparently the child's intervention on my behalf fell on welcoming ears, for the girl's grandfather – as I soon learned that he was – at once invited me to climb into the wagon. A word to the old horse and we were off at a languid four to five kilometers an hour. No sooner were we off than Anya ("My name is Anya and what is yours, please?") reached behind her and took two apples from a sack and offered them to me. What nectar of the Gods they were!

Within a half-hour and just as the night was closing in, we arrived at a small dwelling, the home of my new friends. There we were greeted by the mother and grandmother of Anya, who rapidly explained who I was, how they had met me and asked if I could spend at least a day with them. Yes, indeed I could and with a warm welcome. The food, simple but plentiful gave me a new lease on the uncertain life I was struggling through. I explained that I hoped to reach a Romanian Black Sea port and the grandfather drew me a rough map and with instructions to take roads leading to Rovno, Ternopol, and Ivano and thence to Clug – or Kolosvar - as the Hungarians called that Translyvanian town. These were not simple and uneducated peasants; nor were they of the upper class, as their modest land holding consisted, as they explained, of only about ten hectares (about twenty-five acres). When they asked me to what parish I belonged, I readily explained that I was from the church of St. Vaclav in Liberec. Indeed, having had many acquaintances in that parish I could have supplied many details had such been requested.

The best outcome of my brief stay with that family was that they suggested that I try to find close friends of theirs who lived some forty kilometers on the way to Rovno, and the grandfather drew me a detailed map showing me how to find those people and then he gave me a letter to give them. I learned that Anya's father had been killed by the Nazis the previous year and it was clear that the man in that family was sorely missed."

After almost exactly fifty years, following that long recital by Jacob, I have difficulty in remembering the details of the rest of that young man's odyssey to freedom. He did find the other Polish family, which supplied him with enough provisions to last him several days – that food to supplement what Anya's grandfather had pressed on him. Traveling mostly at night – at one stage on a bicycle he had found leaning against a village inn closed for the night - he finally reached the territory the Germans had given to Hungary (i.e., taken from Romania and then known as "Goerring's Gulf"). Once in Hungary, the danger of arrest was less, as the land of the Magyars was allied to Germany. Just to the east of Kolsovar, Jacob, noticed that a freight train, its engine with steam up preparatory to chugging ahead, was about to move eastward. He managed to climb into one of the cars without being detected and traveled thus as far as Brasov. Then he had still another fortunate day. Just to the east of that town there was another train parked on a siding. There were about thirty flatcars each with about twenty to twenty-five men and that train was headed east. As unobtrusively as possible, Jacob asked in German where they were going and why. The ready replies were that they were headed, some for Ploie°ti and some for Constanta, the Black Sea port, for work at the oil field and docks, respectively. "Could I join you?" Jacob asked as ingenuously as the situation seemed to demand. "The foreman is over there," one of the men replied. So, convinced now that his lucky star would continue to light his way, Jacob walked up to the imposing foreman and asked, "Sir, may I join your crew of men bound for Constanta?" Jacob soon learned that the foreman was missing two men and as his responsibility was just to deliver a certain number of men to two places, he seemed relieved that here was a replacement made to order, so to speak.

It was thus that our friend was able to reach Romania's main port. He apparently had little trouble separating himself from his new acquaintances and walked down to the docks where a Turkish freighter was being loaded by stevedores. A few minutes later, he was carrying quite a heavy bundle that contained cheese. He lost no time in concealing himself in the hold as soon as he had carried his load to its assigned place. The ship left at the end of that day and Jacob reported to the captain and with the aid of one of the officers who spoke German, explained his predicament. And it was thus that Jacob arrived in Istanbul and, immediately upon landing, sought the United States Consulate General.

Teddy Kollek promptly arranged to put Jacob up and, I soon learned, managed then to smuggle him down to Tel Aviv. I would venture a guess that our redheaded escapee eventually ended up in Moshe Dyan's army, which thirteen and a half years later was to save Israel.

The day after listening to Jacob's story, I reported the substance of his adventures to the Department and it is believed that this dispatch was among the first to be received in Washington on the subject of Auschwitz and the infamous treatment of Jewish internees at the hands of the Nazis in accord with Hitler's *Endlösung* (final solution).

After I had been in Istanbul for a year, I decided to take lessons in Russian. The first teacher I employed, who was originally from Kiev and claimed to know no English, was extraordinarily able, and had I continued working with him I believe I would have acquired a fluency in that language. But then I met a Polish family, Prince and Princess Mirski and the princess's sister, Countess Bninska. Somewhat beguiled by the latter, I allowed myself to be coaxed away from the Ukrainian professor by Mirski, who doubtless needed the money and who assured me that my knowledge of Russian would rapidly improve under his tutelage. Very soon after the Mirski lessons began, a dispatch arrived from Washington to inform Foreign Service officers that those who wished to become experts in the Russian language by dint of immersion in a crash language program in Washington should inform the Department. The dispatch stated further that those who were accepted for the program would eventually be assigned either to the Soviet Union or to a country having close contacts with the USSR. I talked this opportunity over with my chief, Burton Berry, and he at once made it clear that he did not wish to have his "listening post" weakened, as he phrased it, by my departure; and he persuaded me not to apply for that special State Department Russian immersion course.

Since that time of long ago, I have often felt that the most costly mistake I made during my years of Foreign Service was in turning down the challenge to become a Russian language expert. My facility for learning a language by ear would very like have ensured a fluency in Russian within a year or two. And, in retrospect, I would thus have avoided problems which loomed ahead; but which I could not have foreseen at that time. One of my good friends who entered the Service at the same time I did, chose to volunteer for the Russian language program. A year after finishing the course, he was killed in a plane crash flying to Moscow. That was another road of destiny. Was I right or wrong?

In mid-April, 1944 a dispatch arrived from the Department transferring me to Baghdad. At that time hardly anyone had the least doubt as to the certainly of victory over Germany, so it was natural that all of us at our listening post were looking forward to assignment to our countries of respective specialty after the end of the conflict. Hence, this instruction out of the blue to report to Iraq came as a deep disappointment. It was nevertheless gratifying that Burton Berry urgently requested

Washington to rescind my transfer instruction, but that was to no avail.

My successor in Istanbul, who came across as a pompous, pretentious know-it-all, arrived from Baghdad well before I was ready to leave Turkey. I made attempts at briefing this officer, but he paid little attention. Moreover, his attitude toward George Palozi Horvath, my Hungarian friend and most valuable and ablest collaborator, was equally uncooperative and pretentious, with the result that, in effect, he cut himself off from the advantage of a close working relationship with George, that keen, versatile expert on all things Hungarian.

A few days following receipt of the Department's refusal to leave me in Istanbul, I boarded the Taurus Express at Hydarpasha. I had very little luggage or other impediments; no furniture and no belongings other than an impressive Suzani embroidered tapestry I had purchased from the fascinating Germaine Senni, the Italian-Levantine mistress of von Pappen, the German Ambassador and a 3 ½' by 5' Shirvan prayer rug I had bought the year before. Herb Cummings and Lee Metcalf came to see me off as did Rezan, the Circassian beauty. And there, also, (I had not expected her to be there) was Hayrieh.

The journey to Baghdad took two days and two nights, for, though called so, this was no express train, and some of the time we moved very slowly. During the first afternoon, I wrote a love-letter of sorts to Rezan – in French, as she knew no English. I then asked the *wagon-lit* conductor if he would do me a special favor. "Mais, certainement, monsieur," he quickly replied. I explained that I had left a special lady friend back in Istanbul, and would he, upon his return to that city, deliver my letter to the address on the envelope. I hoped that my generous tip would ensure the safe delivery of this billet-doux. How wrong I was. This rather trivial event would not be mentioned were it not for the sequel that was not only embarrassing, but also rather humorous.

Chapter Ten

Baghdad
(Fortunately, much less than a thousand and one nights)

I arrived in the former capital of Haroun al Rashid's Empire on a very hot mid-morning in late April of 1944. Bill Moreland, one of the FSO's of our legation, was on hand to meet me and we drove in his car to the quarters in the U.S. Legation complex we would be sharing.

In those days, many of the U.S. diplomatic missions in small (and relatively unimportant to us) countries were known as legations (rather than embassies), headed by ministers (rather than ambassadors). Baghdad was one of these. So it was to the legation in Baghdad to which I was now assigned. We had a legation compound that was entirely surrounded by a wall some ten feet high. This enclosure embraced the office (chancery) that was connected to the minister's residence, and two residences for legation staff officers that were situated at the far end of a garden that separated these houses from the above-mentioned chancery. As Moreland and I were unmarried, we shared one of these houses with another single officer, the agricultural attaché. The other house had been assigned to a third officer, who was married.

Before leaving for Baghdad, I had heard that the minister under whom I was to serve was one of the most brilliant officers in the Service. Indeed, I found Loy W. Henderson to be unusually facile, an excellent writer, a good listener and possessed of the ability to remember everything he had heard during a long session involving conversations with foreign officials. In retrospect, however, I very soon understood that Loy was anti-Semitic, anti-British, and, at least to my mind, handicapped by his Latvian wife, Elise, who, though very pretty, was also vain and not very intelligent. It should be added that Henderson was also outspokenly anti-Soviet. The latter was not unusual, as few of my colleagues of those days trusted the Russians. In view of Mrs. Henderson's origins and taking into consideration Henderson's tour of duty in Moscow just before his assignment in Baghdad, their dislike of the Soviets was understandable. However, bearing in mind the allied status of the U.S. and

U.S.S.R. at that time – well before the Cold-War era – some believed that their frequent uncomplimentary remarks about the Soviet Union and its leading officials should have been restricted to very small audiences.

Perhaps the best remembered remark – at least one made by Mrs. Henderson – was on the occasion when the Iraqi Minister of Foreign Affairs gave a large reception in honor of the recently arrived Soviet Minister following the re-opening of diplomatic relations between the USSR and Iraq.

When the Hendersons came to the receiving line, Mrs. Henderson was wearing long white gloves despite the one hundred degree temperature (no-air-conditioning in those days) – or perhaps because of it. The wife of the Iraqi Foreign Minister suggested that Mrs. Henderson might like to remove her gloves and thus be more comfortable. The Soviet Minister and his wife were standing a few feet away for they too were greeting the guests. In reply to the Foreign Minister's wife, Mrs. Henderson was heard by all within a radius of five yards or so when she replied, "I rather not take gloves off; I might have to shake hands with Soviet Minister."

With regard to Mr. Henderson's anti-Jewish and even stronger anti-Zionist bias, this, too, could be understood in view of the wide-spread anti-Semitism which had existed in the United States since the early 1900's, especially in New York and some of the other large cities. Moreover, it would probably be safe to estimate that at least three quarters of the Foreign Service Officers in the 1940's were at least to an extent anti-Semitic. That having been said, Loy Henderson was serving as a leading American diplomat in an Arab country at a time when the Palestine question, a homeland for the Jews, and bitter anti-Jewish feeling in all Arab countries, were salient factors.

During the fifteen months of my assignment in Baghdad, Henderson, always accompanied by one or more of us F.S.O.'s would be invited to a banquet offered by a Sheikh or by an important government official. Invariably, the host would launch into a diatribe denouncing the presence of the well-organized and increasingly militant Zionist Jews in Palestine. On every one of these occasions, the host would request that Mr. Henderson report these views to Washington. These diatribes would include such statements as, "If the final solution to the Palestine problem – that is, the continuing build-up of the Jewish population in that territory – is unacceptable to the Arabs, I can assure you, Mr. Minister, that all Arabs will rise up as one man and drive every Jew living in Palestine – men, women, and children – into the sea, thus killing every one of them."

What made this kind of remark especially offensive was that just at that time the information about the Nazi atrocities at Auschwitz and other death-camps was beginning to seep out to the West. And this was especially the case at the end of my tour in Baghdad when the full horror of the liquidation of several million Jews became common knowledge.

One white-clad sheikh, as he held a piece of sheep in his greasy fingers prior to shoving it into his mouth, intoned, "The Jews were forced on us by the British and we will not tolerate it. I ask, as does the leadership of Iraq, that the United States side with the freedom-loving Arabs and find a solution to the settlement of the Jews somewhere other than in Arab-Palestine." And so went these tent-banquet speeches time after time.

To my mind, Loy Henderson's special ability as mentioned above lay in his facility for being able to store in his keen mind virtually every word which was said to him at a meeting – this, without taking any notes. Hence, Henderson reported almost every sentence verbatim, as it had been spoken to him. Not only did he send these exact reports of what important Iraqis had said to him, but he added suggestions of his own such as that the United States should not take decisions that would alienate the Arab World, for that world stretched from Morocco to Iran and it was a world which could be expected henceforth to speak with one voice and act in unison, determined to prevent the founding of an independent Jewish state in Palestine.

Mr. Henderson saw many things clearly and other things not so clearly. For example, he at once grasped the significance of Communist involvement in the partisan movements of German-occupied Europe. Well before many of his colleagues understood what was going on and what was in store for the future, Loy Henderson saw that Chiang Kai-shek would be driven out of China and that Marshal Tito would gain complete control of a Communist Yugoslavia, though he did not seem to foresee Tito keeping Moscow at arm's length. What he did not grasp – as it appeared to me – was that the Arabs, at least in the foreseeable future, would not be able to work effectively together and that the Jews in Palestine were a potentially strong ally of the U.S., whereas the unpredictable Arabs could not be counted on. Henderson seemed obsessed by the conviction that basically the Jews in Palestine were friendly to Communism and the Soviet Union and thus would tend to act against the interests of the United States.

When it is borne in mind that every Communist movement in Europe had been (or in the case of soon-to-be Soviet satellites, would be) organized by Jews, Henderson's views on that subject can be explained. Besides Lenin, Trotsky and Litvinov in the USSR, the Jewish leaders of the Communist movements in the East-Central European countries included the following: Anna Pauker, Romania; Slansky, Czechoslovakia; Berman, Poland; and Rakosy, Hungary. What we had, therefore, during the period when Loy Henderson was our Minister in Iraq, and following his assignment back to the Department in the spring of 1945, was an exceptionally able FSO who was greatly respected in the Department and who was in a position to exert a powerful influence on U.S. foreign policy. Hence, at that time, and indeed even for many years and up to the present, the Department of State has tended to be pro-Arab – at least as far as favoring an eventual independent Arab Palestine, thus restricting Israel to unrealistic borders.

What prevented the anti-Zionist movement, encouraged by Henderson from taking root as U.S. policy, was Harry Truman, who soon proved himself to be an outstanding president. With regard to the Palestine problem, he understood that the freedom loving Jewish settlers would be natural allies and that they abhorred any dictatorship including that of the USSR. He also respected the voting power of U.S. Jewry.

I had never thought of myself as being pro-Jewish, but even long before I had ever set foot in an Arab country, the idea of a Jewish homeland, as envisioned by Lord Balfour during the First World War and enunciated in his famous *Declaration* of 1917, appealed to me. When I found myself in Baghdad and knowing then about the Nazi atrocities against the European Jews, that idea of a homeland made even more sense.

In connection with my position, I inevitably made any number of contacts, not only in Iraqi Arab circles, but among Baghdad Jews as well. In connection with the latter, bear in mind that these few tens of thousands were descended from the exiled Jews of the Babylonian captivity who had never returned to their homeland of Israel. As might be expected, the Baghdad Jews were far more enterprising than the Baghdad Moslem Arabs and they controlled most of the business in that city of a *thousand and one nights*. The most helpful Jewish contact I had was Leopold (Ari) Chill – ostensibly an employee of a British engineering company, but actually a secret representative of the Haganah, the military arm of the Jewish Agency. As my boss understandably occupied himself mainly with reporting on the actions and points of view of the Iraqi government officials and other leaders, I thought that I might as well write a dispatch to Washington about the Jewish community of Baghdad, what their ideas were on the subject of a Jewish Palestine and about their relations with the Moslem Arabs.

With regard to Arab-Jewish relations in Baghdad, it should be borne in mind that for some four centuries the territory for what is now Iraq had been part of the Ottoman Empire in which many non-Moslem races had lived in peace. Indeed, as Columbus set sail for what was to become the New World, virtually the entire Jewish population of Spain was expelled from that country by the Inquisition. Tens of thousands of these displaced Jews found refuge in Turkey which at that time was far more tolerant than most of Christian Europe. While these refugees were never considered by the Turks first class citizens, they were never persecuted and were allowed to engage in trade and of course to maintain contact with co-believers elsewhere. Hence, the Jews of Baghdad, that outlying province of the Turkish Empire, prospered and were unmolested by the Moslem Arabs in whose midst they lived.

Then came the First World War, followed by the British protectorate. During the troubles and anti-Jewish riots in Palestine in the 1930's, some anti-Jewish sentiments began to surface in Baghdad and this anti-Jewish feeling, mainly restricted to the Moslems of the poorer class, was, of course, encouraged by the Nazi propaganda which had sought to enlist Arab support from the time of Hitler's ascent to power in early 1933. When the Rashid Ali revolt of 1941 brought that anti-British revolutionary to temporary power in Baghdad, the Arab mobs began more frequently and almost systematically to loot and attack Baghdad Jews. Just before the British Persia-Iraq Force, based at the Habbaniyah Air Force Base recaptured Baghdad, the mobs openly attacked the Jewish quarter in what

Jews later referred to as the *Farhoud* or Looting. My Jewish friends as well as some of my Christian Arab acquaintances told me that they could hear the screams of Jewish women in the night.

This anti-Jewish feeling among the Arabs, however, seemed to have been of short duration. Palestine was seven hundred miles across the desert and the British were still in control. That situation existed during the time I was in Iraq (1944-45). It should be borne in mind that with the possible exception of a handful of high Iraqi officials, the Iraqis were not friendly toward the British and there can be no question that the British mandate over Palestine during the 1920's and 1930's and up to 1948 – not to mention the Declaration which had been voiced by British Foreign Secretary, Lord Balfour, further enflamed this feeling.

Well do I remember driving out to a desert oasis where I was to attend a banquet. A minor Arab official was riding in the front seat of my small car. Suddenly, a dog ran across the road in front of us and this Arab remarked that the dog reminded him of the English, all of whom he thought of as dogs. Comparing a person to a dog is the worst insult an Arab can make.

As mentioned above, I drafted a dispatch to Washington outlining what I had learned, including contacts that were maintained between members of the Baghdad community and Jews living in Palestine. As was customary procedure, Mr. Henderson signed all dispatches destined to the Department. He called me into his office, handed my dispatch back to me saying that he would not sign it, but that I could sent it in over my own signature. I never did learn just what it was that the boss objected to in that report; in any case, I did sign it and sent it to the Department.

As I look back on that time, there is no doubt that my most valuable contact in Baghdad was Alec Waugh, then chief officer of RAF Intelligence. Alec was the elder brother of Evelyn Waugh, the noted writer. Alec, too, was the author of novels and achieved a modest fame after the war in the literary field. Whenever I needed any kind of information, I called on him and he was always helpful. My other valuable British contact was Stewart Perowne, "Oriental Counselor" in his country's embassy. This reference to my English friends leads me to set down the unusual sequel to the letter I wrote to Rezan while on the Oriental Express.

Shortly after arriving in Baghdad, I was invited to a large reception given by Tommy Thompson, the British Counselor of Embassy (i.e., second in command after the ambassador). During this reception, Mr. Thompson came up to me and said, "I say, Birge, could I have a word with you?" Thompson walked with me to a secluded part of his garden and spoke as follows. "You will recall writing a letter on your way to Baghdad and handing it to the wagon-lit conductor for delivery to a woman in Istanbul. This letter came into my hands, as that conductor is one of *our men*. We have strict regulations that all mail is to be sent through regular postal channels so that it can be subject to normal censorship. Will you kindly adhere to this regulation in future?" In view of the steamy prose I had written in that *billet-doux*, I was understandably embarrassed. I shook hands with Mr. Thompson and assured him that in future I would use regular postal channels.

After I had been in Baghdad three months or so, I requested permission to take a month's leave in Istanbul, as up to that time I had had no vacation at all since leaving the United States and the summer climate, moreover, was pretty unbearable. Lee Metcalf, loyal and generous friend that he was, insisted that I take over my old apartment that he had occupied since my departure and he moved back with Herb Cummings with whom he had previously lived. Lee wished to ensure that I would thus be more comfortable and in a position occasionally to entertain Rezan or anyone else more satisfactorily. I had brought my tennis racquet and had several games with Herb Cummings and those four weeks were especially enjoyable. When I bid Rezan farewell upon my departure at the end of that leave, which was the last time I saw her, I survived very well. I came to agree with Tom Whittemore that indeed Rezan would have been a star in the harem of Haroun Al Rashid or of Suleiman the Magnificant.

When I got back to Baghdad, I realized that I had left my tennis racquet behind. As tennis loomed large in the leisure time of Baghdad, I wrote to Lee and asked him to hand the racquet to the wagon-lit conductor for delivery to me in Baghdad and I specified the date so that I would know just which train to meet. So far, so good. I collected my racquet and resumed my daily late afternoon games. Many months later, that is, in June, 1945 at the end of my tour of duty in Baghdad, Bill Moreland

and I gave a cocktail party at which one of our guest was Wing Commander Dawson Shepherd of the RAF. The latter drew me aside. "Could I have a word with you, Birge?" he asked. What he said, in brief, was that British Intelligence had discovered that Rezan, the young woman to whom I had written numerous letters following the wagon-lit conductor episode, was a close friend of a woman whose lover was a German diplomat. It was suspected, therefore, that I might be passing information to this enemy official. Then, when I had my tennis racquet sent to me by unofficial channels, the British feared that I might have a message hidden in it, so had it thoroughly examined – probed, x-rayed, etc., before returning it to me. They then had me followed for several months! "Sorry, old boy," went on Dawson Shepherd, "but you see there *was* a war on and my people were being especially careful in view of the fact that one of your code clerks at the U.S. Embassy in London had been found to be a German agent. It was also noted, I might add, that you danced the Viennese waltz so perfectly that many were convinced you had to be Austrian, or German yourself! So we just could not take any chances."

Of course, my British friends must have informed not only Mr. Henderson, but our OSS staff member as well. By the time I heard this bit of intelligence Henderson had left for Washington. While it is doubted that this rather silly episode did me any harm, I do not think it did me any good either.

Not long after my arrival in the fabled city of the Abbasids, Archie Roosevelt (grandson of Teddy Roosevelt) arrived to assume the duties of Assistant Military Attaché. When I was in the sixth form at Groton, Archie was a first form boy, hence some five years younger than I. Archie was perhaps the finest scholar I have ever known. He was thorough, painstaking and brilliant. During those incredibly hot summer days of 1944, he would study Arabic in his hotel room – that is, during the weekends when not in the office. I introduced Archie to some of my acceptable Iraqi friends, notably Madame Afnan, one of the relatively few *civilized* Arabs of that city.

Archie went on to become a fine intelligence officer of the CIA and ended his career as a political advisor to the Chase Manhattan Bank. When I knew him, he was married to his first wife, Katherine Tweed, reputably an attractive WASP type. Albeit separated from this wife for long periods, including the fifteen months when we were in Baghdad together, Archie never sought out any young women for a special relationship and in this regard he was like Herb Cummings. While in Baghdad, Archie established any number of valuable contacts among the British, Arabs and even Jews. For example, he, too, got to know Leopold Chill, the brilliant Israeli operator. Some forty odd years after our Iraqi experience, Archie wrote an interesting book about his time spent in the Middle East. The title of this volume was *For Lust of Knowing*. This saga was a fine scholarly achievement though a bit ponderous and hardly a book to entertain one when there is nothing else to do. What this book does show, however, is the keen mind and facile pen of its author.

Archie and I became good friends though we did not have much in common. While I played tennis almost every day after the office closed in the early afternoons of the hot months, Archie never played. Neither did he ever play poker with me and my habitual partners in that pastime – namely; Colonel Converse, the Military Attaché, George Moffit, and diplomatic colleagues from the Polish and Chinese legations. We did, however, have several Iraqi friends in common, notably the intelligent and broad-minded Madame Afnan, and Fadhil al Jamali, who often invited guests to listen to his classical records, while enjoying the cool air on the flat roof of his house after dinner.

As an operator in Military Intelligence, Archie, of course, enjoyed the considerable advantage of being able to converse adequately in Arabic. This not only served to broaden his contacts, but it tended also to give Arabs the impression – which was correct – that he liked and admired them and favored their point of view as opposed to that of the Zionists. I had respect for Archie's opinions, though I did not agree with all of them. But one remark he allegedly made did mean a lot to me. When I returned to Iraq on a short business trip in the early 1960's, I looked up Bedia Afnan, who, as mentioned above, had been a good friend of Archie back in the mid 1940's. She made a point of repeating to me what Archie had said to her not long after my departure from Baghdad in 1945; namely, that "Walter Birge wrote the best reports to the Department from Legation-Baghdad." I doubt that Madame Afnan would have fabricated this remark by Archie; whether the latter really meant it might be open to question.

Any discussion involving Iraq must perforce stress the importance of the British and their protectorate over Iraq in those days. The reader may recall that soon after the First World War and the founding of the League of Nations, England was granted a mandate over Iraq until such time as that country was thought to be able to manage its own affairs. A similar mandate over Palestine was also granted to England on conditions that the latter promise eventually to create there a homeland for the Jews. It soon became apparent that England's acceptance of these mandates was based on its plan to create a network of client Arab states friendly to and dependent on Britain. Hence the actions of local British officials in Palestine; calculated to encourage Arab riots against the Jews in that province and the policy shortly before the outbreak of the Second World War of drastically cutting down on the number of Jews allowed to settle in Palestine. In this regard it should be noted that the local British officials administering the Palestine mandate were, almost to a man, anti-Semitic. Of course, during that time many Americans were no less so.

In Baghdad, during World War Two, it was also obvious that a sort of sleeping anti-Semitism among the local British officials also prevailed. In effect, the British controlled Iraq absolutely – through their ambassador (the only diplomat there with that diplomatic rank) and through *Paiforce* (Persia-Iraq Force). This impressive military presence worked closely with, or at least maintained close liaison with, the British forces in Egypt. It should be mentioned that an important part of this British military force was made up of Assyrian Levies, as they were called. At that time, at least a sizeable number of Christian Assyrians lived in the vicinity of the Iraq-Turkish border. As these people were Christian, they were looked down upon by the Moslem Iraqis. As was the case with the famous Ghurkas, many of these Assyrians had been inducted into the British army and turned out to be loyal and hard-fighting men. When Rashid Ali revolted against the British-dominated government in Iraq in 1941, it was largely the Assyrians who prevented the capture of the important Habbanya airbase and when the British reinforcements from India, and presumably Egypt, defeated the Arab forces of Rashid Ali, loyally assisted by the Assyrians, the latter proudly marched through Baghdad wearing their distinctive broad brimmed hats and occasionally hurling insults at the crowds which lined Rashid street.

The Iraqi government during the war was, in effect, a show of musical chairs that featured periodic changes of ministers shuffling in and out of the government, but with no substantive changes in policy. Nuri al Said was usually prime minister and he owed his position entirely to his close relations with his British sponsors. The titular head of the Iraqi government was the king, at that time a young boy of about nine whose mantle of power was exercised by his uncle Abdullah, the regent, a member of the Hashemite family whose father, uncles and grandfather had moved north from the Arabian Peninsula during the First World War.

Tragically, both Abdullah and Nuri al Said, along with Abdullah's nephew, by that time ruling as King Faisal II, met with violet death in 1958 when Baghdad was temporarily taken over by a revolutionary group. Nuri tried to escape in women's clothes but was apprehended when someone noticed that he was wearing men's socks. He and the regent were dragged feet-first behind a car through Baghdad until death finally put an end to their suffering.

I came to know the regent fairly well as he often joined a jackal hunting group which met every Friday and which my good friend, Ghazi Dhagestani, a prominent young Iraqi of Circassian origin, had encouraged me to join. I was able to join the hunt, for Ghazi made available a beautiful white gelding, which he personally led to our legation compound on those Friday mornings. I had not been on a horse since 1936 and very little then, and my horsemanship was pitiful compared to the magnificent Arab horsemen. It can be imagined how sore I was that first time I rode with the hunt. I was barely able to get through that morning. One other occasion I remember well. My horse suddenly stopped just before he was meant to jump over an irrigation ditch – with the predictable result that I took a nose-dive over his head into the water. And looking down at me with a broad smile was the regent. I could not blame him for being amused.

Sir Kinahan Cornwallis (1883-1959) was the British Ambassador – a direct descendant of the famous (to American schoolboys) General Cornwallis who surrendered to General Washington at Yorktown, but who in later years became England's brilliant general involved in the conquest of India. His American misfortune was merely a prelude to a great career in the building of the *Empire*.

With further regard to the British presence in Iraq, there must be mention of the Alwiya Club. Until 1941, only English families had been allowed to join. This changed immediately following the suppression of that above-mentioned 1941 revolt. When the forces of Rashid Ali were closing in on Baghdad at the start of that conflict, many British families, including officials and others whose lives were in danger, took refuge in the American Legation compound, which, it will be recalled, was surrounded by a high wall. As the United States at that time was a neutral and perhaps for other logical reasons as well, the forces of Rashid Ali did not dare penetrate into the Legation by force. When the troubles were over and the British resumed their control over the country, the board of the Alwiya Club voted henceforth to allow Americans posted to the U.S. Legation to become members of the club. At the same time, it was decided to allow a limited number of leading Iraqis also to become members.

That club was a godsend, for it provided the opportunity for tennis every day, not to mention a swimming pool in that awful one hundred plus degree heat, and occasions to meet with British friends.

Mention has already been made of Stewart Perowne, the Oriental Counselor of the British Embassy. A few comments about these counselors are in order. It was the British custom in those days – and had been for some time, that each diplomatic mission in the Middle East had assigned to it at least one counselor who was fluent in at least one of the local languages and who was knowledgeable as to the history and customs and the personages of the country of assignment. In a small number of cases, the United States has emulated the British in this regard, but with a few exceptions our equivalent officers did not attain the level of expertise of their U.K. colleagues. Archie Roosevelt was perhaps a good example of one of these exceptions.

In the northeast part of Iraq lived the Kurdish tribes, a nation totally different from the Arabs in race, language, and customs, though they did have Islam in common. One of the British Oriental Counselors not only spoke the Kurdish language but had spent many months in their midst. During the entire time of my sojourn in Baghdad, there was a civil war of sorts going on between the Kurds, a tough, intrepid mountain dwelling people, and the Iraqi army. Usually the Kurds got the better of the sporadic fighting. This intermittent war has been going on since the 1940's. The chieftain-leader of the Kurds was in the 1940's until quite recently, Mulla Mustafa who with his men and womenfolk was fighting for survival, whereas the Iraqi conscripts, it was generally believed, did not really care too much about whether or not the Kurds were defeated. The Kurds have for centuries been known as fearsome fighting men. Indeed, during the Second Crusade, the great Saladin, who ruled over Egypt as well as Palestine when Richard the Lion Heart led the crusaders to the Holy Land in 1190, was a Kurd.

It should be borne in mind that the nationhood of each of the Arab states, notably Iraq, Jordan, Syria, Lebanon, Saudi Arabia, etc., has not always been a deep-seated, keenly felt emotion. After all, Turkey had been the ruling power in the Arab Middle East for over four centuries, and this should be especially remembered when there is a discussion of the Palestine-Israeli situation. There has never been – prior to recently – an independent Iraq or Jordan or Saudi Arabia or Lebanon or Syria. There has been a large Arab *nation* of relatively primitive people, some sedentary and some wandering, a people having a language and religion and some customs in common, but until less than a half-century ago Arabs tended not to think of themselves as loyal Iraqis or loyal Syrians or Jordanians; rather, they usually thought of themselves as Arabs. The Egyptians were an exception. The national feeling in the abovementioned Arab countries seems lately to be stronger than a generation ago and this is especially true of the Palestinians, for there is nothing like a common enemy (Israel) to draw a people together.

In general, it might be said that while Arabs of one country tended to empathize with Arabs of another country, unpredictability has been a characteristic of the Arabs. Indeed, it could be said that the most predictable thing about them has been their unpredictability. The following patterns of Arab behavior have generally held true since the time I was in Iraq: Arabs of one country tend to empathize with other Arabs especially when policies having to do with Israel are involved; Shiah Moslems of one country tend to encourage cooperation with Shiahs of another Arab country and in general the antipathy between Sunnis and Shiah has continued down to the present. Hence, the frequent strained relations between Shiah Iran (a non-Arab country) and Sunni Saudi Arabia. Iraq, it should be noted is about forty to forty-five percent Sunni and fifty to sixty percent Shiah; however, the Sunnis have continued to dominate the seats of power.

With regard to cooperation between the Arab states, this has been strikingly lacking. This situation has been helpful to Israel, for had the Arab states worked in close unison, militarily and otherwise, Israel might not have survived as it has.

Mention has already been made of Turkish tolerance of the Jews living within their empire, so that gradually the Jewish population of Palestine increased during the centuries of Turkish suzerainty. During the year and a quarter of my service in Baghdad, it became apparent that the Jews of that city were becoming increasingly worried and uneasy about their future status and even personal safety. By the summer of 1945, there had even begun a trickle of Jewish emigration to the Jewish-occupied section of Palestine.

During the reign of the great Haroun al Rashid in the early eighth century, the population of what is now Iraq was at least three times what it was in 1945. Baghdad was a thriving city and it was said that one could walk across the Tigress River stepping from one pleasure craft to another. In the twentieth century, the population of Iraq was perhaps four to five million with 25,000 deaths a year from malaria. In that distant time of the early Middle Ages and the Dark Ages, there was a strong pan-Arab presence – the unifying factors being religion, race, and language. Those factors remained, but for many centuries, a large part of that Arab world had been over-run by successions of conquerors: Turks, Egyptians, Mongols, Crusaders, Persians, and more recently, the British and French. These serious disruptions had stifled an all-embracing Arab unity – which was further made difficult by the geographical factors of the deserts of Arabia and North Africa. When Timor, the Mongol conqueror, laid waste Baghdad, he not only built a pyramid of one million Arab sculls, but also destroyed all the irrigation ditches. To make matters worse, all the trees which had managed to grow in the land stretching between Baghdad and the Sea of Galilee in the time of the Abbasid Empire had long since been cut down. That land was now all barren desert. So most of the Arab world in the early twentieth century consisted of wandering shepherds and tribes who gained a livelihood preying on each other, robbing and stealing. There was no cohesion, only customs, language, race and religion in common, but that was not enough.

When I was in Baghdad, the colonial period was drawing to a close and within about five years both the British and French had withdrawn from Syria, Iraq, and Palestine. There then emerged two powerful cohesive factors: hatred of Israel and distrust of (in some cases hatred also) of pro-Israel America and of the former colonial powers. There also emerged the powerful weapon of oil, which on the one hand provided the Arabs with a weapon to counter the Israeli presence and to gain added respect and concessions from the western oil consuming powers. This oil also tended to divide the Arab world into haves and have-nots, for some of those Arab states had no oil: viz, Syria, Jordan, and Lebanon.

On balance, the events of the latter part of this century have tended to bring greater unity to the Arab world. The Arabian Gulf sheikdoms have imported Egyptian and Palestinian and Lebanese teachers and technicians and this has been a unifying factor. Then, as stressed above, there remain the ever-present varying degrees of hatred of Israel. As these lines were being written [1991] there emerged the powerful threat of Saddam Hussein of Iraq who has just overrun Kuwait and cried out for the unity of all Arabs. Clearly this dictator wished for three things: to gain control over all the oil of the Arabian Gulf; to unite all Arabs under his command; and to drive Israel into the sea.

That having been written, it is reiterated that with the Arabs nothing is certain. What is written is written in sand.

Now I shall set down some comments of how I spent some of my time in Baghdad. As to the routine of life, I played tennis almost every day, even in the one hundred degree heat, but as the humidity was desert-dry heat, that activity was bearable. My tennis clothes were rinsed out after each use and hung up sopping wet; within fifteen minutes they were bone dry. During the hot-dry season of mid-April to November, we worked from seven a.m. right through to about one-thirty without a break. On Fridays (diplomatic pouch day), we would return to the chancery to get our dispatches finished, signed and put into the diplomatic pouch.

As mentioned above, I shared one of the two staff houses with Bill Morland and Bill Robinson. We had two Arab servants,

Alwan and Mohammid. These men would serve lunch at about two, after which I took a nap for two hours, then tennis, etc. Even in the hottest weather this routine worked well, for the dry heat was not too enervating and the daily exercise kept me in shape. Occasionally, we would give a cocktail party that might include a buffet supper. It was the custom during the dry summer months to bring all rugs, furniture and lamps out onto the lawn. We would connect these lamps to electrical outlets in the house and in this way, in effect, we moved our living quarters out of doors. The lawns remained green by means of narrow irrigation ditches, for it never rained during that hot time of year. For some reason – probably owing to the dryness – there were no flies or mosquitoes at that time of day. But with the coming of dawn, the flies would come, and with a vengeance. "Flies are the messengers of Allah," insisted my Arab friends, "for they ensure that you awaken to say prayers." Flies did not seem to bother the Arabs as far as concerned food being invaded by those black winged pests. On one occasion, when I was invited to a desert mid-day feast, I was ushered into the large tent where the food was to be served and there in the middle of the low banquet table was a large roast sheep that seemed overcooked, so black was the meat. But then the host waved a cloth at this succulent *pièce de résistance* and suddenly the roast sheep was no longer black, for it had been an army of flies feasting on that sheep which had been responsible for that somber hue. No one except us, the American guests, which included Archie Roosevelt and Colonel Converse, was at all put out by such an incident.

No sooner had we been seated around this low table than the host, a Sheikh of the Shammar tribe, took hold of a morsel of sheep, held it in front of me and then pushed it into my mouth which I had no choice but to open to prevent the grease laden delicacy from smearing my face with an unwelcome gloppy goo. Then, a few minutes later, another denizen of the desert grabbed one of the sheep's eyeballs and performed the same ritual. This factual description of what took place at that desert luncheon is not intended to cast aspersions on Arab customs. For indeed, what I have described was intended as a show of ardent hospitality and respect for an official American guest.

Another out of the routine, but not al all unusual activity, involved accompanying Loy Henderson on a visit to an outlying part of Iraq. The visit had to do with the holy Shi-ah towns of Najaf and Karbala, which are situated about seventy miles south of Baghdad. What I best remember about that excursion was being invited to the house of a local dignitary. This dwelling had four floors: the main one at ground level with a flat roof used for sleeping in summer, and three other floors, all below ground. In the center of the lowest floor was a well, and as one descended from one floor to the next, the air became progressively cooler so that in the lowest floor the temperature was quite comfortable whereas on the main ground level floor it was almost unbearably hot.

On that occasion as well as others suggested above, our host got off the usual tirade against the Jewish presence in Palestine with the urging that Mr. Henderson report to Washington the already mentioned warning of an inevitable massacre of all Jews in the Holy Land in the event of an unacceptable (to Arabs) solution to the Palestine problem.

Upon our return to Baghdad, Mr. Henderson began drafting a lengthy dispatch all about the Shiah Moslems. In view of the fact that very few Shiah politicians in Iraq had any influence, it seemed to me at the time that this long message might be a waste of time.

Not long after our return to Baghdad, Henderson told me that he intended to take me with him for a visit to the Kurdish area of Iraq, i.e., Kurdistan. Unfortunately, he changed his mind about this, as Bill Moreland had complained that as he was senior to me, it was unfair that I should be chosen to accompany the minister on all the interesting trips. There was, of course, logic in his complaint but it was nevertheless a disappointment, as I would have much preferred to visit Kurdistan than the Shiah holy cities. Mention has already been made of these mountain-dwelling Kurds and of their leader, Mulla Mustapha. This was a subject worth writing about. The British, when they were in a position to help draw the post-World War One boundaries of Arab areas formerly part of the Ottoman empire, should have seen to it that Kurds not be placed under the suzerainty of Iraq.

A few Kurds had entered into the mainstream of Iraqi official and social life – notably, the Haidari family. Daud Pasha Al Haidari, for example, had at one time been Iraqi ambassador to England and when I was in Baghdad, was an influential voice in Iraqi political circles. But his was one of very few Kurdish voices speaking in that Arab wilderness.

It is generally perceived that Arabs tend to be fanatics. There are, of course, exceptions, but it can be said that these exceptions prove the rule. One evening, while dining in the garden of Dr. and Mrs. F.A. (I leave out their name as there is always the remote possibility that the following account might result in harm to them or their descendants), we were discussing this Arab trait of fanaticism, and the doctor, a Christian Arab, told me the following story about an experience he had had many years before. This is what my friend – one of the most civilized, well educated and thoroughly decent Iraqis I met during that fifteen month posting – had to relate.

"The year was 1930 and I had just returned to Baghdad following four years of study at P. & S. Medical School in the United States. I remember the time and year well because I was to be married that month and I was looking forward to entering into my medical career in this city. I was listening to some classical music on records I had brought back with me when there was a loud knock on the front door. I turned the phonograph off and opened the door. There, filling that doorway were two masked men, each holding a revolver pointing at me.

'You are Dr. A____?' one of the intruders asked. When I replied that I was and then obviously enquired why I was being disturbed by two strangers wearing masks and threatening me with revolvers, one of the masked men replied, 'Have no fear, doctor. If you follow our instructions you will come to no harm. Kindly accompany us, for we wish you to make a medical diagnosis. We wear masks as we do not wish you to recognize us at any future time.'

I had no choice but to accompany these men outside who placed a blindfold over my eyes and told me to lie down on the floor of their automobile which was parked in front of my house. One of the men sat in the back seat and he placed his feet on me to ensure that I not try to get up or remove the blind. The car then moved off and after a drive of about ten to fifteen minutes, punctuated by many turns and some slow and some fast driving, we came to a stop and I was allowed to sit up. The man in the driver's seat then said, 'Dr. A___, we have brought you here to our house to examine a young female of our family. We will lead you into the house after which we will remove your blindfold. We believe that the young woman you are to examine is pregnant, though she insists that this cannot be the case.

After you have completed your examination of this young woman, you will tell us what her situation is. If you tell the truth, it will be as though nothing has happened; if you do not tell the truth, we will kill you, but no harm will come to anyone else, whatever you say.'

After being led into the house and my blindfold removed, I could see at once that this was the dwelling of very well off people. The rugs and some of the furnishings were obviously expensive – notably the closely woven silk rugs, three of which adorned the walls. Almost immediately after our entry, a young girl of about seventeen or eighteen was led into the front hall by an older woman. "Dr. A____,' one of the men said, 'Kindly accompany these two women into that adjoining chamber,' and he pointed to an open door. 'Our aunt will remain with you while you make your examination, in accord with our instruction. Kindly tell the older woman when you will have come to a conclusion as to your diagnosis involving this young woman's condition. She will then notify us and we will join you to listen to what you have to say.'

The older and younger women then led the way into the adjoining room and the door was closed after us. I could instantly see that the girl was terrified. Even as I looked at her and before beginning my examination, I was almost certain that she was indeed pregnant, and not in the first stage of that condition either. It was clear, however, that I had no choice. If I said that she was not pregnant and it was soon found that I had not told the truth, my life would be forfeit. Also, I had been assured that no harm would come to the girl. As these were clearly affluent and presumably civilized people, they would probably marry the girl off or otherwise find some way to remove her from any public eye. After thinking all this over, I decided that I should do exactly as I had been trained to do; that is, examine, come to a conclusion, and give my diagnosis. I informed the aunt that the examination was concluded.

The aunt arose, opened the door and beckoned to the men who had disturbed me on that never-to-be-forgotten evening. The men entered the room. One of them – the one who had been the driver of the car and the principal spokesman – was now garbed in a voluminous *gallabiya* robe. His arms were folded in front and his icy gray eyes behind the mask looked first at the girl and then at me and he asked the question. 'Dr.

A____, kindly let us have the result of your examination of our sister. Is she pregnant and, if not, what is it that has conspired to alter her form and bodily functions?'

Having come to the decision that nothing could be served except personal disaster by withholding the truth, I said, in what I am sure was a shaky voice, 'Gentlemen, I find that without any doubt, this young woman whom I have just examined is about five months pregnant. She should have no problem in bringing this pregnancy to term.' What immediately ensued happened so rapidly and was so shockingly horrible that I just stood there fixed to the spot, powerless to move. One of my captors, the one *not* dressed in the gallabiya – moved forward with the rapidity of a striking snake, seized the girl by the hair and yanked her body over a sort of coffee table. The other man opened his voluminous gallabiya, drew a scimitar that had been hidden within the folds of that garment and then, in one swift movement, raised this weapon and brought it down on the exposed slender neck of that poor girl whose scream was suddenly cut off by that deadly, razor-sharp blade. Her body fell to the floor where her bright red blood gushed forth and mingled with the red, blue and yellow of a priceless carpet.

'The honor of our family has been saved,' spoke the murderer of that defenseless girl. I almost fainted away, overcome as I was by the gruesome scene I had just witnessed. All I could manage to say was, 'You swine!' I have a vague recollection of being blindfolded again, driven home, helped from a car and left there by the two executioners. The following morning, I found five 100-dinar notes in a side pocket of my jacket, the frightfully acquired fee, which I gave at once to a Catholic priest with the request that it be used to help young children in need. I never knew who those evil men were. And that, Walter, is an absolutely true story of Arab-Moslem fanaticism."

Female companionship was not exactly a hallmark that characterized the attractiveness of Baghdad. In fact, the city was not attractive at all. During the time spent in that city, I established a close relationship with four young women. The first was an emancipated Iraqi Moslem a few years older than I whom I had met at one of the diplomatic receptions. *Fahtma* was very attractive, talkative, quite sophisticated, sexy and argumentative. I well remember a particular buffet party where Alex Waugh noticed her helping herself from a food-laden table and then eagerly digging into the contents of her plate. Alex remarked how attractive and intriguing Fahtma looked with a little grease on her face, like a mischievous child. She was really the nicest Iraqi female I met in Baghdad; but finally, misunderstandings and silly quarrels brought an end to our friendship. The next was also an emancipated Moslem, the daughter of a prominent Kurd who enjoyed a close relationship with the royal family as well as with the ruling politicians. Majeda H. occasionally went to the Alwiya Club, but it was not there that I met her. She telephoned me one day to say that she had heard about me from some of her friends who were the wives of officials I had met at a reception. At first, she refused to identify herself, but finally did so and agreed to drive to my house. I suggested an hour when I knew that Bill Moreland would be out with his English girl friend, the secretary of a British businessman. Even though Majeda was in a way emancipated, she did not dare to be seen with me in public. Hence, our only meetings were in secret. This had its aura of excitement and intrigue, but did not make for a satisfactory situation. She came a few times to the two rooms I occupied in my shared house. We also occasionally drove out for very short outings into the desert outskirts. On one such occasion, I saw three cars approaching us from the direction in which we were going. Majeda also saw those cars, one of which was flying the royal standard on its left front fender. She at once with speedy agility left her seat and crouched down onto the floorboards, covering herself with the light coat she had with her.

When the three open cars drew abreast, I could clearly see his royal highness Abdullah, the Regent. Though the moment of our passing was brief, I could see his curious glance at my car. He may have momentarily wondered what this American was doing driving by himself in the desert, before realizing that, of course, I was *not* by myself.

The problem with this daughter of Kurdistan was that she developed possessive traits. While she was sexy and desirous of an ongoing relationship that would be close and clandestine, I was not sufficiently interested in her to run the risk of having to deal with the problems that might ensue. In brief, she was intelligent, quite well educated, sure of herself and conceited. She was also a sexually frustrated young woman. Had she been prettier, I might have looked differently at the situation.

There was also another problem. I was sure that Majeda was in the habit of repeating remarks I made to her – though I was careful to be discreet – and probably regaled a few of her close female friends about our meetings. I also felt that some of these tales might reach the ears of Mrs. Henderson during the afternoon teas she shared with Iraqi ladies. Basically, however, the problem was that Majeda's family was too prominent; that, coupled with the arrogance that this descendant of Kurdish chieftains often displayed, gave me some warning signals.

Toward the end of my tour in Iraq, still another young woman entered the scene, Mary Abdini. She was a good-looking American girl of Armenian descent who divided her time between the U.S. and Beirut and had come to Baghdad to visit Lebanese relatives. We met at that most convenient Alwiya club, where we had dinner together on one occasion. Even though she was of American birth, we did not meet publicly from then on, for that was still Baghdad and there was still Majeda, who, sensing the gradual demise of our romance of sorts, had begun to voice thinly veiled threats. And there were also the very conservative relatives of Mary (my new friend) to be considered.

These entanglements both ended in an embarrassing climax. One Sunday afternoon, I picked Mary up at a convenient (for her) meeting place on a corner of Rashid Street and drove her to my place. She had been there for perhaps a half-hour when my phone rang to interrupt the diverting exchanges between us. It was the imperious Majeda on the phone and she said that she would like to drive to my place for an hour or so. I said that I could not see her just then as there were several guests present. She may have had an inkling as to what was actually going on, though I was reasonably sure that she did not know anything about the identity of the woman involved, if, indeed, that was what she suspected. I hoped that I had succeeded in putting Majeda off, but I was wrong.

A few minutes later, her car drove up to my house. As no other cars were there she correctly assumed that my story about several visitors was untrue, so she began blowing her horn. I told Mary to arrange her clothes for a getaway and then we both escaped from the house by the back door from which I intended to proceed with Mary through the Henderson's garden and thence to the main road. We had gone about fifty feet toward that garden when who should appear but a very irate Majeda, who, suspecting something like this, had left her car and walked around the house in an attempt to discover just what I was up to. I did not care much whether she knew I had been entertaining another female, but I certainly did not want her to discover the identity of the latter. I instructed Mary to make her way through the Legation garden and wait for me beside the main Legation gate. I had no choice but to then tackle Majeda and bring her to the ground to prevent her from catching up with the fleeing Mary. I then forcibly led her into the house where she pretended to faint away. Alwan, my servant, then materialized and I told him to attend to Majeda's needs while I absented myself for a few minutes. I then leapt into my car, picked Mary up in front of the Legation, drove her to the residence of her host and rapidly returned home. That, I am glad to relate, was the last I saw of Majeda; and she did not have one of her minions attempt to murder me, as I feared she might do.

Another summer was unfolding with its searing heat. Loy Henderson had recently been transferred back to Washington to become head of the Department of Near Eastern Affairs. His wife apparently refused to leave with him. I say *apparently refused* as she remained in the Legation living quarters for almost two months during which time she insisted on having the American flag flown on the fender of the Minister's car whenever she sallied out for any purpose. Much more embarrassing, she occasionally received afternoon calls from a Major Moger of the British army who ostensibly came for tea, but no member of the Legation staff had any doubts as to the special reason for the major's afternoon visits.

Shortly before leaving Baghdad, Mr. Henderson, probably prodded by his wife, had approached Mike Zia, the owner of the Hotel Zia, with a view to selling Mike two-dozen or so bottles of Scotch whiskey. During the war, the British had very kindly made available to Chiefs of Mission limited stocks of whiskey which were otherwise unavailable or, at best, difficult to come by. The American staff (notably the Foreign Service officers) at our legation had hoped that Loy Henderson would distribute this whiskey among them at his cost of about $2.00 a bottle. Mike Zia later told me that he had paid $10.00 a bottle for this scotch. It goes without saying that we of the legation staff were irritated at this skinflint behavior by a U.S. minister. We suspected, however, that it was Elise who had talked her husband into this shabby deal, but even that was a poor excuse. Before her departure, Mrs. Henderson also sold a few gifts that had been presented her husband by Arab sheiks – notably daggers, the sheaths of which were encrusted with semi-precious stones. These sales had been made to a curio shop, which had then put these items on display in their window.

Aside from tennis, swimming, and very occasional and clandestine meetings with females, there were a few other quite enjoyable diversions. There were official receptions, of course, as well as cocktail parties and dinners. I will never forget the first time I was invited to Alec Waugh's for dinner. I was a novice concerning wine, and still am no expert. We were served a series of wines during the repast, and owing to the extreme heat and the strong effect it had on me in the heat, I added ice and water to my red wine. I look of horror crossed the face of Alec, who said, "No need to baptize the wine, old boy." I learned later that Alec was considered one of the great connoisseurs of wines (he wrote *In Praise of Wine* and the wine and spirits book for *The Time-Life* cook-book series, among others) and had somehow managed to bring out to Iraq a large cellar. I apparently was icing and gulping down a Château Haut Brion '29! From then on, I sipped my red wine slowly at room temperature.

I was quite often invited out to play bridge, notably at the house of Hassan Makzoumi, a congenial Lebanese who had been in Baghdad for business reasons since the 1930's. Hassan had a small wooden platform in his garden, the walls of which consisted of netting to prevent any unwelcome inroads from the insect world. Hassan spoke only French (with a typical Lebanese accent), aside from Arabic. I sometimes think that I played better in French than in English, but it might have been because of the unusual setting.

In addition to those games at Hassan's house, I also played bridge with a few Polish refugees who had come to Baghdad from Yakutsk, to which far distant Siberian freezer they had been shipped in 1940 after the Soviets had overrun the eastern half of Poland. It will be recalled that following the German invasion of the USSR, the Soviets, in dire need of closer relations with and assistance from the Western Allies made the gesture of allowing these Poles to leave the Soviet Union and reach allied-controlled territory – including Iraq.

We also had poker sessions, usually attended by George Moffit, at that time a clerk (later to become a very able Foreign Service officer), Colonel Paul Converse, the Military Attaché, and two non-American members of the diplomatic corps. Often, these two other players would be Mr. Yu and Mr. Ma of the Chinese Legation (before the communist takeover of China). As might be expected, Moffit and I often commented to them, "I done it all for Yu, Ma!" Two members of the Polish Legation also played often with us: Malhomme and Dobrolski (or some such names). George and/or I usually won, first because we noticed that whenever Colonel Converse had a good hand, he would reach for a cigarette and say something like, "Who is going to open?" or he would take special pains in arranging his cards. We would also often change the nature of the game, thus taking some advantage over our foreign guests. First of all, they had to get used to *high-low*, then we would change to *low only – deuces wild*, or *one-eyed jacks wild*. Of course, we did not play for high stakes so even big winners seldom walked away with more than eight or nine dollars.

Colonel Converse was an unusually fine, unselfish, decent man for whom I had great respect. He rarely came away from our games a winner, and thus to a very modest extent he helped finance George and me, but he was invariably a good loser. When I look back on that post and those games and try to judge the people I met there, it is the good colonel who comes out on top as the most likeable man.

One day in mid-1944, when I had been in Baghdad about three months, I received a letter from Ambassador Steinhardt by diplomatic pouch marked *Personal and Confidential.* In brief, the ambassador wrote that from time to time he would enclose in a letter addressed to me, another letter destined for Betty George, the wife of Air Vice-Marshal George, then the commanding officer of the British airbase at Habbanihah, which was situated out in the desert some sixty miles west of Baghdad. The ambassador went on to explain that I should hold any notes for Betty until a young British officer identified himself to me as Mrs. George's confidential messenger. The Air Vice-Marshal, I recalled, had been British Air Attaché in Ankara. At least five or six such letters were passed along to Betty George via the young officer. Several years later, I met, quite by chance, Bobby and Betty George in a fashionable Paris restaurant. By that time Steinhardt had become deeply involved with still another beauty, Countess Cecilia Sternberg.

During the time of these exchanges of letters (for I also forwarded Betty's letters to the ambassador, likewise via diplomatic pouch), Steinhardt wrote me a note asking whether I would like to serve with him in Prague to which post he was to be assigned as soon as the war was over. As can be imagined, I replied at once in the affirmative, not only because I liked the Steinhardts, but also because I had no wish to remain any longer than necessary in Iraq. I later ascertained that when the Department demurred, Mr. Steinhardt called on Cordell Hull, the Secretary of State, to stress how able I was - well, that was what Larry Steinhardt told me later. Steinhardt, as already mentioned, was the type of man who placed personal loyalty ahead of everything else. It is possible that the discrete handling of his letters to Betty George and hers to him might have contributed to his perceiving me as personally loyal.

About a month after writing back to the ambassador that I would be delighted to serve with him in Prague, I received an official notice from the State Department of my transfer, but also ordering me to proceed first to Dhahran, Saudi Arabia, on temporary duty to act as consul in charge of the Consulate during the absence of the officer in charge who was being assigned, also temporarily, to San Francisco for the first meeting of the newly organized United Nations. This instruction arrived in mid-June, 1945, that is, about a month after VE-Day, but we were still at war with Japan.

Meanwhile, Loy Henderson had been transferred back to Washington that spring and his replacement was Jim Moose, a very able expert on that area. As I had by then been in Baghdad a little over a year, I had become knowledgeable enough to draft two or three dispatches to the Department. One of these had to do with the Communist movement in Baghdad. Perhaps the most gratifying comments I received on the subject of these reports were a personal letter from Mr. Henderson, who commented that he was "delighted and surprised" at the excellence of my dispatches; also, Mr. George Kennan, then Counselor in Moscow, to whom the Department had sent a copy, wrote to me a congratulatory letter. I guess I should have kept copies of these kind messages to show them to the Department Chief of Personnel, for, after writing this kind note to me,

Henderson had commented to Personnel that he perceived me as being rather immature. Of course, in some ways I was, but thinking back on those days, I believe that what Henderson defined as immaturity was an enthusiasm, a continuing wish to see American girls, and perhaps also an understanding that the Jewish Agency would in future years be more of an ally to America than the unpredictable Arabs, especially those of Iraq.

In reflecting back on those fifteen months spent in the city of Harroun al Rashid, it comes to mind that many of the people I met made a lasting impression on me, for varying reasons. First, Loy Henderson for his keen mind and ability to set down on paper in clear English and with a forceful style exactly what he wanted to say; Archie Roosevelt, for his brilliant scholarship and disciplined dedication to his work; Paul Converse, for his affable and winning personality; Alec Waugh, for his ever friendly cooperation, outgoing personality and perceptive understanding of political developments; and Ghazi Dhagestani, the most attractive Iraqi I met, for his all-around good nature which resulted, I am sure, from his Circassian genes. Among other Iraqis it was always a pleasure to be with were Fadhil al Jamali, who later became Foreign Minister, and of course, the worldly and pro-western Madame Afnan, who sent her daughter Furugh to Wellesley. Of my female girlfriends, the American-Armenian, Mary Abdini, easily took first prize. And this might well have been the case wherever I might have met her.

Mention has already been made of the Jewish community of Baghdad, which controlled a high percentage of the business and commerce of that city. Now, virtually all are gone – the great majority to Israel. Their distant ancestors should have returned to the Holy Land immediately following the *Captivity* of 500 BC, but most of them finally made it. Many of those who did not succeed in returning to the *Promised Land* of their forefathers were executed by the *Waters of Babylon*.

Once my orders of transfer to Prague via Dhahran arrived, I lost little time. My small Studebaker car that had been shipped to me not long after my arrival in Baghdad, I left behind until such time as I would pick it up upon my return from the Persian Gulf and en route to Europe. At that time of early summer, 1945, I could have sold this car for about $30,000, but then, how would I have gotten to Prague? Moreover, such a sale involving that unusual profit would hardly have gone down very well back in Washington or anywhere.

Chapter Eleven

Saudi Arabia

I set off for Dhahran by air in late June, 1945. The war in Europe was over and the United States was rapidly reinforcing its land, sea and air power in the East for the final attack against Japan. My plane stopped at Abadan, Iran, where the airport was teeming with grim-faced American paratroopers, female khaki-clad nurses, and airmen – all walking rapidly to or from aircraft. It was clear to see that great forces were being brought to bear against the Land of the Rising Sun.

Dhahran, my new, albeit temporary post, was a U.S. oil company (Aramco) camp situated on the outskirts of an Arab village on the shore of the Persian Gulf. The staff of the U.S. Consulate consisted of four Americans, including me, and I was to be in charge. Our duties consisted primarily in providing services for about two hundred or more American citizens who were working either in the Aramco office or in the nearby oil fields. At that time Aramco was owned by Standard Oil of California and Texaco on a fifty-fifty basis. The Consulate was also involved in maintaining frequent contact with the local sheikh as well as with the British Resident on the island of Bahrain which was situated about twenty-five miles off shore.

I could not have arrived at a worse time of year from the standpoint of climate; for every day the temperature soared to at least 110 and occasionally to 125 degrees Fahrenheit. Inland the humidity was low, but where we were, a few hundred yards from the water, it was always humid.

Just at that time a new airfield was in process of being planned and not long after my arrival, a ceremony marking the start of construction was held, with the local Sheikh in attendance. There ensued many flowery speeches on behalf of the United States government, of which one of the least impressive was contributed by me.

The four of us in the Consulate shared one rather small bungalow – two to each of the two bedrooms, with the office situated in an adjoining chamber. The air conditioning was primitive compared to what is now available. Throughout the

Foreign Service, Sunday was observed as a full holiday; during the war, Saturday was a workday. I was therefore surprised to find that as the Dhahran Consulate was in a Moslem country, my predecessor (that is, the Consul I was temporarily replacing) had decided to change the Consulate weekly holiday to Friday, the Moslem holiday. There was logic to this change as Aramco also took its weekly day off on Friday to facilitate its dealings with the Arabs. I might not act now as I did then, but felt that as the Consulate was part of America, we should do as Americans do. So I changed the day off to Sunday and this seemed not to cause any untoward problems.

Three of the oil company men (and wives) are well remembered: Floyd Ohliger, the Aramco president; Gary Owen, the head of liaison with the Arabs, and his deputy, Tom Barger, an unusually knowledgeable executive, who with his beautiful wife became my closest Aramco friends.

Mrs. Owen, who was of Russian origin, like to *receive* visitors while still in bed, in the eighteenth century style. By this I do not imply that her behavior was anything but perfectly correct; she just loved company and gossip, and in that social desert those visits were always enjoyable.

By far the most significant event – for me at least – of that three-month duty in Dhahran involved the strike at Ras Tanura, the site of a refinery being constructed to produce fuel oil for ships. In view of the fact that this oil, as soon as available, was destined for the United States Pacific fleet then poised for the invasion of Japan, it was essential that nothing impede the rapid construction of that refinery.

The situation at Ras Tanura was as follows. There were about four thousand Arab unskilled workers and some four hundred Italian skilled workers who had been recruited in Eritrea following the defeat of Italy and while they were still in a prisoner of war camp. It was these Italian workers who had gone on strike. According to the labor contract of these men, any future disputes involving an impasse were to be arbitrated and settled by the officer in charge of the American Consulate in Dhahran.

It was my custom, in step with the precedent which had been set by Parker Hart, the temporarily absent Consul, once a week to take a boat to cross the water to the island of Bahrain, where I would be at the service of Americans employed by the oil company in that small sheikhdom; I would also make a point of paying my respects to the British Resident, for Bahrain was then still a British Protectorate. In Short, Bahrain was part of my consular district. Bahrain was even more humid than Dhahran and the temperature just as hot. This climatic condition was compensated for by the break in the not-too-exciting routine. As it happened, it was while I was on one of these Bahrain visits that the Ras Tanura strike episode began for me.

I was having lunch with the British Resident in the small dining room that adjoined his office when a native messenger entered the room, bowed his head and announced that he had a message for the Honorable Mr. Birge, the American Consul. I lost no time in opening the envelope, which contained a short note from Floyd Ohliger, as follows.

"Dear Walter,

The four hundred Italian skilled workers at Ras Tanura have gone out on strike for a variety of reasons – none seemingly crucial. As you may be aware, according to the labor contract we made with these men when they were recruited last year, in the event that any dispute should arise over any aspect of labor conditions or for any other reason, it is mutually agreed by the company and by the workers that the officer in charge of the American Consulate at Dhahran shall arbitrate the dispute and his findings and recommendations shall be binding on both parties. Would you be good enough, Walter, to board the launch I have sent for you and meet with me in my office as soon as you land here – that, preparatory to your proceeding to Ras Tanura to do what you can to get those skilled workers back on the job. As I am sure you are aware, it will be the oil from that Ras Tanura refinery, when completed, which will supply the bulk of the fuel for our fleet in the Pacific. As the U.S. invasion of Japan is imminent, the stakes are high.

See you soon,
All best, Floyd"

What better opportunity could one ask to show that he had something on the ball? It took about forty-five minutes for the launch to reach Dhahran. I quickly stepped ashore and hurried to Floyd Ohliger's office that was only a quarter mile from the dock. Floyd's welcoming smile revealed relief at my arrival, for he and Aramco were in a predicament. Victory over Japan would be far more costly if Ras Tanura were to remain inactive. Floyd explained that the Italians had gone on strike because the Aramco office at Ras Tanura had failed to provide satisfactory answers to their several complaints. Floyd did not have all the details and went on to say that I would have to inform myself first hand in any case. I set off for Ras Tanura five minutes after leaving the Aramco office. Our Consulate had a four-by-four truck, that is, four wheels and four-wheel drive. A sand storm was just then starting so I donned a sort of Arab head-dress and light sunglasses both of which I would need during the upcoming fifty-mile drive up the coast road.

Ras Tanura refinery under construction was situated on a neck of land jutting out into the Gulf and I reached there in about an hour and forty-five minutes. I proceeded at once to the local Aramco office where the three top executives were awaiting me. There were no pleasantries, just dead-earnest faces and nervous concern and this was understandable. As soon as I had sat down opposite these men, I asked them to explain what the main gripes were that had brought about this strike. The local manager replied that there were a lot of things, and began to enumerate these complaints. I suggested that the best thing would be for me to call on the Italian spokesmen right away so that I could thus obtain an exact account of what they wanted.

It was only a short distance to the small building where the Italians were waiting for me. A company car drove me over. I was ushered into a sparsely furnished room measuring about twelve by fifteen feet; there were two open windows, but the air was stifling and dusty that early evening, with the thermometer registering 110 degrees. Five spokesmen for the strikers greeted me and motioned me to the only comfortable chair available. These men then sat down on camp chairs facing me, with Mr. Giulino, the leader (who resembled a small edition of Mussolini), in the middle of that group. He was the only spokesman, as his English was quite fluent, but laced with a marked Italian accent.

There was a moment of silence. Then I noticed that the two open windows were filled with a sea of faces – workers who did not want to miss anything going on. Unfortunately, their massed presence also prevented any air from entering the room.

I spoke first. "Mr. Giulino! I want you to understand that I do not represent the oil company. I am here as the representative of the United States and I am here to do what I can to settle the differences which have arisen between Aramco and the skilled workers from Italy." When Mr. Giulino had translated for his colleagues, I asked him to explain the nature of the complaints so that I could be in a position to negotiate with the Aramco representatives.

During that first meeting with Mr. Giulino and his team, I learned that the Italians wanted the following: 1) the construction of a social hall where meetings and occasional entertainment could be held, 2) lower prices for items on sale at the company store, such as shaving items, tooth-brushes and toothpaste, lotions, etc., 3) transport to and from work, 4) a clothing store, and 5) a continuing supply of milk. There were one or two minor requests.

When I had taken notes on the salient points raised by Mr. Giulino, I excused myself and promised to return within a half-hour and after consulting with the company officers.

There was no trouble about lowering the prices on the toilet articles, but at that first meeting with the Aramco men I did not receive satisfactory replies as to the other demands. I returned by my Italian friends. (I had begun to think of them as friends, for I felt sorry for them working long hours in that frightful climate with no transport and no diversions). When the small room became quiet save for a low buzz of whispered comments from the open windows. I said the following to Mr. Giulino, who in turn translated for his group. "Mr. Giulino, the company is prepared to lower the prices on all but a very few articles on sale for your skilled workers at the Aramco store. The company is also willing to set aside a fairly large room adjacent to the main dining hall for social events. The company has also agreed to provide transport to the refinery site on alternate days, as explained in the memorandum I am giving you now. By this system, two hundred workers will be transported each day. While this arrangement may seem cumbersome – that is, somewhat complicated – the company's urgent transport requirements for the movement of supplies prevents the company from transporting all four hundred workers each day." Mr. Giulino shook his head and then translated. There was a rapid exchange between the Italian spokesman and his colleagues. "Mr. Consul," then said Mr. Giulino, "we thank the company for lowering the prices on the necessary articles that our men must buy from time to time. However, our people as well as I, myself, insist that the recreation hall must be much larger than that suggested by the company. Moreover, we must also insist that transportation of all our men must be provided to and from the refinery every day. Will you kindly tell the company leaders what we wish?" I again took my leave in order to obtain answers to these counter-demands.

Back at Aramco local headquarters, I told the Aramco executives that I could not understand their inability to provide full transport for all Italian workers especially as the distance involved was not great. I also pointed out that as there were no outlets in the way of entertainment for the Italians, the company should certainly build a simple hall which would be large enough to hold all four hundred men; moreover, the company should arrange to obtain moving pictures with Italian sub-titles for shows at least twice a week in that hall. The company men somewhat reluctantly agreed to my suggestions. I then commented that as no mention had been made about a supply of milk during my last talk with the Italians, perhaps they would drop that subject. I then returned to the 110-degree room that felt like a small Chinese laundry on a mid-August day in New York. Immediately, there was silence, even from the curious listeners filling the windows. I informed Giulino that the company had agreed to his request for a large enough recreation hall with movies, and for daily transportation to and from work for all his men. Mr. Guilino and his men smiled broadly. I then addressed him again. "My friend, are you and your colleagues satisfied now by the company's proposals and are you prepared to return to work?"

There was still another moment of silence and then another exchange of rapid talk between Giulino and his men. "Mr. Consul," he then said, "you forgot about the milk, and our people also complain that the water we drink is salty – not sea water, but just salty enough so that it does not taste right." I then asked the Italian leader if he had any more requests to make. There was another exchange between Giulino and his men. "Yes, Mr. Consul, we have no more requests." I could not help grinning, as I was reminded of the early 1920's popular song, *Yes, We Have No Bananas.*

I went back again to the company men. "What can you do about a milk supply?" I asked. There was no answer. I went on. "How about getting hold of some goats? I heard somewhere that there are goats being raised somewhere between here and Dhahran. Could you arrange to bring goat-milk a couple of time a week for these men?" - "Hey, that's an idea," said the local general manager, "We'll do it, whatever problem may be involved." Then I added, "And what can you do about the salty tasting water the Italians object to?" - "There is nothing we can do about that, but tell the Italians that a little salt is the best protection against heat stroke." I was a bit dubious on that score, but I went back, hopefully for the last time, to the negotiating room to try to bring all this to a satisfactory conclusion.

Again, there came an abrupt silence when I entered the Ras Tanura *laundry.* "Mr. Giulino, you will get your milk – goat's milk, which is actually better than cow's milk." -"That's-a right, Mr. Consul, in-a my village, we drank-a goat's milk."

Then came again the question of the somewhat salty water, and the workers of Italy silently awaited my reply. "Gentlemen, there is nothing I can do about that drinking water, but the company doctor assures me that this slightly salty water is actually healthy in this hot climate. I tell you what I will do. I will persuade the company to supply free of charge one bottle per man, per day of bottled spring water or Coca Cola. How about that?" Of course, I had no idea whether my Aramco friends would agree to this relatively small extra expense, but I felt they would, given the high stakes involved.

Then came a near shocker from Mr. Giulino. "Mr. Consul, we have one more problem and please try to help us. Could you please arrange for beer to brought here? In this climate, wine is not so good, but beer would make our men so happy."

My back was against the wall. I well knew what the Saudi Arab government's policy on alcoholic beverages was – absolutely none! It was true that the American Aramco officials did smuggle in a few bottles of whisky, but other than that, nothing. "Mr. Giulino", I replied, "I am sure that you must know how strict the Saudi Arab government is about importation of alcoholic drinks. I do not want to see any of your men condemned to prison or even death. No, Mr. Giulino, I cannot help you on this question." - "All right, Mr. Consul, I agree; I understand. But

I do not know if all my workers will agree and understand!" – "Mr. Giulino, I am confident that a man with the qualities of leadership which you possess will be able to persuade his men to agree on this fundamental question. So, are we in accord on all questions?" – Yes, Mr. Consul, and thank you for what you have done to help us."

With that, I shook hands with each of the Italian leaders, waved a goodbye to the score of onlookers crowded at the windows, and took my leave. All that remained for me to do then was to go back to the Aramco Ras Tanura headquarters to report the good news and then drive back to Dhahran. I drove those fifty miles back to Dhahran with a light heart and the next morning – actually the same morning, for by then it was about one-thirty a.m., work resumed at the refinery and the future supply of oil for the Pacific Fleet was assured.

As it turned out, the significance of that little arbitration sank out of sight, for one week after that evening's work, the A-bomb was dropped on Hiroshima and there was nothing of further prime importance for our Pacific Fleet to do.

Floyd Ohliger wrote a very commendatory letter to the State Department on my behalf giving me a praise I did not deserve. I figured that this welcome addition to my personnel file in the Department would bring a promotion. Less than a year later when I was back in the United States on my first leave in four years, I stopped by the Department of Personnel in Washington. Not a word was said about Ohliger's laudatory letter; nor was mention made of Henderson's *delighted and surprised* comment – only a mention that the latter thought me *immature*. But that was later. This was still the summer of 1945 when I was riding high and believing that I had a great career ahead.

As I write these lines many years after the above-mentioned events, Dhahran is again front page news; Ras Tanura is shown on TV as a huge refinery; Dhahran is shown as a large flourishing town with high-rise buildings. But then the refinery – a far smaller one – was not quite yet built and Dhahran was a little settlement. A few days following the Italian workers strike episode, the Department cabled that a congressional delegation led by Senator Mundt of Minnesota was scheduled to fly to Dhahran for a short visit en route to Riyadh where they would visit for two days with King Ibn Saud. I was instructed to accompany the delegation to Riyadh.

The first event of that exercise which looms large in my mind's eye after all these years is the impressive reception when we were all ushered into the great king's presence. First, we passed between two lines of guards, each holding a gleaming scimitar pointing upward, faces expressionless yet somehow purposeful. King Ibn Saud was seated in a large armchair, which could be described as a throne, at the end of a long chamber that measured perhaps seventy by twenty feet. The delegation, plus U.S. Embassy officers and I sat on either side of the room, along with sundry Saudi officials.
The king remained seated and his utterances were translated by an impressive white-robed individual whose fluent English had obviously been learned in England. The great king, resplendent in his long white robe and gold-bound head-dress, held up his hand for silence, for there had been a low buzzing of muted conversation. The king spoke thus. "Good friends from the great United States. I give you greeting. According to Islamic tradition, guests remain with their hosts three days. This applies especially to guests as honored as you, and your colleague, Senator Mundt." The Senator then addressed the interpreter. "Please explain to his majesty that it will not be possible for us to remain for three days as we are scheduled to be in Beirut the evening of the day after tomorrow." The king replied to this rejoinder, "Senator, the customs of Islam are strict and explicit. It would be insulting to you and your delegation for me to allow you to leave before the three-day period. I expect, therefore, that I will have the continued pleasure of your company for two more days." The senator replied, "Your majesty, President Truman has ordered us to adhere to a rather strict schedule and he expects us to obey, as, indeed, you expect your subjects to follow your orders. We are deeply honored to be the recipients of your hospitality, but ask your indulgence on this occasion so that we can take a reluctant departure tomorrow afternoon." All of us Americans there looked at one another and almost held our breath during this exchange. The king raised his hand. "I relent, - so be it. I will allow you to follow the orders of my esteemed friend, President Truman." The major domo (or whatever his title) then motioned for coffee. Each of us was given a small cup of that very special mocha. The servants raised the gleaming copper container about two feet above the cup, and without spilling so much as a drop, filled each cup to exactly the right level. This feat must have required weeks of practice.

That same evening everyone – that is, all except Congresswoman Edith Bolton of Ohio – had dinner with King Ibn Saud and all his grown sons at an elaborate banquet held on the roof of his palace. Mrs. Bolton (whose grandson, Charlie, became a close friend thirty years later) had dinner with all the king's wives in a separate chamber. The king sat with his many sons on one side of the long table, with Senator Mundt and the interpreter directly opposite, and the other American guests sat on either side of the Senator, so each of us sat opposite one of the king's sons. It so happened that I found myself seated opposite Prince Fahd, who later ascended the throne.

That night, the senator and congressmen and I slept on the roof of the guest quarters to which we had been assigned. The beds were rather narrow, but comfortable. Dawn was just breaking when I opened my eyes the next morning, and the venturesome flies, now becoming active at first light, began to alight on any exposed skin – that is, face and arms – thus making fruitless any thought of further sleep. Then from the top of the steep stairway that led to our roof, there emerged three white-clad figures, moving noiselessly. Each of these men carried a dagger and seemingly other things which, in the semi-darkness I could not identify. They moved quietly from bed to bed. At first I feared – in the sleepy and semi-conscious state I was then in – that we were about to be silently put to death, but within a second or two I became fully awake and realized that these messengers of the king were bringing gifts – one for each of us.

Most of the American guests received rather costly presents. As I was the lowest of the low in rank and certainly the least important of those men on that roof, my gift turned out to be an Ingersol watch made of nickel. It was, however, a gift from a king and I later presented it to my eight-year-old son.

One more event seems worthy of mention before I take leave of my duty in Dhahran. As the reader is probably aware, the Koran, as well as ancient Jewish custom, instructed that *an eye for an eye and a tooth for a tooth* should be the guide for punishing evildoers. Hence, if you ran over and thus killed someone – with the driver presumably at fault – you, the driver, were to be put to death. Not long before my departure, Joe, one of the subordinate Aramco officials, known to me as a decent sort, entered our Consulate building by the back door, accompanied by another American dressed in the rough work clothes of a driller. Both men were out of breath and obviously distraught. I greeted them and asked what I could do for them, as they seemed upset. Two minutes of rapid talk by my two visitors revealed that the driller (Jim) had run over an Arab as he was driving his company truck back to the motor pool. As Jim had been traveling at about thirty miles and hour when he ran over the Arab, who was very seriously injured or, more likely, dead, and as an angry crowd had rapidly begun to gather, he left the scene and drove to the company hoping to find Joe to help him.

I instructed the two men to remain where they were, having first ascertained that as far as they knew they had not been followed to our Consulate. I then walked to Floyd Ohlinger's office. My father would have admired Ohlinger, for here was a man who never hesitated in coming to a decision. After I had briefly explained the oil driller's dangerous predicament, Floyd replied in the tone used for command in an emergency. "Walter, one hour after sunset – that is, in about an hour – our launch will be ready at the small and not-often used Executive's Pier which, as Joe knows, is at the foot of Suleyman Street. Please get our *eye for an eye man* down there at the appointed time. That will be at eight o'clock and we'll get him over to Bahrain. All right?"

When I got back to my office, my three Foreign Service colleagues, Joe, the junior company executive and the by now sought-after driller, Jim, were all in my bedroom. The office lights had been extinguished as the Consulate had been closed already for an hour or so. I explained what we were to do and we all just sat there and helped ourselves from the bottles of Scotch whiskey that had been provided to me at cost by the British Resident on Bahrain.

A few minutes after eight o'clock, four of us left the Consulate: the two company men, Dave MacIntosh, my very able deputy, and me. We first carefully made sure that no one was around and then very quickly got into our four-by-four truck. A small American flag was attached to the foot-high staff on the right front fender as was customary. The driller-fugitive immediately crouched down on the floor to my right and the other two men – for I was driving – sat to my right on that wide front seat, with their feet on him.

As we drove out of the Aramco camp we could see a few cars being stopped by Saudi police. On reaching the first roadblock, I showed my Saudi identification card and pointed to the flag. The policeman peered into the truck, but it was almost dark; moreover, Jim had been carefully covered by a canvas tarp. We were waved on and when we arrived at the small dock, the company launch was waiting, her powerful twin engines idling with their purposeful, characteristic growl. All four of us boarded the boat, but Mac and I disembarked immediately upon hearing the sound of shouting. Just as we were climbing back onto the pier a couple of running figures materialized about a hundred feet away, where the road ended a the foot of the dock. They had perhaps been alerted by the sound of the idling engines. That, however, became academic, for with a roar – a most comforting sound – the twin Chrysler marine engines were already propelling the launch out into the Gulf and the driller to safety.

Neither Mac not I could understand a word of the staccato Arabic directed at us by the pair of armed men who rushed up to us gesticulating and pointing to the vanishing launch. I assumed that they were police out of uniform, so I just pointed to our small flag and we drove off. And that little escape episode was a harbinger of what I was to encounter about three years later and fifteen hundred miles to the northwest in far-off Bohemia.

My tour of duty in Dhahran came to an end in mid-September, 1945, when I received a telegram from the Department that Parker Hart would be returning the following week to resume his duties as officer in charge of the Consulate. By that time – the end of my duty on the shore of the Persian Gulf – the great war was finally over; V-E Day had come and gone in early May of that momentous year, and with the destruction of Hiroshima and Nagasaki by the atom bomb in early August and V-J Day which followed a few days later, calm came again to the Pacific and the world was once more at peace.

While long-range travel at that time of post-war disruption would undoubtedly pose problems, I did not expect serious difficulties, provided I could find a freighter that could transport my car and me to an Italian or French port. I gave the few bottles of Scotch I had purchased to my three colleagues, bid farewell to Floyd Ohlinger and my other Aramco friends and took off for Baghdad on a U.S. military transport flight of which there were many during that period.

I stopped over in Baghdad for ten days which gave me enough time to bid many friends goodbye, draft letters of commendation on behalf of my Dhahran staff and play a final game of poker with Colonel Converse, George Moffit and our two Polish friends. I also briefed a visiting American army officer who was gathering intelligence information. With regard to that briefing, this major commented that my comments on the general political situation in Iraq was the most valuable he had received from anyone, and he asked whether I would like to have him write to Washington to that effect. I made a mistake by simply thanking the major and suggesting that he not take the trouble, for I was certain that Aramco would have commended me for my part in the settling of the Ras Tanura strike, and I remembered Henderson's "delighted and surprised" letter. Floyd Ohliger did write a strong letter of commendation to the Department about my arbitrating the strike, so when I left Baghdad, I was confident that all was right in the future on my career.

Chapter Twelve

Baghdad to Prague

I had left my small automobile in Baghdad. This practical four-door sedan, a 1944 model Studebaker, had been shipped to me by the Department for the logical reason that a car was well nigh essential in that post. At that time, this car cost me about $1300 in view of the fact that the department enjoyed a special discount. Soon after arriving back in Baghdad, as already mentioned, I was offered $30,000 for that car by a well-heeled Iraqi. I never gave more than a momentary consideration to this tempting offer for two reasons: first, it did not seem right to profit because of the special post-war situation; second, how could I reach Czechoslovakia with a trunk and other impedimenta unless in my own car? There were no air flights and I would not chance trying to go by train to Turkey and then through an Eastern Europe in chaos, determined to cross the desert in the little Studebaker and try to find a ship in either Beirut or Alexandria.

The day before my appointed departure, Colonel Converse suggested that he supply me with *Military Orders* in view of the fact that I would be passing through areas controlled by the Allied armies. Not only would such a pass ensure a safe passage, but it would also enable me to obtain gasoline at Allied fuel stations. How right the good colonel was! Had it not been for his very official-looking pass, I would have had a difficult time indeed.

The day before leaving Baghdad, Frank, a young clerk in our legation asked whether I would give him a lift to Damascus. It seems that he was due two weeks leave and my transport offered the least expensive way for him to reach the Syrian capital.

Another interesting sideline was that Memminger, one of the more decent FSO arrivals in Baghdad, suggested that I take with me a huge Colt revolver that had been in the Legation inventory for many years – doubtless a relic of the First World War.

For luggage, I had a flat steamer trunk and two suit cases. The trunk fitted perfectly on the floor in front of the back seat. As a precaution against desert hazards, I brought along a *jerry tin* of gasoline and another of water.

Just as I was about to depart, the two Arab houseboys, Al-Wahn and Mohammed, rushed up to bid me tearful goodbyes. I was very touched by their outpouring of sentiment, for I had become quite fond of them as I think they had of me. I was aware that Al-Wahn had almost certainly made away with my blue cummerbund, but I could not be provoked with this devoted character for more than a few minutes.

There was only one road connecting Baghdad with Jordan, Palestine and Syria. This narrow, seven hundred mile long highway to the Dead Sea followed the Iraq Petroleum Company pipeline, which at that time connected the Mosul oil fields with Haifa, the Palestinian port on the Mediterranean. After the founding of the State of Israel of which Haifa was the main port, that pipeline route was no longer used owing to the enmity of the Arab States against Israel. At the time of my trip the trans-desert pipeline had several pumping stations placed about a hundred miles apart. The Iraq Petroleum Company had made arrangements for me and my young passenger to spend the night at their H4 pumping station, about 350 miles west of Baghdad.

We cruised along at a fairly steady pace of sixty miles an hour. From time to time Frank would light up a cigarette, which proved to be unwise and almost disastrous. We were driving with all the windows open and unfortunately an ash from Frank's cigarette blew back and onto the rear seat. The first thing we knew of this was a smell of smoke and from the rearview mirror I could now see smoke rising from that seat. I at once pulled over, leapt out, opened the rear door and could see that black fumes were pouring out from a charred hole in the seat. There was only one thing to do. I opened the car trunk, made sure which Jerry tin contained water and poured a half-gallon down the burn hole. Luckily, that seemed to take care of our little incendiary problem.

That episode brings to mind the Arab method of keeping water cool in the hot desert while traveling. They would fill a porous earthenware jug with water and attach it to the side or front of their vehicle. As they drove along, the slight dampness on the outside of that jug rapidly evaporated in the hot, dry wind, thus cooling the water inside the jug. Even on the hottest day, they had available a cool drink and with no refrigeration involved. I was not far-sighted enough to have brought such a jug along with us, but I had brought a thermos container and that helped to an extent.

We arrived at H4 in the late afternoon and were warmly greeted by the British staff of the firm, which at that time was controlled by the Anglo-Persian Oil Company. We had arrived at near the westernmost part of Iraq and early the following morning we set out for Damascus, the Syrian capital, via Jordan, first due west and then abruptly north, while the pipeline continued westward on to Haifa. At that time, (1945) there was a daily bus – a small vehicle by today's standards – run by the Nairn Bus Company, a British concern that provided the only communication and means of public travel between Baghdad and Syria or Lebanon. At that time, also, Jordan was still called Transjordan, a kingdom which the British had carved out of Palestine immediately following the end of World War One to provide Sheriff Hussein with a kingdom, notwithstanding that the Balfour Declaration of 1917 had stipulated that all of Palestine (which included the Transjordan area) was to be turned over to the Jews for their homeland.

I arrived in Damascus in mid-afternoon and I saw for the first time the *Street called Straight*, surely one of the oldest and best known streets in the world, which is logical when it is remembered that Damascus is reputed to be the oldest continually inhabited city in the world.

The following day, after lunching with Mr. Wadsworth, the American ambassador, I set out for Beirut – alone now. It was first across the Syrian plain and through ancient Balbek, then up into the mountains of Lebanon, which rise to some six thousand feet overlooking the Mediterranean Sea, and then down to Beirut, that civilized (as it then was) city, called the *Paris of the East*, where Christians and Moslems still lived in harmony.

There were three reasons for my visit to Beirut; first, to ascertain whether there might be a vessel available which could transport me and my car to a western European port; second, because Mary Abdini had moved back to that city where her parents were then living; and third, because I remembered Beirut to be an unusually pleasant place that was not out of the way.

I did not find a ship for me and my car, but I did spend a pleasant week in Beirut and saw Mary three times. I was very fond of her, but not quite in love, so our relationship did not progress. I was then full of the adventure of going to the new post in Central Europe and Mary belonged to another world, so we parted amicably. I was destined to see her once again about seventeen years later when I was on a business trip to that part of the world. She was then married and living in a large, elegant mansion but she was still a beauty and I daresay still is at this writing. [c.1990]

When it became clear that there would be no vessel for transport, I decided to try my luck in Alexandria; but the fates conspired to usher in another interesting episode. Two days prior to my departure I was invited to a cocktail party by a Lebanese official I had met at a reception given by the U.S. ambassador in Beirut. This party was held high in the mountains in an impressive dwelling that looked over that sea some four thousand feet below. There were several attractive young women there, all Lebanese girls with one exception, Clothilde, and she was the star of that party. After being introduced, I asked the usual opening questions which revealed that she was Egyptian but descended from one of the beautiful Circassian girl slaves which Mohammed Ali had imported from the Caucasus Mountains ("pour embellir cette race", as he said) to marry off to leading Egyptian men. She was quite tall and slender with rather dark blond hair like burnished gold. She informed me that she was from Alexandria, had been visiting friends and was planning soon to return to Egypt. We spoke French, as her English was poor, and I informed her I was leaving for Alexandria in two days and would be happy to give her a ride. She accepted readily and I picked her up at the St. George Hotel, where I was staying. Her suitcases were stowed on the back seat and we set off via Tyre, Sidon, and Tel Aviv.

In the days of my generation's youth, the first move when you wanted to *make time* with a girl (as we used to say) was to hold her hand, then caress it. Of course, while driving, and especially when a long trip was involved, there was not much else you could attempt. I was somewhat discomfited, however, when Clothilde, my beautiful companion, withdrew her left hand that I had gently taken hold of with my right hand, the steering having been temporarily entrusted solely to my left hand. It was thus clear to me that she wished to establish the travel rules, leaving no doubt that there was to be no chance of more intimate contact.

This gentle withdrawal of my comely passenger's hand posed no problem at all inasmuch as by far the first priority was to keep moving south, and second, to enjoy the scenery with its fleeting glimpses of the picturesque coast. It was not a long trip to Tel Aviv, and we arrived at that bustling Jewish city at about five that afternoon. I noted that the doorman looked much more Slavic than Jewish – a logical introduction to my upcoming new post.

I requested two rooms in that hotel; Clothilde clearly expected this outcome as the natural result of her *hands-off* behavior. My companion had informed me that she had good friends in Tel Aviv, a family that had emigrated from Alexandria a few years before. When we re-met in the lobby twenty minutes later, after getting settled in our respective rooms, Clothilde said that she had telephoned her friends and that we were invited to their apartment for supper.

That evening turned out to be enjoyable and interesting, probably because it was my first visit in that country about which I had heard a great deal from both Teddy Kollek and Ari Chill. To my mind, it seemed also noteworthy that an Egyptian Christian girl was apparently on such friendly terms with Jewish expatriates from Egypt. The reason may well have been that Christians and Jews at times were drawn to each other for survival in a Moslem-Arab sea. That had not been the case in Baghdad, so I figured that Egypt was different owing to the more than a thousand year old international flavor of Alexandria.

In that year – 1945 – the Irgun and the Stern Gang were becoming increasingly active, as well organized, sub rosa and often-terrorist elements dedicated to the eventual creation of an independent Israel. Sometimes they operated in tandem with the Haganah; often they did not, but the ultimate aim of all Jews in Palestine was the same. The British occupying power was then seeking to prevent any further Jewish immigration – this, notwithstanding the recent liberation of the few survivors of the Nazi extermination camps and the revelation that millions of men, women, and children had been gassed and cremated in Hitler's *Endlösung*.

I am and have always been pro-British. I do not fault my island-dweller cousins on much; however, their handling of the Zionist settlement in Palestine and their policy of seeking to appease the Arabs with a view to setting up an eventual network of client Arab states was ruthless behavior in view of the Balfour Declaration, which had been enthusiastically endorsed by the leading Arab ruler, King Hussein, the Hashemite ruler of Transjordan. Also, Zionist leaders had reminded Downing Street of the invaluable contribution during the First World War, not only of the brilliant Jewish chemists who had shown the British how to obtain nitrogen from the air, thus obviating the necessity of bringing nitrates all the way from Chile, but also bearing in mind the very significant contribution of Aaron Aaronson to British victory over the Turks in Palestine during that war when he organized the *Nili Group*, an intelligence service for the British behind the Turkish lines. This intelligence proved indispensable. The British General Gribbon later expressed the opinion that in the crucial battle for Beersheba, it had saved 30,000 British lives.

Despite these factors and in accord with its pro-Arab stance, it was still in 1945 British policy as the occupying power in Palestine to delay as long as possible the establishment of an independent Jewish state in that part of Palestine, the population of which was predominantly Jewish.

Notwithstanding this policy of the British occupying power, the infiltration of Jewish survivors of the holocaust continued. Even more significant was that the Jews in Palestine became superbly organized. Especially noteworthy, the Haganah – the army of the so-called Jewish Agency – gave promise of becoming a first-rate fighting force. A special problem for the British during 1945-47 was the undercover Stern Gang and Irgun, which began a series of retaliations against the British. If, for example, a Jewish leader was arrested because of some action prepetrated against the British, one or two British officers were likely to disappear and be held hostage until the Jewish arrestee was released. Some of those who were adults during that period will remember those occasions when those hostages were executed as soon as the British put to death Jewish prisoners who had been accused of committing a capital offense. At the time of my passing through Tel Aviv five months after the end of the war in Europe, the situation in Palestine was not yet explosive, but it very soon would be, with the culmination of violence in the year 1948, a year fraught with turmoil in the Middle East where the fledgling Jewish state was fighting for existence and surviving, though outnumbered ten to one.

But now, *revenons à nos moutons,* as Clothilde might have said. (Let's get back to the subject).

The morning following our visit in the apartment of her friends, we set out for Gaza and the Sinai. While packing my effects that morning, I noticed that a very beautiful gold cross and chain, a parting gift from Alexandra, my Russian friend in Istanbul, was missing and not to be found. Anyone of the hotel staff could have stolen it and there was nothing to be done. That treasured remembrance probably found its way eventually into the hands of a tourist. By me, it was and still is sorely missed.

Most of our journey to Alexandria was through sparsely settled lands. Between the desolate strip of land that would later be called *The Gaza Strip* and Egypt, nary a soul was to be seen. Then a sand storm blew up and the visibility became so poor that twice I strayed from the narrow road, but somehow managed to get back onto terra firma. Had we become stuck in that country, it would have been a long time before any help would have arrived; furthermore, that help might well have been ominous.

Clothilde and I got on very well; while sometimes we both were silent, most of the time she was quite talkative and entertaining, so the hours of that otherwise rather boring drive passed quickly. As we had started out early, the little Studebaker purred into Alexandria in the late afternoon. I began to ponder what I should do that evening and I glanced at Clothilde who, despite the long, dusty, sandy, hot trip looked every bit as attractive as when I had first seen her. "If you are free this evening, would you like to have dinner with me?" I asked. With an enchanting smile she replied "Mais, oui, Walter, avec plaisir. Je connais un très bon restaurant.

As I had never been in Alexandria, I asked my companion to suggest a hotel, which she did and it turned out to be quite elegant - the best in the city - I was assured by the American Consul General when I called on him the following day.

Clothilde told me that she lived not far from my hotel and would meet me there at eight o'clock. First I drove her to the apartment house where she lived with her parents and I helped her remove her two suitcases from the car. A doorman of sorts then took over and I drove back the three blocks to my hotel. I had two hours to kill so I took a bath, changed my clothes and descended to the lobby where I struck up a conversation with a quite attractive telephone operator who worked at her switchboard that was right next to the check-in counter.

Then came a unique experience – for me, that is. It was not important, but it did tell me something about the nature of some females. It was unique because it never happened again.

Clothilde arrived at my hotel a little before eight and we set out on foot as she explained that her favorite restaurant was nearby. I have remembered that meal, but not because of its excellent cuisine. During the dessert course, Clothilde became increasingly pensive. Then with a hesitant, shy smile, she looked into my eyes and said in a low voice, carefully articulating every word in her perfect French, "Walter, I have something very personal to say and then an important question to ask. Do you mind?" I placed my hand over hers and assured her that I was interested in whatever she wished to say. Clothilde swallowed as one sometimes does before making a significant statement. "Walter, I have decided that I would like very much to marry you and I ask if you look favorably upon what I have just said?"

It would be an understatement to say that I was taken aback. I replied quietly, "Clothilde, you are an unusually attractive young woman and I am deeply touched as well as flattered by what you have just said. However, I have known you only three days and marriage is for a lifetime. Also please understand that I will be leaving this city very soon. Moreover, our Foreign Office still has in effect a regulation that an officer of the Foreign Service must submit his resignation at the same time that he requests permission to marry a foreigner." Clothile did not change her expression, but I could see the hurt in her eyes. "Tell me, Clothilde," I then said, "how is it that you have honored me by what you have just said and asked?" She replied, "My parents have often told me that I should marry a gentleman; and I know that you are a gentleman by the respect you treated me with on our trip from Beirut. That is why I spoke as I did."

Soon after our dinner together, I bid a final farewell to the beautiful Clothilde. I wondered if her head would always rule her heart as she followed a path planned by her parents. I would never know, but I imagine that she remained a dutiful daughter.

The following morning, I drove to the United States Consulate General to inquire about the availability of a freighter to transport me and my car to a South European port with convenient overland access to Prague. The Consul at once made a telephone call and then turned to me. "You are in luck. There is a 1,000 ton (that is, very small) British freighter due to sail tomorrow for Naples." The Consul then telephoned the ship's agent and ascertained that this vessel could take my car, so all I had to do was drive to the pier and leave the Studebaker in charge of the agent. The ship was scheduled to sail at eleven the next morning. Thus, I had the better part of a day to kill.

That afternoon of mid-October was memorable for I came by chance to know another young woman – a Slav this time – whose heart seemed to be her guiding force. After leaving the Consulate, I returned to my hotel and struck up anew my conversation with the telephone operator. After a few minutes of talk spasmodically interrupted by her plugging in and taking out her lines on the switchboard, this friendly operator suggested that I meet her at six o'clock at which time we could go together up to the room of a friend, a young woman who worked as an older woman's companion, but who was free at that hour and liked to make the acquaintance of new people.

I agreed to meet my new friend at six and I set out on foot to explore that polyglot city where Greek and French were spoken by all educated people and even by many uneducated ones. Here had ruled in turn many empires: the Pharaohs, the Greeks, the Romans, the Turks, the Arabs, the English, and in 1942, almost the Germans under Rommel, *The Desert fox.* The British hold was now being loosened. There was nothing typical about Alexandria except that it was very different from any other city of the Middle East. Not long after the time of my visit, there would begin the emigration of Jews to Israel, a people who had lived there for a millennium and a half.

Shortly after six, my switchboard acquaintance guided me to the room of her friend whose name was Anna Cherchich, an unusually appealing young woman, of Yugoslav nationality. Apparently, these two women had planned things so that I was to remain in Anna's room for an hour or so after which I would leave and the operator would return to spend most of the evening with Anna. It seemed a little complicated, but everything worked out well, as far as I was concerned at least. Anna was blond and blue eyed, with typical Slavic features. We spoke the lingua franca of Alexandria – French – and established instant rapport. The *telephoniste* left and told Anna pointedly that she would return at six-thirty. Anna then served us an excellent sherry and we chatted amicably for a while. I then got up to leave, but asked if I could return later, after the telephone girl had left. Anna replied with a certain smile, "A dix Heures".

I dined alone, returned to my room, and tried to read a book, while I awaited the hour of ten. I then descended the stairs (she was one floor below me) and knocked on her door. It opened gently and there stood that young woman whose eyes and smile welcomed me without words. In a moment, she was in my arms and scarcely left them until early the next morning. At another time and with none of the problems involving urgent departure and the exigencies of my Foreign Service career, this lovable girl might have become more important to me than the circumstances permitted. Special mention has been made about this warm hearted Yugoslav girl because her out-going nature, spontaneous show of affection coupled with an innate dignity made an impression, notwithstanding the very short time I spent with her. Time would not stand still, however, so I bid her a reluctant farewell, never to see her again. I could not bear to take my departure, however, without leaving some sort of gift for Anna to remember me by. Back in 1939, Grace's new Indian husband had given me a set of gold cufflinks set with stones, which appeared to be diamonds. Over the years I had given away two of these links, and, in fact, had never used them. So I wrapped up the two remaining links and while having breakfast handed the small package, together with a note, to my waiter for delivery to Miss Anna Cherchich. Perhaps this gift may seem luxurious for such a fleeting contact, an ephemeral acquaintance, yet I felt sympathy for Anna, obviously a girl of good family come upon hard times, exiled from her homeland, alone in the world and the paid companion of an older woman. A month or so later, in answer to a note I wrote to her from Prague, she informed me that she had had an attractive pin made from the cufflinks and would always think of me and remember our night together when she wore it.

At noon of that day when I checked out of my hotel, I boarded the small freighter. My car had already been safely stowed in that ship's only hold and it barely fitted. We slowly steamed out of the harbor at six knots and that was the speed at which we proceeded to Naples and for that reason it took us six days to reach that port.

When I climbed on board, I was greeted by Captain Hughes, who said, "You're to bed down in the pilot's cabin. It's only big enough for you to change your mind in, but I hope you will be reasonably comfortable." The captain was right. The cabin was miniscule, but the bunk was comfortable.

I took my meals with the very few officers of the ship – five in all – and they were a pleasant group; joking, telling off-color stories and ensuring that I felt at home. What was noteworthy on that trip was the radio broadcast from England announcing that Clement Atlee had defeated the great Winston Churchill in the election for the office of Prime Minister. None of these officers seemed surprised at this election result and their comments made it clear that their loyalties lay with the Labor Party. They were hardly a conservative group. To me, it seemed incomprehensible that only five months following Britain's great victory – a triumph made possible by the tenacious courage of this great man – one of England's all-time heroes – he would be turned out of office. I had never heard of Atlee. Not long after this election, Churchill is said to have remarked, "Clement Atlee is a modest man and he has much to be modest about." Many were to agree with this assessment.

Our ship moved slowly into the harbor of Naples on the sixth day at sundown. There we remained motionless at anchor for a day and a half. Finally, impatient at this delay, I hailed a taxi-oarsman and had him row me to shore. Nothing was gained by this move except for a welcome change of scene. I did use the occasion to call at the American Consulate General and chatted for a few minutes with Bob Newbegin, a Foreign Service Officer whom I never met again.

Not far from our vessel and tied to the main piers were large U.S. passenger ships taking on thousands of soldiers about to be repatriated. The decks were a sea of khaki uniforms and large signs were affixed to the side of these transports with messages such as *Here We Come U.S.A.* and *Goodbye War.* It was a scene not soon to be forgotten. But for me it was not a farewell to Europe and hello America, for on the second day our small freighter slowly moved to a pier and my car was hoisted out of the hold. That was in the morning and I set out up the coast road, bound for Rome. I drove through country that had been bitterly fought over for two years when General Mark Clark's army had slowly but relentlessly forced back the hard fighting defenders led by Marshal Kesselring. Perhaps a third of the way between Naples and Rome, there loomed to my right the ruined monastery of Monte Cassino, the strong point perched on a high hill, which had finally been subdued, partly owing to the valor of the Polish contingent under Allied command.

Ten or fifteen miles further on, I noted a woman by the side of the road motioning that she wanted a lift, so I stropped the car and motioned to her to get in. I might not have done so had I realized that she was carrying two live chickens in a sack. She had hardly taken her seat next to me when both of these birds somehow got loose and tore around the car, shedding feathers and making a frightful racket. That was bad enough, but what almost caused an accident was the sudden move of one of these fowl to the windshield directly in front of me so that I could not see to drive and I came to a stop just in time to avoid hitting a telegraph pole. Happily, the good woman's destination was only a few miles up the road.

Some fifty miles short of reaching Rome, I noted that my fuel gauge showed almost empty. At that time there were very few, if indeed any, gas stations on the Italian highways, so my only hope was to get to a military post of some kind and I was then grateful that I had been given that military pass by Colonel Converse – a document that requested any Allied military command to give aid and assistance. Fortunately, I soon came to a large command post which was under U.S. jurisdiction and I drove up to the main gate where I was met by an impressive looking non-com whom I easily identified as a member of a Polish contingent, for he wore a Polish emblem on his sleeve.

I got out of the car and began to explain who I was and where bound. He obviously spoke no English, so I showed him my special pass, but that made no impression either. Foolishly, I made a move to walk past him in what appeared to be the command post general headquarters and with that the Polish guard lowered his rifle so that the fixed bayonet was an inch from my chest. I then had the good sense to step back and I spoke the few words which I hoped would be effective, namely, "American, Chicago, America-Polska" – the last while clasping both hands together to indicate friendship. At once, a broad grin replaced the menacing scowl on the countenance of that Slavic warrior and he brought his gun down, then leaned it against the small guardhouse and seized my arms in a gesture of friendship, and a tear of emotion, or perhaps of joy gave mute evidence of what he felt at that moment. I had met several Poles in Istanbul and in Baghdad, refugees from Soviet internment camps, and I was to meet more of these fine people in Czechoslovakia. I can say that I never met a Pole who did not have warm feelings for the United States. The actions of this lonely guard, far from home and probably with an uncle in Chicago or Buffalo, said it all.

The camp commander took one look at Colonel Converse's special travel document and promptly gave orders to let me have all the gasoline I required. I not only filled my tank, but two jerry tins as well.

This was not a sightseeing trip so I had no intention of remaining in Rome any longer than absolutely necessary. I arrived in that fabled city to which all roads lead, in late afternoon and in that October of the VE year there was no trouble in finding a suitable hotel. I asked the desk if they could recommend a good restaurant conveniently located and with some form of entertainment for someone traveling alone. The effusive clerk replied that he knew just the place and rapidly wrote the name and address on a sheet of hotel stationary. He then said, "Also, please tell the *Maître d'Hôtel* that I sent you."

Almost half a century after that time, I do not remember much about that restaurant. I do recall, however, that there was an orchestra playing dance music; I also see in my mind's eye the head waiter asking me whether I might like to dance with a young woman who was unescorted. "Certainly," I assured that solicitous minister to what I might wish. And lo and behold, within a minute, he escorted to my table an attractive young woman of about twenty-five, quite tall for an Italian, with a good figure, dark hair, but the blue eyes of some Nordic ancestor. Not surprisingly, her name was Maria. The headwaiter introduced her as Signorina Agnelli – Maria Agnelli. This evening's companion spoke passable English, probably owing to exposure to the American Army of occupation during the previous year. I naturally invited Maria to have dinner if she had not already dined. She accepted and we enjoyed an excellent repast together with a bottle of Chianti.

I told Maria about my upcoming departure for the north via Florence, Venice and Austria and when she asked whether I could give her a ride to Venice as she had been planning to go to the north of Italy about then, I replied that this was a fine idea and asked if she could meet me at my hotel on the morrow at nine in the morning. When I spoke these words, I thought back to my experience of ten days before on the eastern Mediterranean littoral. There were a few but not many similarities between the two excursions. Maria was a pleasant companion, but her halting English prevented meaningful conversation and exchange of ideas and experiences. Moreover, there seemed to be lacking that special spark of warm rapport, which is sometimes described as the chemistry of mutual attraction. There was, of course, a certain physical attraction and the trip with Maria was much more enjoyable than would have been the case without her company.

In Florence, we spent a half-day sight seeing – a totally inadequate tribute to that fabulous city – followed by an expected and enjoyable, albeit not earth-shaking, intimite encounter between us.

Before reaching Venice, we made one short and uneventful stop at mid-morning in Bologna, recently the Communist stronghold in Italy, before arriving in Venice in early afternoon of the third day. I thought back on my visit to that city back in 1924 when mother, Claire, Julius, Grace and I spent three days there. On that occasion mother made a few purchases of glassware, linen, and, as already mentioned, some lovely antique painted Venetian furniture, two pieces of which my wife and I now have. On the fourth morning of our trip, I put Maria on a bus bound for Rome via Ferrara, where she had relatives, with enough money to cover her passage, plus a little in addition – and I set forth for Austria and my final destination, *Golden Prague.*

My route took me first to Villach via Udine and Treviso. A look at my map seemed to indicate that the shortest and logical way to proceed was to the left from Spittal – a small town a few miles north of Villach – then right and up over the Grossglockner Pass. So that was the route I took – that is, until I reached an inn situated a few thousand feet high and perhaps ten kilometers short of the pass. As it was already dusk, I decided to spend the night at that inn where I made the acquaintance at supper of two very pleasant and friendly Austrians. These table companions got out dozens of photos they had taken a week or so before and insisted that I keep a few as a remembrance of our meeting and of the beautiful scenery which surrounded us.

In Venice, I had purchased a kilo and a half of cheese with the thought that there might not be a lot to eat in the Austria and Germany I was about to traverse. This excellent provender was a fortunate addition to that evening repast. When I removed some of this cheese from my briefcase, I could at once see by the expression on the faces of my new friends that they were hungry, so between us we finished off about half of that cheese. We might well have eaten all of it but I made a point of saving half for the next day.

I learned from my dinner companions the discouraging information that the road over the Grossglockner was blocked by "zwei Meter Schnee". I had no choice, therefore, but to retrace my way back down to the main road where I turned left toward Spittal. There was no other way to get over those mountains. At Spittal, I soon learned that it was necessary to have my car transported through a long tunnel by rail. So I drove up a ramp and onto a flatcar and there I just sat behind the wheel of my car while an electric engine pulled our twenty-car train through the tunnel, which was about five miles long.

I was driving a few miles north of the tunnel outlet en route to Obervellach, when I saw a solder in a German uniform thumbing a ride. I pulled over to the side of the road and motioned for him to get in, which he did after I had indicated that he should stow his knapsack on the back seat. "Wohin fahren sie?" I asked in my best German-A fluency. "Nach Deutschland – Aschaffenburg", he replied. This was a big, powerful young man in his early twenties, so it seemed. He looked a bit undernourished, but otherwise healthy. My German was hardly fluent, though I had a good accent with what I did say. So we understood each other quite well and my young German acquaintance came in very handy indeed; for at one place, between Mallnitz and Badgastein, the road became very steep, so steep that the heavily laden Studebaker would not make the grade, even in low gear. Johann – all 195 pounds of him – got out. I somehow managed to turn the car around and, with the soldier pushing and in reverse gear, I managed to get up that steep rise.

We proceeded through Badgastein, Golling, and Frankenmarkt until we came to a crossroad where Johann left me, for to the left was his road to Bavaria and ahead was my road to Ried and the Czech border.

About a half-hour after dropping off my ex-Wehrmacht companion, there materialized fifty yards or so down the road a tall, and from that distance, good-looking woman thumbing a ride. In those days that inexpensive and often necessary means of transport was characteristic all over a recently war-torn Europe. I slowed down and drew to a stop next to the – as I could now verify – very comely hitchhiker. I opened the passenger side door and the young woman who was carrying a small suitcase and a light overcoat asked in German if she could put these things in the back. "Aber natürlich," I assured her. My new passenger identified herself as Clara Deindorfer who wanted a ride to a small town, Ried. As I had to pass through Ried in any case I assured her that I would be happy to deposit her practically at her doorstep. Clara then informed me with obvious pride – all this in German – that her father was the Bürgermeister of Ried and would I not like to drive her not just practically to her doorstep but, indeed, right up to her father's doorstep, for she was sure that her father would be happy to put me up for the night, it then being late afternoon of the first day of November and already almost dark.

I assured Clara that I would be proud to accept her father's hospitality if it were offered, and that is what did happen. I was warmly welcomed by the mayor of Ried. He thanked me profusely for having given a ride to his daughter and thus having ensured her arrival in time for dinner and then said, "We hope and we insist that you will share our evening meal with us and do us the honor of spending the night, Herr Botschaft-Sekretär" (Mr. Embassy-Secretary). My acceptance of this kind invitation came with alacrity and I was ushered to an attractive guest-room that was simply but tastefully furnished, if you like rather heavy furniture, which I do.

Two other guests were also invited for dinner – two "GI's" from the nearby American garrison. There were outgoing, friendly, typical American boys, who obviously knew Clara well.

After dinner, the phonograph was turned on and another girl materialized to join us for an hour or so of dancing to some of those wonderful tunes of World War Two vintage, such as *I'll*

Be Seeing You, In The Mood, and *Sentimental Journey,* among others from records that the GI's had brought with them.

During that evening one of the American GI's suddenly asked me if I could use 150 Deutsch marks that he no longer needed as he was due to leave for the States the following day. He went on to explain that the little get together at the mayor's house was a sort of goodbye party for him. I have sometimes wondered why this money was offered to me, a total stranger, instead of, for example, to the mayor's daughter. Perhaps it had been offered to Clara but she had refused to accept the money. I did accept the two bills of 100 and 50 marks, respectively, with many thanks and the promise to make good use of them.

The following morning I bid farewell to the Bürgermeister and his wife and Clara and set out for Bayerisch-Eisenstein, a small town on the border, which separate southeast Bavaria and Czechoslovakia.

I could not have been more than five kilometers from Ried when there by the side of the road stood still another female hitchhiker. So, of course, I stopped, and this one was a beauty, notwithstanding her somewhat bedraggled appearance, caused no doubt by many miles of walking, a lot of meager meals and the all too frequent importune advances of men attracted by a lone woman. My passenger was a Hungarian who was returning to Budapest from Munich where she had been employed as a hairdresser of all things. I did not even learn this appealing girl's name for, as we were in effect heading in almost opposite directions, she did not ride with me for more than a half-hour. When we came to a fork in the road and we could note that the right branch of the Y led to the East, we parted company, but before she opened the door to get out, I asked whether she might be able to use some extra money and before she could answer, I pressed into her hand the 100 D-mark note and GI had given me the previous evening. The look of surprise and delight on this beautiful wayfarer's face was a pleasure to behold and well worth anything I might have purchased with that money. I had a piece of paper and pencil handy and took down the young woman's name and address on the chance that I might eventually visit Budapest, but I did not visit her city until a quarter of a century later and she disappeared into that bright morning of the second of November. I have cherished the hope that the one hundred marks made a difference in enabling her to reach home safely.

Believe it or not, a few kilometers further on I picked up still another female thumbing a ride, a German this time, who explained that she was bound for Bayerisch-Eisenstein where the American Army post in that frontier town was putting on a dance that evening and she planned to show up, drawn, as it were, by the lure of good food, cigarettes (later to be used for barter), drinks and GI companionship.

As I would have no use for the 50-mark bill that remained and as my hitchhiking traveler looked as though she could use a bit of extra cash, I pressed this money on her as we entered Eisenstein. She got out of my car with a word of thanks, too surprised to say anything more, and I proceeded to the border checkpoint. Then I entered liberated Czechoslovakia. The road I was on led first to Plzeò and then east to Prague. The long journey was almost over. I was about twenty miles within the borders of this country of my new assignment when there again ahead of me I saw yet another hitchhiker, a young man this time, and the last I was to encounter. I slowed down, noted that this lone traveler looked like a clean-cut youth, so I motioned for him to get in the car. He was a traveling salesman from what I could gather, who was also going to Prague, but via Plzeò, where he wanted to stop for just a few minutes to see someone on business. When he asked whether I would be willing to wait for him a short time and then take him to Prague, I agreed, inasmuch as Mr. Foukal, for that was his name, had insisted that he would be happy to direct me straight to the American Embassy when we reached the capital city.

As we traveled that road my companion kept repeating, "Prima Wagen, prima Wagen", which, of course, means *super car, great car.* Of course, there was nothing super or prima about my little buggy, but after all, few Czechs had seen, or much less, driven any cars of post 1939 manufacture. American cars made since 1936 were rare.

There were few vehicles on the road and we made good time, but when I arrived in Plzeò, U.S. army vehicles were everywhere to be seen. According to the May, 1945 agreement between General Eisenhower and Soviet General Zukov, General Patton's Third Army was to occupy the western tenth of Czechoslovakia whereas the Soviets were to take over the rest of the country as well as annex outright the easternmost province of Ruthenia.

This Eisenhower-Zukov agreement or arrangement was to have unfortunate results. The problem was that Roosevelt had just died in April and Harry Truman, his able successor, at that time had had very little exposure to international affairs, a deficiency that he lost little time in making good. Ike was a soldier; he was not a statesman, and he apparently did not in 1945 understand what Stalin had in mind. This agreement need not have been made and the U.S. Army was strong enough to have prevented the virtual handing over of Czechoslovakia to Soviet control.

I later learned from our number two CIA man in Prague, Kurt Taub, who became a close friend, what happened just prior to the end of hostilities. Major General Ernie Harmon was in command of the 22nd Corps of General Patton's Third Army and he had captured Plzeò and all Czech territory west of there. He called Kurt in for a conference and this was logical as Kurt, a native Czech, spoke German as well. He had fled his native country shortly before the Nazis had taken that country in 1938, had become a U.S. citizen and joined the U.S. Army. "Kurt", said General Harmon, "I want you to drive a jeep, accompanied by a GI to man the vehicle's machine gun, through the German lines to Prague. I am told that the Germans are in total disarray and I think you will be able to get to Prague. Find out what the situation is there and return at once to report." Kurt, one of the most self-reliant and enterprising men I have known, did succeed in reaching Prague, notwithstanding several informal encounters with German detachments seemingly bent on surrendering to the Americans rather than to the Soviets who were rapidly approaching Prague from the east.

When Kurt reached Prague, he immediately made contact with resistance groups who expressed joy at the sight of the small American flag affixed to the right fender. "When are you going to liberate us?" asked these partisans. It took Kurt only an hour or so to become convinced that Prague was ripe for capture and that all General Harmon had to do was roll east with his armor. He sped back to Plzeò and reported his finding to the General who at once telephoned to his commander, General Patton, who, in turn, called General Eisenhower. "I can move on Prague and formally liberate Czechoslovakia, General. Will you give me the order to move now? Our 22nd Corps can be in Prague within three hours." "No, General," said Ike. "Stay right where you are. I have made an agreement with General Zukov by which the Soviet Army is to liberate Prague and occupy the eastern nine-tenths of Czechoslovakia. Your 22nd Corps is to occupy Plzeò and the western tenth."

That ill-advised order to General Patton from Ike was to bring misery to millions of Czechs and Slovaks. It was to cost many lives and for almost a half century would undo the work of Thomas J. Masaryk and of countless other men of that republic. It was also destined to have an impact on me and many of my friends.

Following a short stop while Foukal met with his business associate, we set out on the fifty-five mile drive to Prague. About two miles east of Plzeò, we entered the Soviet zone of the republic where my documents were examined and we were waved on. I was thankful to have Foukal to guide me, as I know it would have taken me a long time eventually to find the U.S. Embassy. I bid goodbye to my affable guide whom I was never to see again. I passed beneath the arched entrance of the old baroque palace, which housed our embassy, parked the little Studebaker and entered the building.

At that minute, it could be said that World War Two was over and another war of sorts – the Cold War (though not yet called that) began for me. The enemy was no longer the now crushed Germans, but increasingly the Soviets. The three and half years in Czechoslovakia that lay in store would bring a brew of pleasant living, many new and outstanding friends, excitement and the gut-feeling that worthwhile things had been accomplished.

Chapter Thirteen

Prague

The Czech period of my Foreign Service lasted from November 2, 1945 until May 9, 1949. That time marked the beginning and crescendo of the *Cold War* – the regaining of freedom following the long German occupation and then the stifling of that short-lived freedom under the tyranny of Communist rule.

As soon as I entered the embassy building, I was at once led to the office of Ambassador Lawrence Steinhardt, whose first words were, "I did not expect to see you so soon, Walter." As far as I was concerned, it had taken me too long and I had been a bit apprehensive lest I be taken to task for the length of time spent en route. The ambassador was seated behind a large desk and he motioned me to a chair opposite. He continued, "You are going to find the Czech girls attractive." I was somewhat surprised at this remark immediately upon my arrival. I recall thinking at the time, however, that this was a normal observation by this unusually able, but somewhat freewheeling chief who had been entrusting letters to me for clandestine delivery to his lady friend in Iraq. Moreover, Steinhardt saw me as a bachelor with an understandable interest in young women, a sort of kindred spirit. I assumed also that during the Istanbul period one or two members of his embassy staff had kept him posted as to my proclivities. Unlike Loy Henderson, however, who, while understanding, tended to disapprove of such extra-curricular activities, Steinhardt saw things differently. (Perhaps, also, there might have been the thought that I might eventually be envisioned as a suitor for the hand of his by-then seventeen-year old daughter).

The ambassador characteristically continued to monopolize our conversation. "I am appointing you my administrative officer. I have reason to expect that very soon the State Department is going to limit the number of people employed in the embassy; they may even order a ten percent reduction of staff. For this reason, I want you to hire at least ten or twelve additional people – off the street, if necessary. This will result in our ending up with just the number of employees I want us to have." "Yes, sir," I replied.

The ambassador then called into his office a young and very personable junior member of the administrative staff, Jack Guiney. Jack, who was to be my right-hand man, was instructed to guide be to the Hotel Alkron, where I was to live for the ensuing three months. During the next three and a half years, Jack became a good friend and an able assistant while I was in charge of administration. It was during my stay at the Alkron that I saw Jack outside the office a great deal for he was also unmarried and living in the same hotel.

Almost directly across the street from our hotel was a public dance hall where every night that fall there was dancing to American big band and jazz tunes, and even to the then popular Russian Cavalry song. During the war, no such activity had been allowed, so it was understandable that the young people of Prague made up for the lost time and lost dancing opportunities. The crowd on the large dance floor was always so thick that there was barely enough room to move at all; hence, the dancers seemed just to bob up and down without moving forward in any direction.

I well remember one occasion when everyone was meant to come in some sort of costume, the idea being, "A minimum of effort and a maximum of effect." Jack came, wearing attached to his belt a Nazi dagger encased in a sheath on which was the swastika emblem of the crooked cross – the former property of an S.S. officer. One of the Czech dancers hopping up and down close to Jack grabbed the handle of this dagger, probably just because he wanted to look it over, but Jack wanted none of that, and grabbed at the knife as it was being withdrawn. The result of this by-play was that the razor-sharp blade cut deep into Jack's hand and at once there was blood all over the place. That put a stop to the evening's festivity, but the next day, in spite of a cumbersome bandage wound around his right hand, Jack said he was as good as new and ready for another dance.

During that November, and indeed since the end of hostilities in May, the Soviets, in accord with the Eisenhower-Zukov arrangement, had an army of occupation in Prague, as well as in other cities and towns of the eastern nine-tenths of the country. It was natural, therefore, that every evening, members of the Soviet armed forces – mostly officers – were to be seen in the nightspots. Soviets, when sober, are usually well behaved, but in those days, it was just a question of time before problems involving drunken Russian officers would arise and this was apt to involve touchy problems when girls were present, for there was nothing worse than a Soviet soldier, no matter what his rank, when he had had too much to drink.

Shortly after my arrival, Jack and I, along with four others from the embassy, including two of our American secretaries, visited a popular, but rather small bar, where you could have drinks and short-order food. One of the girls with us was Norma Darling, from Chicago, a pretty, giggling, joking, effervescent type who very soon caught the attention of one of the Soviet officers seated at a nearby table. Jack and I very soon noticed that this Soviet was leering at Norma, calling to her in Russian, motioning her to join his table and otherwise alerting us that there was serious potential trouble ahead. "Let's get out of here before we have a problem with that character," I said to Norma. "But he and his friends are our allies," chirped Norma. "This is it - school's out. Let's go!" I said, and Jack and I at once plunked down sufficient money to cover our bill and hustled the girls out of there, and none too soon, for the Norma-admirer, obviously plastered, had arisen, red in the face and obviously angry at our sudden move toward the door. One of the other Soviets was unsuccessfully trying to restrain him as he shouted and lunged toward us shouting, but being sober and fleeter of foot, we were out of his reach in time to avoid a denouement.

The Czech Communist Party, in its determination to get control of the government, made the most of the Soviet army of occupation. This occupation lasted six months and the Soviet presence of several hundred thousand men greatly facilitated the work of the communists and their fellow travelers bent on seizing control. It was not that the Soviet army intervened at all in the post-war political life of the country, but the presence of this force was intimidating and helped clothe the Communist Party with an aura of invincibility.

What took place inter alia following the liberation of Czechoslovakia was as follows, in brief. First of all, the Agrarian Party, which before the war had been the largest political entity in the country, was almost immediately outlawed because it was accused of having collaborated with the German authorities during the war. Four parties were authorized: the Communist Party, the National Socialist Party, the Social Democratic Party and the Peoples' Party.

Shortly after my arrival, in an apparently free election, the Communist Party received about 42% of the vote, the Social Democrats, 12%, the National Socialists, 30% and the Peoples' Party (closely affiliated with the Roman Catholic Church), 16%. These percentages may not be accurate, as I am relying on my memory. The two significant factors to bear in mind, however, are that while the Communist Party was the largest, it did not by itself constitute a majority and thus needed the close cooperation of a compliant Social Democratic Party to achieve a de facto majority and thus the effective control of the country. Second, the National Socialists, under the able leadership of Dr. Peter Zenkl, was the largest anti-communist political party in Czechoslovakia. Dr. Zenkl had been mayor of Prague before the war and had, soon after the German occupation of his country, been thrown into a concentration camp.

When I arrived on that, to me, very important day in early November, the prime minister was a shifty-eyed, pro-Soviet collaborator, Zdenek Fierlinger, who had spent the war years in the Soviet Union, being groomed for the key role he was to play following the defeat of Germany and the "liberation" of the Czechs and Slovaks. It was, of course, a clever ploy for Fierlinger to join the Social Democrats rather than the Communist Party for that served to create the impression that the government was democratic and not dominated by a foreign power. Of course, Fierlinger was known to be working closely with the USSR and the Czech Communist Party; hence, for over two years the collaboration between those two parties was close.

On November 30, the Soviet occupying armed forces and the 22nd Corps of the U.S. Third Army withdrew from the eastern nine-tenths and the western tenth, respectively, of the country in accord with the agreement of the previous spring.

The Soviets and their Czechoslovak minions, mindful of this impending evacuation had prepared the ground well. In addition to the action involving the Agrarians, immediate steps had been made to expel all the Sudeten Germans and all Germans living in other parts of the republic – a process that took about a year to be accomplished and which, by the time of my arrival was already in full swing. In view of what had taken place in 1938, when Hitler had threatened war unless France and the U.K. (not to mention the Czechs) agreed to the cession of the Sudetenland to the German Reich, it was understandable that all Czechs from the reinstated president Edward Beneš on down through all four parties were adamant that these Sudeten Germans, and those whose mother tongue was German, be expelled.

There were 3.5 million Germans in Czechoslovakia in 1938, or 22.5% of the total population of the country – this compared to 7.5 million Czechs. These unfortunate people were uprooted from the lands they had lived in for centuries. There were two main results of this draconian policy: first, it gave the Communist Party an opportunity to take credit for bestowing farms, formerly owned by Sudetens, to Czechs who seemed likely to become good communists - and it was reasonably certain that this bribery did win votes for the Communist Party - second, as the Sudeten Germans were largely skilled workers – as well as prosperous farmers, their expulsion was to deprive the country of valuable skills, notably in the textile, glass and costume-jewelry industries.

With regard to glassware, whereas the Czechs had been primarily glass blowers, the Sudetens had provided the glasscutters and glass etchers. As for the costume-jewelry business, the Sudetens had virtually dominated this activity. Hence, the expulsion of these industrious workers and managers was to deprive post-war Czechoslovakia of a significant segment of its exports. It should be noted also that those Czech Jews who had survived the war and whose mother tongue was German were not expelled to Germany.

One interesting aspect of this situation came to light during that winter of 1945-46. One day a Jewish woman came to the Embassy and asked to see the ambassador. "What can I do for you and can I be of help in any way?" asked Mr. Steinhardt. The woman replied, "Mr. Ambassador, I am Jewish, my mother tongue is German and I would like to join other Germans being expelled from this country. I want to be sent to Germany." - "What! You want to be expelled to Germany, the country that murdered millions of Jews?" - "Mr. Ambassador," the woman replied, "I consider myself a German; that is my mother language, that is my culture. Hitler was an aberration for a short time. I want to be allowed to remain German in a German-speaking country."

When he recovered from his momentary amazement, Steinhardt agreed to intercede on behalf of the German Jewess who was in due course allowed by the Czech government to join a contingent of German expellees. If this attitude was at all typical of those Jews who had somehow survived the holocaust, it can be appreciated how high was the cost to Germany of the virtual liquidation of this dedicated, highly intelligent people.

A question that is often asked is how could the Communists gain control of a freedom-loving people whose democratic government since 1918 had been a model of success?

Mention has already been made of the arrangement by which nine-tenths of the country was "liberated" by the Soviet Army and of the indoctrination in the USSR during the war of Zdenek Fierlinger. There were many others like him, and when these Soviet-trained men returned to Czechoslovakia, they knew exactly how to go about ensuring that their native land would remain a loyal ally of the USSR under a communist dominated regime.

First of all, Fierlinger saw to it that the top command of the Czech army, which was rehabilitated after VE-Day, was revamped with men friendly to Fierlinger and the USSR. The same was true in the Department of the Interior, where Mr. Nosek was named Minister. It should be noted that the Department of the Interior (as is the case in most European countries) was in charge of state security and the national police. Hence, seemingly with a minimum of effort and within a very short time, the army, police and the STB (the equivalent of the KGB) became, in effect, extensions of Soviet policy.

Still another useful tool for control used by the Communist Party was the *Narodny Vybor* (National Committee). In each community, in each factory and even eventually in each trade union, even in small villages, *Narodny Vybor* was established. The leaders of each of these so-called committees were totally under the control of the Communist Party. Eventually, so-called *Akšny* (pronounced Akshny) *Vibors* were set up in sporting clubs such as in the *Czesky Veslarsky Klub* (Czech Rowing Club) to which I belonged. These *Action Committees* were set up to ensure that when the time came for a Communist take-over, the organization presumably led by that Action Committee, would cooperate closely with the Communists

So far, no mention has been made of President Edward Beneš and Jan Masaryk, the son of Tomaš T.G. Masaryk, the founding father of the country. During the war, Dr. Beneš had served as president of the Czechoslovak government in exile in London, and Jan Masaryk had been Foreign Minister in that government. Naturally, both men returned to Prague after the war and owing to the prestige that they commanded, they assumed the same posts in the post-war government. It was, of course, well known that both of these men, whose names were household words in their country, were devoted to the democratic ideals for which their homeland had firmly stood since 1918. The Communist Party and the Soviet ambassador, Zorin, bided their time and gradually hemmed in these patriots in such a way that eventually they were eliminated from the power structure of their country. This process required about three years. Both Dr. Beneš and Jan Masaryk were of national stature with an impeccable record of unyielding hostility toward the Nazis. Hence, their prestige, especially that of Dr. Beneš, throughout the republic, at the time of their return and even until early 1948, was strong and, except in the case of die-hard pro-Soviets, unquestioned.

In addition to the ministries of Interior and Defense, the Communist Party, closely allied to the Social Democrats, also took control of the Ministry of Propaganda, hence, the press. In other key ministries, such as Education and Foreign Affairs – of which Masaryk, a member of the National Socialist Party, was the Minister – they placed pro-Soviets in key subordinate posts that enabled them to exert pressure when issues important to them were involved.

One of the first significant moves that that post-war CSR government made was to nationalize the large key industries, which included such firms as the Skoda Works in Plzen, the Vitkovice Steel Mills, the large textile factories, glass works, etc. Needless to add, any firms which had been owned by Sudeten Germans were confiscated without remuneration, and nationalized. Aside from the latter, compensation was meant to be paid and when U.S. citizens of Czech origin were involved, our embassy intervened on behalf of these stockholders - with limited success. On the whole, these claimants did not fare well.

A few Jews who, before the war had realized soon enough how the Nazi wind was blowing, had sold out in time and had thus been able to get at least part of their money out of Czechoslovakia before the German take-over in the spring of 1939; but there were not many of these. One of my good friends,

Jan Stiastny, the son of one of these Jewish escapees who had been able to move some of his fortune out before 1939, came back to Prague as a member of the staff on the CIA in the embassy. Following the 1948 seizure of the government by the communists, there were no restitutions.

As already noted, I moved into the Hotel Alkron the day of my arrival and lived there for about three and a half months. The best thing about that place was that I was assured of hot water at any time of day or night, a special luxury that winter. Mention is made of this, as not long after moving in, I met the Rohan family, that is, the mother and her three daughters. Mabille, the daughter I knew best, was the eldest at age twenty-two. The father, who had allegedly been a German collaborator, had fled to Austria shortly before the German surrender. The de Rohans were descended from the famous French noble family of that name which had escaped from France during the French Revolution of 1789-1794. They had remained in exile ever since and had become totally Austrianized having acquired a large estate in Bohemia.

I befriended Mabille and her mother and sisters mainly because they were civilized and seemed to represent what I had always seen as the best qualities of the Austro-Germans. One day, Countess de Rohan asked whether I would lend her a key to my room so that she would thus occasionally be able to take a hot bath. Every other day she availed herself of this opportunity and one or more of her daughters may also have been involved. I felt that these good people caught in the mesh of that difficult time deserved this small luxury I could provide.

Through the de Rohans, I met the Czech Bubela family, notably the older son, Ctibor (Bobby). Bob called me one day and said that the de Rohans would like us to share a simple evening meal with them. He suggested, moreover, that if I could bring along some preserved food such as tinned meat, etc., this would be much appreciated, as adequate food was not always easy to obtain in those post-war months. As our embassy regularly sent a truck to one of the U.S. Army commissaries in the U.S. zone of Germany, we were regularly supplied with such staples as bacon, eggs, milk, cheese, macaroni, cereal and tinned meat. On that occasion, I brought along a package of bacon, some hard cheese and a dozen eggs. The eyes of the de Rohans lit up with pleasurable anticipation at the sight of this American provender and with little delay, they attacked the pound of bacon, which they ate raw. When I suggested that they might enjoy it more if it were cooked, they all quickly explained that during the war, they had had so little fat that this raw bacon was now a godsend. Never again did I suggest that bacon be fried.

While I did invite Mabille for dinner a few times, I never got to *know* her in the Biblical sense, and my acquaintance with her and her family was rather short-lived. There were two reasons for this: first of all, this family was not well regarded by the Czechs and this information seeped through to the Steinhardts, who thus suspected a pro-Nazi past, and second, the de Rohans, before long, moved to Vienna.

Bobby Bubela, who was ten years younger than I, became a good friend and was helpful, not only by introducing me to many interesting people, but also as a translator on several important occasions.

In the early spring of 1946, the Czech government sponsored a *Folk Festival* in a picturesque town called Liberec by the Czechs (pronounced Liberetz) and Reichenberg by the Germans. Several embassies were asked to send a representative and the ambassador asked me to do the honors for the United States.

Liberec was a town of some 40,000 which, up to 1946, had been inhabited largely by Sudeten Germans, then being rapidly replaced by Czechs, who were delighted to be moving into apartments and houses which had been left spotlessly clean by the former owners. I asked Bubela to accompany me as an interpreter and he was happy to do so as that bestowed on him a certain prestige in the eyes of his contemporaries.

While we were checking into our hotel as guests of the Festival, having parked my car nearby, someone had seized the opportunity to bend double the thin metal rod on my right fender to which a small American flag was attached. This childish, albeit annoying, deed had obviously been done by a communist apologist who might have been egged on by a communist functionary to commit this act of minor sabotage. I promptly reported to the police what had happened and to my surprise, within an hour, a policeman led a twelve-year-old boy up to me, the boy having allegedly confessed that it had been he who had been the saboteur. Of course, I shook hands with the boy and, as was obviously expected, asked that he not be punished. The thought did cross my mind that the lad had had nothing to do with this peccadillo.

The following morning, several thousand people, all dressed in colorful, traditional costumes, crowded into the large town square for the formal ceremonies. The dignitaries of the town, as well as the British and French diplomatic representatives and I, made our way to a large balcony on the second floor of the town hall which overlooked the square.

First, the mayor gave a five-minute speech of welcome, after which he introduced Alan Shukburgh of the British embassy. While Alan was delivering his already prepared speech in passable Czech, the mayor whispered to Bubela that I was scheduled to speak after monsieur de la Geneste of the French embassy. Obviously, both my British and French colleagues had been informed well ahead of time that they were expected to say a few words – but not I.

As a result of this being-taken-by-surprise situation, I had two or three minutes to think about what I would say to ten thousand listeners, a sea of up-turned faces – happy, good humored, expecting some special message from these men from the West and especially from the American. Having marshaled my thoughts, I asked Bob to translate sentence by sentence. This he did and very skillfully.

As a great many of these colorfully garbed listeners had at least one relative in Chicago or Pittsburgh, Youngstown or Cleveland, etc., there were loud cheers and a thunder of applause following each sentence spoken. I could have said almost anything, including, "the flowers that bloom in the spring, tra-la" and there would still have been that enthusiastic response. While many Czechs and Slovaks were grateful to the Soviet "liberators", there was no question that America, despite organized efforts to down-play its role in the war as compared to that of the USSR, was the most popular foreign country with most of the people. After all, it had been T.J. Masaryk, married to an American woman, and speaking in Philadelphia, who had announced the birth of a free Czechoslovakia in 1918.

Illustrative of this widespread sentiment, every city and town of 50,000 or more inhabitants – and even a few smaller communities – boasted a *Friends of the USA Society* and up to the time of the Communist take-over in early 1948, our embassy sent me to many of these places to represent the embassy and to speak at gala parties organized by these societies. This folk festival at Liberec was my baptism of fire as a propagandist for the USA, but never again did I have to extemporize.

On or about the first of December, 1945, by which date the Soviets had moved several hundred thousand men out of the country, Roy Sheldon, who worked in the economic section of the embassy, invited me to join him, his fiancée, and a twenty-year-old lady friend of the latter, for dinner in his apartment. Roy and I had become quite good friends, especially after he commented one day that he was from St. Louis where the name Birge was a household word in his family. The name of Roy's fiancée's friend was Pusina Kapsova, the daughter of a prosperous construction engineer. She was quite tall, blond, and despite being a little overweight, had the good looks of a Nordic type and a fine sense of humor. As I had so far met no one of interest – of the female sex, that is – we began to see a lot of each other and she invited me to spend Christmas week at her parents' chalet at Spindelmühl (the German name for that attractive village), a small ski resort in the *Giant Mountains* (Riesengebirge). I was obliged to attend the Steinhardts' command-performance invitation of Christmas Eve, but on Christmas Day, I picked up Pusina, along with a huge amount of family laundry which had been accumulating preparatory to being washed by a Sudeten German laundress who still lived in Spindelmühl.

That week was enjoyable and memorable. I was much impressed by Pusina's father with whom I conversed in German – he fluently, I haltingly, but that marked the end of our acquaintance for a week later, Mr. Kapsa died of a heart attack

Pusina was not afraid of anything. We would sometimes *luge* down a steep trail lickety-split. While I was petrified, she would just laugh and insist that we climb back up the hill for another run. There were no ski lifts in that primitive resort, so if you wanted to ski, you just had to climb up to whatever height from which you wanted to ski down. This meant a paucity of skiing and a whole lot of exercise.

After our return to Prague and following Mr. Kapsa's death, I was able to do Mrs. Kapsova a favor. When she told me that she would like to rent out two rooms on the second floor of her rather large house in the fashionable Bubenech section of Prague, I suggested that the newly arrived military attaché, General Koenig, would be a logical and desirable tenant. This arrangement worked out well until the general (by then demoted to colonel owing to elimination of temporary wartime ranks) was replaced by the far abler Colonel Michela, who rented a house elsewhere in the city.

I ran into a problem with Pusina, however, for one afternoon as she was accompanying me into the Hotel Alkron, where we occasionally met clandestinely, we were spotted by the prime minister's chauffeur who was parked near the hotel door. Apparently the chauffeur lost no time in reporting what he had seen to Mrs. Fierlinger who, in turn, passed this intelligence along to her friend, Mrs. Kapsova. As they say nowadays, *the shit hit the fan.*

First of all, Pusina's mother told General Koenig about this. I assume that the general filled in the ambassador who almost certainly commented that this was a tempest in a teapot and that he was sure that I had no long-range intentions. I must confess that as of that time, I did not have what is often thought of as honorable intentions – not yet, at any rate. What happened could have been predicted; Pusina was packed off to England where the Czech ambassador found a job for her. Within a year, Pusina began to study nursing in England and settled down in the U.K. permanently. So it all worked out for the best for this fine Bohemian girl.

For the first six months following my arrival – that is, the last two months of 1945 and up to the spring of 1946 – there was a food shortage in Prague. The embassy truck, manned by G.I.'s on loan from the U.S. Army, did bring some supplies in from the U.S. zone of occupation in Germany, but it was the end-use of this food that was the problem. Some of the American clerks at the embassy, notably the stenographers, were not allotted as much food as they should have received. Those girls who lived in hotels were meant to hand over to the management the food received from the embassy, with the assurance that this extra provender would be made available to them for breakfast –eggs and bacon, for example. This extra food, however, was limited and our young women often were still hungry when reporting for work.

As already reported, as soon as I arrived, the ambassador told me that I was to be his administrative officer. For some reason, he had gained the impression during the time I had known him in Turkey that I was efficient. Perhaps I was in some ways; however, I had never really worked for him, but rather had occasionally carried out spasmodically given instructions during the summers when he worked on a reduced-time basis in Istanbul. In any case, there I was in Prague supposed to carry out Mr. Steinhardt's non-substantive policies. One of these was to see that extra food was made available sparingly. Needless to say, this placed me in a difficult position as many of our stenographers were continually complaining to me that they were not getting enough to eat. When I would discuss this situation with Steinhardt, his customary reply was that I was too softhearted. I suppose this was at least partly true, but I could see no impelling reason to take available food away from our hungry girls. So I cheated a bit – at least enough – thus seeing to it that our girls received adequate extra supplies of bacon and eggs.

During that very cold winter of 1945-46, when zero F. temperatures were not at all unusual, a rather amusing occurrence unfolded which served further to bring into relief the ambassador's reactions to breaks with normal routine and what was expected. Fortunately this story had a happy ending.

One of the embassy's military staff was a young Italian-American Pfc by the name of Mario Bertelli. On the day when this story begins, there had been a sleet and snowfall the night before and on that morning it had turned very cold so that the roads were almost a sheet of ice. A U.S. Army general had been visiting the ambassador for a couple of days and he was due to fly back to Rome; and this is where Mario comes into the story.

As soon as I reported for work on that icy morning, Mario, somewhat deferentially, albeit purposefully, came into my office. "Mr. Birge," he said, "I want to ask a big favor of you." - "What about Mario? I'll be glad to help you if I can," I replied. Breathlessly, Mario continued, "Mr. Birge, I hear that General Stetson is flying back to Rome this morning and I want to ask him if he will take me with him. Is that OK?" I then naturally asked him why he wanted to get to Rome. "You see, Mr. Birge, I was in General Clark's army and before leaving Italy, I got to know this girl. Her family knew my parents, so she promised to marry me, but then I was transferred out. And, Mr. Birge, if the general says it's OK for me to get a lift with him, is that OK with you?" "Sure", I replied, "but General Stetson has already left for the airport. In five minutes, I am to meet General Koenig, our military attaché, and accompany him to Ruzine (name of the airport) to bid farewell to him. But I'll tell you what I'll do. I'll ask General Koenig if you can ride with us."

Five minutes later, General Koenig, his assistant military attaché, Lt.-Col. Tom Foote, Mario and I started out for Ruzine. Just outside the embassy gate, the road descends for fifty yards or so – not steeply, but enough to make driving hazardous in icy conditions. Almost at once the general's car skidded completely around so that we ended up facing the way we had come.

"To hell with this," cried Koenig. "We're not going anywhere and general or no general, I'm not going to risk breaking my neck on these icy roads." So we all got out and walked the short distance back to the embassy.

And now there enters into this tale Frankie Volek, the watchman of the embassy, who lived in the stone gatehouse that formed one side of the arched stone entrance. Frank had a jeep, which had been supplied by the embassy. I had learned that Frank was obliging, positive in attitude and afraid of nothing. As we walked back through the gateway, I saw Frank standing at the door of his lodging. I immediately took him aside, having asked Mario to stand by, rapidly explained to him how Mario wanted to get on the departing general's plane, how so far Mario had not had an opportunity to ask the general's permission to ask for a ride to Rome. "Will you drive Mario to Ruzine in your Jeep?" I asked him. With a man such as Frankie, no sooner was it asked than it was done, and despite the miserable driving conditions.

I did not accompany Frank and Mario, but I later learned what happened. Frank was a skillful driver. Moreover, the Jeep handles better than a normal passenger car on slippery roads. When Frank and Mario got to the airport, they at once ascertained that the departing general's plane was already taxiing out to the main runway preparatory to takeoff, but Volek never hesitated for a moment. Fired up by Mario's fervent desire to get to Rome to marry his girl, he drove his jeep right onto the runway where General Stetson's plane was beginning to rev up its engines immediately before gunning them to full power. The general, looking out his window, saw a jeep speeding toward his plane with the passenger of that vehicle waving his arms. He promptly ordered his pilot to delay takeoff for a moment as someone apparently had an urgent last-minute message for him.

The twin engines were throttled down and the jeep pulled up to the door of the aircraft, which opened, revealing the stalwart figure of the puzzled general. "What's going on?" asked that imposing officer of America's powerful army. According to Frank Volek's report later that morning, Mario replied, "Good morning, General. My name is Mario Bertelli and I work at the embassy here. Please excuse me, sir, but could you give me a ride to Rome? I promised my fiancée I would get down there somehow to marry her and she lives in Rome and I can't get there any other way. I'd surely appreciate your help, sir." With that, the general's normally stern countenance took on a broad smile, thinking back perhaps to the day, shortly after leaving West Point, when, on a short furlough, he had dashed off to meet his girl. "Come along, Mario. We'll get you to Rome, barring an act of God to prevent it."

That is how Mario got to Rome. He did marry his girl and he brought her back to Prague by train. The problem that served to cloud this happy ending was that Steinhardt, who had been driven to the airport by Andy, his Greek chauffeur, had witnessed the scene of the Jeep driving out onto the runway and of one of his embassy GI's boarding General Stetson's plane. To put it mildly, the ambassador was fit to be tied. The first person he called onto the carpet was his administrative officer, i.e., me, who was, as a rule, held responsible for things he did not like and who did not always receive credit for positive developments.

"Did you give permission to Mario to be driven to the airport by Volek and to stop the general's plane just as it was about to take off?" he thundered. I was still standing in front of Steinhardt's desk, not having been asked to sit down, and I replied, "Mr. Ambassador, yes and no. I told Mario that if he asked the general for a ride to Rome and if he received a positive reply, he could ride to Rome with him." "Do you know what happened at the airport?" he shot back. The information about Volek's driving his Jeep onto the runway, the aborted takeoff, and how Mario had been seen to enter the plane had reached me just before my entry into the ambassador's office. "Yes, sir, I have just been informed about what happened and, of course, that was not what I had intended to have take place." Then Steinhardt let me have it with both barrels of his unleashed fury. I was too "soft-hearted". I should never have allowed this GI to seek the general's permission at the last moment. Of course, the ambassador was right, I suppose, but I did not regret for one moment doing what I could to assist Mario in getting his betrothed to the altar.

About two weeks after the above-mentioned meeting with Mr. Steinhardt, Mario suddenly appeared without warning in my office. Word had apparently reached this Pfc. that the big boss was angry with him. Mario said, "I have brought a gift from Italy for the ambassador. Could I go to his office to report back and give it to him, and will you please go with me, Mr. Birge?" – "Sure Mario, and welcome back," I replied. "Wait a minute. I'll call the ambassador to see whether he has a minute free."

Five minutes later, I accompanied the young swain into the large and – to Mario, I am sure - frightening office. Steinhardt was seated behind his large flat top desk that was flanked on the right by the *Stars and Stripes* and on his left by the flag denoting his ambassadorial rank. He had on his special look of disapproval reserved for occasions such as this, with no suggestion of a smile of welcome for the returning bridegroom. Mario was clutching the small package he had brought as a gift of appeasement. I broke the silence. "Mr. Ambassador, Bertelli wants to report back. He got married in Rome and brought his bride back with him." The ambassador, after a few seconds of silence, in a sarcastic tone, replied, "Glad you're back, Bertelli, and I assume that this time you used a normal method of transport." Mario swallowed hard. "Mr. Ambassador, I picked out a little present for you. As Mr. Birge told you, I got married." Then, as I had briefly coached him to do, he added, "I'm really sorry about how I got on that general's plane. He was real nice about it though and treated me real good." The ambassador replied, still with the voice and expression of disapproval, "Private Bertelli, I do not feel that under the circumstances, I can accept your gift though I appreciate the thought. I have not yet gotten over my strong disapproval as to how you boarded the general's aircraft. That will be all."

Later that week, Mario invited me to have "a real Italian Spaghetti dinner" in his apartment, where I met his pretty wife. The aura of happiness that filled that small and sparsely furnished room was well worth incurring the displeasure of Steinhardt. Who knows, perhaps Mario and Lucrezia would never have reached the altar had Frank Volek not driven that GI in his Jeep over icy roads to the airport on that frigid winter day.

After I had been in Prague about two months, I began the search for a suitable apartment, a quest that was not easy, as I did not have much spare time to devote to this project. The married members of the embassy staff, whose wives had ample time to look around, had an easier task in this regard. Finally, in February, I did find an apartment on Nabrezi Legii, the road that followed the bank of the Vltava River. This apartment had a large living room and quite a large bedroom, plus two small bedrooms suitable for guests or servants.

On the day I was meant to move in, I passed by Carla, the embassy receptionist, who was chatting with an unknown man. She stopped me and said, "Mr. Birge, are you still interested in employing a cook?" I assured Carla that indeed I was, and she introduced me to the man who was destined to work for me for two and a half years. His name was François Ryšavy, and he had walked in just a few minutes before to enquire whether anyone needed a cook. I promptly ascertained that François spoke fluent French, having been trained in Paris, and having worked many years in Tunis. After about one minute, I said, "You're hired," and I never regretted this. Ryšavy (pronounced Ryshavy) was of medium height and his almost perpetual smile revealed a mouth full of gold teeth, worthy of an ambulating branch of the Bank of France.

François turned out to be a superb cook. If I wanted to invite a few people for dinner all I had to say was, "Demain, il y aura cinq pour diner," and he did the rest. At the time he was hired, he was separated from his wife, Jeannette, but within a month, she moved into the apartment with their five-year-old daughter.

François and Jeannette worked for me until the autumn of 1948, that is, until the day I drove them and their eight-year-old daughter to Germany on the first stage of their move to the United States. Before leaving Prague, I had seen to it that he was well supplied with impressive letters of recommendation from Charles Katek, chief of American Intelligence, from Colonel Michela, and from Tom Foote, assistant military attaché, among others. François first employers in the U.S. were my old friends, Count and Countess de Limur, who were still living in Washington. After a few years, he entered the employ of another prominent and very well off couple, the William Burdens, who also lived in Georgetown. François later related to me when I met up with him in the mid 1950's that one morning, while shopping in the meat-market, he overheard one of his chef-colleagues remark that the White House, just recently occupied by President Eisenhower, was looking for a chef. That was all this enterprising character needed to know and he landed that prestigious job in the White House where he remained as chief culinary artist during Eisenhower's administration and for a while with the Kennedys. Afterwards, he wrote, with the able assistance of a ghostwriter, a book entitled *White House chef*, an account of his life and the people he worked for, and including many of his wonderful original recipes. In it, he had some very kind words about the time he worked for me. From Washington, François moved to Hollywood, and I lost track of him.

So, from February, 1946 until May, 1949, when I was transferred by the State Department, I lived very well indeed, owing mainly to François' culinary ministrations. Thinking back on those days, I understandably divide my three and a half years into two distinctly separated periods; before the communist seizure of power and after that coup d'état of February 22, 1948. I look back on that first period – a little more than two-thirds of my sojourn in the *Golden City* – with nostalgia. There were problems, of course, and the Soviet armed forces of the USSR, poised just across the borders of Czechoslovakia, prevented what could have been a full recovery economically and politically, for the people continued to look over their collective shoulder, so to speak, and the Communist government, prodded by the Soviet ambassador Zorin, was interested primarily in preparing the groundwork for an eventual take-over rather than in doing everything possible to encourage economic recovery and the full reestablishment of democracy. On the surface, however, living in that beautiful city was a pleasant experience. When the Soviet army left at the end of November, 1945, there was a feeling of relief that those two occupations, first the German and then the Soviet, were over. The economy picked up and there was very soon plenty to eat. In general, there was optimism, and most of the citizens of that land of Dvorak and Smetana, the Moldau and the sun-drenched fields - with the exception of the few who were in a position to doubt a happy ending – felt that before too long, the political parties which were the strongest opponents of the Communists (notably the National Socialist Party and the Peoples' Party) would obtain a majority in the Chamber of Deputies.

As a bachelor and an American, my personal situation was enviable. As mentioned above, most towns of any size had a *Friends of the USA Society*, which held at least one big evening party a year. I was usually chosen by the ambassador to represent the embassy at these receptions and they were always enjoyable. Among those cities thus visited were Plzen, Moravská, Ostrava, Pardubice, Brno, Tábor and Liberec. Usually at these balls, on which occasions I wore full dress (i.e., white tie and tails), some twenty pretty girls would form a circle around me and as a large orchestra played a Viennese waltz, one after the other would cut in to dance. What a workout this was during those non-stop waltzes. It was fortunate that I was in good shape, for these dances were the equivalent of a two thousand meter crew race.

Mention is made of these pro-American societies, as they were a tangible proof of the general pro-American feeling throughout the country. The pro-Soviet regime of Zdenek Fierlinger, advised and backed by Ambassador Zorin, was well aware of these extensive ties to America and set about doing everything possible to counter this devotion to the democratic ideals of America. It will be recalled that Tomas J. Masaryk, the founder of the Czechoslovak Republic, had married an American woman; moreover, his son, Jan Masaryk, had also married an American; and Jan, who had served as Foreign Minister in the Czech government in exile during the war, was now serving in the same capacity.

How did the Communist Party go about counteracting this widespread fascination with the political fabric of the West, with its democratic traditions, with its popular jazz, its movies, its free speech, its wealth? How was Fierlinger going to cope with the ties binding countless American relatives with their homeland? This task was not going to be easy, but the minions and henchmen of Joseph Stalin (perhaps the greatest mass-murderer of all time) set about the job with the cunning and dedication which were characteristic of Soviet actions in post-war Eastern Europe.

The preparation for the eventual Communist Party *D-Day* (i.e., takeover day) was many faceted. First of all, as has already been briefly described, virtually all of the three and a half million people of German extraction were expelled – most of them to the U.S. Zone of occupation and lesser numbers to the British,

French and Soviet zones of Germany. Then their vacated farms and other former German properties were either taken over by the State for permanent ownership or – notably in the case of small farms – given to "worthy" Czech farmers who presumably had professed fervent loyalty to the CSR Communist Party and naturally a heart-felt thankfulness to the great Soviet Union, which had single-handedly liberated them from the Nazis.

At the same time, the Agrarian Party was outlawed. This served a dual purpose. It removed an organized, conservative anti-communist political entity and even some of these former Agrarians were lured into the Communist Party ranks via the offer of former German farms; but most ended up in the National Socialist and Peoples parties.

Among the other carefully planned moves by the Communist Party was the well orchestrated move to gain control of the re-established labor unions, which had been banned under the German occupation. This was relatively easy, as the radio kept blaring out how the fraternal Soviets had liberated the CSR, that the Communist Party was the friend, protector and hope of the working man and anyone who voiced sentiments other that these was either shunted aside to a status of little import – or even expelled from the union.

Hand in hand with this well orchestrated union mobilization, was the equally skillful formation of Communist-dominated factory milititias (Zavodny Milice). Each sizeable factory – notably the Skoda Works, Vitkovice Iron Works, Zlin shoe factories, etc., soon had its own militia which worked loosely with the labor unions, and its officers, all C.P. henchmen, stood ever ready to obey the dictates of the Czech or Slovak Communist Party. There were, as already noted, the Narodny Vibors (national committees) and Aksny Vybors (action committees) that were prepared to move into action on *D-Day*.

Aside from the above, there was the close alliance between the C.P. and the Social Democratic Party, headed by the intrepid and wily ex-miner, Vaclav Meyer. Together, the C.P. and Meyer's party controlled about 55% of the vote. Hence, for the time-being at least, the Communist hierarchy (Gottwald, Slansky, Nosek, and a few others) made a point of working with the Socialists – however, as will be seen, Vaclav Meyer was becoming increasingly disenchanted.

In the early spring of 1946, four years after my departure from New York for Istanbul, I applied for and was granted two months home leave. There ensued visits with Claire and Fuller, a delayed tenth Harvard reunion, a visit with my parents in the Adirondacks and of course, a visit with my son Walter III, then seven and a half years old. During this leave, I met Hannah Bradley, a beguiling Boston charmer, then in her first year of Radcliffe, who would occupy most of my thoughts for the next two and a half years and until I received her *Dear John* letter, which aside from bringing keen disappointment to my life, brought in its wake a rebound liaison and ultimately a disastrous marriage to a young Czech woman who was beautiful, alluring, lacking in character and totally self-serving.

Before my departure on this home-leave, Ambassador Steinhardt asked me to do him a special favor, as follows. "During your leave, Walter, you will naturally report to the Chief of Personnel of the Department. During that meeting, I want you to point out to the director that I do not wish to be *inspected* by Mr. Merle Cochran. Moreover, if Mr. Cochran should be sent to Prague to inspect the embassy, I will refuse to see him." The reason which impelled the ambassador to issue this instruction was that two years or so before, when Cochran had inspected the embassy in Ankara, the inspector had filed a damaging report on Bob Kelly, Steinhardt's right-hand man and Counselor of Embassy. This had infuriated the ambassador. It may also have been that the ambassador subsequently learned of detrimental remarks about him that Merle Cochran had reported to the Personnel Department.

The ambassador's request placed me in an embarrassing position, as I was a very junior officer. Be that as it may, the Chief of Personnel listened politely and understandably made no comment. What was discouraging about this meeting in the Personnel Department was that no mention was made about my having arbitrated the strike at Ras Tanura; no mention was uttered about Mr. Henderson's having been "delighted and surprised" with the reports I had drafted following his departure from Baghdad; no mention was made as to Mr. George Kennan's letter complimenting me on my report on the machinations of the Iraq Communist Party.

By 1946, it was known to a few - notably to Loy Henderson – that I was part of a very small minority in the Department that favored the Jewish-Zionist cause in Palestine. Virtually the entire Middle East section of the Department was pro-Arab and the stature of Henderson was such – and on the whole deservedly so – that very few, if any, in the Department dared take a pro-Jewish stand. Fortunately, president Harry Truman lost little time in recognizing the State of Israel after its founding in 1948, the first chief of state to do so.

The ship that took me back to Europe stopped at Southampton for a few hours and I took the opportunity to go ashore, find a bicycle shop and purchase a Raleigh three-speed bike. The day of the ten-speed two-wheeler had not yet arrived. I remember it cost me one-pound sterling for the ship to transport the bike to Cherbourg.

In Paris, I stayed for two days at the Crillon and during that time I met, through the embassy, another American girl, Barbara MacGruder, the daughter of a U.S. Army general. What I remember about this young woman is that she was unusually attractive and that had it not been that I was carrying a torch for Hannah Bradley, serious interest might well have been in store. As it was, Barbara helped me get my luggage and the bicycle from the Crillon to the Gare de l'Est. The taxi had no way of transporting the bicycle, so Barbara rode the taxi with my luggage and I followed riding the bike through Paris. The taxi had been instructed to drive slowly enough to enable me to keep pace. Barbara was still another beautiful girl I never saw again. There were so many goodbyes during those Foreign Service years.

When I arrived back in Prague in the early July of that beautiful, sunny mid-European summer, the Ambassador gave me the choice of working in either the Political or Economic Section. I chose the latter mainly because Jim Hodgson was the Director of that branch and he had urged me to join him as the successor to Jim Sheldon who had left the embassy during my leave in the U.S. Hodgson was a colorful individual – able, bluff, and humorous. Although he was about twenty-five years older than I, he was not a career Foreign Service officer and thus had an insecure future in the Service. I decided to join Jim not only because we had had a friendly relationship since my arrival the preceding November but also for the negative reason that the de-facto head of the Political Section was the Counselor, John Bruins, a career FSO of obviously limited ability and known by all of us as an apple-polisher who was continually yessing the ambassador. All this notwithstanding, I should have borne it in mind that the so-called Political Officers cut a lot more ice in the Department than the economic specialists, at least in those days. However, working with Jim Hodgson was enjoyable and I did receive several *excellent* grades from the Department on my reports, not that these tangible results bore any special fruit of advantage as far as I could judge. I worked with Jim Hodgson for about a year, that is, from early summer of 1946 until the early fall of 1947 following a short leave in the U.S.

From my return from home leave until the end of 1947 was also my most enjoyable time in Prague. During that year and a half, one of the highlights was my affiliation with the Czech Rowing Club (Cesky Veslarsly Klub or CVK). I had heard about this club even prior to my departure for the U.S. in April; and immediately upon my return in early July, I applied for membership. After two or three tryouts, I found myself rowing in the number four seat of the first boat. One problem was that the coach spoke no English and my Czech was virtually nonexistent. However, a young twenty-two year old oarsman, George Romovaèek, who became a very good friend, had a fluent command of English, so he acted as go-between with the coach and that was a big help.

While our stroke oar was not as skilled as I remembered Eric Beresford to have been, the Czech boat was probably more powerful than the Thames rowing Club crew of 1937-38 and, I would say, probably the equal of an average U.S. college varsity crew.

At the beginning of the training season, as was apparently the custom every year, the coach called all the oarsmen together and sternly admonished us to adhere to the three basic rules: no alcoholic beverages, no smoking, and no sex.

It is, of course, unwise to generalize as to the behavior, conduct and characteristics of any nationality. I would venture the opinion, however, that Czechs tend to be serious-minded and this applies especially to athletes of that country. Hence, I am reasonably sure that no one of that group which was gathered together that day either smoked or drank (barring an occasional beer perhaps) during the rowing season. As for sex – that was undoubtedly reduced, and from what I was able to gather from a reliable source, this diversion was eliminated on the one or two, or perhaps even three, days preceding a race. After all, Czechs, being pragmatic, usually know what their priorities are.

In that fall of 1946, there took place the annual ten-kilometer (6.2 mile) race down stream on the Moldau River (the Vltava), from the village of Zbraslav to Prague. I had never been to Zbraslav, but had been informed that the composer of the then-popular polka, *Roll Out the Barrel*, had come from that small town.

On a cool September afternoon we paddled up to the Zbraslav starting dock. Astern of me rowed Joe ("The Bear") Schebal, a powerful 6'2", 195 pound, at number five, who had the habit of making humorous comments in the middle of a race. Ahead of me at three, rowed Vaclav Robik, a strong, smooth oar who, à la Bert Haynes, the Harvard freshman coach, always transferred his thoughts to the end of his oar blade.

There was a small crowd at the take-off point, including monsieur de la Geneste of the French embassy, accompanied by his two young children. "Allo, Walter," he called to me, "Je ne savais pas que vous ramiez avec cette équipe." ("I didn't know that you were rowing with that team") Then, turning to his small boys, "Regardez bien. Voilà mon collègue américain, un grand rameur. Et voilà le CVK don't je vous ai parlé." I was very flattered by this gross exaggeration of my prowess.

As that narrow inlet was not wide enough to enable two crews to line up abreast, it was the custom, for that race, to send the crews off one minute apart. Our opponent, *Blesk* (which means lightning) *Rowing Club,* started first; then one minute later, it was our turn.

The Czechs start crews off with these words (phonetically spelled) – *Psi Praventi, Pshett.* We did not give much of a racing start, perhaps because there was no opposing crew right along side. I think we started off at about a 35 strokes per minute, and then quickly settled down to a 30 or 31 for that 6.2-mile row. At about the four-mile mark, Schebal, as was his wont, began one of his humorous soliloquies. By that time, our cox calmly informed us that we were closing in on *Blesk.* As for me, I saved my breath by keeping silent and did my best to keep it "long in the water".

I had rowed four-mile time trials, Putney to Mortlake with the Thames Rowing Club, and that had been tough enough, but this ten-kilometer grind was exhausting. I realized then why the Czechs had the reputation of being super athletes and thought how crazy I was to be rowing with guys over ten years younger, and prayed my strength would hold out for the last two miles.

Soon, out of the corner of my eye, I could see a few landmarks of the city, then a familiar bridge, then up went the stroke to about 35 and we caught up with *Blesk* just as we crossed the finish line – s few hundred yards short of the old 14th century Charles Bridge. So, we had beaten *Blesk* by the equivalent of about fifteen lengths. Not bad!

In the early spring of 1947, we started training again – first in two fours and then back into the eight. We had been in the latter not quite a week when Dulcie Steinhardt came up to me one evening at a British Embassy reception. "Walter, why is it that I did not see you at either the Dutch Embassy reception the day before yesterday or at Colonel Michela's cocktail party last week?" I started to voice my reply when Mrs. Steinhardt continued. "And the Ambassador mentioned today that when he called an impromptu staff meeting today at five you had already left the office!"

I offered the explanation that every afternoon shortly after five, I trained with the CVK crew and that as I was the only non-Czech in the boat, I considered the time well spent, not only for my physical well-being, but because of the added exposure to and close association with representative young Czechs, several of whom appeared to be well informed as to the political situation. While there was some logic in what I had said, I saw at once that Dulcie was not at all impressed.

Knowing well that Dulcie habitually discussed almost everything which was on her mind with the Ambassador and mindful that the latter valued his wife's judgment – about relatively unimportant things, that is – I was sure that Mr. Steinhardt would himself broach this subject with me before very long. Sure enough, later that week, he called me into his office to suggest that I represent the embassy at a *Friends of the USA* reception scheduled for later that month and, in a rather offhand, but also purposeful way, questioned the advisability of my continued involvement in a sporting activity which could be expected to conflict with my effectiveness in the embassy.

The very next afternoon, I asked George Romovacek to explain the situation to the coach, namely that I would no longer be in a position to continue rowing in the CVK crew. As it turned out, George took over my number-four seat and rowed effectively. While he lacked experience, he was a bit taller and about ten pounds heavier – not to mention, ten years younger.

When next I saw Dulcie, I told her what I had done. "You know, Walter," she replied, as she warmly pressed my arm with her bejeweled hand, "You are at this post as an American diplomat and not to take part in crew races with a Czech rowing boat." I supposed that she had a point. It was then that I decided to take up sculling, as I would not be tied down to training at a particular hour. So I ordered a single skiff from the Sims Company in England to fit my 6'1" height and 175 pounds.

The CVK first boat went to Henley in July of 1948. Schebal had made his escape from Czechoslovakia following the Communist take-over and had been replaced by a powerful new oarsman in the number-five seat. Another big and effective crewman, who had recently moved to Prague from Brno, took over at number-six and Romovacek was moved to number-two. This boat had handily won the big two-kilometer race in Prague for the Czech championship and much was expected of them at Henley. They tried to talk me into accompanying them to England in a duel role: a spare, in case one of the men became ill, and interpreter/spokesman. For many and obvious reasons, however, this jaunt was out of the question, especially as by then that crew was representing a club in a Communist-ruled country. My friends narrowly lost at Henley owing to their cox's error in steering off course.

The problems with turning into a sculler were that I had no coaching and not enough time to train adequately. I did manage to win one race, just barely, but that was about it. In my last regatta on Czech water, I had a two-length lead at 1200 meters, but then inadequate conditioning took its toll. Had the Almighty handed down a heavenly ukase that I hold that lead, I still could have done nothing to hold off the boats which were moving up on me – not enough time on the river; a paucity of time-trials; too many afternoon meetings and obligatory functions. But it was all well worth it. I made some good friends and played a part, albeit a very minor part, in the athletic life of

Czechoslovakia. I came to know them as a friendly, fun-loving, very sports minded people, devoted to a democratic form of government and to the freedom that such a government ensures.

Schebal was just as good an ice hockey player as he was an oarsman. Soon after the Communists seized power, he swam the Danube to safely in Austria and at once made his way to Klagenfurt, where he joined that town's professional hockey team. Robik managed to cross the Giant Mountains safely and enter the haven of the U.S. zone of Germany. After Schebal had played with Klagenfurt for the better part of a year, he was recruited by the Zurich team and remained there for a short time. When next I heard from him, he was in Australia and he asked me to write a letter of recommendation to the U.S. Consul General in Sydney – this in connection with Joe's application for a U.S. immigration visa. I wrote back that Foreign Service Officers were not allowed to write such letters, but I went on to comment in that letter that I was especially sorry about this rule, as he was one of the finest men I had met in Prague – very anti-communist and an admirer of the United States. Of course, he showed my letter to the Consul General and soon after, armed with his visa, he reached New York, where I met up with him several years later. Robik also ended up in the United States, where he obtained a good position with an American international company.

In setting down this CVK interlude, I have it in mind that it was probably a rather unusual experience for a U.S. diplomat; moreover, it provided a sequel to the pre-war rowing experience in London. A few months ago, when Charlie Hamlin, the president of *The Friends of Harvard Rowing* and I were attending a meeting of the Executive Committee of the Harvard Varsity club, I briefly mentioned to him some high-lights of those experiences. He soon asked me to send him an article about my post-Harvard rowing days. The above report as well as the one included in that covering my time at LSE in London is the same as that which appeared in *Blade on the Feather* in the spring of 1990.

At this juncture, it seems logical that I should comment at some length about the outstanding men who served with me in the *Iron Curtain* post. The impact of these people was especially noteworthy in view of the length of time I spent in Czechoslovakia and the onslaught of the *Cold War* there.

As might have been expected, the best informed men in the embassy were Charlie Katek, head CIA man there, and his right-hand man, Kurt Taub, whose daring exploit of driving a jeep through the German line from Plzen to Prague just before the end of the war has already been described. Had the ambassador listened carefully to these two men, he might have given the State Department a timely warning as to what was impending, prior to the Communist take-over in early 1948. Charles Katek, the Czech born, powerfully built, ex-Chicago piano mover, I remember as truly outstanding. Unfortunately he was declared *persona non grata* not long after that momentous February of 1948, and so had to return to Washington.

On the whole, I would say that the diminutive Kurt Taub (later known as Charles Taylor) had the keenest mind of anyone. Born in Czechoslovakia of Jewish origin, he managed to get to the U.S. well before the war. He, too, was expelled from Prague in the spring of 1948, and fortunately for his adopted country, went on to continued exploits in the CIA.

Another American FSO who started out in Prague, but was soon transferred to Bratislava, where he was instructed to set up a new consulate, was Claiborne Pell, many years later the Democratic senator from Rhode Island. His wife, Nuala, was also outstanding and charming indeed, albeit at the outset a bit unconventional. I never thought of her as such, but soon after arriving in Prague, she lit up a thin cigar following the dessert course at a diplomatic dinner and that brought a speedy rebuke from Dulcie Steinhardt, which was ignored by Nuela, whose aristocratic social background allowed her to choose which conventions, if any, she would follow. Despite their transfer to Bratislava, I saw the Pells quite often and our friendship carried over to much later times, notably when I was assigned to Washington and Claiborne was no longer in the Foreign Service. I have thought during the long years following those days in Prague that the Pells represent the best and finest of our country. I disagree with many of his votes in the Senate, but there has never been a doubt as to his decency, intelligence and honor.

In late spring, 1947, I met Lt.Col. Tom Foote and his attractive wife, Foss. Here was also a couple, not only handsome, but also bright, educated and always enthusiastic. Then there was Colonel Mike Michela, the man who became involved with me in several escape adventures. Unfortunately, he and Tom, his assistant, did not get on very well. Of course, I was able to stay out of this situation, but it was distressing, nevertheless, as I feared that Michela's dislike of Tom might harm the latter's career.

The Footes had an adorable young daughter – at that time an only child – (a son was born a few years later in Washington). I remember her best during the period when I was assigned to the Department in Washington in 1952-53, by which time she was about fifteen – a beguiling, amusing young girl and, as was her mother, beautiful, even at that age. Three years later she died of leukemia.

The list of outstanding men and women in that embassy was truly impressive, and too long to go into, but I must note Milton Fried, the Labor Attaché, and the son-in-law of Sydney Hillman. While Milton's political proclivities were far to the left of mine, I admired his keen mind and articulate expression of his ideas.

Meanwhile, François continued to look after my every need. At the beginning of his service with me, when good food was still scarce, he would produce the most marvelous meals and parties from food and beverages bartered for with chefs from other embassies. He knew that I was looking for a house to rent and helped in the search. He showed me a beautiful place in the country, but despite its idyllic setting, it was too far from the center - over an hour's drive - so I had to forego its advantages. Finally, in the early summer of 1947, I rented an unusually attractive modern house, situated in the Barrandov area some four miles south of the embassy and overlooking the Moldau (Vltava) River valley. It was a beautiful setting and the house was perfect for me. The living room was spacious and with high ceilings. There were two large bedrooms, one of which I used as an occasional guest-room. There was also adequate room to house François, his wife, Jeannette, and their daughter. Another intriguing advantage was its basement living quarters, made available, by universal custom involving fairly large houses, to favored pensioners who had the right to occupy that space rent-free. The benefit for me, of course, was that if I entertained, my *dumovnik,* Miroslav, and his wife could be at my disposal if needed. This man also kept up the garden in return for his free rent; so it was an ideal arrangement.

When I moved into that house, I acquired a collie that I called William. That name was really bestowed by Marjorie, an English girl whom I had met a party and who had read about another collie called *Just William*. This collie had a perfect temperament, was affectionate and loved to ride in the car, his head stuck out the window to catch the breeze and myriad smells. Sad to relate, that canine companion died of distemper on Christmas Day, 1947. If there is a dog-heaven, William is surely there, joyously barking and chasing sticks hurled by the angels for him to retrieve.

During that summer, I came to know well two outstanding Czechs, Veleslav Wahl and Major Nechansky, both of whom had been parachuted into German-held Czechoslovakia by the British during the war. They became heroes of the resistance, their exploits having been legendary. Indeed, it was Nechansky who had been involved in the slaying of one of the top Gauleiters in Prague.

I best remember two occasions in Wahl's company. One day during the summer, he invited me out to his summer retreat, which was situated about fifty miles north of Prague. We spent most of the day walking in the woods. Each of us carried a shotgun in case we saw any game, but we spent most of the time just talking, so we saw no quarry save a swift-running hare at a distance.

In the course of our walk, Veleslav (called Vaclav) showed me an underground shelter that he and other partisans had used just three years before as an occasional safe-haven when sought by the Nazis. So well concealed was the entrance that I would never have noticed it, even standing a few feet away, had not Wahl pointed it out. The other occasion involving Wahl was the Christmas Eve of that year when I gave a party for a few Czechs and Americans. I think back often on that evening, as I still have the two gifts Vaclav and his wife brought for me: one, a statuette of King Wenceslas (a reduction of the famous one in Prague), and the other, a silver chalice commemorating a victory of the middle ages in 1331 with the initials, C.B. The chalice has the Austrian hallmark of between 1830 and 1850, so I imagine it was made to commemorate the 500th anniversary of some happy event, probably to do with his family, but have never been able to trace exactly what.*

---

* Possibly, it may refer to Charles IV of Bohemia, (original name, Wenceslas).

That year of 1947 was a watershed of sorts. On the one hand, the country was staging a rapid recovery from the war, both economically and, in a way, politically; but on the other hand, many observers, including Katek and Taub and Wahl and "Gibby" Gibson, chief of intelligence at the British Embassy, did not feel easy in their minds, for they were not oblivious of the fact that the Communist Party and Soviet Ambassador Zorin would not be content to let things continue as they were, with the communists not completely in power.

Perhaps the first tangible sign of what might be expected to lie ahead was the reaction to what took place at the memorable Harvard Commencement of June, 1947, when Secretary of State Marshall (formerly Chief of Staff of the US Army) delivered his key-note address which in effect launched the Marshall Plan. Without delay, Jan Masaryk, the Minister of Foreign Affairs, accepted this generous gesture of aid from the United States. However, it was soon clear that Masaryk had not consulted the communist controlled prime minister; and he certainly had not consulted Ambassador Zorin. As a result, Masaryk was summoned to Moscow for a talk with "Uncle Joe" Stalin (as a few fellow travelers used to call him). And as soon as Masaryk returned from the USSR, he made an official statement to the effect that the Czech government had decided on second thought *not* to accept any US aid under the auspices of the Marshall Plan. It was from that moment that my Czech friends and acquaintances began to feel uneasy. The communist leaders, however, were also as yet undecided as to what action their party should take to ensure its ultimate victory.

Free elections were scheduled for 1948. The Communist Party was fearful of losing votes in that election; moreover, the Social Democrats, under the able leadership of Vaclav Meyer were, it was reported, growing restive, and Meyer was increasingly resenting his role of being a *yes-man* to the prime minister.

Also, in that summer of 1947, a group of anti-communist partisans called Menderovskis, having been driven out of Poland, was now operating in the mountains of Slovakia. This, too, troubled the communist leaders.

In view of these uncertainties and with a view to finding out what the results of the upcoming open election might be, the Soviet ambassador instructed the prime minister to arrange for a quiet, secret Gallup-poll like enquiry to determine as to what probably lay in store if the formal open elections were held as scheduled. The fears – or one might more accurately say the suspicions – of the communists were apparently justified, for this secret sounding out of popular opinion revealed that they would suffer almost certain defeat at the polls in an openly-held, free election.

There thus remained only one action for the communists to take – activate the plan to take over the government by coup d'état. This did not present much of a problem, for as previously mentioned, they already controlled the all-important Ministry of the Interior, the army, the prime minister's office and of course, the Ministry of Propaganda. They at once began the process of infiltrating their own men into all the top posts of those ministries and where any factory did not already have a factory militia (Zavody Milice), one was formed. All National Committees (Narofny Vyborgs) were scrupulously examined to ensure that all leaders were loyal communists. These moves did not go unnoticed by the leaders of the anti-communist parties, namely the National Socialist Party led by Dr. Zenkl, and the People's Party, headed by Monsignor Sramek.

These men apparently came to the conclusion that something had to be done without delay to thwart the obvious communist plans to terrorize and then take over the country. Unfortunately, the counter-move made by the National Socialists and People's Party men backfired and played into the hands of the communists. What happened was that by February 20, all the cabinet ministers belonging to the two above-mentioned anti-communist parties, resigned from the government. Now there were no longer any officials to stand up to the Communist Party. The stage for the take-over was set.

By February 23 - the day after our Washington's Birthday – the citizens of Prague woke up to see the streets patrolled by detachments of the Communist-controlled police and *Zavodny Milice*. Now, Communists filled the vacated ministries. A notable exception – that is, until March 10 – was Jan Masaryk, who during those two and a half weeks continued as Minister of Foreign Affairs. Jan Masaryk ceased being Foreign Minister on that 10th of March, 1948, for early in the morning of that fateful day he was murdered, defenestrated, by two communist thugs who overpowered him, having gained forced entry into his apartment in the Cernin Palace, and threw him out the window onto the cobblestone court below.

It has never been firmly established as to why Moscow and its henchmen in Prague decided to eliminate Masaryk on that particular day. It is known that Marcia Davenport, the well-known novelist, and Masaryk's mistress and fiancée, was at that time in London, presumably waiting for Jan to join her there. (She confirmed this later in writing and also told me of it when I visited her a few years later in New York) It is also almost certain that Masaryk had decided to defect and escape from Czechoslovakia. As there have been conflicting reports as to how Masaryk was to escape and to which country he was planning this escape, it would serve no useful purpose to go into any detail about it here. Probably the escape was to be by air. Otto Springer, who had been active in Czech resistance during the war, and since then had kept in close contact with my friends, Wahl and Nechansky, informed me many year later that the escape plane was about to land at a small airstrip, but at the last minute, not seeing the all-clear signal, aborted the landing and took off for the West.

The important factor is that somehow the Communists learned of Masaryk's escape plan and that was enough for them. Jan was a folk-hero and his successful escape would grievously harm the reputation of the new order. So immediately, the new Communist government loudly proclaimed in the press and radio that Masaryk had died accidentally or committed suicide; and there was no one in a position to contradict this fact. (The window was too high to have fallen out of accidentally and human feces found on the windowsill indicated extreme terror on the part of Masaryk) An elaborate funeral was arranged, with an impressive cortege with a band playing funeral dirges moving through the principal streets of Prague.

With the illegal seizure of power by the Communist Party, that beautiful country of Czechoslovakia changed overnight. An interesting sidelight – and not such a sidelight at that – was that Vaclav Meyer, the titular head of the Social Democratic Party, which since the war had collaborated closely with the communists, finally made up his mind no longer to walk in lockstep with them; so now it was the Communist Party alone which, in fact, ran the country.

Dr. Beneš resigned from the presidency in June rather than accept a new Constitution legitimizing the Communist regime, and spent the short remainder of his life at Sezimovo Ustí, his country estate, dying September 3, 1948.

While my life, from that day of February was no longer as pleasant and relatively carefree as it had been up to then, it did take on more excitement, for from that day on, I became increasingly involved in a sort of *Scarlet Pimpernel* kind of activity which did not bring danger to me, but did enable me to remove many Czechs from danger of imprisonment or even death. .

I had no sooner arrived at my office on the morning of that fateful day when Mary Klementik, the ambassador's secretary, called on the inter-office phone to say that the boss wanted to see me right away. I was not at all taken aback by this summons as I had noted during my drive to the embassy that there were far fewer pedestrians than usual; moreover, I had been aware that Factory Militia detachments, armed with carbines were patrolling with the regular police. I had also noted that Karla, the embassy receptionist (who married an American Marine officer two years later) looked frightened. After bidding me good morning, Karla said, "Mr. Birge, one of my boy friends in the university was arrested early this morning. His mother phoned me at seven o'clock. Do you know what is happening? I guess this is what we have been expecting."

Within one minute after receiving Mary Klemintik's call, I stood in front of the ambassador's desk. Steinhardt's usually serious expression was positively grim and his eyes, flinty. "Walter," he barked, "are you ready to drive to the German border?" "Yes, sir," I replied at once. He continued, "Do you know Joe Hartmann?" "No, sir, I don't think so, but I may have met him at one of the diplomatic parties," I answered. – "Well, this is the situation. Hartmann has been a prominent member of the National Socialist Party and has been the leading sugar merchant in the country. While, of course, not as rich as before the war, he has been, I understand, the leading financial contributor to his party, is staunchly anti-Communist and pro-West. Do you remember *Gibby* Gibson from the time you were in Turkey?" I replied that I did remember this British Intelligence operator by reputation, though I had never met him. Steinhardt went on, "It seems that there is a warrant out for the arrest of Mr. and Mrs. Hartmann. Gibson informed them of this about an hour ago and the Hartmanns are at this moment in Gibson's office. Gibson has just sent a message to me to ask if I could arrange to get the Hartmanns to our zone in Germany. I sent word back that you would take care of it." "How would you like me to proceed, Mr. Ambassador", I asked, my thoughts not at all in step with the calm assurance my voice sought to convey. "Just this, Walter. Drive over to the British Embassy and park in front of the main entrance. The Hartmanns will be expecting you and when they get into your car they will instruct you as to how you will proceed to get them into Germany. One more thing! Do not stop at the Hartmann's apartment to pick up any luggage as we are sure it is being watched!"

It was cold that morning, maybe 15 or 20 degrees F., and there was a light snow falling, seemingly the harbinger of a long-lasting winter.

I had been parked for three or four minutes in front of the British Embassy when two warmly clad figures emerged from the embassy gate – a man of middle height, of early middle age and a somewhat young and quite comely woman. Well, here we go, I thought and little did I know, or even guess, what was in store on that cold, first day of the Communist revolution, a morning which would mark the beginning of forty years of travail for the freedom-loving Czechs and Slovaks.

"You are Mr. Birge? Yes, of course you are. I remember you now, and Mr. Gibson described you perfectly." This little speech of Mr. Hartmann caused me to wonder just what that *007-type* had said to enable this stranger readily to identify me. I suggested that Mrs. Hartman get in the back of my Cadillac (bought new in Basel the preceding year for $3000) and that Joe sit beside me. Mindful of what the ambassador had so recently said about instructions, I enquired of Mr. Hartmann, as soon as the doors had been closed against the wintry air, how he would like me to proceed and what route I was to follow so as to reach Germany without interference from the STB (State Security Police). Hartmann raised both hands in a gesture of surprise. "But, Mr. Birge, Mr. Gibson told us that *you* would know exactly what to do and that in your hands we would be safe and that we should not worry."

While this accolade from one of England's ablest intelligence operators would have been nice to hear under any other circumstances, at that particular time I felt neither pleasure nor satisfaction. Rather, it scared the hell out of me. There I was, sitting in my car which bore US Embassy plates, in the middle of Prague with two passengers for whom there was a warrant out for arrest. And I had no idea as to what to do next.

What probably brought about this parlous state of affairs was that the messages – or talk – that had passed between Steinhardt and Gibson had not been very explicit. Steinhardt had probably described me as resourceful and a man of action, or something like that, and Gibson had probably said that Hartmann knew his way around and had good contacts.

"Mr. Hartmann," I asked, "did not you and Mr. Gibson have any discussion as to just how I was to get you over the border and into Germany? Did Mr. Gibson by chance suggest that he might have a colleague or collaborator with a house close to the border?" Hartmann thought for a few seconds. "Oh yes, Mr. Gibson did speak of a smuggler, Nicco Papadopoulos, whom I also know, a man who does have some sort of dwelling at Cheb which is right next to the border, but he also said that if you had a plan, it would be best for me to follow that, as he reposed great confidence in the Americans." I then asked where this Greek smuggler lived in Prague and if he would be at home at this hour. Joe Hartman replied that the Greek would indeed be at home as a backstop for us. "I'm relieved to hear that, Mr. Hartmann, so just show me the way and we'll go directly there." Then Mrs. Hartmann, who up to that moment had remained silent, interrupted. "Please, Mr. Birge, could you stop at our apartment to pick up two suitcases which are already packed – and my fur coat?" I was mindful of having been specifically instructed by Steinhardt not to stop anywhere for luggage. I turned my head and looked back at this frightened lady who was preparing to leave her native country forever. When I mentioned my instructions about not picking up any luggage, she clasped her hands together and in a low but anguished voice begged me to allow her to collect a few items which she treasured – all carefully packed. So I relented – and I never told the ambassador about this later – and Joe Hartmann showed me the way, which was not far, to their apartment. Within ten minutes the suitcases were safely stowed in the trunk and the couple back in their seats, Mrs. Hartmann clutching her mink coat. Just then, a car arrived at the entrance of the apartment and two men emerged. Fearful that they might be STB agents, I told the Hartmanns to duck down and we lost no time in pulling away.

We set out for the apartment of Nicco, the Greek. I wondered whether he might have been awaiting us for I assumed that this was possibly not the first operation of this nature in which he had been involved. Indeed, I learned many years later that Harold W. Gibson, that same man as *Gibby* Gibson, ostensibly the head of the British Embassy Visa Section in 1948, had, nine years before, in 1939, when he was a major in M16, spirited out of Prague the eleven top officers of Czech Intelligence – along with their invaluable files.

When we picked up the Greek smuggler, the latter sat in front with me, and Joe Hartmann joined his wife in the back seat. It was getting colder and although only eleven am, the sky was a somber gray. Despite the presence of the obviously resourceful Greek, my misgivings were increasing apace; we had a long road to travel and the big unknown factor was how far behind the STB was with their arrest order. My own personal safety was in no danger and I was sure that Nicco would be able to take care of himself; but my new friends who occupied the back seat could still be arrested before reaching safety.

We crossed most of the city and set off on the main road that led to Karlovy Vary (Carlsbad) and from there to the small town of Cheb (Eger) where Nicco told us he had a safe-house. On that road we continued to risk being stopped by either the regular police or the much more dangerous STB. It was still snowing, albeit less heavily than before, and the visibility was pretty good. I could see in the mirror over the windshield that Anna Hartmann was asleep. Joe and Nicco were chatting in Czech. As for me, I was trying to make up my mind as to what I should do in the probable eventuality that we would be stopped on the road for a check of our identity papers.

Several factors were involved. First of all, at the beginning of any coup d'état, there is apt to be some confusion with regard to the issuance of commands from the top leadership down to the middle and eventually lower ranks of the police and other security forces. This was to our advantage. Second, the order for the Hartmanns' arrest had probably not reached down to all ranks – if, indeed, the order had actually been issued yet. If it had been sent out, the first step would be to inform all border-crossing transport, notably railways. The third factor, I like to believe, was that at least a few members of the police forces – especially those in the lower ranks – were pro-USA, inasmuch as tens of thousands of Czechs and Slovaks had relatives in Pittsburgh or Chicago or Cleveland, etc., so the chances of reaching Cheb safely were not altogether bleak.

By way of mention – and this probably turned out to be an important factor – I was dressed in a long, suede Hungarian overcoat with *frog* button fasteners, plus a white Sheepskin hat, which I had bought in Bratislava while visiting Claiborne and Nuala Pell the year before. So I decided on a plan of action that had its degree of risk in case we were stopped but which might well be successful.

While in Istanbul, I had taken Russian lessons, and while hardly a great grammarian, I have always had a good ear and have a facility for mastering a good accent in the languages I have studied. What I intended to do, if stopped and asked for an identity paper, was to reach into my wallet (already placed in the readily accessible car-pocket for maps), pull out my 4" by 6"gray diplomatic card, place two fingers over the words "21-5-13, St. Louis, USA" and say "Sovietsky Posoltsvo" (Soviet Embassy). Even assuming that my Kiev accent acquired from my teacher in Istanbul was not perfect, the Czech police would almost surely not know the difference. While driving along, I also dreamed up a back-up ploy; if the police insisted on closely examining my identification card, I would treat it as a joke and admit that I was an American diplomat after all. At the last moment, I would decide on whether or not to try this plan – or simply to hand over my card, with the almost assured certainty that the cards of my three passengers would also be examined.

This reasoning may seem odd to a reader nowadays, but at the time of this story and in view of the Hartmanns' situation, plan-A seemed to merit a try. Basically, it would all depend on what kind of man might be stopping us.

Sure enough, a few miles east of Carlsbad, I saw dead ahead two uniformed men, one with a lantern, slowly waving their arms over their heads as a signal to come to a halt. Both men were standing in the middle of the road. I came to a stop on the right-hand side of the road and rolled down the left-front window. These men were regular policemen and not STB – that I could see at once. I also noted that the officer who was not holding the lantern and who was now moving toward my window was a pleasant looking man in his mid to late 40's. He looked like he might have a sense of humor; but he also moved in a disciplined sort of way. I had only a few seconds to decide what to do, so without further delay, I quickly removed my wallet from the map-pocket. As the officer said "Ridicsky prukaz, prosim" (Identification document, if you please), I removed my document, held it in my right hand and in a quiet and I hoped purposeful tone, spoke the two mentally well-rehearsed words, "Sovietsky Posoltsvo." The policeman slowly came to attention and saluted and as he did so, I thought I detected a slight smile on the man's face. He then said in Czech, "Everything is o.k. You may go." As he said these words his fellow policeman moved up to him and seemed to remonstrate, but by then I was already shifting from first into second speed and we were not stopped again. "What possessed you to tell that policeman you were from the Soviet Embassy, my three passengers demanded, almost in unison. "What if our friend asked to see all our documents and had already been informed about your arrest warrant," I replied. That rejoinder brought a dead silence as we sped along the road toward the west and the border town of Cheb.

We arrived in that small factory town – which the Germans call Eger – at about 1:30 pm. A hundred or so workers were walking home following their last shift and a disturbing number of Zavodny Milice was much in evidence, as might have been expected in a center situated so near the western border. And there we were, slowly driving down the center of the town with a man sought by the authorities, sitting in the back seat of a large American car. Undoubtedly, the communications problem, which so often characterizes the first day of a sudden seizure of power, probably contributed to our having avoided a second hold up by the police or STB or Factory Militia. I asked Nicco how much further we had to go before reaching his house. He said that we had about ten more kilometers and to take the right fork just ahead and follow the signs leading to Franciskovy Lazne (Franzesbad), and to Aš (Ash). We drove right through the watering place of Franzesbad and twenty minutes later, entered the village of Aš, which is situated in the center of a sliver of land surrounded on three sides by Germany. Nicco held up his hand and pointed – "That is my house – the big one with the iron gate in front."

The snow was now about four inches deep. Nicco jumped out and managed to open the gate, the bottom of which was fortunately an inch or so above the snow level. I drove in; the luggage was brought into the house and we all shook hands at the successful conclusion of that first phase of the operation.

I turned to Nicco. "How far to the German border and in what direction? I think we should go across as soon as possible. If we wait until dark, any light we use would attract attention. Don't you agree?" "Absolutely, Mr. Birge," replied our Greek friend. "I plan to send my guide-assistant with the Hartmanns to show the way. It is not necessary for you also to go, Mr. Birge. In fact, an additional person would increase the danger of the Hartmanns being apprehended by a Czech patrol." I then asked him when we could expect the guide as it was already nearing three o'clock. Nicco assured me that he would be there at any minute, as had had been due back at two.

Twenty minutes passed and there was still no guide. "Nicco," I said, "the Hartmanns have to get going as it will be dusk before long. Are *you* able to escort them?" Nicco waved his hands in front of his face and in a low and regretful tone, replied that unfortunately, it would not be possible for him to accompany the Hartmanns "In that case," I declared. " I will go with them – not as a guide, but to assure myself and to be able to report to my chief that this escape mission has been accomplished." At first, Nicco tried to persuade us to wait a day, but finally explained how we should proceed. "I am going to take you in my car up a road which leads through the point of Czech territory that juts into and is surrounded by Germany. There I will leave you. It would be highly inadvisable for you, Mr. Birge, to drive to that point in your car for it would be too conspicuous during your absence. Before the three of you leave my car, I will give you exact instructions as to how you should proceed."

Within a few minutes we were on our way and it took us only five minutes or so to arrive at the spot where Nicco stopped his car. It was still snowing lightly, but there was light enough to see clearly the surrounding fields and wooded patches. He then gave us our final instructions. "When you leave this car walk straight ahead across the fields westward. Here is a small compass to ensure that you do not deviate from your westward direction. The border of the US Zone lies approximately two kilometers from this spot. On your way, you may see two deserted barns with signs in German attached to them. One of these barns is in the former Sudeten area of Czechoslovakia and the second one is just over the German border. Here are three white sheets with which to cover yourselves in case of need. You will not be able to carry the luggage with you, but do not worry; I will see that you get it. Mr. Birge, I will await your return in about an hour – not exactly here, but at a spot on this road about half way back to my house. Good luck." Each of us took one of the sheets and we set out across the snow, which was some five inches deep. It was cold, but it had stopped snowing.

I led the way. For a moment we stopped and agreed that if one of us saw anyone who might see us, one would say "Down!" and we would all at once drop to the snow and cover ourselves with a sheet. Joe Hartmann held the compass and on two occasions directed me to turn slightly, once to the right and once to the left. All of a sudden Joe whispered, "Down". The three of us instantly dropped to the snow-covered ground and as I covered myself with my sheet, I discerned some fifty yards away a dog being chased by three running figures. We lay motionless; then I heard voices and then a dog's wet nose invaded the sanctuary of my sheet cover, sniffing curiously. I raised the sheet and there were three children aged about ten or eleven, who had followed the dog and were now doubtless wondering what those three sheets were hiding. I promptly asked Joe to put the kids off with some logical explanation as to what in heaven three grown-ups were doing there. Joe smiled broadly as he told the children (I could understand enough Czech for this) that we were exploring, and that in a few minutes we would all play hide-and-seek with them, but in the meantime, would they run back to the adjoining woods and hide for five minutes, after which we would see if we could find them. The children seemed to like what he was suggesting, so they called their dog and made off across the field.

We set off again, a little faster now. Then five minutes later, Joe saw two figures carrying carbines, to our left, and a little ahead of us. He pointed them out to his wife and me. They were partially concealed by the fir trees which formed a thinly wooded part of that frontier area. The three of us quickly dropped to the snow-covered ground. As I lifted a corner of my sheet, I could see that Joe's vigilance had undoubtedly prevented our arrest. There were indeed two Czech militiamen. They were not walking toward us, but seemingly following a path that led around us. Moreover, they were busy talking to each other and fortunately the path along which they were walking was leading them away from us and in the direction of the village of Aš.

Within a minute, we were on our way again. It was now almost dusk and it was getting colder and colder. After about another five minutes of trudging through the snow, we could see ahead of us a small barn on which was painted in capital letters, "Achtung – Hunde!" (Look out – dogs!) Was this the barn in the Sudentenland or was it the barn on the German side of the border? Logically, the Czech authorities would have removed any signs in German. Just then, as we were looking at that sign, two green-clad men in uniform, rifles at the ready, emerged from the back of the barn and walked slowly in our direction. "Wer da?" (Who goes there?), one of them commanded. No Czech border guard would speak German (I hoped), so I raised my hand and replied in German thus. "I am from the American Embassy in Prague. My two companions are Czech refugees who seek asylum in the US Zone. Would you be good enough to inform Mr. and Mrs. Hartmann how they can get to the nearest U.S. Command Post?" "Herzlich

Willkommen," both Germans called out. They then informed us that the area command post of the U.S. Army was only three kilometers distant and that they would drive the Hartmanns there in their jeep.

I retraced my way back to the road we had left an hour or so before. All I had to do was follow our still barely visible footprints in the snow. Then I turned right on the road and walked about a half mile until I came to Nicco's car. It was by then deep twilight.

I retrieved my car and set out for Prague. En route back to the embassy, I had two flat tires; the first I was able to change with my spare, but when the second tire went flat (right in front of the police station in a small town), I was able to telephone the embassy where Walter Burke, the Security Officer on duty that day, answered the phone. I explained where I was and asked him either to drive me to Prague or to bring a spare tire. While I was waiting for this rescue of sorts, the policemen were all gathered around their radio listening to a government spokesman telling about the *glorious* revolution. Before long Burke arrived with a replacement tire and, very hungry and tired, I was able to get to the ambassador's residence in time for their dinner party to which I had been invited the day before. I could briefly report to the ambassador, "Mission accomplished!"

Several weeks later, I learned that the Hartmanns had settled in Canada. I also learned that the luggage they had left with the smuggler never reached them. Under the circumstances, that was perhaps understandable. Had I known at that time what I was to learn during the course of that year, I would have suggested that the luggage be left with me for eventual delivery in Germany or elsewhere.

Just a day or two following the Hartmann's escape, while walking toward the Mala Strana from the Charles Bridge, I ran into an acquaintance who was on the Prague police force. From time to time, he had made a point of letting me know that he was anti-communist. This officer came up to me and said conspiratorially, "Mr. Birge, I think that you should know that there is a warrant out for the arrest of Mr. and Mrs. Josef Hartmann and that the STB is looking for them!" I thanked my well-intentioned acquaintance for his information. Within a year, this officer made good his own escape to the West and eventually to the U.S. where he entered the service of the International Red Cross.

My rescue of the Hartmanns led eventually to another adventure of *derring-do* – this time concerning Dr. Peter Zenkl, the pre-Communist chairman of the National Socialist Party. During the war, Zenkl had spent most of the years of that conflict in the Dachau Concentration Camp, a few miles west of Munich. From the Nazi point of view, this incarceration was logical – indeed essential – inasmuch as this courageous and outspoken champion of his country's freedom had been mayor of Prague and was occupying that office when the German Nazi regime forcibly occupied Bohemia and Moravia and set up a protectorate over *Independent* Slovakia in the spring of 1939.

Shortly after the Communists seized power in February, 1948, Dr. Zenkl and his wife were placed under house arrest. This meant that they continued living in their Prague house, but they were guarded twenty-four hours a day by three shifts of two guards each. They were allowed two short walks a day, accompanied by their guards; otherwise, they had no contacts with anyone. In this way, the Communists hoped to silence Dr. Zenkl for the foreseeable future, as they had – by more drastic means – ensured the permanent silencing of Jan Masaryk.

My two close collaborators in the saga of the Zenkl's escape were Colonel "Mike" Michela, Military Attaché, and Reinhold

Pick, my half-Czech, half-Russian assistant during my tenure as Administrative Officer up to April, 1946. The latter had worked as an interpreter for General Harmon, commander of the 22nd Corps of Patton's 3rd Army. When the US forces were removed from Czechoslovakia at the end of November, 1945, General Harmon asked Ambassador Steinhardt to hire Pick if possible, as the latter wanted to remain in his own country. Reinhold had proved to be an unusually able, efficient, and imaginative member of the staff.

As for Michela, he had served as Military Attaché in our embassy in Moscow until early 1942 and had at that time come to know well Larry Steinhardt, our ambassador there prior to his assignment in Turkey. Colonel Michela, who arrived in Prague in mid-1947, let it soon be known that he had a burning hatred of Soviet communism. "Drop the bomb on them," he often growled, but beneath this bluster there lurked a keen, calculating, analytical intelligence. We became good friends, partly, I supposed, because he knew that the Steinhardts and I had served together in Turkey and also as we shared a hatred of the Soviet international and scheming Communism.

One day, several months after the Communist take-over, I met with Michela in his office and we had a long talk about what was shaping up as a *Cold War* and about the robust possibility that before long World War III might break out. What we had to do, we agreed, was to ensure that at least one Czech statesman of stature, such as Dr. Zenkl, escape to the West – preferably to the U.S. - and thus to be in a position to head a Czech government-in-exile, as president Beneš did in the U.K. during World War II.

After a few days we met again, this time with "Noldy" Pick (Noldy being our nickname for Reinhold), whom we could count on the get a job done with dispatch. We decided that the logical way to bring about the escape of Dr. and Mrs. Zenkl was to have someone approach one of their guards with a view to persuading him to defect along with his colleague on his shift. As their guards were rotated every week, it would be necessary to plan the escape for the week during which the defecting guards would be on the eight a.m. to noon duty. We then discussed the possible advantages of having the Zenkls leave the country separately – Dr. Zenkl via East Germany and Berlin (at that time, the *Wall* had not yet been built) and Mrs. Zenkle straight into the U.S. Zone of Germany.

Mike Michela then suggested that if that plan were adopted, Mrs. Zenkl should spend a few days in my house which was more remote than his house; moreover, my servants were considered to be completely reliable, as, indeed, they proved themselves to be during the ensuing months. We were aware that Mrs. Zenkl had a rather bad heart condition. "What if she dies while staying in my house?" I asked. "Bury her in your garden," shot back Michela. After mulling over that possibility, even though such an eventuality was remote, we gave up this separate escape idea, mainly because there would be little chance of concealing a burial in my garden in view of the residence in my basement of my *Dumovnik* and his wife. They gave the impression of being fine, decent, loyal people, but I could certainly not guarantee their total trustworthiness as far as our political activity was concerned. Hence, the decision was made to attempt a double escape straight into the US controlled section of Germany.

The first and most ticklish job was how best to approach one of the guards. As it turned out, this was not as great a problem as we had anticipated. Pick, as it turned out, was a good friend of the barber who periodically cut the hair of one of the guards. In addition, Pick was also acquainted with that guard. So there now began a series of rather comical conferences between Pick and the guard as they sat in adjoining chairs in the friendly barbershop. As these conferences took place at least twice a week, Pick and the guard soon were all out of hair to cut, but the obliging and anti-communist barber went through the motions of assiduous clipping and snipping.

In the interim, we had a talk with Frank Volek, the obliging embassy gate watchman who had driven Mario Bertelli to the airport to board the General's Rome-bound plane. Colonel Michela and I decided that Volek would pick up the two guards at the moment of their defection. The Zenkles themselves would be taken out of the country by Mike and me.

Then came the first stumbling block, which for a few days seemed formidable indeed. Just as Pick succeeded in persuading his barbershop friend to defect along with his colleague, all the Zenkl guards were changed. So Noldy had to begin all over again. This presented not so much a real difficulty as inconvenience and waste of time (not to mention, possible permanent baldness). Pick's friend lost no time in getting Noldy together with one of his replacements. Not content with that, the first guard asked Pick to allow him to defect along with the replacement guards. It is a tribute to Pick (who in succeeding years became an outstanding CIA operator) that within two weeks, he again succeeded in talking the new guards into full cooperation and enthusiastic agreement to defect (along with the girlfriend of one and the wife of the other) on a given morning and then to ride out of Prague and west to the Giant Mountains in Frankie Volek's jeep, accompanied by a staunch friend of Volek. Naturally, Volek drove only as far as a spot in the mountains a few kilometers from the border.

Now all we had to do was plan the details. Aside from Volek, three of us were involved: Mike Michela, my former assistant, Jack Guiney, and I. Jack was unmarried, in his late twenties, tough and always ready for action. First of all, a final meeting place was selected in a small pinewood close to the Plzen highway and about eighteen kilometers west of the capital. At that spot, we would *load* Mr. And Mrs. Zenkl into Mike's car and my car, respectively.

The plan was simple enough. Guiney in his Plymouth and Volek in his jeep were to meet on a certain street and at a specified spot on that street close to the Zenkl house in the Bubenech district. They were then to await the arrival of Dr. and Mrs. Zenkl taking their morning constitutional accompanied by their two about-to-defect guards. The Zenkls were immediately to get in the back of Jack's car and the guards were to get into the jeep.

With a view to lessening our visibility, we decided that Mike and I would drive separately to the pinewood rendezvous, that is, not in tandem. First of all, other essential arrangements had to be made. As my car was an Alfa Romeo sports roadster (this vehicle having been acquired since the Hartmann escape operation) with a rather small trunk in which Mrs. Zenkl was to ride, the spare tire had to be removed to make room. Hence, to guard against the possibility of getting a flat tire, my spare was placed in a small trailer which was to be towed by Michela's car. It should be added at this juncture that during the post-war years of the late 1940's, the quality of automobile tires was very poor – no radials and with inner tubes –so that flat tires were a frequent occurrence.

In view of the very limited space for an occupant of my Alfa trunk, I had to do whatever possible to make it as comfortable as possible for the two hours during which it was to be occupied. First of all, I took François into my confidence, for I was convinced that he was trustworthy, not only because he was loyal to me but also owing to his determination to emigrate to the United States as soon as possible. Moreover, François would not only be of help in transforming the car trunk into a cozy hideaway, but also, being a very observant see-all, know-all individual, he would have guessed that something special was in the works, so it was much better to enlist him rather than having him think that perhaps he was not trusted.

In order to ensure that plenty of air could flow into the trunk, I made two holes through the upholstery that separated the trunk from the small rear seat. We also placed three small pillows for the escapee's comfort. So, all was prepared for the execution of the most significant of all the Pimpernelian escapes. For at that time when the cold war was becoming increasingly hot, so it seemed that Zenkl was perceived as a key figure.

On the appointed day, I drove away from my house at nine in the morning and proceeded down the winding road that led to the main highway on the Vltava River shore. My house on the heights of Barrandov was accessible only by that one winding road. Barrandov was a relatively new development built following the establishment of the Czech moving picture studios there in the 1930's. Just before that one road of access or egress came to the river road, it crossed a branch railway track. There was very seldom any railway traffic on that track, but that morning was an exception. As that crossing came into view, there appeared all too clearly a line or eight or ten freight cars which were blocking the intersection. A steam locomotive puffed and wheezed at the front of this small train. Was it going to move out of there or not? There was nothing to do except sit there and wait.

In situations such as this each second is like a minute and a minute is a quarter of an hour. Finally, after about four or five minutes of this torture, the locomotive gave out a shrill whistle, then slowly chugged forward with those cars clanking and thudding behind. The instant the road was clear, the little Alfa leapt forward and I set off in the direction of the Plzen road.

When I had driven some five or six miles west of the city, I looked at my watch and noted that I was probably a few minutes ahead of schedule. I was not thinking so much that Michela might not be ahead of me; rather, I wanted Jack Guiney to be in front, for in the very unlikely eventuality that he had a breakdown, I wanted to be in a position to gather in the Zenkls. My reasoning was perhaps specious. In any event, I stopped by the side of the road, got out, raised the hood and pretended to check on the engine. Within two or three minutes Jack Guiney's Plymouth passed me doing at least sixty. In the back seat was a large newspaper being held up in such a way as to make it seem as though someone was reading it, but also ensuring that the person seated behind the paper – Dr. Zenkl, that is - could not be seen. I quickly slammed the hood down, leapt into the driver's seat, pulled the heavy doors shut and was off. Jack momentarily reduced speed until he could be sure that I was following him on that straight road and I caught up with him after about three miles of fast driving.

When we arrived at the pinewood-meeting place, Mike Michela was already there. Few words were spoken and we lost no time in getting the Zenkls out of Jack's car. Peter Zenkl crawled into the trunk of Mike's olive-drab army vehicle and Mrs. Zenkl was helped into the smaller Alfa Romeo trunk, her temporary place of refuge until she would alight in Bavaria. So we set out for Eger, the border-crossing point. No one stopped us on the way. When I knew we were fairly close to the German border, I called back to Mrs. Zenkl, "In zehn minuten – Deutschland!" "Dobry," came back her muffled reply.

Mike's army sedan and trailer pulled up to the guardhouse at the Czech border-crossing control and I drew up a few yards behind him. Twenty yards in front of us a solid telegraph pole-size barrier about twenty-five feet long rested on a large hinge on the right side of the road with a heavy weight attached to the short end – in such a way that the long end that blocked the road could easily be raised by applying extra weight on the short segment.

As we drew up to the control post, an officer of the Border Patrol stepped up to the driver's side window of Mike Michela's car, saluted and, according to customary procedure, asked to examine his identification papers. Just at that moment, a subaltern walked quickly down the steps leading from the guardhouse, came up to the inspecting officer and informed him that he was wanted on the telephone – an urgent call from one of his superiors in Prague. At that time neither Mike not I understood anything more than that the man was wanted on the phone. Dr. Zenkl, however, could clearly hear from his hiding place the reference to "an urgent call from Prague." Of course, as can be imagined, both Mike and I at once feared that somehow word of the Zenkl's escape had reached the STB, with immediate warnings sent to all border-crossing points.

Fortunately, our worries were groundless, for as it turned out, the examining officer soon returned, handed back our documents and ordered that the massive barrier be raised to let us through.

Two hundred yards down that road, we drew up to the US Army border control post, were quickly waved through and the Zenkls were in the free West and under the protection of the United States. We stopped when we were a mile or so within the US Zone. We helped the Zenkls from their respective hiding places. They embraced and then rode together in the back seat of Mike's car and we all drove to Bayreuth. Mike Michela then drove the Zenkls to Frankfurt and I returned to Prague by a somewhat circuitous route. The Zenkls eventually settled in Washington, where Peter was employed by one of our government agencies. About ten years later, after I had moved to Columbus, Ohio, I arranged for him to fly to that city to take part in a radio program having to do with the *Iron Curtain*. I visited him twice in his Washington apartment, where he and his wife lived quietly yet in continuing contact with the growing number of refugees from their mother country.

The Zenkl's successful escape in early August had been preceded by another adventure, about four months earlier, this time involving Miloš (pronounced Meelosh) and Karla Hanak. This very personable and attractive middle-aged couple had been in Turkey during the war where Miloš was Counselor of the Czechoslovak embassy representing that country's government-in-exile. While in Ankara and in Istanbul, the Hanaks had become close friends of the Steinhardts and I, too, came to know them well. After the war, Hanak was assigned to the Czech foreign office in Prague at about the same time that Steinhardt was transferred to that city.

It was of course well known to Mr. Nosek, Minister of the Interior, that Hanak, as a close friend of the Steinhardts, was strongly pro-West. This alone was enough not only to jeopardize his diplomatic career, but also to place him in danger of eventual arrest, for the line separating close association with the US embassy and espionage was a thin one.

One morning in April, 1948, the ambassador sent for me – much like a repeat performance of the Hartmann episode of two months earlier. "Walter", began the ambassador, "Miloš Hanak told me yesterday that he has good reason to believe that it is only a question of time, and a short time at that, until he will be arrested. He and Karla have decided that they should escape to Germany. Miloš went on to tell me that he has made contact with a reliable friend who has connections near the German border. He wants to be driven to a small village south-west of Prague which is off the beaten path and from which his "connections" will organize his move to Germany." The ambassador went on to explain that the Hanaks had full information as to contact, pass-words, route to follow, etc. All I had to do was provide transport.

This Hanak operation was set for the following day. On this occasion, I did not use my own car. Incidentally, I now had two cars: both the Cadillac and the newly acquired Alfa Romeo. My idea was to keep the former until I had an opportunity to sell it profitably and that was accomplished in midsummer. I did not want to take the Hanaks in my car, so as thus to minimize the chance of attracting attention. One of the newly arrived junior embassy staff members had brought with him a small beat-up Ford and I asked him to lend me that vehicle for a day, the day following my talk with the ambassador. I also took the precaution of taking with me an extra set of license plates that I intended to attach in place of the regular plates, while en route. The idea behind this ploy was that if an unduly vigilant policeman reported ahead that such and such a vehicle bearing a given plate number had passed by, my replacement plates might serve a useful purpose.

I picked up the Hanaks at a pre-arranged spot in the Malastrana. They were carrying only raincoats – nothing else for they had already deposited luggage and a few treasured belongings with the Steinhardts. Our route was to Plzen, then south to Klatovy, then south and west on a smaller road to

Nyrsko and then due west on an even smaller road to a very small community about two or three kilometers from the border. As we drove along, Hanak explained that when we reached our final destination, he was to enter a butcher shop and give a password to the owner. The latter was then to issue exact instructions as to how they were to proceed to the nearby frontier. Miloš then requested that I please try to wait for at least a half-hour at a spot we would decide on when we parted – just in case something went wrong or they had a change of heart. This was a logical suggestion, as two strangers near the German border and with no transport would look very suspicious to an enquiring Czech border patrol or newly installed local policeman.

In due course, after some two and a half hours driving, we came to the village where Hanak was to find the butcher shop. Sure enough, it was right there where it was meant to be – *Ivan Plesko, Butcher.* Hanak pointed to a tall tree that was about a hundred yards up the narrow road by which we had come, to indicate he wanted me to wait there for him and Karla as their back-up safety alternative. The Hanaks got out of the car, quickly said their goodbyes and entered the small shop. I at once drove slowly up the road, pulled over to the side next to the tall tree and settled down to wait. I had a Czech newspaper with me and on the three occasions when someone walked past me, I pretended to read. If one of these citizens had stopped to ask me even a perfectly innocent question, it might have proved very embarrassing, not only to me, but also for the Hanaks.

Forty minutes after I had parked beside that tree, I said to myself that to be on the safe side, I would wait at least five more minutes. Then the Hanaks materialized out of nowhere. Miloš quickly opened the car doors; Karla got in back and Miloš climbed in beside me. I gunned the engine and lost no time in starting on the trip back to the capital while Miloš told me the story of what had transpired. They had entered the shop, he said, and had seen a large, burly individual with a bloodstained apron standing behind the counter reading the *Rude Pravo* (the Prague Communist Party newspaper) sports section. Miloš than gave the prescribed greeting, "Nazdar, Ivanko, how are things in Kdyne?" The butcher then replied, as agreed, "Long live Stalin!" These ridiculous passwords having been dispensed with, the butcher shook hands with the Hanaks and asked them to follow him, leading them to nearby woods. There, he told them to keep out of sight and await the arrival of another man by the name of Franta, who would lead them to Germany, only two and a half kilometers due south. But then the Hanaks had misgivings. Neither of them liked the looks of the butcher. Moreover, Karla mentioned that he had said, "Long live Stalin", whereas she reminded her husband that the phrase should have been, "Long live Josef Stalin." Not liking the looks and feel of the situation, they began to fear for their lives and retraced their steps to my car. Greatly relieved to see it still there, they thanked me profusely for having waited for them. Then Miloš said, "A diplomat and his wife in a strange village and close to the border would have been sitting ducks for the STB."

The story ended happily, for a few days after their return to Prague and following a meeting with the Steinhardts, the latter decided to take personal change of their friends' move to the safety of the West. This was a decent thing for Lawrence and Dulcie to have done. It was really quite simple; they placed lap robes over the prone bodies of the two Hanaks who lay at the feet of the ambassador and his wife. Andy, the Greek chauffeur, drove them. No one inspects the car of the U.S. ambassador and so Miloš and Karla reached the safety of the West.

Steinhardt interceded with the State Department and the US Customs on behalf of our friends. When I arrived in Washington in May, 1949 for a six-month temporary assignment, the Hanaks were settled. They had managed to save a few thousand dollars – this also probably with the help of the ambassador – and with this sum had a large enough down payment for the purchase of a modest house that had several bedrooms. These they rented out to other Czech refugees, and so they were able to keep their financial heads above water.

During my relatively short temporary assignment in Washington immediately after leaving Prague, and two and half years later, in 1952 to 1953, when I was assigned on loan to the Department of Commerce, I saw a lot of the Hanaks. In fact, they stored a few of my belongings in their basement during the interim of my absence in Dakar. This couple epitomized the finest qualities of the Czech people. They were well educated, patriotic, organized, loyal, and incapable of a mean act. One does not forget such friends.

The next Pimpernelian operation that I was involved in had to do with the escape of Jan Stransky, who was the son of the pre-coup d'état Minister of Education. Jan was a good friend, but he was especially close to Charley Katek, the CIA chief at the embassy, and Kurt Taylor (originally called Taub). As I was never closely involved with any CIA activities, I do not know whether Jan was ever more than just a friend of Katek and Taylor. The fact remained, however, that the Czech STB undoubtedly tarred Jan with the same brush as that used in their active tarring of Katek and Taylor.

In June, following the Communist seizure of power, Katek asked me to come up to his security-safe office. What he and Kurt wanted to talk to me about was whether I would help them by allowing Jan to stay in my house for a few days until they could devise the best way to get him out of the country. Charley had apparently learned via his many contacts that the STB was about to arrest Jan for espionage. As both Katek's and Taylor's houses were kept under close surveillance and as mine was, so far, reasonably safe on that score (probably because the STB expected François to report to them about any untoward activity on my part), the plan to put up Jan in my Barrandov house was logical.

On the appointed day of that June, Jan showed up, dressed in informal clothes as though he was just out for a walk. It so happened that just at that time I had planned to drive to Holland to meet my best girl, Hannah Bradley, who was due to land at the Hook of Holland accompanied by another Boston charmer, Emily Caner. The fact that I was due to take off the day following Jan's arrival at my house made no difference, as François was able to take good care of Jan, who later related to me that he had been served his favorite drink (dry martini) and excellent food during my absence. Before my departure, Jan asked whether I had a spare jacket I could "lend" him. As he was almost exactly my size, this presented no problem and I supplied him with a gray-blue outfit that had been made for me in 1935 preparatory to my ocean voyage to Buenos Aires. I never saw that jacket again, but its service was a distinguished one.

None of the other exploits involved the most unusual way Katek and Taylor devised to get their friend out of Bohemia. One of Charley's cars was a pre-war Hudson. How and where he had acquired that car, I had no idea. Perhaps it had been "liberated" from a Nazi just after the war or maybe one of Charley's staff members had brought it over. Whatever the circumstances, this vehicle was to play a key role in saving Jan Stransky from prison or even from death.

What was most unusual about this 1939 Hudson was that between the radiator and the front grill there was an unusually wide space. I suppose that the engineer who designed that model wanted it to have a racy look, for if the grill had been placed a few inches, instead of about fifteen inches in front of the radiator, this Hudson would have looked stubby, but at that time was the *last word* in an automobile soon to be extinct. It was Kurt who came up with the ingenious idea of hiding Jan in this space between the radiator and the grill. Suffice it to say - it worked. Katek and Taylor stuffed Jan into the front end and without incident, drove him out of Czechoslovakia and into the safety of the US Zone.

The next most perilous and almost doomed-to-failure escape, I often think of as *Operation Flying Fiancée*. This episode began with Reinhold Pick. Not long after his arranging the defection of the two guards watching over Dr. and Mrs. Peter Zenkl (August 7, 1948), word came to us that the STB was closing in on Pick. It was imperative, therefore, that something be done to get him out of the country as soon as possible, and we hit on a logical and seemingly safe way to accomplish this. Once a week, the embassy sent a truck into Germany to obtain supplies from the U.S. Army PX in Germany. We were using U.S. Army drivers – two for each trip – so we decided to pretend to substitute Reinhold for one of these drivers. The problem that had to be solved was that in order to travel, Pick would require a Czech passport. To obtain this passport, the embassy had to apply to the Ministry of the Interior.

A week went by – no reply. Another week passed and still nothing from that ministry. At that juncture, Steinhardt instructed John Bruins, his deputy, to make an official call at that ministry to enquire why such a routine request for a chauffeur's passport was being ignored. When John got the runaround, the ambassador decided on more positive action. Whenever a Czech exporting firm wished to ship goods through the US Zone of Germany, or to the United States as the ultimate destination, they had to obtain a US consular invoice. Within a few days of Bruins' fruitless call about Pick's passport, a minor official from the Ministry of Foreign Trade called at the embassy with documents covering the export of textiles to the United

States. These papers, including the consular invoice, were to be returned to the ministry within a day or two – but that did not happen. A week went by and then a higher official called to ask whether the export documents had been prepared. He was given a dilatory reply. Finally, after a further few days of request and delaying tactics on our part, the Minister of Foreign Trade himself called the ambassador to ascertain why this routine export permit was not forthcoming.

The gist of Steinhardt's rejoinder was more or less as follows: "Mr. Minister, for several weeks now, we have been waiting for your Ministry of Interior to issue a Czechoslovak passport to enable the recipient – one of our minor Czech employees, to drive to and from the US Zone of Germany with our supply truck. We, too, have asked why a simple request of this kind should not meet with a quick and positive result. I suggest, Mr. Minister, that you approach Dr. Nosek, your Minister of Interior, and arrange a *quid pro quo* – a passport for an export visa." The result of this action was that Pick's passport was delivered within two days. The ambassador then took special pleasure in relating to us how shortly before the war, when he was ambassador in Moscow, he had obtained a positive result by using exactly that tactic. It seems that the embassy physician needed some special implements, but for some reason, the Soviet government would not allow their importation, or were delaying issuing the necessary permit. Whereupon, the ambassador prevailed upon the State Department to arrange for the Panama Canal authorities to delay issuing a permit for a Soviet vessel to use the Canal. Within a few days, the embassy obtained what it wanted and even Mr. Molotov, the Foreign Minister, was rather amused at this effective Steinhardt ploy.

Within a day of receiving his passport (August 30), Pick was on his way to Germany, driving with Spencer Taggert. He was not to see his native land again - at least not until the advent of president Havel over forty years later - for when Taggert returned, Pick remained in Frankfurt where he entered the employ of a US agency and we had to report his defection, "much to our surprise".

I thought the problem had been solved, but when I returned from a trip to Paris via Frankfurt, I had a brief get-together with Reinhold, who had written to ask that I meet with him as soon as possible. He lost no time in getting to the reason he wanted to see me. He had left his fiancée, Milada, behind in Prague and he desperately wanted her to join him in Germany and asked if I would see what could be done to get her out safely. I told him that I would do my best and would, if necessary, enlist the help of the ambassador, himself.

I had known Milada slightly, since purchasing a suit in 1946 at Knize's branch in Prague (a very upscale and well-known men's emporium from Vienna), where she was the cashier. Immediately after my arrival back in Prague, I started to work on the problem. The first thing I did was sit down with Mike Michela to discuss all possible solutions. As the fates would have it, a week or so before my return to Prague, Steinhardt received word that he was being transferred to Ottawa as ambassador. That, as it turned out, was a stroke of luck – at least seemingly so – and bid fair to give us a solution to the Milada problem.

The day following my meeting with Michela, the two of us sat down with Larry Steinhardt. First, I told him about my meeting with Pick during which the latter had voiced his determination to be reunited with Milada. I stressed what Pick had said as I left him; namely, that if a way could not be found to get Mila (short for Milada) out, he himself, would return to Prague clandestinely to get her out, somehow. This rash plan could only end disastrously with Pick's arrest.

After informing Steinhardt about Pick's determined view on having Milada join him in Germany, I asked the boss whether he would be willing to take Milada out of Czechoslovakia in his plane when he left Prague en route to his new post if a feasible way could be devised to bring this about. Steinhardt was unpredictable, but this was the kind of adventure that appealed to him and which, if successful, would bring to him the accolade of an intrepid hero. If the operation proved unsuccessful, he would logically find a way to disassociate himself from it. When he replied, "If you can get Pick's girl on my plane safely and undetected, I'll go along", that was all I needed to know and that was all Spencer Taggart (the one remaining CIA man in the embassy following the expulsion of Katek and Taylor), wanted to know.

Ten days intervened between the time of this meeting and *D-Day*. Our plan seemed quite simple. On every occasion of an important departure such as that of a diplomat of Mr.

Steinhardt's stature, the Foreign Office organized a champagne reception at the airport to which all diplomatic chiefs of mission were invited, plus leading Foreign Office officials and most members of the departing ambassador's staff.

Our plan, to which perhaps seven or eight, beside myself, were privy, was to arrange for the four female office workers in the embassy to carry bouquets of flowers for Mrs. Steinhardt to the reception. These young women were to follow closely Mrs. Steinhardt to the aircraft and with her onto the aircraft where they were to leave the flowers and then immediately leave the plane. Two days prior to the departure date of September 20, I called the women into my office and outlined the plan to them, stressing that they were to remain close to Dulcie Steinhardt at all times, that is, at the reception, walking to the plane, etc., until they finally left the plane. Above all, they were to bear in mind that a life was at stake and that one careless word could mean prison for Mila.

'The next task for me was to outline to Milada exactly what she was to do. I paid a visit to her at Knize's and told here that it was imperative that we meet during her lunch-hour. We did not have our talk in a restaurant; rather, we talked while strolling on Vaclavske Namesti. I explained that I had met with Pick that I had a plan to get her out of Czechoslovakia and into Germany where her lover would marry her, that I was to accompany her to the airport reception in honor of the Steinhardts, that she was to carry a bouquet which I would supply, and so on, exactly as our office girls had been instructed. But, of course, there was one very large difference. Mila would remain on the plane, locked in the lavatory by Mrs. Steinhardt. "Above all, Mila," I admonished, "Never for even an instant leave Mrs. Steinhardt's side; she is your passport to freedom and to your future with Reinhold." I stressed also that Mila was to bring absolutely nothing with her – only the clothes on her back. I was to pick Mila up at exactly ten o'clock on the morning of *D-Day.*

Aside from the Steinhardts, those in the know about *Operation Flying Fiancée* (as we called it) or simply, *Double F,* were Colonel Michela, Spencer Taggart, Jack Guiney, and Mark Ballenger, the pilot of the ambassador's plane. Mark was destined to perish along with Mr. Steinhardt in the crash of that same aircraft a year and a half later in the spring of 1950. On the departure day, all went well at the outset. Mila was standing on the sidewalk in front of Wilson Station at the appointed hour. In a jiffy, she opened the passenger-side door of the little Alfa Romeo, slid onto the seat, pulled the door shut and we were off – back to the Square of Good King Wenceslas, down to the foot of that long square and then onto the road leading to Ruzyn Airport.

When we parked not far from the entrance to the main building, there were already many parked cars. The main entrance seemed filled with well-wishers and the reception room, as we entered, was a buzz of conversation, of guests greeting each other, and of platitudinous diplomatic exchanges. The champagne was already being passed to fifty or more guests from the western embassies. Mrs. Steinhardt, standing in the center of the large room, was almost hidden by a circle of flowers. Mila and I moved up to this ambulatory garden and were warmly greeted by Dulcie. Mila at once melted into this group of flower-bearing girls and I began unobtrusively to reconnoiter. There were two doors leading into or out of the reception room; the one where we had entered led to and from the main hall of the airport; the other led directly out to the parking runway where passengers got on or off aircraft. I first sauntered to the latter exit-door through which the Steinhardts and the reception guests were to pass to the ambassador's plane. I tried the knob and found that the door was locked. I also noted through the glass panel that two leather-coated police were stationed outside. This unexpected discovery did not seem to bode well for our plan, for it was probable that when the door was unlocked to allow passage to the ambassador's plane, those security agents (probably from the STB) would carefully scrutinize everyone who passed through, for it was customary for well-wishers, on occasions such as this, to bid a final farewell right at the steps leading up and onto the aircraft.

One minute after this alarming discovery of the locked exit door, Jack Guiney came up to me and said, "Walt, it looks like we are going to have to cancel operation *Double F.* "Why?" I asked, and thought that Jack might also be worried by the locked door. Jack went on to explain, "Did you know that according to the flight schedule on the flight board in the main hall, the ambassador's flight has not been cleared?" I at once followed Jack out to the main hall and there was the terse announcement: *Private flight – US Embassy aircraft. Destination: Frankfurt.*

Awaiting clearance. "We are not giving up, at least not yet," I said. Jack turned to me, "Walt, I am afraid they suspect something." I replied, "Jack, that might be, but I am going to see the boss about his flight's clearance, and first, I am going to double check at the Airport Control Center over there."

The small control office was not far from where Jack and I were standing and I moved quickly over to the counter where Captain Novak, a slight acquaintance, was in charge. I found him in deep conversation with a subaltern. "Could I have a word with you, Captain?" I asked. He left off his low and urgent conversation. "Of course, Mr. Secretary. What can I do for you?" I was sure he knew very well what was bothering me. I shook hands with Captain Novak. "I see that my ambassador's flight has not yet been cleared for take-off. Could you please explain this unusual situation? As you must be aware, both embassy aircraft – one carrying luggage and the other waiting for the Steinhardts to board - are now ready for take-off which is scheduled for five minutes from now." Captain Novak's eyes momentarily left mine, and his previous look of confident composure became one of worry touched with embarrassment. In a tone tinged with what he hoped would be taken as one of friendly advice from one officer to another, he said, "Not to worry, Mr. Secretary. There seems to be a short delay and I am sure that the clearance will be forthcoming very soon – just a technicality."

Having heard enough of this line of baloney, I immediately returned to the reception room, went up to the ambassador and briefly explained the situation – that is, the locked door of egress and the delayed flight clearance. "Take me to Captain Novak," fumed the ambassador of the most powerful country on earth. Like a panther approaching its intended prey, he rapidly covered the short distance to the airport office. "Are you in charge here, Captain?" was the ambassador's greeting – this, in his most menacing tone. "Yes, Pane Velvyslance," replied the Captain, at once obviously very nervous. Steinhardt continued, slowly enunciating every word in tones of thinly cloaked fury, "Mr. Birge tells me that my flight to Frankfurt has not been cleared. What is the explanation, Captain?" Novak replied what he had already reported to me barely a minute before, but now in a conciliatory and quaking voice.

"Get me General Boèek (Chief of Staff of the Czech Army) on your phone," peremptorily ordered Mr. Steinhardt. Captain Novak did not need a phone book to call the correct number. In a voice breathless with worry, urgency, and fear, he told the person on the other end of the line that the American ambassador wished to talk with the general. Within ten seconds the Captain spoke again. "This is Captain Novak at Ruzyn, General. I pass you to Ambassador Steinhardt." The ambassador seized the phone and spoke as follows: "Is that you, General Boèek? Ambassador Steinhardt here." A short silence from this end of the line ensued. Steinhardt then said, "Thank you for your good wishes, general. Now, would you kindly explain why my flight to Frankfurt has not yet been cleared for take-off? I assume that a flight such as this on the occasion of my departing from Prague for my new diplomatic post comes under your jurisdiction." Again, there were a few seconds of silence during which I could see that Steinhardt was getting even angrier. "That is no explanation, General, and is an insult, not only to me, but to the United States. Now, let me tell you something, General. If my flight is not given immediate clearance, do you know what I am going to do? I am going to call the US Air Force base at Rhein-Main and I am going to ask the officer in command of that base to send a flight of fighter-bombers over here to bomb the hell out of your Ruzyn airport. And do not labor under the illusion that my request will not be acted upon!" There followed a few more seconds of silence, and then Steinhardt handed the telephone to Captain Novak, saying, "General Boèek wants to speak with you, Captain." Another few seconds passed. Captain Novak closed the phone circuit and turned to the ambassador, smiling obsequiously. "Mr. Ambassador, the technicalities which have delayed your flight clearance have been overcome. Your flight to Frankfurt is now cleared."

To a reader nowadays, this bravado and seemingly incredible threat by Ambassador Steinhardt seems utterly fantastic. I was there and I can vouch that those were Mr. Steinhardt's words. It is to be remembered that this incident happened at the beginning of the *Cold War*. The USSR had only just obtained the secret of the atomic bomb. The United States, only three years after Hiroshima, was the most powerful country in the world. Of course, Steinhardt would never have requested a flight of fighter-bombers to let loose a lethal storm of bombs on Ruzyn.

However, General Boèek was taken by surprise and probably, he believed he had to act without delay to avoid an embarrassing incident. Whatever the reason for the STB's request to delay the clearance of the ambassador's flight, the latter could not be put off much longer in any case, so why run the risk?

So the flight clearance problem had been resolved; but what about the outside door which, as it seemed, was going to prevent free access to the ambassador's plane. Clearly, the Czech intelligence people suspected we were up to something. I tried that door again and it was still firmly locked. Jack Guiney sidled up to me. "Walt, someone must be on to us. I have never heard of that door being locked on an occasion such as this. Now I really think we have had it." "Hold on, Jack," I replied. I then asked the ambassador if Jack and I could have a word with him. I briefly explained the locked-door situation. "What I am now going to do, Mr. Ambassador, is look around, especially at the far side of the customs area. I think there is another way out to your aircraft. I'll let you know in two minutes."

I then left the reception room by the inside door, turned right to the customs area and walked the fifty or sixty feet to the far end of that hall. There, I spied an open sliding door, normally kept open to allow the almost continuous movement of baggage and airfreight into and out of that area.

It was at once obvious that if the Steinhardts and their friends were to reach their plane without a meticulous search being made on each person, it would be necessary for everyone to use this custom areas door now being guarded by a soldier who seemed to have a very menacing mien. At least, the Soviet-made *drum* Tommy gun slung over his shoulder looked forbidding. Indeed, the special circumstance that led me to this conclusion - that is, to try to use that sliding door – was that such a move would, I hoped, be unexpected.

The guard looked especially grim and tough, not only because of his facial expression and his lethal weapon, but also by reason of his burly physique, for his legs were like oak trees and his neck, that of a heavyweight prize fighter. This powerful mass swayed ever so slightly from side to side as though daring anyone to pass through that door without permission.

I pondered how I was going to get around this seemingly immovable obstacle. The guard was apparently paying no attention at all to me – probably owing to the continual movement and inspection of incoming and outgoing cargo – a fortunate break for me. I had to depend on timing, surprise and luck to keep that sliding door open until it was too late for that armed guard to close it.

I walked rapidly back to the reception room where the Steinhardts were already shaking hands of farewell and with the short little speeches characteristic of such functions, bidding goodbye to the foreign ambassadors and especially to Dr. Heidrich, the Secretary-General of the Ministry of Foreign Affairs, whom we knew to be pro-western. I managed to catch the ambassador's eye and he promptly extricated himself from the group surrounding him, thus giving me the opportunity to quickly explain the exit plan I had in mind. "Do you think it will work?" he quietly shot at me. "Yes, sir. It's not fool-proof, but even if a problem arises, no one will guess what we are up to." "All right, Walter," whispered Steinhardt, "let's go!" I then asked him, "How long before you arrive at the customs area?" The boss replied that they would start moving in three minutes, as almost all the farewells had been said. And then I said to Jack Guiney, who was standing beside me, "Jack, you know the customs hall. See that our floating garden gets there safely. I'm pretty sure I can keep that sliding exit door open". "Move it!" were the ambassador's last words to me.

It was now clearly up to me and as I walked back to the escape-room (as I thought of it), I was worrying about two things: would Mila follow instructions and stay close to Mrs. Steinhardt and would I be able to keep that door open? When I arrived back, the oak-tree legged guard was standing to the right of the sliding door with the opening at his left. To block the door, I would place my left foot in its path to prevent its sliding closed.

I took up my station as close to the door as I dared (there were many employees milling around) and waited, keeping my eyes glued to the far end of the hall where I was expecting momentarily to see Dulcie Steinhardt and the flower girls.

Then it all happened quickly. There was a sudden cessation of movement in that hall; then a buzz of talk, and Mrs. Steinhardt came into view at the far end of the customs area, surrounded by the moving garden and – most important – there, waddling beside them was Dr. Arnost Heidrich, all three hundred pounds of him.

I turned my eyes from that procession to see how the guard would react. First, there was a look of incredulous surprise from that imposing individual, then he - and I, too – moved toward the sliding door – he to pull it shut and I to block its closing. As I placed my left foot in the path of the door, I instinctively let loose a stream of invective at the guard, mostly swear words, not one of which would have been understood by him. That burly line-backer-built soldier, taken by surprise, must have wondered for a moment who the devil was this foreigner shouting at him like a top-sergeant. But then he began unlimbering the sub-machine gun from his shoulder, ready to defend the exit door. Fortunately, the element of surprise, which is so often the difference between failure and success, sustained us, and by the time he got his weapon ready, Mrs. Steinhardt, the bevy of flower girls, and Dr. Heidrich were already up to the door. He couldn't very well shoot the wife of the ambassador or the office girls, or the secretary-General of the Ministry of Foreign Affairs. When the frustrated guard realized what he had allowed to happen, the above mentioned, plus all the US embassy people and other diplomatic officials had streamed through the door, and I, too, lost no time in joining them.

This van of some fifty people, plus Jack Guiney, Spencer Taggert, and I reached the ambassador's parked aircraft within thirty seconds of leaving the building. It was gratifying to note that two STB leather coated individuals were still standing in front of the reception room door through which we originally were meant to have passed. One of these men had just hurried over to the plane and his two colleagues were just starting their move to join him. But by now, Mrs. Steinhardt and the five flower girls were mounting the steps that led into the plane.

For the STB men, this was a scenario unlooked for. They understandably must have assumed that their superiors had for some reason allowed the ambassador's party of distinguished personalities – his family, foreign diplomats, Dr. Heidrich, among others - to leave the airport building by the customs area door. Perhaps the regular exit door could not be unlocked. In any case, by the time the chief STB officer reached the aircraft, it was too late; or was it? The flowers had been deposited in the plane, the flower girls, having bid Mrs. Steinhardt goodbye, had descended the steps, and the ambassador himself had climbed half way up those steps, and now he turned to face the party of diplomats and other well-wishers gathered below in a semi-circle to bid a final farewell.

At that moment, I was standing at the foot of the access steps beside Spencer Taggart. I was as nervous as the proverbial grasshopper on a hot plate and obviously Spencer felt as I did. I remember him asking me, "Walt, do you have a cigarette?" - this, despite his having quit smoking "for good" some months before.

At the moment now being described, Mila was already locked in the small washroom, and one could see Mrs. Steinhardt up there just back of the aircraft door, her arms folded in front of her in a sort of protective and perhaps defiant gesture. It was plain to see that the STB security men were in a quandary. They had obviously been taken completely by surprise owing to the sudden, puzzling and unorthodox exit from the reception room. Moreover, they had not had the time or opportunity to check on just how many girls had carried flowers onto the aircraft and how many had come down those steps again. And no check of any kind had been made as to the identity of the individuals standing beside the plane to say goodbye. Of course, they recognized almost all of those diplomats, but not all. In short, it was a colossal communist snafu.

As the ambassador stood a few steps below the plane's entrance door, the STB colonel in charge of security in connection with that departure informed Mr. Steinhardt that he would like to inspect the aircraft – "A normal procedure, of course, and for the ambassador's protection." I had no idea as to the extent of that STB man's suspicions that someone was about to escape from the Czech communist paradise on the embassy plane. The peculiar exit via the customs chamber would have been grounds enough for his suspicions, but as I look back on that day, I believe that one of our girls might have unintentionally leaked to a Czech boyfriend that something was in the wind, so to speak. The locked door and the delay in granting flight clearance lent credence to this explanation. It later also came to light that one of our stenographers, who shall remain nameless, did spend a lot of time with a Czech man some years younger than she. As this individual was an adept charmer and our girl was in her mid-thirties and not especially attractive, our State Department security people eventually came to suspect that this girl had possibly been an unwitting mole for the STB.

When the STB colonel made his inspection request, the ambassador, with a grim half-smile, invited that leather-coated henchman to ascend to the plane if he wished. Then, with characteristic bravado, Mr. Steinhardt said to the crowd gathered below, "He seems to think I have a stowaway on board!"

A few of the diplomats gathered below laughed, but not many. For those of us who were trying to pull off this escape operation, the moment of truth was at hand. The inspecting colonel climbed to the aircraft door where he was confronted by Mrs. Steinhardt. Behind her was that lavatory door. The colonel looked to the right and to the left. No one was to be seen except Dulcie Steinhardt and her daughter, Dulcie-Ann and around them, all those flowers. The colonel may not have had his mind set at rest. He was checking on the aircraft that was about to transport the ambassador of the powerful United States of America. According to custom and international law, an ambassador's residence and mode of transport were inviolable. A fruitless search could bring a stern reprimand.

Under the circumstances, the STB colonel probably made the wise decision. He nodded his head and began to descend the steps. "Are you quite satisfied?" Steinhardt shot sarcastically after him. The colonel saluted and continued his descent to the tarmac.

That was it. Mark Ballenger, the ambassador's pilot, and André Duchaene, the pilot of his air attaché's plane that was carrying a mountain of luggage, both raised their right hands, thumbs pointing upward. The ambassador's aircraft door was firmly closed, the powerful engines roared into life, and the two planes taxied to the main runway and within five minutes were airborne en route to Frankfurt. A week later Reinhold Pick and Milada were married. Pick, who later changed his name to Ronnie Parker, gave many years of distinguished service to his adopted country, the U.S. of A. He, too, is one of the ablest and finest men I came to know, not only during those parlous years, but also during my lifetime.

Two days after this *Operation Double F*, the Czech Foreign Office sent a strongly worded message to our embassy protesting the uncalled-for and rude and unacceptable behavior of Mr. Walter W. Birge, Secretary of Embassy, in shouting at and preventing the guard at the airport from performing his duty.

It will be recalled that Dr. Arnost Heidrich, the Secretary-General of the Ministry of Foreign Affairs, had represented that office on the occasion of Ambassador Steinhardt's departure from Prague. We had known for some time that Arnost Heidrich was anti-communist and friendly to the West. He had spent the war years in England, but he was basically a professional functionary rather than an activist politically. His political party allegiance had been that of Dr. Zenkl's National Socialists.

It was natural that this high-ranking official would attend many diplomatic social functions, so our contacts with him were frequent, and with the passage of time following the communist takeover, increasingly cordial. We gradually gained the impression that this very knowledgeable individual would eventually seek asylum, probably in the United States. We were not kept waiting long, following the departure of the Steinhardts.

It was at a British social function that Dr. Heidrich made his move. Colonel Mike Michela and I were chatting together, somewhat apart from the other guests when Heidrich came up to us and said, "Could I bother you gentlemen for a moment?" "Of course, Dr. Heidrich," quickly replied colonel Michela with his ready and slightly questioning smile which was to disappear forever within a year; for Mike was to die of a sudden heart attack in mid-1949.[*] Dr. Heidrich continued, "Since the seizure of power by the Communist Party, my wife and I have become ever more strongly convinced that we should seek asylum in the United States. I see no happy future for us here and both Milena and I want our son,[*] who is now two years old, to grow up in your freedom-loving country. Will you help us, Colonel?" As an understandable and polite sequel, he added, "And you, Mr. Birge."

Without a moment's hesitation, Mike Michela, replied, "You can count on us, Dr. Heidrich. I will phone you at your apartment one week from today at six pm to arrange a meeting. I suggest that we meet at the Mala Strana end of the Charles Bridge. The key to the time of our meeting will be one hour and a half later than the time I will mention over the phone. When we get together, I will give full instructions as to how your family's escape to Germany will be implemented." Deeply moved by this

---

[*] As Dr. Heidrich was at this time 59 years old, the comment was made by someone who knew him that this boy was more likely his grandson.

[*] According to information from a CIA agent, this was not a heart attack, but an assassination.

assurance of help, Dr. Heidrich, in a low voice – though no one was near enough to hear – said, "I know that our small boy's nurse will want to accompany us. Could you include her in your plans? "Of course," replied the Colonel. "By the way, is this nurse small, medium, or large?" "She is quite small, Colonel. She comes up only to here," and Heidrich indicated a spot on his vast anatomy which indicated that his small boy's nurse was about five feet tall. "Fine," replied Michela, "That is all I need to know right now."

The reason for the curiosity about the nurse's size was that Mike was thinking in terms of using three cars for the operation: one for dr. Heidrich, one for his almost equally large wife and one for the nurse and boy. Had the nurse been described as large, that would have presented us with a problem.

The day following our brief talk with Dr. Heidrich, Mike and I met to decide whose cars should be used. One vehicle would have to have a trunk large enough to hold the massive Arnost; another car would need to have almost as large a trunk to hold his bulky wife. The third car would not present a problem. We knew that Frank Sisco, the recently arrived Assistant Commercial Attaché, had a large American car and we checked with Frank to make sure that, first of all, he would be willing to work with us and second, that his car did in fact have a large trunk. My own little Alfa Romeo was adequate for the transport of the little boy and nurse, provided that Mike again took my spare tire in his trailer, as in the Zenkl operation. So we were all set as far as we were concerned. Now all we had to do was arrange with Heidrich as to the exact time of the Charles Bridge meeting.

Colonel Michela telephoned Dr. Heidrich at exactly six p.m. on the day that had been set for that call, and the following day they met on the famous six hundred year old bridge. As soon as there were no pedestrians within earshot, Mike asked Heidrich how many days he would need for departure preparations and was told two days were sufficient. So Mike then made plans for the Heidrichs, the boy, and his nurse to meet at Mike's house at ten-thirty in the morning. He added that if they had valuable personal effects to leave them with a trustworthy friend who would then leave them at his or my house to be eventually delivered to Germany or Washington. What worried Michela was the possibility that the little boy might start to cry at an inopportune time, and suggested that they bring sleeping pills with them for him to take just before leaving for the border.

So, we were all set. My spare tire was placed in Mike's small trailer and I made sure that the fabric separating the back of the trunk and the very small jump-seats was partly opened so as to allow an adequate flow of air for the destined occupants.

On that appointed morning, a Thursday in the early fall of 1948, I left the embassy at nine-thirty to allow myself plenty of time and arrived at Colonel Michela's house some fifteen minutes later. What the Heidrichs did was split up. Dr. Heidrich left his apartment for the office at eight-thirty. Mrs. Heidrich, the nurse and small boy left their apartment at nine and took a streetcar that conveyed them to a park conveniently situated about a half mile from their destination. They strolled in this park for a few minutes and then slowly wended their way up the sidewalk that led to Michela's house. From 9:45 o'clock, Michela, Sisco, and I began watching for the arrival of our friends.

The three cars to be used in our operation could not be seen from the street, so we had no worries as to getting our escapees into those vehicles. At 9:50 Mrs. Heidrich, the boy and his nurse materialized at the driveway entrance and ambled up to the house as though they did not have a care in the world. As for Heidrich, at a quarter before ten, he told his secretary that he had an appointment, first with a physician and then with a foreign diplomat, and not to expect him back until early to mid-afternoon. "Don't worry if I am a bit late," he called to her as he walked out the door carrying his briefcase. No Czech who works in an office is ever without his briefcase.

Dr. Heidrich first walked to a taxi stand that was situated on a street corner a quarter of a mile from the Foreign Office. The taxi then took him to the small park mentioned above. From there he walked to Michela's house where he joined us at precisely ten-thirty, with characteristic Czech promptitude. Few words of greeting were spoken. Mike Michela said, "Good morning, Doctor. Do you have the pills for your boy?" Dr. Heidrich took a small bottle from his coat pocket and withdrew two white capsules, saying, "My physician, a lifelong friend, told me that one pill given before departure and a second pill two hours later should keep Milan asleep for at least four hours, but he added that in the morning, this time might be somewhat shorter." "Let's get going then," ordered the Colonel, as though he were preparing a battalion for an advance into battle. The first pill was quickly administered. Michela raised the heavy cover of his car's trunk and Dr. Heidrich was, with some difficulty, placed in that space. "Are you reasonably comfortable, Dr. Heidrich?" asked the Colonel. The Secretary-General, with a smile of resignation assured us that he could last until he heard the voices of the American border patrol of the US Zone. The prospect of a free life in the West, he quietly assured us, would keep him comfortable. Mike did not have a François Rysavy to help make his car-trunk comfortable, but he had done a good job in the strategic placing of blankets and pillows. We next helped Mrs. Heidrich into Frank Sisco's rear trunk. That obviously frightened lady said nary a word except a thank you; and the lid was closed over her. Next came the important role about to be played by my black Alfa with the green canvas top. I had, of course already copied as well as I could the well-remembered ministrations of my ex-chef, whom I had already driven to Germany on the first leg of his journey to Washington where he was to work for H.M. de Limur's parents. The two-year-old was not yet drowsy, but almost so. First, the nurse hopped into my trunk and we handed Milan to her for the beginning of his game of hide and seek, or the Czech equivalent. And we were off, with Mike, as was natural on any exercise in which he was directly involved, leading the way in his olive-drab army car. Our convoy moved at a fairly steady pace of about forty miles an hour. We took the Plzen road and then the highway to Doma•lice, which lead to the German border town of Fürth-im-Wald. On the occasion of this operation, over a half year following the Communist take-over, we expected to meet one or more security patrols, and our expectations were justified. We were stopped twice - the first time not far from Plzen. We were directed to pull over to the side of the road and asked to present identity papers. These policemen were in no hurry and when they saw that we were from the capitalist USA, they moved even more slowly; but they were not going to do any inspecting of American embassy vehicles. We set out again and on the southwest side of Doma•lice, we ran into still another patrol. This took more time. It began to rain and the STB men returned to their car to fetch raincoats. No smiles here – just grim following of orders to stop all vehicles traveling toward the border. Time was passing. It was now over two and a half hours and the clock hands were moving well past one p.m. As my car was the third in line, I was the last to present my *prukaz* document, but there was no problem, just rather impolite stares, then salutes. I waved my hand out the window to give Mike the all-clear signal and again, we were en route. It was not far now from the border command post.

I called out in Czech to the nurse, "Vshetsko Dobri?" (Is everything o.k.) "Ano," came back the muffled reply from the nurse. So far, not a sound came from her small charge. Then I asked myself why the doctor had prescribed just two pills – why not three or four? I was feeling more and more uneasy.

At length, our small convoy reached, without further incident, the Czech border-control post near Fürth-im-Wald. As our cars bore diplomatic plates, we were not required to get out, but had only to show our documents to the officer who came to the driver's side window of each vehicle. At the time, I thought this seemingly lax control was at variance from the highway controls, but this made sense as no vehicles which had not already been cleared by the highway police check-points would get as far as the border-control, right next to the US Zone. We were now in the clear, but only just. The officer in charge of the checkpoint motioned to the soldier stationed at the barrier to raise this heavy pole. We started our engines. Mike gunned his heavy vehicle past the raised telegraph pole-size barrier. Frank followed closely behind. My own 2.5-liter engine was purring at about a thousand revs just prior to my start forward when a child's shriek, high-pitched and clearly audible, emanated from the trunk of my two-seater. I was already in first gear and gave the gun to that Italian-made jackrabbit. I was now some fifty yards from the barrier and, as the piercing cries of that now fully awake two-year old reached their crescendo, I was already in second speed and moving fast. One of the customs officials cried out to the barrier guard – as the nurse later told me – a peremptory order to lower the boom, and that boom was massive enough to put out of commission any vehicle on which it suddenly descended. However, my little car was accelerating rapidly by the time the last yard of Communist-held territory was reached and just before the barrier-pole could be brought down in time to prevent my moving further. I was already some forty feet past the barrier and doing about fifty, when it reached its lowered road-blocking position. That was the closest shave I or any escapees ever had, for what if that massive contraption had landed on my trunk, thus possibly crushing the nurse and little boy?

Our three cars reached the US Army border control post in twenty seconds. There was a rapid look at out identity papers and we were off again, no one saying a word. A mile or so down that road to Fürth-im-Wald, we pulled over to the side and at once released our friends from their cramped confinement. By this time, the boy had stopped his shouting, though at that juncture I felt like shouting myself – shouting for the joy and relief of our having succeeded in getting those fine people to the safety of American-controlled territory.

So ended this chapter of Prague adventure. We drove onto Nürnberg where the US Army Intelligence people took over. I promptly drove back to Prague via Waldhaus, Bor, Støibro and Plzen.

The next day, when I was removing the pillow and blanket that I had placed in the trunk of my car for the comfort of the small boy and his nurse, I noticed a small white object about the size of a pea. On closer examination, it was clear that the boy must have spit out the second sleeping pill; hence, the near tragedy.

The probability is that the commanding officer of that Czech border post never reported the child-shrieking incident. Not only would such a report have gotten him into trouble, but also, nothing could have been proved. Dr. Heidrich and his little family soon arrived in Washington where the doctor was soon given employment in the Department of State. We met again in Washington and I shall report later about one such (for me at least) memorable occasion.

The next escape episode that I vividly remember even after a half-century later did not involve me at all. As mentioned earlier in this story, the smallest and most conservative political party in the immediate post-war period in Czechoslovakia was the *Lidova Strana* (Peoples Party). As mentioned above, this political group was the Catholic Party with close ties to Rome, and militantly anti-communist. The leader of this Peoples Party was Monsignor Šramek – a politician-priest – very able and energetic and a loyal servant of his church.

We have already noted that not too long after the illegal seizure of power on February 22nd, 1948, the Communists placed

Dr. Peter Zenkl under house arrest, from which he and his wife were extracted by the combined efforts of Michela, Guiney, Pick, and me. Whereas Dr. Zenkl had looked to the United States for help and salvation, it was natural that Monsignor Šramek sought to maintain close, albeit semi-clandestine, rapport with France, in view of that country's Catholic ties, its political presence, and its close collaboration with the US and U K solidifying bloc dedicated to opposing further Soviet seizures of power. Most important of all, the main thing that made for the special but unofficial relationship between the *Lidova Strana* and France was the towering figure of Charles de Gaule, then establishing himself as one of the great leaders in modern French history.

In view of this scenario, it was understandable that French political leaders, including the French ambassador in Prague, would come to the conclusion that the safety of Monsignor Josef Šramek should be assured – if possible – before he was placed under restraint.

It came about, therefore, that the French ambassador arranged to meet with one or more leading men of the Peoples Party with a view to planning the escape of Monsignor Šramek to France. This plan, which subsequently came to light, was to have France send a small plane to an obscure airfield in Bohemia where it would pick up the Monsignor and fly him to safety.

The problem that intervened was that there was a diplomat in the French embassy who was either a member of the French Communist Party or a least a "fellow-traveler". This was monsieur de Villeneuve, an impressive looking Secretary of Embassy. It should be borne in mind that for several years following the Second World War, approximately twenty-five per cent of the electorate in France belonged to the Communist Party. We do not know for certain, but de Villeneuve may have found out about the above-mentioned escape plan and informed his contact in the Czech Communist Party.

The sequel was obvious. The French plane flew into Czech territory at a low altitude to avoid the Czech radar and landed at the appointed field. Monsignor Šramek, accompanied by a few of his fellow *Lidova Strana* party members, was there awaiting the plane's arrival. Also waiting, but concealed in the woods which surrounded the field, was a squad of STB security police. No sooner did the leader of the Peoples Party begin to walk toward the aircraft than the Communist operatives closed in from both sides of the field, and a few hours later the house arrest of Monsignor Šramek began.

I never learned what happened to monsieur de Villeneuve. The French diplomat who told me about de Villeneuve's probable connection with this abortive escape did not know it for a fact, but was fairly certain that he was the betrayer.

In mid-summer of 1948, the Czech government officially informed the embassy that Charles Katek was no longer *persona grata*. This communication had not been unexpected, and we immediately went ahead with plans for a farewell party to be given at my house, an event to which all embassy officers were invited. It so happened that Claiborne Pell, who had been vice-consul in Bratislava the preceding two years, was in Prague for consultations just at that time, so naturally, he, too, was at the party.

As we had anticipated, several STB men took up posts in the vicinity of my place, not that this bothered us. Claiborne Pell's night train for Bratislava was scheduled to leave at half past eleven and the party had run its course by the time I set out for the station with Pell. Many of the other guests were to follow.

We had noticed that an STB Tatra with its Porsche designed V8 air-cooled engine was parked some thirty yards below my house, pointed uphill, thus in the opposite direction we would be taking downhill en route to Wilson Station. We decided to play a little game with those black leather-coated henchmen of Gottwald, the Communist president. When we were all set, I backed my car out of my gate and accelerated down the hill. At once, the two lurking STB men literally dove into their Tatra, but to follow us, they first had to drive at least forty yards uphill before a driveway enabled them to turn around. In the interim, we were speeding down the Barrandov road, which at the bottom of the hill led to the main highway, Praha-Zbraslas. As soon as I reached this road, I turned right toward Zbraslas, then pulled over, braked to a stop and turned off the lights.

A few seconds later, that Tatra passed by us and sped onto the thoroughfare, turning left toward Praha obviously trying to overtake us; for not only was Pell in my car, but Kurt Taub (Taylor) and his wife, Betty, as well. In short, they were apparently interested in just where we were going. What they did not realize was that six more cars carrying Katek and other guests were following them at a more sedate pace – all destined to meet us at Wilson Station. At that time, this little byplay seemed hilariously funny to us, especially when our leather-coated friends turned up at the station as we were bidding Claiborne goodbye.

Charlie Katek left for Washington later that week and one by one, the other Americans in the CIA office were whittled down. Finally, only Spencer Taggart remained. Soon after the *Flying Fiancée* exploit (September 20), however, Spencer informed me that he, too, had been declared *persona non grata* and would be departing for Washington within two days. Would I be willing, he asked, to act as a conduit for secret communications between him and his principal Czech collaborator, Veleslav Wahl? Wahl, who for over a year had been one on my best Czech friends, was an extraordinary man. Aside from his courageous exploits during World War II, previously discussed, and his efforts to bring about a free Czechoslovakia, he was a man of many talents, not the least of which was his expert knowledge of ornithology.

Veleslav ostensibly worked for Czech Military Intelligence, but was, in fact, a double agent, working with Taggart and the CIA. After his forced departure, Taggart would periodically send a message to me, via the secure diplomatic pouch, with the understanding that it be delivered to Wahl in person. Almost always, on the occasion of this message delivery, Wahl would read his message and then take a few minutes to pen a reply. Sometimes, he would write for twenty to thirty minutes during which time Mrs. Wahl would serve tea, or drinks, depending on the time of day.

Wahl was not the only local agent involved. One day, he informed me that I would occasionally hear from a young woman when he had an urgent message to send to Taggart. Three times, a very good-looking young woman in her mid-twenties came to my house, having telephoned first, took about a half hour to write a message, handed it to me and lost no time in making her departure. She was clearly a close collaborator of Wahl and used by him to decrease the number of my visits to his apartment. As I was a bachelor who at times entertained female visitors, this arrangement was logical, and I only hope that this attractive woman came to no harm.

I now relate the most painful experience relative to my Prague assignment. Following my return to Washington in late May,

1949, the department requested me to give a series of talks that autumn in Atlanta at local high schools on the subject of the Communist takeover of Czechoslovakia. In late October, while driving through Virginia en route to Atlanta, the broadcast of classical music to which I had been listening was abruptly interrupted by a special news announcement as follows:

"The Czechoslovak government has just issued a communiqué to the effect that two American spies, Veleslav Wahl and Major Nechansky, have been arrested (they were arrested in August, 1949) for treasonable contacts with Walter Birge, a former diplomatic Secretary in the American Embassy and also a spy."

Upon my arrival in Atlanta, a telegram from the State Department was awaiting me with a terse instruction neither to give any interview nor to make any comments on that espionage subject to anyone

The horrible and, for me at least, heart-rending sequel to this dismal news, was that several months later, following a four-day trial – about which at that time few details were available – both Wahl and Nechansky were hanged (June, 1950). Many years later, it came to light that the Czechs, seeking to copy the Stalinist policy of forcing individuals on trial to give pat answers – well rehearsed beforehand – had sought to force Wahl to recite carefully prepared testimony, but they had not realized the kind of man with whom they were dealing. Wahl refused to cooperate with his accusers and, when on trial in the presence of the press and hundreds of onlookers, he said exactly what he wanted to say with no admission of guilt as in the Soviet show trials of 1936 and 1937.

For this unheard of behavior, he was subjected to repeated torture and beatings. His teeth were knocked out and he was repeatedly flogged into unconsciousness. At the end, he was barely recognizable. Somehow, Wahl's widow got out of Czechoslovakia, emigrated to the United States, remarried and settled in California.

What is even sadder is that in the late spring or early summer of 1949, Spencer Taggart had reason to suspect strongly that those two intrepid agents were in real danger of arrest and he sent a message strongly urging them to leave at the earliest possible moment. It is a tragedy that my friends did not heed this warning. The double tragedy is that two of Wahl's brothers had been executed by the Nazis. So perished these men who had the courage to put their lives on the line of action and danger to defend the freedom of their country and to do what they could to break the Nazi or Communist shackles that bound them and their countrymen to tyranny.

This story would not be complete without an account of the activities of another tough, imaginative and courageous Czech whom I met under unusual circumstances and whose real name I did not learn until almost twenty-five years after my departure from Czechoslovakia.

One day in the early fall of 1948, I received a telephone call at the embassy from a man I did not know. The caller, who did not tell me his name, spoke fluent English and asked if I would meet him in a small park that was not far from the embassy. I would not know who he was, he went on, but he knew me by sight and would identify himself as the individual who had telephoned. We were to meet that same day in the late afternoon.

At the appointed time, I sat down on one of the park benches and waited about five minutes. There then materialized a short, slender figure, rapidly walking down the path from the interior of the park. As this person approached, I could see that he was a man in his mid-thirties. He came to my bench and casually sat down, and without looking at me, he said in an educated English, which had obviously been learned in England, "I am a bit late as I have been watching to make sure that you were not being followed. Mr. Birge, this, our first meeting will be short, as its purpose is to set up procedures for what I hope will be other meetings. Would you be good enough to note the following: if I say we are to meet Wednesday – I mean Tuesday – always one day before the day I mention on the phone. If I say we are to meet at five o'clock – that means six o'clock – one hour later than the stated time. Remember - the day is earlier, the hour is later."

I was about to ask the purpose of these future meetings, but he forestalled me. "As you know, Walter – please excuse that from now on I call you by your Christian name. Many Czechs are seeking ways to escape from my country. I am sure that you will be approached – if not already many times up to now – by friends or officials you know, with a view to enlisting your assistance for their flight to the West. I have a small organization set up which is in a position to see that those you want to help get out will indeed get out. However, it takes money to plan these escapes. Some men must be bribed; temporary lodging must sometimes be arranged." I replied that I was sure he could eventually, if not very soon, be of great assistance. "I do not want to know your name," I added. "I will know you as *Blackwood*." And that was how we parted on that day of our first contact.

I do not know why I chose *Blackwood* as the name for this stranger who was to become a good friend in the time to come. Perhaps I was thinking of the "Blackwood" convention in the game of bridge. I also gave him the first name of George. It was clearly in his interest that I not know his name, for it was always within the realm of possibility that I might let it slip to someone – even to one of the embassy officers – and even that could be dangerous, for it subsequently came to light that "L.S.", one of our political foreign service officers was seeing a lot of a Czech, who, we later learned, was a Communist plant.

I worked with Blackwood on three escapes. On two of these occasions, men whom I did not know very well, but whom I wanted to assist, asked whether I could help get then out. Blackwood had stated at one of our early meetings that he would require the sum of 30,000 Czech crowns for each escapee. At our black-market exchange rate (almost always readily available), this amounted to between $60 and $100 depending on whether the rate was 500 or 300 to the dollar. At the official rate of fifty-to-one, it amounted to $600.

On the third occasion involving Blackwood, I was surprised when Jim Penfield, who in the late summer of 1948, following Mr. Steinhardt's departure, became chargé d'affaires for a few months, came to me for help, asking whether I could suggest a way to get a friend of his out of the country. I was surprised at this request by Jim, as what I was doing was strictly unofficial. Of course, I explained about my arrangement with Blackwood and told him that the latter would need 30,000 crowns to ensure that Jim's friend would be assisted into Germany.

Blackwood was calling me once a week, as I had no way of getting in touch with him. We arranged for a meeting on our park bench at a day and hour in accord with our code. I had obtained the required money from Penfield, and well do I remember Blackwood's instructions even after over forty years. "Tell the man," he said, "to come to the Wilson Station a week from today at eight am. He is to board the eight-thirty train for Plzen and he is to wear this red wool scarf," whereupon Blackwood handed me a crimson neckpiece and continued, "He is to carry a briefcase and he is to wear a green felt hat which, if necessary, can be obtained in any clothing shop. I will approach him on the train and I will say, 'Nazdar, old friend, are you going to Plzen or to Karlovy Vary?' He is to reply, 'How are you, Janek? I am getting off before Plzen to visit a small paint manufacturer.'"

In each of the three escapee episodes, the same routine was followed and in each case the escapees reached the US Zone of Germany safely with no slip-ups. I later found out that Blackwood used safe houses and bribed border patrol guards

I met with Blackwood about a half dozen times. I learned that he had flown with the Czech Fighter Squadron with the RAF during the war and then had returned to what he had hoped would be a free, democratic homeland. Hundreds of his compatriots had the same disillusioning experience.

In connection with these Blackwoodian escapes, the escapees were warned and admonished not to reveal to anyone – not even to American or British, or any western official - how they had managed to make good their escape. At least one of Blackwood's escapees, however, could not keep his mouth shut. During the winter of 1949 I made a short trip to the U.S. at my own expense. I stopped in London on the way back and called by at the U.S. embassy where I was informed that the Security Officer wished to see me before my departure for Prague. I was not a little surprised when this man, who had a pretentious and pompous air, told me that a certain Stejskal (not his real name) had called on him soon after arriving in London and, upon being questioned about how he had managed to get out of Czechoslovakia, had revealed in some detail how Mr. Birge had arranged for a Mr. Blackwood to engineer his escape. That security officer then recounted in detail all about the safe houses and the Border Patrol operator who had presumably been bribed to cooperate.

I had, of course, no choice but to admit minor involvement in Stejskal's escape and I assumed that this whole episode was being reported to the Department. I gained the impression –not from anything the security man said, but by his attitude and voice inflexion - that State Department personnel were not going to be pleased by this extra-curricular activity on the part of an FSO.

As already mentioned, I completely lost track of Blackwood for some twenty-five years. Then out of the blue in 1974 I received a letter from him. How did he find me? He had started enquiring among his Czech friends in England after he had finally succeeded in reaching that haven in 1968, and eventually was able to ascertain that I had settled in Columbus, Ohio. "You will remember me as Blackwood," he wrote. "My real name is Josef Hybler." In that first letter (which took many months to reach me) and in subsequent ones, and when we finally met again in England later that year, Josef brought me up to date on the saga of his adventures.

Josef's undoing was brought about by his much younger brother and sister, who were ardent Communists. Somehow they became convinced that their war-hero brother was involved in some sort of anti-government activity and, as the Party urged its loyal members to do, when even close friends or family members were suspected of anti-government activity, they reported their brother to the authorities. Josef was arrested at once. One of the first questions Josef was asked by the burly STB interrogators was how he had come to know Walter Birge. Hybler knew that I did not know his name so he felt confident in replying that he did not know Birge. "How is it that you were seen raising your hand in greeting as Birge was driving past, when you were standing on the sidewalk near the foot of Vaclavsky Namesti?" Josef replied that he remembered having met the man to whom he had waved in friendly recognition at some official reception, but that he had not even recalled his name or exactly what his job was – only that he was an American. That was when Hybler was thankful he had not revealed his name and thus could be assured that no involuntary slip of the tongue could have made known to the STB that there existed any kind of close relationship between us.

The betrayal by Josef's brother and sister, however, was enough to have him thrown into Pankrac prison for eleven years – three of them in solitary confinement. Joe (as he was also called) soon realized that above all, in solitary, he had to keep his sanity. He had been a good musician and before the war had played the violin for a time with a symphony orchestra in Prague (I do not believe that it was *The* Prague symphony). So, in addition to subjecting himself to a severe regimen of setting-up exercises, he scheduled a continuing series of make-believe concerts, acting as the conductor of Mozart, Beethoven, Brahms, Schubert or Dvorak symphonies, among others, whose scores he knew intimately. On one such occasion, while he was "conducting" Dvorak's *New World Symphony*, a guard loudly knocked on the cell door as he slid open the small aperture through which he shoved the mid-day meal of black bread, water, and cheese. "What are you doing?" asked the guard. "Don't bother me now," answered Joe, "I am busy conducting my symphony orchestra." The astonished guard moved rapidly away in search of the prison doctor. Although exercise, music from memory and humor (he had many other funny stories of prison life) were important, Joe said that he mainly owed his survival to a devout belief in Jesus Christ. While many of his fellow political prisoners – some much stronger physically – perished in the harsh prison, Joe kept his sanity and his life by praying often and by being sure of God's help and continuing presence near him.

About 1961, Joe was released from Pankrac prison and found that his stipend from the RAF (he was a war hero) had been confiscated by the "State". He was forced to work at menial jobs. Finally, when Dubcek came to power in 1968, during the so-called *Prague Spring,* Joe was able to obtain a visa to attend a reunion of his RAF buddies in England. When the political picture once again began to darken, he decided not to return and asked for and received asylum, just before the Soviet tanks rolled into Prague. He found work with Lucas, a high-tech engineering firm.

In 1974, when my wife and I and my stepsons visited England, we finally met with Joe. He was living very simply and frugally in Hemel Hempstead with a much younger Czech, a woman named Lydia. Lydia was fluent in Russian, had a chemical engineering degree from a Czech university, and worked for a Texas company in London. She too, was a refugee and had an interesting escape story.

She was a Communist Party member (the only way she could get a university degree), and by dint of frequent attendance at party indoctrination sessions had established herself in the good graces of the Communist bosses. This good conduct also had made it possible for her to join a student group that was to visit England (about two years after Josef's arrival). Before leaving Prague, she had informed her mother that she would try to defect. In London, the student group was put up in one of the inexpensive hotels where, as luck conspired, there was a chambermaid who soon was identified as a Czech national – a girl who informed Lydia that she had defected to England the year before. Lydia lost no time in obtaining the maid's advice as to the safest and easiest way she, too, could find official refuge in England. The maid advised Lydia to postpone her defection until the day of the scheduled departure of her visiting group. As Lydia knew almost no English, her new friend wrote down very explicit instructions as to what bus to take, where to get off and exactly how to find the safe house where she would find several fellow Czechs, most of whom were recent escapees. The maid also drew a rough map to ensure Lydia's eventual safe arrival at what she hoped would be her haven of refuge. All the money Lydia possessed was thirty shillings (about £1.5). Her relatively short odyssey to the safe house passed without untoward incident and within two weeks, Lydia obtained employment in the same hotel where she had been staying.

Lydia met Josef at a gathering of their displaced countrymen and they soon began living together. We saw them in the summer of 1974 in London and then took a trip to Wales with them. The next year, they came to the United States and visited us in Columbus, Ohio, where we were then living. They had already been to Florida where they were married in the presence of some old friends, also Czech expatriates. When we moved to Brussels, Belgium from 1975-1980, they visited us there. We also traveled to southwestern France with them (Rocamador region) and we saw them in London and Hemel Hemptead.

During all those years, and somewhat distressing, was Josef's obsession that he might eventually be murdered. During that time, there were a number of suspicious deaths of defected Czechs from sudden heart attacks or strange, rapid, deadly diseases. It was found out later that many of these were actually murders by cyanide or injecting victims with deadly bacteria through a needle in the end of an umbrella. Josef constantly asked us to be very suspicious if he should die suddenly of a heart attack. He also told us both before his marriage and afterward that he had been warned against Lydia by a few of his Czech expatriate friends. They claimed that she was very likely a Communist STB agent and to be very careful. He was, after all, fifty-seven years old when he met her and she, only about twenty-eight. They thought she was trying to find out if he had joined the *M16* in England (a possibility) in order that she might pass information back to the Communists. This may have been, although Lydia always seemed devoted to Josef and after his death, to his memory and to his RAF squadron companions.

In connection with his death, a very odd thing happened. I had a beautiful old German "onion" clock of silver and copper that suddenly stopped a few minutes after two p.m. on January 9, 1984 (we were then living in Massachusetts, our final home). We couldn't find the key anywhere to wind the clock and decided to wind it with the key from the French clock in another room, but kept forgetting to do so. Three days later, my wife, my stepson and I were looking at a movie on television, the remake of "The 39 Steps". It had an authentic setting in London in the first apartment building built there in the 1850's and where we had visited the Czech sister of a friend of ours. During the most exciting part of the film when the hero is hanging on to the minute hand of *Big Ben* to keep a bomb from going off before it can be disconnected, we suddenly heard ticking from the antique German clock. Not only was it running without being wound, but also the hands had moved forward to the correct time of day – 4:30pm!

About two weeks later, a letter arrived with a London postmark. My wife immediately said, "Josef is dead!" and sure enough, the black-bordered letter inside from Lydia related how Josef was struck down by a heart attack like a huge oak tree being felled and died a few minutes after seven pm on January 9. Our clock had stopped at exactly that time (five hours later in London) and date. A service was held for Josef three days later at the exact time the unwound clock started running again. I cannot help but think that it was more than coincidence.

We have kept in touch with Lydia, mostly at Christmas card time. Josef was also terribly worried about his future, as Lucas was to pay him only a small pension of £1000, hardly enough to live on. Luckily, more money must have been obtained from some source or other, as Lydia stopped working right after his death, and although continuing to live in the simple "council house" in Hemel Hempstead, was also able to maintain a rustic country retreat in southwestern France for a few years. She kept up with Joe's old squadron mates and after the *Velvet Revolution* in Czechoslovakia in 1989, had a "memory book" with his name placed in a cathedral in Prague. She later published his wartime diaries. She was also able to visit her mother often in Prague and travel frequently. In the early 90's, she stayed with us in Massachusetts and then with other friends in California before going on to New Zealand to visit old RAF buddies of Josef. A few years later, she planned to visit us again, but was unable to obtain a visa to enter the United States. We always found it puzzling that after his death, Lydia denied vehemently that Josef's siblings were responsible for his betrayal – in fact were friends of hers – when Josef told us clearly that they had been the reason for his imprisonment.

In any case, thus passed away a courageous enemy of Communism, a Czech patriot, a brave fighter pilot, and a man who had the guts to throw the pain of a solitary confinement into the face of his jailor. How tragic it is that this man could not now see his native land free again. Would that I could walk with Joe in King Wenceslas Square – and with Veleslav Wahl, too – and see the Czech people laugh and joke again.

A year or so following my arrival in Prague, the ambassador asked me to represent the embassy at the annual ball given by the Friends of the USA Society of Plzen. There would have been nothing especially note-worthy connected with that event had it not been for the presence there of Bozena (Beatrice), a beguiling vivacious, lovely blond girl of about twenty. I danced with her many more times than with anyone else, as the large orchestra, lacking the scores for the latest American dance music, played over and over again, *It's a Long Way to Tipperary*, for that was the song that everyone had heard time and time again during the war over the BBC. Of course, I did not get to Plzen often, but Bozena did occasionally come to Prague to visit a relative. When she came on those visits, she would let me know a few days ahead of time and the hours spent with her – in my house, walking along the river or in a café were always fraught with pleasure and exciting. Bozena was a laughing, passionate, intelligent young woman. Perhaps if she had lived in Prague and I had not met and become seriously enamored of Hannah Bradley of Boston at that time, the story that unfolded might have had a different ending.

The last time I saw Bozena was on a summer day in 1948, after the Communist take-over. We went for a long walk and then, not far from my house, sat down on the warm ground.

Behind us and on either side were flowering shrubs and before us was the panorama of the gently flowing Moldau. At first, we sat there very quietly and close to one another, when suddenly Bozena, in an anguished tone, said, "Why must I live in a country ruled by tyrants? Why cannot my beautiful country be free?" Then she lay back on the ground, her arms stretched out on either side, then up toward me as though urgently seeking comfort to assuage the pain that I could see in her eyes which so perfectly matched the blue of the sky above us. I did what I could to bring her out of her mood of despair.

That same evening, I put her on the Plzen train at Wilson Station. As she said goodbye after a long embrace, she said with an enigmatic half smile, "Maybe the next time we meet, it will be in the West." Then her train pulled out taking that dear girl away forever.

It was about two months following Bozena's visit that I ran into an acquaintance from Plzen whom I had met at that *Friends of the USA* ball those two and a half years previously. "How are you Stepan," I said, "and have you seen Bozena lately? How is she?" My acquaintance clasped my hand in a firm grip and pulled me down to the bench beside him where he had been taking a coffee. "Prepare yourself for a shock, Mr. Birge." And set forth below is what that Plzen businessman (most of whose property had recently been confiscated by the government) had to say about Bozena.

"Several weeks ago, a cousin of mine was approached by a casual acquaintance who suggested that he had perfected a plan for escape to Germany. So far, three friends had enlisted to make good their escape and would my cousin like to join them – along with three or four others for whom he could vouch. The two arranged to meet again two days later and during that time my cousin spoke with Bozena and two others to ascertain whether they might wish to join the small escape group. Bozena at once leapt at the chance to reach the West and she in turn persuaded three of her close friends – two young women and a young man, the brother of one of these friends – to join her. On an appointed day the group met together with the *escape artist*, whose name was Bohumil, as well as with me, even though I did not yet want to take the escape step owing to a family problem involving illness. I was not impressed by the looks of the prime mover of the planned exploit – but then, looks can be deceiving.

I made a point of asking Bohumil a few details as to how the escape was to take place. He stressed that his main weapon was the bribing of guards who were not only lukewarm communists, but also greedy for money. At that meeting each would-be escapee paid over to Bohumil the sum of five thousand crowns, and an additional five thousand was to be paid by each escapee upon reaching the border. Bohumil stressed that no luggage should be carried. The escape group was to meet at a certain place on Black Lake, which, as you may know, is in the foothills of the Giant Mountains. Having met there they would proceed on foot over the low mountains via paths already well memorized by Bohumil.

"The following day, the group left Plzen. I expected to receive a letter or card from one of the escapees who was thus to let me know that all was well and that they had reached the safety of the U.S. Zone. No such letter arrived. However, a Czech border guard, within two days, reported to his commander that he had come upon eight bodies, all of which showed that death had resulted from bullets fired from an automatic weapon. Identification papers found on the bodies revealed their identities to be the same as those of Bozena and her fellow would-be escapees. No valuables of any kind were found in the clothing of the deceased victims. Thus, it can be assumed that the alleged guide had murdered in cold blood the defenseless young men and women in order to gain possession of money and any other valuables the victims carried. As far as I know, the murderer, at least as of now, has disappeared."

Thus perished my dear young friend, Bozena. To this day, I do not know whether her assassin ever surfaced and ever paid the penalty for his horrendous crime.

I have previously mentioned Hannah Bradley, an unusually attractive Boston girl whom I had met during my first home leave in April, 1946 while visiting Claire and Fuller Albright. While my romantic interest in that Radcliffe student grew apace, that romance, such as it was, and handicapped by the distance separating Prague from Cambridge, was destined to end upon receipt of her *Dear John* letter in October, 1948. The end of that relationship, however, as unfortunate as it seemed at the time, was relatively unimportant compared to results of the rebound in the direction of a beautiful and alluring Czech schemer whom I had met in January, 1947 at the semi-annual ball offered by the mayor of Prague. Mrs. Beneš, the wife of the president of Czechoslovakia, was seated in the box of honor which overlooked the ballroom at one end of which an orchestra played Viennese waltzes half of the time, while at the other end, while the strings were resting, a jazz band blared out tunes which had been popular during the 20's and 30's and even during World War I. The young men were all attired in white tie and tails; the girls were dressed in ball gowns of the 1930's style, most of which had doubtless been carefully stored during the intervening war years in anticipation of future occasions such as this.

Soon after arriving at the ball with a few embassy colleagues, I noticed that a friend from the Czech Rowing Club was dancing with a very pretty girl. A formal introduction soon followed and that marked the start of my relationship with Dagmar Polakova, a nineteen-year old girl who resembled Hedy Lamarr. During the ensuing year and a half, I often met with Dagmar, but there were several other young women whom I also invited out. Until the fall of 1948, none of these girls made any marked impact on my emotions owing to my romantic preoccupation with Hannah. Following the receipt of her farewell letter, I understandably, but as it turned out, foolishly, began to think of Dagmar as a replacement of sorts.

Not long after, when my meetings with her became increasingly frequent, two of my Czech friends tactfully warned me that they knew Dagmar and that on occasion, her behavior had left much to be desired. I listened, but not attentively enough. Then another factor entered into the situation. Two American couples connected with our embassy who had gotten to know Dagmar well at informal parties we attended together began to sing her praises, for Dagmar was carefully preparing that development. Then foreign embassy colleagues, as well as my American friends, began inviting us together to receptions, asking if I would be good enough to escort Dagmar to their parties.

It occurred to me, of course, that Dagmar was mainly interested in getting out of communist Czechoslovakia and finding security in the West. There were these and other warning thoughts, but they did not assail me often enough. Nor did I seriously ask myself the logical question that if one had serious doubts about marrying someone - why do it?

I had some leave coming to me so I flew back home to New York to think things over. That did not help, especially as my father, intrigued by the romantic aspect of my situation, even encouraged me to return to Prague and marry the girl. Mother was far less enthusiastic. After a month's stay, I returned to Prague with the now predictable outcome that definite plans for the marriage proceed apace.

The wedding day was March 26, 1949 and very soon afterward, I was instructed to report to Washington for assignment "on loan" to the Department of Commerce.

Dagmar and I left Prague without fanfare on the ninth of May, 1949. Having sold the Cadillac to Andy, Mr. Steinhardt's Greek chauffeur (who ended up paying only a quarter of the agreed-upon price), we set out in the little Alfa Romeo. Until we reached the German border, Dagmar maintained her charming, winning ways, but once the territory of Czechoslovakia had been left behind, the first words she uttered as we entered the U.S. Zone had a rude intonation. During the ensuing months and years, her character and behavior changed, at first imperceptibly, then spasmodically, and then with increasing frequency – with an almost predictable effect on my personal well-being and career. I had no one but myself to blame for having turned a deaf ear to the inner voice which before our marriage had urged, "Get out of it!"

En route to Cherbourg, where we were to board the SS United States, I had decided to travel via Milan to have a faulty part in my car replaced. While awaiting completion of this work, we joined a small group of Czech refugees then living near that city, a few of whom we had known in Prague. One of these young men, whose name has long since been forgotten, recounted the grim story of his arrest and incarceration in Pankrac, the prison in which political transgressors were customarily jailed. He described his arrest and the tortures he had to endure as follows.

"I had been arrested because the STB wanted to obtain the names of the anti-communist students in the political group to which I belonged. As we used the multi-cell system, I only knew the names of a few members of our organization. My interrogators, however, kept questioning me to obtain the names of my collaborators. When this questioning had gone on for twenty-four hours, they decided to try what they apparently felt might be more effective means. First, they tied a strong string around my testicles. Then one of the henchmen took hold of that twine and started to pull upward as I was again asked to reveal the identity of my friends. The pain, as you can imagine, was frightful. 'All right, all right,' I managed to say between groans of agony, 'I can give you two names. I do not know any others.' I was quite sure that at least one of these men, both of whom had been fellow law students, had probably escaped to the West, and the other had been hardly involved at all in our "reactionary" activities. You in American think of the term reactionary as a pejorative adjective-noun. All of us students proudly thought of ourselves as reactionaries."

The young Czech went on to explain that his guards, satisfied for the moment, put him in a hospital, his injuries being so severe, so that they could eventually continue the torture, but luckily, with help, he was able to be transferred to a hospital in South Bohemia from which he made his escape and crossed the mountains on foot to freedom.

From Milan, we drove over the Simplon Pass, up to Paris and then, three days later, on to Cherbourg where we arrived with only a half-hour to spare; but that thirty minutes was enough to have the car stowed on board the SS United States.

Upon arrival in New York, Dagmar and I spent ten days in my parents' apartment at 580 Park Avenue, during which time I sold the Alfa Romeo and replaced it by a second hand Buick, which arrangement eased my financial situation.

We drove to Washington in early June and entered into a happy arrangement with Burke Wilkinson, my good friend and Harvard classmate, who suggested that we house-sit during the summer in his Georgetown residence while he and his wife, Franny, spent the hot months in their residence in Swampscott, Massachusetts.

While in that very comfortable house, we gave an informal cocktail party that was attended by mother and father, who came down from New York, as well as by three of my escapee friends: Dr. and Mrs. Peter Zenkl, Mr. And Mrs. Arnost Heidrich, and Mr. and Mrs. Miloslav Hanak. Herb Cummings, my able friend from the Istanbul days brought along Hubert Humphrey, then a senator and later, vice-president under Lyndon Johnson before becoming Democratic candidate for president in the election which he lost to Richard Nixon in 1968.

During that reception, messieurs Zenkl, Heidrich, and Hanak came up to father (as he later described it to me) and Dr. Zenkl took his hand in his and in a solemn voice had this to say: "Mr. Birge, we just want you to know that the three of us and our wives owe our lives to your son, Walter." The reason I mention this here is that it meant a great deal to father, who put his hands on my shoulders and said very slowly, "Just remember – one human life is worth any career and then some."

Shortly following our move to Washington, the Department, as previously reported, assigned me to a week's duty in Atlanta where I was to give a series of talks in three high schools about the events which had led up to the Communist Party take-over in Czechoslovakia. It will be recalled that it was during that trip that I heard over my car radio of the arrest of Veleslav Wahl and of my having been accused of espionage. Immediately upon my arrival in Atlanta, several reporters did their best to elicit information from me about this accusation, but I had "no comment" to make.

During my week in Atlanta, I must have talked to several hundred students, most of whom seemed to be intrigued by what had taken place in Prague. Usually I was meant to address one class and then give another lecture to the next group. It did not often work out that way, however. In many instances, the first class refused to leave the room and loudly demanded to hear more, so I wound up talking to two or three classes at a time. This was flattering, albeit somewhat difficult, as I had to recapitulate for the benefit of the later arrivals.

In Atlanta at that time there was an honorary Austrian Consul who had come to the United States some twelve years before – an escapee from the Nazi takeover of his country. At noon on the day after my arrival, he phoned me at my hotel to invite me to an informal reception in my honor to take place at his residence the next evening. A few minutes after shaking hands with my host who was awaiting me at the door of his impressive house, the Consul led me to an immense, lavishly furnished drawing-room where at least fifty other guests were already assembled. The Consul motioned for silence and opened his welcoming speech thus: "Mr. Birge and honored colleagues! I am delightful and thank you from the bottom of your heart for coming here today." My reply was not nearly as effective as this introduction.

In the early summer of that year of 1949, and prior to settling down to the work of my temporary assignment in Washington, I drove up first to the Adirondacks to pay a short visit to Claire and Fuller Albright and then up to Ottawa to pay my respects to Mr. Steinhardt, who, it will be recalled, had been assigned to serve as ambassador to Canada not quite a year before. During our brief stay with them, the ambassador suggested that I might again be amenable to joining his staff. I replied that working with him again would of course be a pleasure. I never learned whether he approached the Department on that subject for that was the last time I saw Mr. Steinhardt.

In March of 1950, not long after reporting to my next post in Dakar, French West Africa, I learned of the tragic death of my friend. He had just taken off for New York in his private plane piloted by Mark Ballenger. A few minutes later, one of the twin engines caught fire. Mark at once ordered everyone to don parachutes, quickly explained how they worked and instructed the ambassador and the other passengers to jump. But Steinhardt, apparently fearful of leaping from the plane, which was only some 500 feet from the ground, refused to move. In any event, he did not jump. The co-pilot then left the controls, came back to the passenger cabin and said that if no one else was going to jump, he would, and with that, at once leapt from the plane. Mark Ballenger would not jump out until the ambassador did, so all the remaining group burned to death as the plane exploded and crashed. The co-pilot suffered only broken ankles on landing. The United States lost an able diplomat, and I, a loyal friend.

At the close of this chapter in which I have sought to emphasize the importance of the three and a half years of service in *Golden Prague* – a few comments on career ambassadors and political appointee ambassadors under whom I served may be of interest.

Although I was not a Foreign Service Officer but merely an unofficial secretary to the ambassador (though recognized by the Argentines as an *Agregado Civil*), I served under chiefs of mission in Argentina, Turkey, Iraq and Czechoslovakia.

The first was Ambassador Alexander Weddell in Buenos Aires, a career FSO and a Virginia gentleman of the first order – handsome, always thoughtful, dedicated and very persona grata with the Argentines. He went on to serve admirably in Spain from 1939 to 1942, before retiring. I do not believe that he was a man of keen intelligence, but it is a near certainty that he made few, if any, mistakes. The two chiefs of mission under whom I served as an FSO were Ambassador Lawrence Steinhardt, a political appointee, and Minister Loy Henderson, a career FSO.

I served indirectly under Larry Steinhardt in Turkey from 1942 to 1944 (indirectly, as he spent all but the summer months in Ankara, while I worked in Istanbul), and as a member of his staff in Prague, 1945-48, when he went to Ottawa. I came to know him very well during those five years. As set forth in the chapter on Baghdad, I worked under Loy Henderson for just about a year, from mid-spring 1944 to May, 1945, when he returned to Washington six weeks prior to my temporary move to Dhahran.

These two men were both outstanding yet as different, one from the other, as they could be. Steinhardt, a wealthy member of the *Our Crowd* New York Jewish community, was always completely sure of himself, an extrovert and usually a good judge of people. He placed special importance on personal loyalty. In Turkey, he was determined, if possible, to bring that country into the war on our side – or at least, to ensure that the Turks not repeat their action of joining Germany, as in World War I. He was fully aware of Turkey's ill treatment of the minorities, yet, it will be recalled, he stressed to Jewish acquaintances that sought his intervention on their behalf, that he was the American ambassador, not the Jewish ambassador. Steinhardt never was slow to act or to delegate authority. For example, he was aware of how able our OSS officers were and he listened to them. Following the Communist Party seizure of power in Prague in February, 1948, Steinhardt did not hesitate to entrust to me the rather parlous task of saving more than one life by bringing about their escape from Czechoslovakia. In a way he was, on a very small scale, a *Schindler* via direct or indirect action. I got the message – sometimes directly and on other occasions on my own – but I always knew that in principle, he approved of assisting Czechs in danger of arrest to escape to Germany and I was guided by the same idea until my departure in May of 1949.

Steinhardt had an outstanding wife who was fluent in five languages; yet he also loved other women and was ardently loved by them (his love affair with Countess Cecilia Sternberg in Czechoslovakia and America is touchingly described in her autobiography, *The Journey*, 1977). I suspect that had he been a career FSO, he might not have ended up as an ambassador in five countries. He would probably have rebelled against the restraints imposed on career officers by the Secretary of State.

As for Loy W. Henderson, his abilities were sharply different from those of Steinhardt. He had been promoted rapidly during the five or six years before his assignment as minister in Baghdad and he was understandably determined to continue the skillful performance that had so impressed the State Department. He realized what had served him well – namely, to write exhaustive, carefully written dispatches. And that was what Loy did, consistently and impressively.

Loy was brilliant as a writer and as a listener. As discussed previously, he could absorb all that he had heard in a meeting and pass on that information in a well-written and accurate report. I was to learn, however, that while he reported the facts in detail, he stressed the significance of those that were in accord with his own beliefs; notably, the certainty that all Arabs would attack the Jews in Palestine and massacre every man, woman, and child there if the final solution of the Jewish problem would not be acceptable to the Arabs. Henderson was not only anti-Semitic, but also convinced that an independent Jewish State would become a close ally of the Communist Soviet Union.

Henderson succeeded in persuading most of his colleagues in the Department and abroad to share his views. Fortunately (I think), president Harry Truman stood in the way of Loy's almost successful aim of preventing the U.S. recognition of Israel in 1948.

In contrast to Henderson, Steinhardt was not a good listener, but an eloquent talker - not a brilliant reporting officer, but more broadminded, more sure of himself. Above all, he did not have any strong prejudice which might have harmed future U.S. foreign policy.

In summary, it is suggested that no one should be appointed to an ambassadorial post just because he or she has been a substantial contributor to either of the political parties. Although we have had many such persons, many others, happily, have also been men (or women) of stature and with a degree of greatness in some field. A good example that comes to mind is

Lewis Douglas, who had been director of the budget under Franklin Roosevelt. The ablest career ambassador in fairly recent times, I believe, was Joseph C. Grew, our Chief of Mission in Tokyo for a few years up to December 7, 1941.

From my own experience, I prefer non-career ambassadors, but that could be explained by my somewhat adventuresome, freewheeling proclivities and the men who happened to be in charge of the above-described posts.

Chapter Fourteen

French West Africa

Dakar, Senegal (then French West Africa), my last foreign service post where I served from early December, 1949 to late February, 1952, had interesting aspects, but was the least challenging in the office and the least enjoyable otherwise of any foreign service post of my FSO years. Had dear Virginia, to whom I have been married since 1966, been my wife at the time that I am about to summarize, the after-office hours would have brought joy instead of recurring trial; but I shall try to avoid further comment on the subject of my marriage during the years 1949-55.

When I arrived in Dakar, the Consul General was Perry Jester, an imaginative and well-qualified officer. One of the first tasks he assigned for me was to pay official visits to Bathurst, British Gambia; to Bissau, the capital of Portuguese Guinea; and to Conakry in French Guinea. In retrospect, those visits had significance, for the time of which I write was the prelude to the liquidation of the British, French and Portuguese colonial empires.

The flight to Bathurst took less than an hour and we were met by a junior official of the governor's staff and shortly conducted to the governor's residence where we were escorted to a spacious, elegant guest room in which photographs featuring members of the British royal family, past and present, were prominently displayed.

The afternoon of Dagmar's and my arrival happened to coincide with the finals of the annual snooker (pocket pool) tournament and a dance was held that evening during which the winner was presented with a handsome silver cup. At least twenty Gambian blacks attended the party and I was surprised to note that there was no evidence at all of any color barrier. Several times during the dance, a *Paul Jones* partner-mixing number was announced, thus making sure that I would dance with several partners including black women belonging to the elite of Gambian society. These women were attractive, obviously sophisticated and were graceful dancers. Until that time, I had been under the impression that the English did not mix with non-whites in their colonies – obviously a misconception – at least in Gambia. Then another instance of British respect for blacks came to light. While I was standing next to the bar, a rather uncouth Englishman, who obviously had had too much to drink, approached me in a somewhat obnoxious manner. Immediately, an African gentleman who had been standing nearby moved to place himself between the troublemaker and me, and in a tactful way told the latter to move on. That Gambian of color had obviously been educated during at least a few years of his youth in England, for his accent and choice of words were those of the ruling class.

On the morning after the snooker tournament dance, the governor informed me that he had arranged for us to take a two and a half day excursion on the Gambia River. An hour later, we boarded *The Lady Wright*, a small freight and passenger steamer that called at every riverside hamlet to deliver or take on mail, freight, and an occasional passenger. In the afternoon of the following day, our ship docked at the last town within the territory of Gambia. We were warmly greeted by the Colonial Service representative, who had recently arrived from India and it was at once painfully apparent that half of his face was caved in. This otherwise most attractive junior official lost no time before explaining that his disfiguring wound had been inflicted by an ax-wielding Hindu militant who had wished to take revenge on the English for creating a new Indian Islamic state soon to be known as Pakistan. It has been my experience that most British colonial officials, as well as diplomats have been capable, attractive, articulate and intelligent – not to mention well educated, albeit sometimes full of themselves. This official with the frightful wound, stationed in a small and very much out-of-the-way post was clearly outstanding – and here, there was no conceit.

On the day before our departure, the governor suggested that I might be interested in seeing what was being done to prepare the ground for a large new development, namely, an experimental chicken farm – definitely the first of its kind in the tropics. He explained that London had decided that good use could be made of land available in Gambia, despite its small area, to raise thousands of chickens for which adequate food could be raised locally and then the fowl shipped to England ready for the market. What we were to witness, said the governor, was the clearing of land by means of giant Caterpillar tractors. A short distance from Bathurst, we saw those tractors at work. In some cases, one of those machines would butt into a tree, thus flattening it down. When a larger tree was to be felled, a heavy chain attached to two tractors, one on either side of the tree, would do the work. If that were not effective, a third tractor would drive into the tree to assist the work of the chain. The English foreman explained that those tractors would before long clear enough acreage to make possible adequate cultivation of feed for the chickens. The man in charge of the project was a chicken farmer from Georgia, USA. With regard to that Georgian, I was told an amusing story which stemmed from a recent episode. Apparently that chicken farmer from Georgia decided to give a costume party at Christmas time. When one of his invitees, a minor English official, turned up disguised as *Little Black Sambo*, he was ordered to leave, as no natives had been invited.

A year or so after my visit, I heard what happened to that project. One of the main problems that the organizers were guarding against was the danger of "fowl plague" that could be brought by wild birds infiltrating the grounds. To keep those possibly disease-carrying birds out, wire netting had been built over the area where the chickens were to be hatched and grown to full size prior to their being killed and frozen for shipment. The first disaster to take place was that somehow a few wild disease-carrying birds somehow gained access through a hole in the wire. That resulted in the entire crop of chickens being wiped out just before reaching marketable size. The next disaster to befall the operation was that the freezing mechanism broke down. In the tropical climate of Gambia, that meant that by the time the chickens were to be loaded on a vessel bound for Britain, the entire shipment had been spoiled. That was enough for the investors. The chicken operation closed down and it is doubted that such a chicken farm would ever again be established in a tropical setting. I suppose that the Georgian chicken farmer returned to Georgia.

The next colony to be visited was Portuguese Guinea. In order to reach Bissau, the capital of that colony, we traveled in a jeep-type vehicle driven by an employee of the Gambian governor, first, to the southern part of Senegal, called Casamance, where we were met by a junior French official who had spent most of the war in the French Resistance. It was his assignment to drive us further south and into Portuguese Guinea. During that trip through the jungle, he provided continuing entertainment by explaining just how he had been trained to kill an unsuspecting German guard when attacking the latter from behind. He went on to point out that on several occasions he had put the training to good use. That loquacious Frenchman also gave an exciting description of how he had disposed of a German soldier in a pitch-black hallway, waiting patiently in stygian darkness. After what seemed like ten minutes, but was more likely one minute, the dead silence was broken by a slight rustling. Frenchie instantly fired three shots at the sound with his Lugar automatic and a body was heard to fall to the floor. He found a light and there, sure enough, was the corpse a German Feldwebel (sergeant).

As soon as our Resistance driver brought us to the territory of Portuguese Guinea, it was as though we had entered a well-maintained park; for both sides of the road were neatly kept up and obviously had been periodically mowed – and this, in the middle of nowhere. There were occasional glimpses of leopards and on one occasion, with a thump-thump, we ran over what appeared to be a huge fire hose, but turned out to be an enormous boa constrictor stretched across the road.

Immediately upon arrival in Bissau, we were driven to the governor's headquarters, which was surrounded by a formal garden. The governor had been awaiting us, for we were met at the main entrance and without delay ushered into his large office that was cooled by a fan blowing air on a porous water container, the effective system used also by the Arabs in those days before universal air-conditioning. As the governor spoke no English and I, very little Portuguese, and he seemed very uncomfortable with French, I tried Spanish, speaking slowly and he answered in Portuguese slowly and we had little trouble understanding one another.

We remained in Bissau only one day, as there was nothing to make a longer stay worthwhile. Shortly before starting the trans-jungle trip to Conakry, one of the governor's young assistants remarked that he was about to fly to Dakar on official business in a small four-seater and asked if Mrs. Birge by chance would like to accompany him, thus sparing her the tedious journey which lay immediately ahead of us. In private to Dagmar,

I indicated my disapproval of this idea, but saying it was a great idea, she insisted on flying off to Dakar with the young man, while I returned with the resistance fighter to French Guinea. At the time this did not seem significant, but in fact was characteristic of what lay ahead.

The trip to Conakry was difficult and tedious, involving many times when we had to either ford small streams or cross larger ones on small, flimsy rafts. We became stuck once in deep mud and were able to extricate ourselves only by dint of the aid of a dozen natives who had miraculously materialized to help us.

Conakry was a thriving town owing to its proximity to the large deposits of bauxite in the nearby hills. As there was a small railway line between those mines and the seaport of Conakry, the movement of that ore was a never ceasing activity and a continuing source of profits for the French mine-owners.

I remained in that town two days, established a cordial relationship with the affable governor, then bid a warm farewell to my very decent and friendly driver and flew back to Dakar, the seat of government for the vast territory of French West Africa. As my plane circled over the town before heading north, I could see below the *tricolore* flying bravely over the Government House. Not many years thence, it would be hauled down forever.

Dakar, while hardly a Paris of the French empire, was not too bad a post in which to spend a little over two years. The French knew it as an important *point d'appui* (a naval base, in this case). In view of its geographical location at the tip of the African continent's most western projection, the city became also an important refueling stop for aircraft flying between Europe and South America. While Dakar was a growing center of many industries, the two leading American firms represented there were Texaco and Mobil Oil. By far the better run of the two was the latter, of which the manager was an Englishman, a Mr. Franks. Happily, because of the assiduous efforts of the Pasteur Institute, as well as its location on the Cape Verde Peninsula, the city was relatively mosquito free.

Aside from rather routine office work, there were three activities that helped to pass the time with varying degrees of enjoyment: tennis, swimming (from March to November), and bridge. Of these, tennis was by far the most enjoyable, and few were the days when I did not spend most of my leisure daylight time at *Le Club de Tennis*. Occasionally, a British warship –

usually a cruiser – would call at Dakar en route to Nigeria, the Gold Coast or perhaps South Africa and on those occasions, a match was arranged between British players and the tennis club team. When these matches occurred, I was usually called on to act as referee, presumably because I was looked upon as neutral and because I could call out the scores in both languages.

Although the whites swam regularly in the season, the natives, who were probably too busy grubbing for a living, used the beautiful beaches primarily as latrines. They also fished and I noticed that when the fishing boats arrived back every day with their catch, a line of natives, with a hand on the shoulder of the man in front of them, was led down the beach to the boats. When I enquired what they were doing, I was informed that they were blind, and that it was customary for the fishermen to give each one a fresh fish for his dinner.

Important government and business officials did not mingle freely with the blacks in Dakar. There was a token native army major attached to the staff of the High Commissioner, a well educated native of Senegal who had spent several years being trained in a French military school; but that was a notable exception. A few clerical and blue-collar employees who worked for French firms in Dakar did mingle occasionally with *les noirs*. In that connection, I heard an amusing story that I was assured was true. Seated in a restaurant was a French couple with three pre-teen age children, one of whom had a *café-au-lait* complexion. An acquaintance, recently arrived from France, entered the establishment and came up to their table to greet the seated couple whom he had not seen in several years. After enquiring as to how his friends had been doing, he commented on how good looking their two children were. He then commented pleasantly on their entertaining one of their children's native friends. The woman at the table then spoke up in a tone she might have used to comment on the weather. "Ah, non, monsieur. Ce garçon est mon petit souvenir de l'Afrique."

We had two native servants, Alicali and Dumbo, both of whom were from the Gold Coast, where they had been trained by the British. As was the case with ninety per cent of the Senegalese, they were Moslems and they let it be known that they attended regularly the Islamic religious services in the *Medina*, the native quarter, over which presided the *Marabou*, the well-known and revered prime-mover of these ceremonies.

On New Year's Eve, 1951, when we were invited to the annual reception held by the French High Commissioner, I decided to wear the crimson-lined opera cape that I had purchased in London before the war. Only during December through February was it cool enough to wear such a woolen garment. At the last moment before setting forth to the reception, my cape was nowhere to be found. A month later Alicali remarked that the previous day, the Marabou had made his customary appearance in a splendid crimson-lined cape, which, it was said, had been presented to him by a devoted admirer. Upon questioning, Dumbo finally admitted that it was he who had presented that cape to the great Marabou, and beseeched me to forgive him. That was typical of Dumbo, but nevertheless, he did have many redeeming qualities.

I made several good friends during my two-year assignment. My best friends were a French couple, Raymond and Nicole Faguer. Raymond was the chief officer of Crédit Foncier for French West Africa. Nicole was a tennis enthusiast and that activity provided a special bond between us. The Faguers had three young daughters at that time, each one prettier than the other ("chaqu'une plus jolie que l'autre", as I used to tell them). Following a short trip to Europe, I brought back for the eldest of these children, a beguiling ten-year old, a Bavarian outfit – jacket, blouse, sweater, stocking, shoes and plumed hat. That darling girl was beside herself with joy. Special mention is made of this otherwise unimportant event, as three years later Raymond and Nicole wrote that my young friend had died of leukemia. I have kept in touch and exchanged visits with the Faguer family over the ensuing years.

Two of my colleagues in the consulate General became close friends: Jerry Levesque, originally from Lawrence, Massachusetts, and Phil Christy. A year or so following my assignment back to Washington, one of the senior officers at that post, who shall remain nameless, sent a report to the Department's personnel department, which was detrimental, or at least meant to be, to Levesque. A young woman in that department whom I had gotten to know quite well asked me what I thought of Jerry. My enthusiastic report in his favor served to eliminate any harmful result from the other report.

And so passed a pleasant two years (if one does not count the difficulties and unhappiness of my marriage to Dagmar).

Not long before my departure, a package arrived from the United States containing a red and black checked woolen flannel shirt, called a lumber-jacket, which I had ordered for Dumbo when he noticed an advertisement of such a shirt and had expressed the hope that he might some day have one just like the one in the ad. It was to be his Christmas present. Dagmar opened the package at once and said that she would like to have that shirt. I reminded her that the article had been ordered for Dumbo, but that did not make any difference to her – she just put it on. I said nothing to Dumbo and could only hope that he did not know that the red and black shirt had been intended for him.

Chapter Fifteen

Radio Free Europe

The six years between March, 1949, the date of my wedding to Dagmar, shortly before we left Prague, and April, 1955, when we were divorced in Munich, was an increasingly heavy millstone for my well being and career to bear - a period marked by an unpleasant and steady deterioration of our marriage. Because of Dagmar's attitude and behavior during that time, - her contemptuous undermining of our marriage - the final outcome was inevitable. In view of Dagmar's self-centered behavior involving promiscuous adventures, often with much younger men (to cite only one example, the Wilkinsons told me many years later of how she was sleeping with the fifteen-year-old gardener's assistant when we lived in their house the summer of 1949), by 1953, I finally felt that I had no choice but to resign from the Foreign Service. In those days (no longer the case), one's wife was an integral part of one's yearly review, and it was suggested that because of her, my future success in the Department looked less than rosy.

Three weeks following my resignation from the State Department Foreign Service, Radio Free Europe offered me the position of Director, Voice of Free Czechoslovakia. That was in September, 1953. I rented the small Georgetown house (unfortunately, as it turned out to two airline hostesses who preceeded to wreck the house and furniture), and boarded a PanAm flight to Paris and then on the Munich, the Radio Free Europe headquarters in Europe.

Radio Free Europe was broadcasting about sixteen hours a day to Czechoslovakia, Hungary, and Poland. The overall management was American, the radio technicians were German and the newscasters, artists, actors, singers and writers were natives of the three respective countries. The basic policy governing RFE was that the programs would be written exactly as though they were to be broadcast from Warsaw, Budapest and Prague.

At that time, the exchange rate was four marks and a few pfennigs to the dollar. As my three-room apartment was free, I lived quite well on a salary of $9000 a year. My duties were mainly administrative, so I all too often had to settle personal problems involving one or more of the 150 people in the Czechoslovak section of the radio station.

Many of our programs were broadcast from places other than Munich – for example, Bolzano in the Tyrol, Paris, Berlin, the Rhineland, Nürnberg, and Salzburg, to mention a few. In all those cases, I accompanied the actors and commentators. We usually traveled by bus. In most of these instances, there was nothing earthshaking to broadcast – just local color, historical background, and occasionally comments by a Czech or Slovak who was living in the area where the broadcast took place.

It should be borne in mind that in the Communist governed Czechoslovakia of those years, practically the only news and commentaries available were Communist dominated and anti-West. Hence, listeners in Prague, Bratislava, Brno or Pilzen were always interested in almost any program we broadcast. We knew this from what refugees told us as well as from hundreds of letters that somehow evaded the Communist censorship.

There were many amusing episodes that took place during my RFE experience. For example, when I arrived in September, 1953, the *Oktoberfest* was at its height. Every evening, thousands of revelers milled about in the fair ground. At the center of these festivities was the large *Löwenbraü* dance hall in which there was continuous dance music supplied by two orchestras which took turns blaring forth the latest (and some not so late) American popular music.

Outside and close to the main entrance to this hall was a large papier mâché lion, the inanimate mascot of that beer company. Once every two minutes, that lion would raise a huge stein and pour the invisible beer into his massive jaws. As the lion did this, he uttered in a very deep voice, *"Löwenbraü"*.

Each year, the Löwenbraü Company held a contest in which any man with a deep bass voice could take part. The winner's voice would then be the one heard thousands of times during the *Oktoberfest* as the lion roared out his *"Löwenbraü"*. The prize for winning that contest was a few hundred marks, plus any quantity of Löwenbraü beer that the winner and his guests would drink on a special evening.

A few days after my arrival in Munich, I was informed that V. Kavan, a news announcer for RFE, had been declared the winner of the contest. On the prize celebration evening, Kavan, accompanied by a girl friend and several RFE colleagues, swilled numerous giant steins of *helles* Löwenbräu. When they left the beer hall at about midnight, Kavan was plastered. His news program at five a.m. ushered in every day's program. Mindful of this, Kavan's friends walked him around, put him in a cold shower, poured a cup of strong coffee into him and otherwise did all they could to get him sobered up.

A few minutes before Kavan was scheduled to make the day's first announcement over the radio that would be heard by tens of thousands of eager listeners in Czechoslovakia, he entered the newsroom. The German technicians were ready. Kavan walked somewhat unsteadily to his customary seat next to the microphone. Fritz Gottwald, the chief technician, pointed first to Kavan, then to the wall clock, and then in a loud voice said, "Herr Ansager (announcer), - ein, zwei, drei, ..." And when he reached the number "zehn", he brought his hand down as the starting signal. Kavan's customary opening words at that very early morning hour were "Dame a panove (ladies and gentlemen). This is the voice of free Czechoslovakia." But that morning Kavan, in his deep resonant voice, blared out, "LÖWENBRAÜ!"

While there were no significant repercussions (except perhaps increased sales of that beer) for that little faux pas, the Czech director of the Voice, Miroslav Kobak, banished Kavan from the air for a week without pay.

At Christmas time, I joined Kavan in the bass section of our choir when we broadcast old Bohemian carols. A short time following my departure from Munich in May 1955, Kavan was killed in what seemed to be a suicide, but may have been an accident.

During the course of my nineteen months service with RFE, on three occasions we sent our messages (of hope, good will, and firm belief in the ultimate triumph of freedom over Communism) by balloon, as well as over the radio waves. On those days, when the strong west to east winds were especially favorable, our ten thousand balloons, each bearing a small package containing our message, were let loose. These balloons had been carefully prepared well ahead of time to ensure that we would be able to take full and immediate advantage of weather conditions.

We released our balloons from a narrow road less than a mile from the border of Czechoslovakia. While that exercise was not expected to bring immediate freedom to the Czechs and Slovaks, it may have played a small part in assuring those people that America had not forgotten them and was determined somehow to bring about their eventual liberation from the godless Communist yoke.

Dagmar and I had a young maid of Yugoslav origin who apparently took a dislike to Dagmar owing to the latter's habit of arrogant treatment of her. One evening in March 1955, when Dagmar was out, Marushka, speaking German, informed me that she had overheard my wife making arrangements with a Mr. K, one of the Czech political writers in my section, to spend a few days with him in an Austrian village – this, during the days when I was scheduled to visit two refugee camps in the US Zone of Germany. Marushka explained that the similarity between Serbo-Croat and Czech languages had enabled her to understand everything Dagmar had said over the phone. This intelligence enabled me finally to obtain evidence and to take action under the aegis of German law to terminate that unfortunate marriage.

Two months later, I resigned from RFE and left for the United States to begin still another phase of my life.

Chapter Sixteen

Vignettes

Jim Gerard and Jean Shevlin

Jim Gerard, a Grotonian two forms behind me, was a member of one of the oldest and most prominent families of New York. It was not until some years after I left school and was temporarily living in New York prior to moving to Washington to study for the Foreign Service exams, that we became good friends. We met up again during the period of my temporary duty in the Department of Commerce.

Jim was over six feet tall and gave the impression of being overweight, but he was an outstanding athlete in the racquet games, having inherited the agility of his father, Sumner Gerard, who had been a star performer on the track team and captain of the baseball nine at Yale.

Jim claimed to be interested in girls, but he seemed shy and ill at ease in their company, and he would occasionally ask me to arrange a double date – the latter when Dagmar and I were separated during the months preceding the Radio Free Europe assignment, i.e., the summer of 1953. Basically, Jim just did not like women, but said that he did plan eventually to get married. He was a loyal friend and he had a lively sense of humor.

Jean Shevlin was from Minneapolis, had been an outstanding scholar at Vassar and was living in New York, where I met her in 1957 through my third wife, Jinx Heffelfinger, who was also from the Twin Cities area and who knew the Shevlins well. When my sister Grace wrote to me from France that a son of an acquaintance of hers had moved to New York to work in the Guaranty Trust Company, we got in touch with him and introduced him to Jean. When that relationship came to an abrupt end, for reasons, which, according to the young Frenchman, were imperative, we introduced Jean to Jim Gerard.

In November, 1957, I left my fortunately brief connection with the stock brokerage business in the big city and moved to Columbus, Ohio. ("Where is that?" mother had asked when I told her of the impending move.) During the half year or so between our departure from New York and our introduction of Jim to Jean, the latter pair saw each other quite often and occasionally, the four of us would spend an evening together for dinner and dancing.

After moving to Columbus (where I was foreign manager of Ranco, Co.), I would make two business trips a year to New York. During one of these times, when I was attending the annual meeting of the Foreign Trade Council, Sumner Gerard phoned me at mother's apartment (father had died in 1952) where I was staying, and asked me to join him for lunch the following day. The reason for this invitation was that Sumner wanted to quiz me about Jean, asking such questions as, "What sort of person is she? Does she have good character? Is she intelligent and serious-minded?" While the son of Grace's French acquaintance had indicated to us that on one of these scores, Jean did not measure up, I certainly was not going to relay that opinion to Sumner. Moreover, I was not going to play God and say anything that might jeopardize a marriage which I hoped would take place – especially when any such remark would be based on hearsay. Hence, I related to Mr. Gerard all that I personally knew about Jean; namely that she was educated, unusually intelligent, very attractive, and from a good family. Sumner already knew that the Shevlins were of an old Yale family and that was a big plus to him.

Jean's mother also began asking me about Jim, notably on one occasion when she visited us. Of course, I explained to her about his outstanding family, their considerable wealth, Jim's decency and fine character, his sense of humor and loyalty. I did not dwell on his oddball characteristics; nor did I say anything about his usually being ill at ease with the opposite sex. Surely Jean would by then have noted that herself. So the plans for the Gerard-Shevlin marriage began to proceed apace. What I did not know during that period of 1958 to 1960, the latter being the year of the planned wedding, was that Jean was involved in a heavy romance with Langdon Marvin, also a Grotonian and former Chief Marshall of his Harvard class. I had met Langdon (he was six years younger than I) at Bar Harbor during the summer of 1956 while visiting the Gerards there. I noted that he was a heavy drinker who had a habit of kissing his partners on the dance floor and was hardly someone I would have chosen to escort a daughter to a party. True, he came of a distinguished family and was related to Franklin D. Roosevelt; but that was not enough.

When the summer wedding date was set, Jim asked me to be one of his ushers, along with his two brothers, and Jim's cousin, Claiborne Pell, my close friend from Prague days and later. (Pell later served as U.S. Senator from Rhode Island for many years).

The wedding in that summer of 1960 was to be a highlight of the Minneapolis social season. My wife, Jinx, and I stayed with the Peavey Heffelfingers. Bill Tenney, a close friend of my in-laws, invited Jim to stay at his house; and Jean, of course, stayed with her mother.

Two days before the scheduled wedding, I was asked to attend the rehearsal at the church. When I arrived promptly at the appointed hour of four p.m., the church was empty except for the presence of a dark-suited, stern faced middle-aged man whose clerical collar led me to assume that he was the cleric in charge.

"I guess I am early," I ventured, as I extended my hand and introduced myself. "Not at all, Mr. Birge," replied the minister, somewhat lugubriously. Then in the same low and very serious voice, as though in prayer at a funeral, he announced, "I am afraid that there will be no wedding, for the bride-to-be has disappeared."

How and why Jean disappeared two days before her wedding came to light later that day and during the next. First of all, at least one person, if not more, who was traveling from New York to Minneapolis by train, noted that Jean, seated in the same car, was obviously accompanied, not by her fiancé, but by another man, later identified as Langdon Marvin.

At about the same time that I was being told by the minister of Jean's mysterious disappearance, the chief of police of Des Moines, Iowa telephoned the police chief of Minneapolis to inform him that a couple from Minneapolis had applied for a marriage license in Des Moines and the woman involved had later claimed to the police that she had been kidnapped.

It was later assumed that Langdon Marvin had persuaded Jean to drive with him to Iowa to get married and that Jean began to have second thoughts about that elopement during the drive and then during the waiting period following the application for the marriage license.

It was then that Bill Tenney played a key role. The Minneapolis police called him, as he was from Wayzata and knew the police chief very well. When Bill insisted to the chief that he was convinced that Jean must have been kidnapped, the Des Moines police promptly drove Jean back to Wayzata. Langdon was left behind to fend for himself.

On the evening of the day following the "abduction", Jean sat beside Jim at the large rehearsal dinner as though nothing untoward had taken place, but at every other table at that party, the disappearance and return of the bride-to-be was discussed in hushed voices.

During the early afternoon before the above-mentioned dinner, Sumner Gerard asked me to join him and Jim's two younger brothers, Jerry (Sumner) and Coster, in their automobile for a private talk to decide whether to advise Jim to go ahead with the wedding or call it off. I recall Coster saying that this was Jim's last chance to get married, and the four of us agreed that this was undoubtedly the case. It was my impression that Jim would probably have gone ahead with his marriage unless his father had argued very strongly against it.

That same day, just before the dinner, Peavey Heffelfinger asked Bill Tenney to recruit two stalwart men from a police-connected undercover organization to station themselves just inside the entrance to the church, thus to ensure that Langdon Marvin not be allowed to disrupt the service and I was asked to join these men in order to identify Langdon, should he make an appearance. Those two agents, supposedly undercover, but dressed in short-sleeved Hawaiian shirts, could have been recruits for the Green Bay Packers. They were a bit noticeable as the guests arrived. As I had to remain in the church narthex (vestibule), I did not get to see Jim and Jean married; moreover, Langdon did not make an appearance. In spite of the wedding party and guests pretending that nothing had happened, the story soon appeared on the front pages of all the leading newspapers and created a sensation.

During the ensuing years, I met occasionally with Jim and Jean whenever business took me to New York and later saw them in Holland when Virginia (my last and ideal wife) and I were living in Brussels.

The Gerards had two children, a boy and a girl. In 1971, they asked Virginia and me to keep James with us in Columbus for a week while they visited members of Jean's family in Minneapolis. This we did, and young Jim got along very well with Brian and Neil, my two stepsons who were about the same age.

Jean lost no time in putting to work her scholarly mind, for she studied law, passed the bar exam and became an important and leading member in the national women's organizations of the Republican party. Generous financial assistance from Jim undoubtedly played a role in this development.

Shortly after the Republican election victory of President Reagan in 1980, Jean was appointed, first as ambassador to Luxembourg and later, as United States representative to UNESCO. As for Jim, he maintained his close connections with many organizations, including the US Army Reserves with the rank of Brigadier General.

The last time we saw Jim was in the early 80's in Kingston, Massachusetts where we had settled, following my retirement in December, 1980. He had driven up to Plymouth to attend a meeting of the Mayflower Society and stopped off to see us on his way back to New York.

He died in a New York hospital in 1987. Two days before his death, according to a telephone report by his brother, Coster, Jean, accompanied by a unknown lawyer, came to Jim's hospital room and prevailed on the dying man to change his will in such a way as to leave his entire estate to her, claiming that the children were too young and immature to handle their portion (which was half, or perhaps even two-thirds) of the estate of several million dollars (the children were then about 23 and 26 years old, and very responsible citizens). They finally brought suit against their mother to overturn the very late change in the will, but the case lingered in the courts for a long time, so that when they eventually were awarded their rightful portion, a great deal of the money had gone to court expenses and lawyers. Needless to say, this event, like the Gerard's wedding, provided sensational front-page news for all the tabloids.

Belgium

In October, 1975, James Rhodes, the governor of Ohio, appointed me as managing director of the European offices for the state of Ohio. The offices, in Brussels and Düsseldorf, had been established a few years before for the dual purpose of attracting direct investments from Western Europe with a view to the establishment of manufacturing plants in Ohio and thus to create employment – also to encourage the sale of Ohio products. A minor aim was the boosting of tourism.

As Brussels was more advantageously situated than Düsseldorf, that is, closer to England, France and the Netherlands, yet only three hours by train from the Rhineland, I established my headquarters there. It should be noted that many of our American states had offices in Europe for similar purposes and that most of them had their main office in Brussels.

At that time (1975), I had been living in Columbus, Ohio since November of 1957 and since 1967 had been a vice-president of Banc Ohio in charge of their foreign department. In December, 1966, I married Virginia, the beautiful, talented, loyal and much younger than I, charmer, originally from Princeton, whom I had met on the Fourth of July, 1961. Ginny inherited her attention to detail and executive ability from her father, a Norwegian engineer, and her artistic talents in music, painting, and sculpture from her mother, an outstanding pianist, of Franco-German origin.

I left for Brussels in early November and Ginny, accompanied by Neil, my step- son, and Oliver, our bull terrier, joined me four months later. Neil attended St. John's School in Waterloo for the remainder of his sophomore year and his entire junior year. For his senior year, he went back to the school he had attended since the fifth grade, the Columbus Academy for Boys. Brian, my older stepson, had stayed to finish his senior year at the Columbus Academy and then entered St. Lawrence University, graduating in 1980. By that time Neil was at Dennison University. Both boys spent most of each summer with us, and Brian, while we lived in Brussels, spent terms in Florence, and at the University of London.

We rented an impressive five-story *hôtel de maître* at number 3, avenue Jeanne, in Ixelles, a close suburb of the old city of

Brussels. The house was luxurious and one of the most beautiful in Brussels. There were high ceilings, beautiful boiseries with silk paneling, a room with tooled leather on the walls and a painted and inlaid coffered ceiling, six fireplaces with *trumeaux* (built-in mirrors) and *grisaille* (shades of gray) paintings above, gorgeous inlaid floors, a magnificent curved main staircase, numerous reception rooms, pantries, bathrooms, cloak rooms, - even a dumb waiter. Although we brought many of our own beautiful chandeliers and wall sconces (standard for European rentals), there were several left in place, including a magnificent *Louis Seize* crystal chandelier and a Venetian glass beauty. We counted at least fourteen sinks and six toilets, but only two bathtubs. (To be sure, one of these was huge and paneled in mahogany). From bottom to top were over a hundred steps, with the large beautifully tiled kitchen in the basement, the dining room on the ground floor, the reception rooms on the second (main) floor, and the five bedrooms on the third and fourth floors. Being much younger then, we did not mind, and we were glad to be able to house our large collection of antique furniture and works of art.

If it sounds as if we were overspending on luxurious housing, that was not at all the case. Of all the houses and apartments we looked at to rent, this one was the least expensive and the only one large enough to hold our furniture, plus the closest to downtown and the office. I had only to hop on a tram on the corner to be downtown in a jiffy, so rarely took the car. Shopping was convenient, also, with a host of little shops around the corner that one could walk to easily. Our veterinarian was around the other corner, and a block and a half away, across the Boulevard Franklin Roosevelt was a beautiful park, the *Bois de la Cambre.*

A few months following my arrival in Brussels, I replaced the two men who had managed the German and Belgian offices before my arrival and who were still there, by hiring Bob Crowell, an outstanding former Foreign Service Officer (by way of the OSS), who was fluent in German and thus well able to manage our activities in Germany, partly from Düsseldorf, and also from Brussels, where he also worked as my assistant. Another fortunate move was the employment of a young, charming, beautiful, and well-connected German aristocrat, the Baroness Gabriele von Glasow de Soucy, who had a nine year old daughter, and had been recently divorced from a French Baron. Gabriele had many sterling qualities, and was fluent in at least four languages: German, French, English, and Portuguese. Karl Koch, a former OSS officer whom I had known, also worked for me.

Crowell and Gabriele made my work easy to perform and when I left Belgium in the spring of 1980, Bob Crowell succeeded me and Gabriele was promoted to be his assistant.

During the four and a half years of my managing the affairs of Ohio in Europe, I spent about a third of my time traveling to and in the U.K., France, Holland, Scandinavia, Switzerland, Germany, Italy, Spain and Portugal. Ginny accompanied me on several of these business trips, and often Oliver, our precious bull terrier, came along, too. Fortunately, we were able to visit with many of our old friends in Europe, as well as relatives, for my sister Grace lived in Mallorca and her six daughters lived in England, France, and Switzerland and Ginny had a niece, Karin Holder, who lived with us for a time before going to Paris, and many cousins in Norway. Our house also became a nice place for many friends from the USA to stop by.

My service for Ohio in Europe was somewhat like that of the U.S. Foreign Service. In this case, however, I was in charge and that had its advantages. I returned to Columbus in late April, 1980 and until November of that year I traveled all over the state, mostly to deliver talks at the chambers of commerce to inform listeners about what the state was trying to accomplish in Western Europe and to suggest how they could profit by the activities and contacts of the Brussels office.

When our move to Brussels was imminent, several acquaintances who had lived there or who knew someone who had spent some time there, warned us to beware of rapacious, money-grubbing landlords – words of advice which we found to be in the department of understatement. When I signed the lease with monsieur Eeman for our dwelling, I was required to enter into an agreement with the Banque de Bruxelles to the effect that I would be responsible for covering the cost of any damages to the house during our occupancy. That is, the bank would pay the landlord and the bank would collect from me. In connection with that agreement, an inspector at once spent an entire day meticulously examining every square foot of the floors and walls of the house – then, carefully listing every scratch or spot in a huge document, the *"Etat des Lieux"*. As the fates were to decree, our landlord, who turned out to be difficult in many ways, died six months before our departure. Had that not been the case, we would, I am sure, have been liable for several thousands of dollars, for Oliver did inflect minor spots to the magnificent inlaid floors and I am sure that there were a few additional spots or scratches which had not been visible when the inspector made out his list. The landlord's son, Thierry, a decent young man, presented us with a modest repair bill amounting to only a few hundred dollars.

In the same general damage-assessment sphere, we had another narrow escape.

After occupying the house for three years, my wife found out from a friendly neighborhood electrician, who was doing some work for us, that furnaces were meant to be inspected every year to make sure that if any problem arose, one would be insured. Our landlord, of course, being a very mean-spirited man, had not mentioned this to us.

Luckily, numerous workers who did repairs around the house liked us, but loathed Eeman (who lived in the house originally), and constantly warned us of his nefarious tendencies. My wife then called the oil company and had the furnace properly inspected, and a pink colored document, saying all was in good condition and well maintained, was duly delivered to us.

A month later, Ginny and I went to the US for a combined business and holiday leave. We had a built-in house sitter, Agnès David, a twenty-one year old French girl, who was studying at the University of Brussels (almost across the street). She boarded with us for two years, as her parents, who had lived across the street, had been sent back to Paris, and Agnès wanted to finish her university degree in Brussels. (Agnès became like a daughter to us and she and her parents have remained good friends since that time and exchanged numerous visits). During our absence, something happened to the furnace, which caused heavy soot-laden smoke to pour out, covering the entire walls and ceilings of our kitchen, back stairway, and much of our furniture and rugs on the upper floors with black residue.

Immediately upon our return, I called the insurance company with which our landlord had a contract, and three adjusters accompanied by the landlord, came to the house. After conducting the four men on a tour to view the extensive damage, we all sat down around the dining room table. The head insurance adjuster spoke, in a voice dripping with insincere sympathy, but with eyes almost gloating with triumph, "Ah, Mr. Birge, I am afraid that *you* will be responsible for the entire damage, unless, of course, you can produce a recent official furnace inspection document stating the furnace was in good condition." When I handed him that document, there were looks of mingled surprise and consternation from them and even fury from Mr. Eeman, for it was not *I* who would have to pay for the substantial expense of the clean-up work. (Unfortunately, the soot damage on our rugs and upholstery never came out entirely). The above story illustrates the typical attitude of the Belgian landlord (and this one was even married to an American!), and the difficulties that most tenants had with them, especially unwary, unwarned Americans.

When we first moved into the number 3, avenue Jeanne house, our telephone was not yet in service (very slow in those days getting it) and we needed some ice, as our transformer was not working properly for our large American refrigerator. (The landlord had only 60-ampere service for the entire house!) I had noticed a sign two houses down, at number 7, which said "Relais Sept", and assumed it was a restaurant, so rang the bell to ask if I could use the telephone and buy some ice. An attractive, well preserved, and well dressed and coiffed bleached blond woman in her early sixties opened the door. She had a somewhat worldly and hard look and reminded me of Claire Trevor, from old thirties movies. When I made my request in French, she gave me an ingratiating smile, and said, "Mais, oui, monsieur, avec plaisir," then added, with another winning smile, that if there was *anything* else she could do for me at any time, to not hesitate to ask. She was, she said, Madame Winant, the proprietor of the restaurant at number seven, and welcomed us to the neighborhood.

A few days later, Tatiana Putzeys, our next-door neighbor at number five, who maintained very friendly hospitable relations with us while in Brussels, asked us over for cocktails to welcome us to the neighborhood. She asked if we would mind if she asked Madame Winant also. But why would we be offended, we enquired? Tatiana then proceeded to fill us in on the intriguing story of Madame Winant.

It seems that during World War Two, she had owned a restaurant-bar in downtown Brussels, where she also provided beautiful companions for dining and *more*. German officers frequented the place, and her "girls" were often able to find out important information from their "customers" to pass on to the Belgian Resistance. More important, rooms on an upper floor provided a sanctuary for British aviators who had parachuted from damaged aircraft and then been guided by the Resistance operators to temporary safety before being spirited out of Belgium, north into Scandinavia, or south, through France, across the Spanish border. Often these aviators were wounded and were tenderly cared for by the girls. It is estimated that not one RAF airman managed to evade capture and return to the UK without help from the evasion lines. Over 3,000 lives were saved thanks to the bravery of these people, many due to Madame Winant's ministrations.

After the war, Madame Winant, (who had married a cabinet minister who was then disowned by his family and who later died of alcoholism), became a heroine and was decorated by the Belgian government. Asked how they could reward her bravery (for anyone caught aiding the airmen was horribly tortured and executed), she asked for a respectable restaurant in a classy neighborhood, and though zoning laws precluded such an establishment, was given it anyway, with the stipulation that the sign by the door be very small and discreet. Thus *Relais Sept*, which refers to her relay station for the transport of these airmen, came into being. The restaurant offered fine dining (and beautiful female companions) for lunch and dinner during the weekdays, mostly to businessmen, and visiting dignitaries, but also to members of the royal family (not the king, Baudouin I, as I had it on authority that he was gay).

So the above story explained why Tatiana wanted to make sure that we would not be offended by having cocktails with the notorious Madame Winant. Of course, we weren't and came to know her fairly well. We dined occasionally at her restaurant, which had superb cuisine, and also had her cater some of our parties. One New Year's Eve, very late, she (through Tatiana) begged us to come over to celebrate again and so we did, and met some of her old friends from Resistance days in her private quarters on the top floors. (Her bed, where we left our coats, was heart-shaped and covered with a zebra patterned bedspread!) There, among others, was her accountant, who had apparently been her original pimp, and an old worn-out *pute* from the 1940's, Paulette, whom she had taken in after she was found wandering, homeless and ill, a few years before. She used her as a cashier in the restaurant, but Paulette was basically useless by that time, and Madame Winant was only being kind. Paulette would sometimes take little José Putszeys, the six-year-old from next door to the *Bois* to watch the skating and to have ice cream, but it was really *he* who guided her across the busy Boulevard Franklin Roosevelt. On Sunday afternoons in the warm weather, the accountant, Paulette, another woman, and Madame Winant would sit in the walled garden (which we could see from our sitting room windows), drink tea and play bridge. It was straight out of a short story by de Maupassant.

When she was sixty-five, her staff at the restaurant threw a fabulous party – great food, wines, a dance orchestra, etc. – and we were invited. Most of those attending had been notified by reading on the front page of the Brussels evening paper that such a party would be held in her honor at such a date, time and place, and invited all her friends to attend – this, by only mentioning her pet name, which as I recall was Minette. Everyone knew exactly who it was. People from all walks of life were there, from government officials, down to simple food purveyors. The Putzeys came with their five children. Even a man whom we used to see coming out of Madame Winant's in the early morning to his parked Mercedes 600 came *with* his wife. We had a wonderful time, and Ginny, my wife, didn't mind at all when beautiful call girls asked me to dance.

Sadly, Madame Winant had an illegitimate son who, in spite of her fame, was ashamed of her and so would rarely see her or let her visit her grandchild. Happily, her exploits, however, became the basis of a very popular BBC series called *Secret Army,* which started in 1977 and ran through 1979. This weekly riveting drama was largely filmed in Belgium and in it, the café owner was changed to a man, Albert Foiret, played by Bernard Hepton, and the café was called the Candide. The proprietor and café were also depicted as a bit more respectable than Madame Winant and her original establishment, but basically the episodes were carefully researched and based on real-life events. It was a superb series, but I do not know if it ever ran on United States television. A few years later, when we would occasionally visit France, we always tried to watch the hilarious spoof of *Secret Army,* which was called 'Allo, 'Allo, and set in Paris.

Oliver

The Belgians love dogs and in fact, we were told before we left for Belgium that one could walk down the street with a beautiful child in a baby carriage and it would be totally ignored, but everyone would come up to look at one's dog, no matter how ugly a mongrel. We found this to be true, at least in so far as Oliver, our champion white bull terrier, was concerned.

No dog was ever denied admittance to public transportation, hotels, grocery stores, or restaurants, and so we generally took Oliver everywhere with us. We did stop taking him along to the grocery after he peed on a box of grapes that were at floor level. We were horrified, but it didn't bother the shop owner at all! I remember a woman who would take her toy poodle to this store (DelHaize) so that it could ride up and down the moving counter where the groceries go. Everyone thought it was adorable.

Once, when we took Oliver to a neighborhood restaurant (where we later realized that we were eating *horse* filet mignon), Oliver, seated in the booth with us (oh yes, dogs were often seated!) leaned over the low divider and started gently nibbling at the ears of two ladies seated in the adjoining booth. They took a fancy to him and proceeded to feed him tidbits from their plates, which he gobbled down delicately with rapid tail wagging. At another neighborhood restaurant, the proprietor would always give Oliver the almost full remains of a leg of lamb, but there, he had to devour it in the courtyard, as, the *patron* explained apologetically, there were some Arab diners there who didn't like dogs.

When the weather was fine, Ginny and I sometimes drove to one of the beaches near Ostende, with Oliver, of course. On the occasion that comes to mind, we had brought a simple lunch of what we had in the house at the time – just peanut butter sandwiches and bottled water. Seated near us, shaded by two large parasols, was a Belgian family. We soon were aware that the picnic fare of that family was far more enticing than ours. We noted smoked salmon, pâté de foie gras, caviar, deviled eggs, parma ham, and other delectable looking viands, with an array of baguettes, pastries and wines. At once, Oliver's tail began to wag with special rapidity and, as was to be expected, all members of the picnicking Belgian family reacted in customary fashion;

"Quel beau chien! Comment s'appelle-t-il? Quelle race est-il? Puis-je le caresser?" (What a beautiful dog! What is his name? What breed is he? May I pet him?) But without waiting for an answer, they started to hug and kiss him. Then both parents and their children began offering bits of food to that happy dog, which proceeded to lunch on the above mentioned delicacies, while his master and mistress had to be content with their plebian victuals, as they were offered not *one* bite.

The French also love dogs, and I remember one trip that we took around Easter time, when we visited, among other cathedrals, that of Laon, accompanied, of course, by the ubiquitous bull terrier. Inside, Oliver decided to pee on one of the huge Romanesque piers, so we thought it better if one of us stayed outside with him, while the other viewed the interior. Outside, a busload of school children pulled up for a tour of the cathedral, but saw me standing there with Oliver and immediately ran up shouting the usual – "Puis-je le caresser? Quelle race est-il?" etc. I then raised my hand and gravely replied, "Vous savez, ce chien a visité toutes les cathédrales de France; il est donc un chien saint." (You know, this dog has visited all the cathedrals of France; hence, he is a holy dog). At once, the children lowered their voices and they lined up to pet with suitable awe that *holy dog*. Of course, Oliver loved that show of deference, even reverence. Within a minute or so, however, the children abandoned their formality and proceeded in turn to hug and pet their new friend with laughing joy. Then they gleefully said to one another, "J'ai caressé un chien saint!" (I petted a holy dog!)

Oliver was very athletic and loved chasing balls. One Sunday afternoon, when we took him to the *Bois de la Cambre* to play, he managed to grab the soccer ball during a game between Brussels teams, and scored two goals before the players were able to wrest the ball away. They really didn't mind though, as he scored for our local (Ixelles) team!

At another time though, Oliver decided to jump incredibly and easily high to grab the Frisbee that was being tossed in a *concours* at the Bois. We got it away from him to hand back to an irate man who then claimed that it was ruined and that we had to pay for it. Although we didn't see one tooth mark, we finally settled on the equivalent of $20. The man (a Swede, by the way) then tried to take the Frisbee back, too. I told him that

I had just *bought* the Frisbee and that it was now Oliver's. Fuming, he decided to keep the money and give up the Frisbee. Later, our neighbor Tatiana, who had four sons, told us that that model Frisbee cost the equivalent of $3, so we had been had. I'm glad the con man was a Swede, though, because I don't like the thought of a Belgian cheating a dog.

On the other hand, there were a couple of occasions when Belgians did take advantage of us. One day, a lady arrived at my office and sent in her card, which read *Bonne de la Kéthulle*. Mistaking *Bonne* for the French word for *maid*, I thought she was applying for a job, as we were looking for a *domestique* (as the French say) at that time. I was surprised to see a well-dressed, distinguished looking woman appear. After a farcical exchange, it turned out that she was a Baroness (*Bonne* is an abbreviation for Baronne in French) and the secretary of the Bull Terrier Club of Belgium, to which we belonged, and she thought that Oliver should be shown in the annual dog show, as he was an American champion. I told her that regrettably, we would be in the U.S.A. at that time, so she very graciously offered to care for Oliver at her country place and show him for us. She asked if we would mind if Oliver slept with her daughter in her bedroom, as their nine-year-old female bull terrier was in heat, and would sleep with her owners in their bedroom. Of course, I did not, and Oliver was duly shown, taking a second, and well cared for while we were away. About two months later, we decided to pay an unannounced visit to the Baronne de la Kéthulle at her country place with a gift for all her trouble and were surprised to see her nine-year-old bull terrier with a litter of pups. The Baronesse, who had said that she was no longer going to breed her bitch, explained that she had gotten loose and mated with a neighborhood mutt. We accepted her explanation, but noted that the pups looked *exactly* like Oliver. We thought that this might explain why Agnès, who knew the Baroness de la Kéthulle, always referred to her as the Baronne de la Quéquette (a slang word for *penis*.)

On another occasion, we decided to visit one of the numerous castles open to the public, - Gaasbeek (castle of the counts of Egmont), an over restored, but beautiful château, accompanied, of course, by Oliver. We were surprised and amused to see a sign in the beautiful grounds announcing, *Please to keep the neck-strings on dog*, as usually dogs ran loose. When we got up to the entrance building (a stone edifice with a large gothic style, stone doghouse attached to the front), a uniformed, combination ticket-seller and major-domo informed us that we could not take the dog inside. I told my wife that she could do the tour while I waited with Oliver, but the major-domo said, "Non, non, monsieur – *I* will watch the dog while you both enjoy the tour. I will attach his neck-string to the ancient dog house." Thanking him for his trouble, we proceeded to tour the building. We eventually got to the large hall of the main floor (U.S. second floor), a huge, impressive room with arms and armour and coats of arms, banners, painted coffered ceiling, huge fireplace and huge windows. We went over to a window to gaze out at the lovely grounds and noticed, by the gothic doghouse below, a large crowd of people gathered around Oliver and the major-domo. The latter, who I am sure had never before seen a bull terrier, was giving a talk to the rapt audience on the *medieval castle dog* who fiercely guarded his master's château, with details about Oliver's ancestry and fame. We could also see that he was being generously tipped afterward. When we finally descended to pick up Oliver, we thanked the major-domo and gave him a tip also, which he *reluctantly* accepted, because the dog had been "very little trouble." Well, we had been had, but in a most amusing way and by a most enterprising Belgian – and Oliver had enjoyed every moment! And we always referred to his leash from then on as his *neck string.*

Many years later, not far from Cape Cod Bay on the South Shore in Massachusetts, Oliver's ashes, in a suitably impressive container, grace the mantel in the master bedroom of our house. For he is now, we are sure, in Dog Heaven.

TO WALTER BIRGE ON HIS EIGHTY-FOURTH BIRTHDAY

May 21, 1997

Four score and four long years ago
In a house on Hortense Place*
Was born a boy with hair of tow
And fair of form and face.

His loving family soon moved east
To Connecticut's elegant shore,
Where life was a perpetual feast;
He could harly ask for more.

With a French governess, Madame Espy,
He dwelled at old "Overbrook",
Where he grew up quite happy and free,
And read many a Henty book.

Doting parents gave him learning,
Sports, fine schools, and travel,
And instilled in him a profound yearning,
Life's mysteries to unravel.

His beautiful mother sent him to Groton,
A school like Eton or Harrow,
Where the Rector, desendant of Mather and Cotton,
Kept boys on the straight and narrow.

Then on to Harvard, illustrious college,
Where he acted, played, and rowed boats,
Crammed his head with useless knowledge,
And occasionally sowed wild oats.

His family moved to 580 Park,
Walter joined the Foreign Service,
Exciting adventures a continuous lark,
No danger could make him nervous.

He traveled often, far and wide,
Collecting numerous wives
Promising to each and every bride
Love eternal in their lives.

At last he met Ginny, whom he soon did woo,
And made her his last and best wife.
He'd finally met his Waterloo,
and was married the rest of his life.

Covered with honors, he's reached a great age,
But with vigor like lads of eleven,
And is now a beloved, venerable sage.
To know him is ultimate heaven!

* In St. Louis, Missouri

Virginia Birge, 1997

Addenda

The following section is comprised of quotes from three books that mention Walter Birge. There may be others, unknown to the editor.

For Lust of Knowing

The following quotes are from Archie Roosevelt's autobiography, *For Lust of Knowing, Memoirs of an Intelligence Officer,* Little, Brown and Company, 1988. Archibald Roosevelt (1918-1990), a grandson of President Theodore Roosevelt, knew Walter Birge slightly at Groton, where Walter was five forms ahead of Archie, and later got to know him much better in Iraq, where Archie was military attaché and Walter, an officer in the legation. Walter's copy of this book is inscribed on the fly page:

"To Walter Birge –
Who plays and important role in certain pages of this book, whose company I so enjoyed during those fascinating and exciting times in Baghdad!
Hoping all goes well with you, that I'll see you again soon –
Archie Roosevelt
Feb 1988"

p. 133 "My principal official contact at the legation, by coincidence, I already knew, though our acquaintance was a distant one: The political secretary, Walter Birge, had been a sixth-former at Groton when I was a "new kid." He was tall and handsome despite a touch of premature baldness, and much more attached to our Groton ties than I. He recalled how he, the tallest sixth-former, had led the choir in chapel, followed by me, the school runt. Recently divorced*, he was starved for female company, not easily available in Baghdad. But he knew how to make himself charming to the few ladies one could meet, and it was he who introduced me to what there was of Iraqi society in the Western sense of the word."

p. 146 "Shortly after my Babylon expedition I made my first foray into tribal Iraq, to the Dulaim tribe of the Upper Euphrates. In our company were Don Bergus and Walter Birge, my friend from Groton, and we took along Badi'a Afnan and her daughter Furugh – not a successful idea but one that at least served to illustrate the gulf between Baghdad and tribal society."

p. 236 - In a section of photographs following this page, there is one showing Walter Birge in the U.S. Legation staff in Baghdad, 1944. From left to right are pictured Don Bergus, vice-consul; Archie, assistant military attaché; William Moreland, second secretary; Walter Birge, third secretary; Minister Loy Henderson; Armin Meyer, OWI; and Colonel Paul Converse, military attaché.

The following is from a letter that Archie Roosevelt wrote Walter Birge from Washington, on February 26, 1988.

"Dear Walter:

What a thrill to get your long letter of February 18! I would answer it in length except that I am, as usual these days, in a terrible rush. The official date of the publication of my book is this Sunday and I have an enormous amount of speeches, correspondence, etc., to take care of in connection with it. Besides all this, I have to hold on to a full-time job at the Chase Manhattan Bank, where I have been working since 1975. You can catch up on my career simply by reading my book, which I hope you will do immediately!

I am, indeed coming to New England, but simply don't know how far Kingston is from Boston. As of this minute, I am planning to make a quick trip to Boston on April 21st because that evening an old girl friend of mine, Mrs. Don Belin, is giving a book party for me, and I'll ask her to send you an invitation. In Boston I shall be seeing my two grandchildren who live there with my son, Tweed Roosevelt, have lunch with my publisher, Little, Brown, and perhaps have some media interviews before rushing back to Wahington. So probably the only chance we would have to see each other would be at Hattie Belin's party.

---

* Walter Birge, by 1944 had been divorced for about five years.

I will be in touch with you within the mext couple of weeks when things get less frantic.
All the best,

Archie

Archibald B. Roosevelt"

The following is from a letter to Walter Birge from Burke Wilkinson in Washington, on March 10, 1988:

"I'll be interested in your comment when you have finished Archie Roosevelt's book. Franny and I both find the non-Arab parts a bit simplistic."

White House Menus and Recipes

The following quotes are from François Rysavy's book, *White House Menus and Recipes*, 1962, Avon, a revised edition of *White House Chef, 1957*. It is an autobiographical account of Rysavy's life (he was born around 1905), especially his years as chef at the White House for Eisenhower from 1955 until 1957, with, of course, many menus and recipes. It will be recalled that Walter Birge had hired Rysavy in Prague to cook and run his household in 1946, which he did very well for two and a half years.

From page 49 – 52: "I was very lonely for my daughter and wife. Little Janet was just starting school. Much as I had grown to like the Americans [Rysavy had been cooking for an American general on the Riviera right after the war] and especially their democratic ways, I left them to return to Prague to see if I could effect a reconciliation with my wife. I heard that the American Embassy was looking for a chef for its First Secretary, Walter Birge. The First Secretary was a bachelor, but as soon as he had acquired me for a family, he moved out of his hotel and set up housekeeping in a mammoth apartment.

"When Jeannette and I reconciled our differences and decided to try again to make a success of our marriage, Mr. Birge, one of the best men the Creator put on earth, moved to a villa with a garden in the suburb so that we could be united and live with him, and so that Janet might have sunshine to play in.

"I often thought that if I could be like anyone I chose, I would choose to be like Walter Birge. He was a connoisseur of fine food and one of the dishes I served him, I later served at the White House."

[Rysavy goes on to give the recipe for *Stuffed Pork chops Rysavy*].

"Another thing which Walter Birge insisted upon having, and which I later made at the White House, were *Croissants* or Crescent Rolls. I served them at the White House for company breakfasts."

[Rysavy then gives the recipe for Croissants, and at the end adds these lines]:

"This is the way the First Family served them for guests at the White House, but Walter Birge liked each triangle covered with chopped walnuts and cinnamon-sugar before rolling. It takes about 1 cup of chopped nuts and ½ cup cinnamon-sugar to fix them à la Birge.

"Almost as soon as I met Mr. Birge I asked to be registered under the quota, because after meeting this wonderful "goodwill ambassador" of the United States, I knew that America was the place for me. Before my quota number had come up, however, the Communists took over Czechoslovakia and I escaped, with the help of Mr. Birge, in the nick of time.

"Walter Birge, bless him, saw me on my way, returning to his diplomatic post while I continued on alone without savings and with Jeannette and Janet – now eleven – looking to me for comfort and reassurance.

"My first American job was with friends of Walter Birge in Georgetown, Washington, D.C. – Count André and Countess de Limur. While Janet was soon speaking a strange mixture of Czech, French and English – *Dej mi penny pour bon bon* – which translates loosely into "I need some money for candy," I was getting nowhere improving my English, because we spoke French in the house."

Rysavy goes on with many recipes and the story of his life. When Walter Birge was posted to Washington in 1953, François gave him a surprise party for his fortieth birthday on May 21st. (He had from time to time come over to help with cocktail parties). The food and wines were fabulous and Rysavy also gave Walter a gift of the very finest Scotch whiskey. Walter was very touched and never forgot François. When Rysavy left the White House in May of 1957, he then went to Hollywood and ended up being the chef for David Selznick and his wife Jennifer Jones. After that, Walter lost touch with him.

Closing the Circle

The third group of quotes about Walter Birge is from the memoirs of Isaac Patch entitled *Closing the Circle*, published in 1996, Wellesley College Services. Isaac Patch had been invalided out of the navy during World War Two and served for a while from 1943 in the Soviet Union as a courier in the U.S.Embassy, and had then served in a U.S. consulate in China. He was not a Foreign Service Officer, but, early in 1949, was sent to Prague as an assistant political attaché, where he was to replace (he says) Walter Birge in the embassy's political division. Luckily, in Prague, he had diplomatic immunity, for he was summarily expelled by the Czech government with twenty-four hours notice in October, 1949, for espionage activities, particularly involving Nechansky and Wahl. Ike conferred with Walter in 1990 about the events of which he writes and the situation in Prague before he arrived. In the mid nineties, he came twice to the Birge house in Kingston and spent the day with Walter, who generously shared all his memories with him and also gave Ike copies of his chapter on Prague, which had been written about 1990.

p. 194 "One evening in March 1949, I was invited by Walter Birge…to meet two of his Czech friends who lived in a flat in the Hradcany. I eagerly accepted as I wanted to make as many contacts as possible to help me in my job on the political desk at the embassy." [Patch then goes on to describe Nechansky and Wahl]

p. 196. "On our way home that evening, Walter Birge said that he and Wahl had been friends for several years. Wahl hated authoritarianism. According to Walter, Veleslav Wahl had said on one occasion: "I would like to bury Communism." Walter dropped a bombshell when he rather nonchalantly said the two men were double agents whom he met with from time to time...."

"Wahl and Nechansky, said Walter, would be important contacts for my political reporting and "for whatever else might come up." I could only surmise that Birge expected me to get involved in certain work which would not be a part of my official duties on the political desk of the embassy. I certainly did not want any part of this intelligence activity, whatever way it was being handled.

"Rumor had it that Walter was a self-appointed intelligence agent who relished undercover conspiratorial work. To my knowledge Walter had no official connection with the CIA or U.S. Military intelligence. At the time of my expulsion, the Czechoslovak government also brought charges against U.S. Embassy personnel, accusing them of smuggling high-level, anti-Communist suspects to West Germany in an underground railway rescue operation. The fact is Americans were involved in smuggling Czech officials in the trunk of a car with diplomatic plates headed for West Germany.

"Perhaps more deeply involved were Spencer Taggert, a military attaché, and Sam Meryn, an employee of the U.S. military, who was arrested by the Czech authorities at the same time I received my expulsion orders and charged with smuggling radio transmitters to the Czech underground. Taggert had left Czechoslovakia by the time I arrived, while I had never met Meryn..."

[Patch then goes on to say that he told the American Ambassador Jacobs of his meeting with Nechansky and Wahl, who then told Patch not to engage in any intelligence activity job. Patch then claims again that he did not get so involved and only reported general political information as well as insights into Czech society and attitudes.]

p.197 "Earlier I met Wahl and Nechansky at the reception following Walter Birge's marriage to a Czech lady in the St. Vitus Cathedral in Prague. We shook hands and enjoyed a drink together. Nechansky commenting on the wedding extravaganza in Communist Prague said: "I am surprised but delighted that such an event can still go on in Prague."

p. 198 "In a front page article on October 22, 1949, rude Pravo (the Communist daily) reported the arrest of Nechansky and Wahl and the charges against them, naming the Americans they had collaborated with – Birge, Shaffman, Patch, and others. Undoubtedly, under strong persuasive tactics, the two Czechs were forced to name certain Americans, including me." [Patch then goes on to describe the "show trial" of these men in April 1950 and their hangings on June 16. 1950. He denies any part of helping the CIA. After his expulsion, Isaac Patch spent several years working for the State Department in Bad Nauheim as an interrogator to debrief Soviet defectors (he spoke Russian) and later in Munich under CIA auspices. Whether or not Patch is telling the truth when he denies any connection to the CIA is an interesting question. CIA employees are known for never admitting their connection, but in this case, I (the editor) believe that Isaac Patch is telling the truth.

Prof. Igor Lukes of Boston University, *"On the Edge of the Cold War"* published by Oxford University Press, has a large section about Walter Birge. Lukes says that *"Walter (whom I admire and respect very much) is a central character of the plot. He is probably the only good guy of the whole lot...Meeting you and Walter at your home in Kingston is a lovely, lovely memory that I'll carry with me for the rest of my life."*

Mabelle Birge [1882-1970] holding newborn Walter or one of his siblings.

Walter Birge aged about four [1917]

Walter Birge aged about seven or eight [1920-21]

Bust of Walter Birge, age 17, by George Rickey, who taught History at Groton and later became a world famous sculptor.

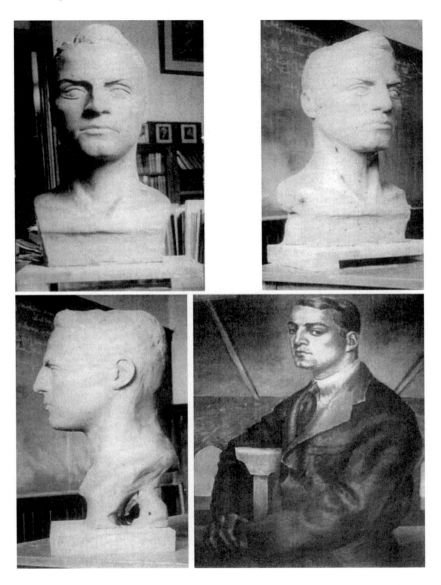

Portrait of Walter Birge 1936, age 23, by George Rickey. Only known oil portrait by Rickey.

1939

Overbrook', the Birge house in Greenwich, Connecticut, circa 1925.

Walter Birge in Iraq, c. 1944 or Turkey 1942.

Wlter Birge in Istanbul, Turkey 1943 [third from left] with Cardinal Spellman [fifth from left] visiting the Papal Nuncio, Cardinal Roncalli [third from right], later, Pope John the XXIII

April 1945 'Foreign Service Magazine' Walter Birge talking with Abdul-Ilah, Regent and Heir Apparent to the Throne of Iraq. They had just been out riding with the Baghdad Exodus Hunt. The hounds which are brought to Baghdad from Habbaniya once a week are bona fide and the jackal is not so very different from the red fox but there the resemblance to hunting in America or England ceases. Instead of rolling fields and fences there is a flat expanse of mud corrugated by inumerable irragation ditches. The Regent, who is a skillful, prudent horseman, almost always takes part in the hunts and paper chases.

Walter Birge in Prague, c.1948

Walter Birge in Prague 1948

Walter Birge with 'William' on the Charles Bridge in Prague, Christmas 1947.

Walter Birge with members of the Czech Rowing Club c. 1947.

Walter Birge [second from right] with other 'marshals' of his class at Harvard 25th reunion 1960.

Walter Birge c. 1960

Walter Birge c. 1984

Walter Birge and wife Ginny c. 1990 and [insert] c. 1968.